Cajun and Zydeco Dance Music in Northern California

Cajun and Zydeco Dance Music in Northern California

Modern Pleasures in a Postmodern World

Mark F. DeWitt

University Press of Mississippi
Jackson

American Made Music Series
Advisory Board

DAVID EVANS, GENERAL EDITOR

BARRY JEAN ANCELET

EDWARD A. BERLIN

JOYCE J. BOLDEN

ROB BOWMAN

SUSAN C. COOK

CURTIS ELLISON

WILLIAM FERRIS

JOHN EDWARD HASSE

KIP LORNELL

BILL MALONE

EDDIE S. MEADOWS

MANUEL H. PEÑA

DAVID SANJEK

WAYNE D. SHIRLEY

ROBERT WALSER

Down At The Twist And Shout
Words and Music by Mary Chapin Carpenter
© 1990 EMI APRIL MUSIC INC. and GETAREALJOB MUSIC
All Rights Controlled and Administered by EMI APRIL MUSIC INC.
All Rights Reserved
International Copyright Secured
Used by Permission

Illustrations courtesy of the author unless otherwise noted

Maps by Bill Pitts

www.upress.state.ms.us

The University Press of Mississippi is a member of the
Association of American University Presses.

Copyright © 2008 by University Press of Mississippi
All rights reserved
Manufactured in the United States of America

First printing 2008

∞

Library of Congress Cataloging-in-Publication Data

DeWitt, Mark F.
Cajun and zydeco dance music in Northern California : modern pleasures
in a postmodern world / Mark F. DeWitt.
p. cm. — (American made music series)
Includes bibliographical references, discography, filmography, and index.
ISBN 978-1-60473-090-6 (cloth : alk. paper) 1. Cajun music—California,
Northern—History and criticism. 2. Zydeco music—California,
Northern—History and criticism. 3. Folk dance music—California,
Northern—History and criticism. I. Title.
ML3560.C25D48 2008
781.62'410763—dc22   2008010801

British Library Cataloging-in-Publication Data available

Contents

vii	Acknowledgments
3	**CHAPTER ONE** Prelude: Down At The Twist And Shout
17	**CHAPTER TWO** Identity Issues, Research Methods, and Ethnography
40	**CHAPTER THREE** Music, Dance, and Social Capital
49	**CHAPTER FOUR** Wartime and Postwar Creole Migration to California
75	**CHAPTER FIVE** Further Creole Migration and Bridging to Other Social Networks
117	**CHAPTER SIX** Folk Revival Connection: The Musicians
161	**CHAPTER SEVEN** Folk Revival Connection: The Dancers
197	**CHAPTER EIGHT** Later Gulf Coast Arrivals
249	Notes
259	Bibliography
267	Discography
271	Filmography
273	Interviews
275	Index

Acknowledgments

The appearance of this book is in no small part thanks to the patience and generosity of several key people who have helped me along the way. Among the first to provide valued assistance in this project were Bonnie Wade and Ben Brinner, ethnomusicology faculty at the University of California, Berkeley. Ben's advising on my dissertation, which served as the foundation for this book, was exemplary, while Bonnie has been a faithful champion and mentor all along and encouraged me to look more closely at the lives of individual musicians. Other scholars who generously spent time reading work related to this book and gave me comments of lasting value include Alan Mason, Elisabeth LeGuin, Steve Pond, David Code, Steve Swayne, the late John Ogbu, Graeme Boone, Rocky Sexton, Timothy Cooley, and Jeff Todd Titon. Jim Hobbs of Loyola University's Monroe Library in New Orleans generously shared his painstakingly compiled Cajun and zydeco discography database, thereby saving me much time in checking facts about recordings. Scott Krafft was instrumental in getting me materials and information from the Berkeley Folk Festival Archive at the Northwestern University Library.

Another level of patience is ever required by one's consultants in the course of field research as the researcher asks necessarily naïve questions, acculturates slowly and partially to subtleties of musical and social interaction, and appears directionless until the relevant issues for investigation take shape. In this regard, I would like to thank all my dance partners and those who played music with me over the years. Jam session stalwarts like Blair Kilpatrick, Steve Tabak, Dwight Shackelford, and Mark Marcin are keeping alive those crucial informal gatherings where amateurs and beginners can gain experience in playing the music. Freida Fusilier and Jolene Adam graciously accepted my "help" in their community research project in 1993, thanks to an introduction from Louisiana Sue, even though at that point I was just beginning to learn about Cajun and Creole culture myself. Freida and Jolene helped me much more than I was able to help them. I am extremely grateful to everyone who sat down with me for a recorded interview, including those whose profiles do not appear here. I learned a great deal from all of you. Special thanks go to Gary Canaparo for permitting the use of so many of his excellent photos from years gone by, and to Jim Block for his cover photographs and design ideas.

If there is one person who inspired this book more than any other, it has to be Danny Poullard. I have attempted to document in the book his historical importance, but it is hard to convey what it was like to know him, to play music with him for hours in his garage, and to see him grow in his role as a master teacher. My personal nickname for him was "Maestro," which never caught on but which captured for me the depth of his musical knowledge and the assuredness of his musical aesthetics, reminding me of teachers from conservatory days. In addition to his musicianship, he demonstrated an ability to bridge social worlds with music that many miss now that he is gone.

At University Press of Mississippi, Craig Gill has been the most patient and supportive editor an author could ask for. Thanks also to managing editor Anne Stascavage and the rest of the press staff who have brought the book through production and to market. Anonymous reviewers of the book proposal and the final manuscript gave several crucial suggestions and corrections.

The grand prize in patience and greatest measure of thanks go to my wife, Sue Schleifer, who has helped me keep body and soul together through the closing years of graduate school, the academic job market, unemployment, and the process of writing this book. She was very understanding of the time and space that writing requires, even as it made incursions on our weekends and travel plans. Her proofreading eye and thoughtful comments on the manuscript, steeped in her own experience as a dancer and three years as executive director at Ashkenaz, were also great assets. To dance through life with her is my greatest joy.

OAKLAND, CALIFORNIA
December 2007

Cajun and Zydeco Dance Music in Northern California

CHAPTER ONE

Prelude

Down At The Twist And Shout

Saturday night and the moon is out
I wanna head on over to the Twist and Shout
Find a two-step partner and a Cajun beat
When it lifts me up I'm gonna find my feet
Out in the middle of a big dance floor
When I hear that fiddle wanna beg for more
Wanna dance to a band from Louisian' tonight.

And I never have wandered down to New Orleans
I never have drifted down a bayou stream
But I heard that music on the radio
And I swore someday I was gonna go
Down Highway 10 past Lafayette
There's Baton Rouge and I won't forget
To send you a card with my regrets
'Cause I'm never gonna come back home.

"Down At The Twist And Shout" by Mary Chapin Carpenter © 1990,
recorded on *Shooting Straight in the Dark*, CBS 46077

When I first heard "Down At The Twist And Shout," it was performed live at a dance circa 1992–93 in Berkeley, California, by a local "swamp boogie" band, Tee Fee. Since that band was performing many original songs, I assumed that this was one of them, and all the more so due to its apt portrayal of how many of the dancers in attendance that night, myself included, had been introduced to the music. I mistakenly thought that the song was a tribute to Ashkenaz, the Berkeley club where we were dancing and where one or two Cajun or zydeco dances took place each week.

In fact, Mary Chapin Carpenter, the singer-songwriter star who began her career playing the coffeehouse circuit around Washington, D.C., wrote and recorded this song for which she earned a Grammy award in 1992 for best country female vocal performance. Carpenter wrote this song one cold, rainy weekend in her Takoma Park, Maryland, apartment when she heard that Michael Doucet and his band Beausoleil would be playing at the Twist and Shout, a D.C. area music venue where she had previously heard other "roots" acts. Without attending the Beausoleil show—and indeed, with little prior exposure to Cajun music except for local public radio programming—she nevertheless wrote this remarkable song. In a dream come true for the songwriter, Beausoleil later agreed to collaborate on its recording.[1]

When I discovered that the song I had first heard performed live in Berkeley was actually a national hit on the country charts, I was both surprised and intrigued. How could Carpenter write a song whose lyrics and manner of musical presentation—a non-Cajun singing in English to a Cajun two-step rhythm, with Cajun musicians (Michael Doucet, fiddle; Jimmy Breaux, accordion; and Billy Ware, percussion) sitting in—fit so well a place (Ashkenaz in Berkeley) that was in no way an inspiration for the song? Its depiction of a dance hall "up north" was startlingly apt for those out west. The song's success as a commodity in popular music culture could be taken as a measure of the songwriter's ability to capture a certain zeitgeist, having to do with the marketing power of the word *Cajun* as a catchall term to signify exotic food, music, and other expressive culture across all historically francophone groups in Louisiana. Louisiana French music has been used in recent years as a soundtrack to promote a wide variety of commodities, including world music recordings, Louisiana tourism, grocery stores, over-the-counter stomach medicine, and automotive parts.

Like the appearance of the Cajun label as a marketing tool and like the popularity of Carpenter's song, the existence of a thriving dance scene for live Cajun and zydeco music some 2,000 miles from the home base of these regional styles begs the questions, how and why? In a region triangulated by Santa Cruz and Sonoma Counties along the coast and Sacramento to the east, dances to live Cajun and/or zydeco music have been held roughly four times a week since the early 1990s when I began my field research. While the focus of the book is an ethnographic study of this local scene, I have chosen to lead off by examining "Down At The Twist And Shout," an item of mass popular culture, to emphasize that this scene did not appear for reasons entirely unique to northern California and to provide a starting point for a discussion of themes that will resurface in other chapters.

Postcolonial critiques of anthropological practice acknowledge that other forms of travel writing have great relevance to ethnography, including writings by colonial governors, missionaries, journalists, and novelists. Why not then also songwriting? It may seem a stretch to associate "Down At The Twist And Shout" with travel writing and ethnography, given that it does not directly portray the writer's experiences of travel or even of attending a Cajun dance at the local club. Still, the romance of travel is a central theme of the song, and the coupling of its lyrical content with its commercial success as a pop song makes it ripe for an analysis of what its success can tell us about its audience(s). In this case, Mary Chapin Carpenter's "Down At The Twist And Shout" embodies a larger trend in popular culture to rehabilitate the image of Cajuns and to treat aspects of their culture as objects of touristic desire.[2]

Francophone culture in Louisiana is the result of the travels of multiple groups, most notably Acadian refugees and African slaves. The traditionally French-speaking Cajuns and Creoles distinguish between their two cultural groups and their respective Cajun and zydeco musics, as well as between themselves and American society. Broadly defined, in southwestern Louisiana *Cajun* refers to a white person with some relation by blood or marriage with French-speaking ancestors who were deported from the region known as *Acadie* in eastern Canada at the hands of the British in 1755; *Creole* refers to a person of color descended from French speakers with a mixture of European, African, and Native American ancestors. Both groups have evolved their identities by absorbing cultural influences over time from many groups of settlers. Furthermore, both define themselves in opposition to *American*, the general term used by Cajuns and Creoles alike for an English-speaker neither related by blood nor assimilated through marriage. They do not apply the term to outsiders in order to disavow their citizenship to the United States, rather to mark differences in language and culture.[3]

The social context depicted in "Down At The Twist And Shout" is not only a romanticized view of Cajun life in Louisiana, but a situation in which a group of northerners with such views gather to celebrate their shared leisure choice with the help of a band from the very place and culture that has them transfixed. In other words, tourists of a sort are included in the travel snapshot that the song provides, but the roles of host and guest have been reversed: the representatives of the culture being visited (the band) have traveled afar while the tourists (the dancers) have stayed close to home. One is left to assume that the dancers are all outsider-enthusiasts like the song subject herself, the band members are all true Louisianians, and that relations between these two groups are completely harmonious.

What does it mean for *this* songwriter to write and record *this* song? Mary Chapin Carpenter herself is no stranger to identity politics. Questions of authenticity have arisen frequently in print concerning the cosmopolitan, prep-school, Ivy-League, white-collar, liberal-politicking Carpenter and whether or not her music can properly be considered country music, a category in which she has enjoyed most of her commercial success. She has said of her early days in country music, "If anything, I felt insecure about fitting into any kind of category. Not because I didn't want to be part of any category, but that I thought that somebody was going to find me out and say, 'You don't belong here. You're a fraud.' Then somebody called me a country musician, and I was scared. I felt like I was credential-poor, but my heart was in the right place." While this issue may be old news in the evolution of Carpenter's career, it is a story that gets reenacted frequently in Cajun and zydeco music, albeit without commercial success and celebrity at stake, as outsider-enthusiasts become deeply immersed as musicians and dancers.[4]

A Louisiana French dancer once described Carpenter to me as an outsider who had taken commercial advantage of trends in popular taste by writing and recording "Down At The Twist And Shout" without knowing very much about Cajun culture. For Carpenter, her association with Cajun music through this one song was enough to land her a spot on the pre-game program of the 1997 Super Bowl in New Orleans, performing it with Doucet's band, Beausoleil, as backup. The division of labor between the Anglo-American star and the Cajun backup band replicates an inequity in social and economic clout that is seen to persist in Louisiana and that parallels a similar division in Paul Simon's *Graceland* and more recent cross-cultural collaborative projects in popular music.[5]

On the other hand, charges of theft and ignorance on the part of Carpenter seem exaggerated—the criticism overlooks the role that Cajun music star Michael Doucet played in the performance of the song, and the fact that this is the only song with a Cajun theme that she has written. Doucet's band Beausoleil, while already well-known and successful enough to employ their own booking agent, received even more exposure by touring with her, appearing in a music video of the song and on stage with her on the Country Music Association awards and the Grammy awards broadcasts, as well as at the Super Bowl.[6]

Furthermore, the songwriting and arranging do not demonstrate ignorance but rather communicate knowledge of Cajun culture at multiple levels of sophistication: casual music listener, country music fan, Cajun music fan, and ethnic insider. Although Carpenter has written and arranged "Down At The Twist And Shout" so that one may easily dance to it as a Cajun two-step, it is evident for several reasons that this is not a newly composed piece of Cajun music, rather a song *about* Cajun music, both in its lyrical and musical content. One might say that it achieves some ethnographic distance from its subject matter. The music establishes a Cajun two-step but is written and arranged more by Nashville standards; after Charles Seeger and Christopher Small, it might be said to be musicking about music. The lyrics for the song are in English, while Cajun dance music is almost always still sung in French. (Zydeco, a related genre associated with Louisiana's

Creole population, by contrast is now mostly sung in English.) Michael Doucet remembers that "people in Louisiana played that song but we never played that song. People would have hired us to do the song. We'd say, we don't do that song! She does that song." While it has been popular with country music audiences, I have never heard this song played at a dance featuring Louisiana French music except by one Bay Area band; Tee Fee bassist Linda Schmidt called it "our Top Forty song." Yet, through the lyrics Carpenter addresses listeners with various levels of familiarity with Cajun culture, and through the music she and the rest of her musicians evoke the feeling of being on the dance floor.[7]

Example 1. Complete Lyrics to "Down At The Twist And Shout." Words and Music by Mary Chapin Carpenter. (c) 1990 EMI APRIL MUSIC INC. and GETAREALJOB MUSIC. All Rights Controlled and Administered by EMI APRIL MUSIC INC. All Rights Reserved. International Copyright Secured. Used by Permission

Chorus

Saturday night and the moon is out
I wanna head on over to the Twist and Shout
Find a two-step partner and a Cajun beat
When it lifts me up I'm gonna find my feet
Out in the middle of a big dance floor
When I hear that fiddle wanna beg for more
Wanna dance to a band from Louisian' tonight.

Verse 1

And I never have wandered down to New Orleans
I never have drifted down a bayou stream
But I heard that music on the radio
And I swore someday I was gonna go
Down Highway 10 past Lafayette
There's Baton Rouge and I won't forget
To send you a card with my regrets
'Cause I'm never gonna come back home.

Chorus

Verse 2

They got a alligator stew and a crawfish pie
A gulf storm blowing into town tonight
Living on the delta it's quite a show

They got hurricane parties every time it blows
But here up north it's a cold cold rain
And there ain't no cure for my blues today
Except when the paper says Beausoleil
Is coming into town baby let's go down

Chorus

Verse 3
Bring your mama bring your papa bring your sister too
They got lots of music and lots of room
When they play you a waltz from 1910
You're gonna feel a little bit young again
Well you learned to dance with your rock'n'roll
You learned to swing with do c'est do
But you learn to love at the fais do do
When you hear a little Jolie Blon

Chorus

Let us assume a casual listener who knows little or nothing about the songwriter, about country music, or about Cajun culture, but has working knowledge of music and regional stereotypes in U.S. popular culture. In the chorus, the phrases "Cajun beat" and "band from Lou'sian'" cue the listener that the song is about Cajun music, even if he or she has never heard the music before. Familiar place names like New Orleans and Baton Rouge reinforce the location of Louisiana as the area of interest, while Lafayette and Highway 10 may go by unnoticed. "Alligator stew and crawfish pie" serve as reminders of the reputation of Cajun food as a distinctive regional cuisine, while "gulf storm" and "hurricane" evoke the region's renowned weather.

For a general pop music listener who has at least heard Louisiana French dance music before, the presence of an accordion on the recording would alone be enough to lead one to associate the performance with Cajun music or zydeco, as opposed to rock or country. The appearance of the fiddle makes it yet more recognizable as Cajun as compared to other accordion styles such as polka, even for the listener minimally knowledgeable about any of these styles. Although the accordion is not foregrounded to the usual extent, it does get a short solo.

Somewhat closer to Cajun culture are listeners familiar with country music, in which this song received most of its attention and with which Cajun music has a history of mutual influences. Country listeners would have in mind a step pattern for the "two-step" that is different from the most common Cajun two-step, but they would recognize the music as a two-step in rhythm and tempo, and would assume correctly that the dance is a partner dance. The verse/chorus pattern of the song and the high proportion of vocals compared to instrumental passages conform closely to conventions of country songwriting and arranging.

While fans of Cajun and zydeco music are heavily outnumbered by the country music audience and cannot by themselves account for the song's popular success, nevertheless there are numerous references that only those who have more than a passing familiarity with southern Louisiana would catch. In contrast to the casual listener, for Cajun music fans the reference to New Orleans in verse one brings relatively marginal associations of tourist-targeted representations of Cajun culture, while the less well-known Highway Ten and Lafayette resonate as the road through Cajun and Creole country and its urban center, a vacation destination for dancers. In verse two, "alligator stew and crawfish pie" are more esoteric examples of Cajun food than familiar dishes such as gumbo, jambalaya, boudin, or boiled crawfish. Mention of Beausoleil, a widely known band that does nationwide touring, might evoke a positive memory of a concert attended. Verse three validates this listener's leisure choice of Cajun dancing as the dance where "you learn to love," and communicates through insider terminology such as "fais-do-do" (an evening of Cajun dance), "Jolie Blon" (the title of a waltz often called "the Cajun national anthem"), and the Cajun French endearment, "*Eh, chère!*"

In addition to these signs, Carpenter also conveys a good deal about the subjective experience of participating in Cajun dances. The subject of the song (not to be confused with the songwriter) in the first verse reveals her vow to herself to make a pilgrimage to the home of the music she loves, a utopia from which she pledges not to return. The word *pilgrimage* is used intentionally here, for while this is a strictly secular dance genre, some of its adherents consider their dancing career in ways akin to a spiritual journey. They may have had an initial conversion experience, as the song's subject did over the radio, by listening or by watching someone else dance or by dancing themselves with a skillful partner. The dance may function for them, following the classical definition of leisure, in terms of self-fulfillment: it allows them to "become more of what their nature intends them to be," or as the song says, "when it lifts me up, I'm gonna find my feet." The beat simultaneously uplifts and grounds the dancer, a striking image underscored musically by the vocalist's accented on-beat articulation of "find my feet" and by band members' "Cajun yells" (so credited in recording's liner notes) in the background following those words in choruses two and three.[8]

The image from the chorus of the dancer being lifted up suggests not only spiritual uplift but also a physical sense of lightness, perhaps even of being suspended above the floor, buoyed by the energy of the beat. This matches what psychologist Mihaly Csikszentmihalyi calls *optimal experience* or *flow*, where a person's skill level is well-matched with the demands of an activity in which goals are clear and feedback immediate. In such situations, subjects report focused concentration, a feeling of control, a distorted sense of time, and a lack of self-awareness. "Irrelevant thoughts, worries, distractions no longer have a chance to appear in consciousness. There is simply not enough room for them. . . . Because the activity forces us to concentrate on a limited field of stimuli, there is a great inner clarity, awareness is logically coherent and purposeful."[9]

A pair of dancers who are comfortably familiar with the basic step can lose themselves in proceeding to listen to the music, follow the beat with the basic step pattern, attend to the bodily contact with each other, synchronize their interpretations of the beat, improvise moves within the basic step, avoid collisions with other couples, and express their reactions on the proceedings by verbal or nonverbal means to each other, to other dancers, and to musicians on the bandstand. At the same time, they also *find* themselves in an activity that "reaffirms the order of the self and is so enjoyable, [they] will attempt to replicate it whenever possible."[10] Betty Leblanc, a Creole who has been dancing zydeco her whole life, explains:

> Zydeco, if you really look at zydeco, zydeco music, it's a darn stress relief. Therapy thing. It really is. Because if you're all stressed out and if you go there, and you get on that floor, and if you don't know what the hell you doin', you still could let that stress out of you. Because I know for a fact, I know how I feel about it. And when I get on that floor, I forget everything. I just concentrate on that music, and I carry it to my heart. And once I carry it to my heart and let it down on that floor, my feet can just go with it. And my heart just goes with the flow. And that's what you gotta do. And if you love people, people gonna see that energy that you throwing out, they love to be around you. They want a part of that energy.[11]

On the second, third, and fourth choruses, Carpenter shouts more than sings the word "beg" in, "wanna hear that music, wanna *beg* for more" on a downbeat, emphasizing the desire with which her dancer wants to re-create that optimal experience. Dancers will confess at times that they have had too much of a good thing; indeed the urgency in the singer's tone of voice reveals a quality of compulsion or dependency regarding the euphoric feeling that occasionally leads a dancer in northern California to attend dances three or four nights in a week.

The third verse transports the listener through time as well as space with its nostalgia for a "waltz from 1910." All generations in the family are welcome (various lines in the verse seem directed at different age brackets), which fits with the image of the traditional dance event in Louisiana, where children, parents, and grandparents all attend and dance with each other. This is an image that would be familiar to Louisiana French people and Cajun music fans alike. However, the nostalgia for 1910 gets somewhat tangled up with the name of the dance club, the Twist and Shout, taken from the name of an actual club but also hearkening back to popular music of a more recent era. Perhaps this reference to the early Beatles (and before them, the Isley Brothers) works to portray a venue that, like its patrons, looks backward. The verse ends with a journey toward sexual and emotional maturity, where a progression in dance styles starts with "rock 'n' roll" (dancing by oneself), continues with square dancing (basic moves with a variety of partners), and culminates "where you learned to love," with Cajun dancing (dancing a whole dance with one partner). This sequence suggests that, just as in Louisiana, Cajun dancing "up north" has a courtship function but (less like Louisiana) for a later stage in life.[12]

There may be more to the progression from rock and roll to square dancing to Cajun dancing than simply the life cycle of a dancer. Musician Eric Thompson has insightfully suggested that part of Cajun dancing's allure to outsiders is its suitability as "safe sex" for contemporary times, that is, physical contact with no risk or commitment. In not-too-distant decades, according to this theory, there was less need to touch one's dance partner or even have a partner at all while dancing, since casual sexual liaisons were fairly common. In the current era of heightened concern over sexually transmitted diseases, people are far more discriminating about their sexual partners, and therefore the physical contact of partner dancing becomes a substitute for other kinds of intimacy for one to share with a variety of partners. Note the similarity to Carpenter's song in musicians Eric and Suzy Thompson's comparisons of the "hippie hop" (dancing to rock music), contra dance (similar in partner interaction to square dancing), and Cajun dancing:

> Eric: You know, a lot of these people had been contra dancers before they got in the Cajun scene.
> Suzy: Or folk dancers.
> Eric: Why had they gotten interested in contra dancing? Because you held someone rather than just standing apart from them, you know. It was couple dancing. And then I said, "I get it!" You know, this really fulfills a need now, where people need to have a . . .

Suzy: Right, whereas in the sixties or the seventies, then they could do the hippie hop and then just go home with somebody.
Eric: Right.
Suzy: But they're not going to do that now.
Eric: They want to *stay* and flirt and have a good time.
Author: Why aren't those people contra dancing now, though? They were contra dancing before.
Suzy: This is much sexier.
Eric: Much sexier, you see.[13]

Another sort of insider, of course, is the Louisiana Cajun or Creole steeped in his own culture. For such a listener, the mention of New Orleans in conjunction with Cajun music could give the impression of ignorance, as the Atchafalaya Basin effectively separates the city from Cajun and Creole country both geographically and culturally. A Cajun song sung in English could be seen to undermine political efforts in southern Louisiana to preserve French there as a living language. In Louisiana, music often plays a role in public relations efforts to persuade people to use their French, and music is a major component of radio programming in French. Therefore, it is significant that Carpenter chose to replace the third chorus in her performance at the Super Bowl in New Orleans with Michael Doucet's French translation of it, albeit an abbreviated one of eight measures instead of the original sixteen. The bilingual gesture is clearly one of respect. The French endearment "*Eh, chère!*" at the end of chorus four could be a charming form of imitative flattery coming from an outsider, or it could be irritating—who does she think she is? Conversely, the musical ending to the studio recording that might sound perverse or "wrong" to an outsider (a song ending on the four-chord or subdominant, D major, instead of the one-chord or tonic, A major) would sound perfectly normal to someone who has been around a lot of Cajun music, since this is how an accordionist playing a Cajun diatonic accordion tuned in D would typically end a song, by pushing in on the bellows to punctuate the ending, which happens to produce a D chord regardless of the key of the song. Doucet describes the decision to end the recorded performance this way in terms of C accordion playing in the key of G (the same chord relationships, tuned down a whole step), and casts it as a subversive tweak of musical convention:

And then I said, well one thing we have to end on the four. And they said what? I said yeah, end on the four. And if you hear the original recording, that's how we did it. Later, somebody says, the producer says, "this is not right." [laughs] And the only reason that Cajun music ends on the four is because of the accordion. Usually if you

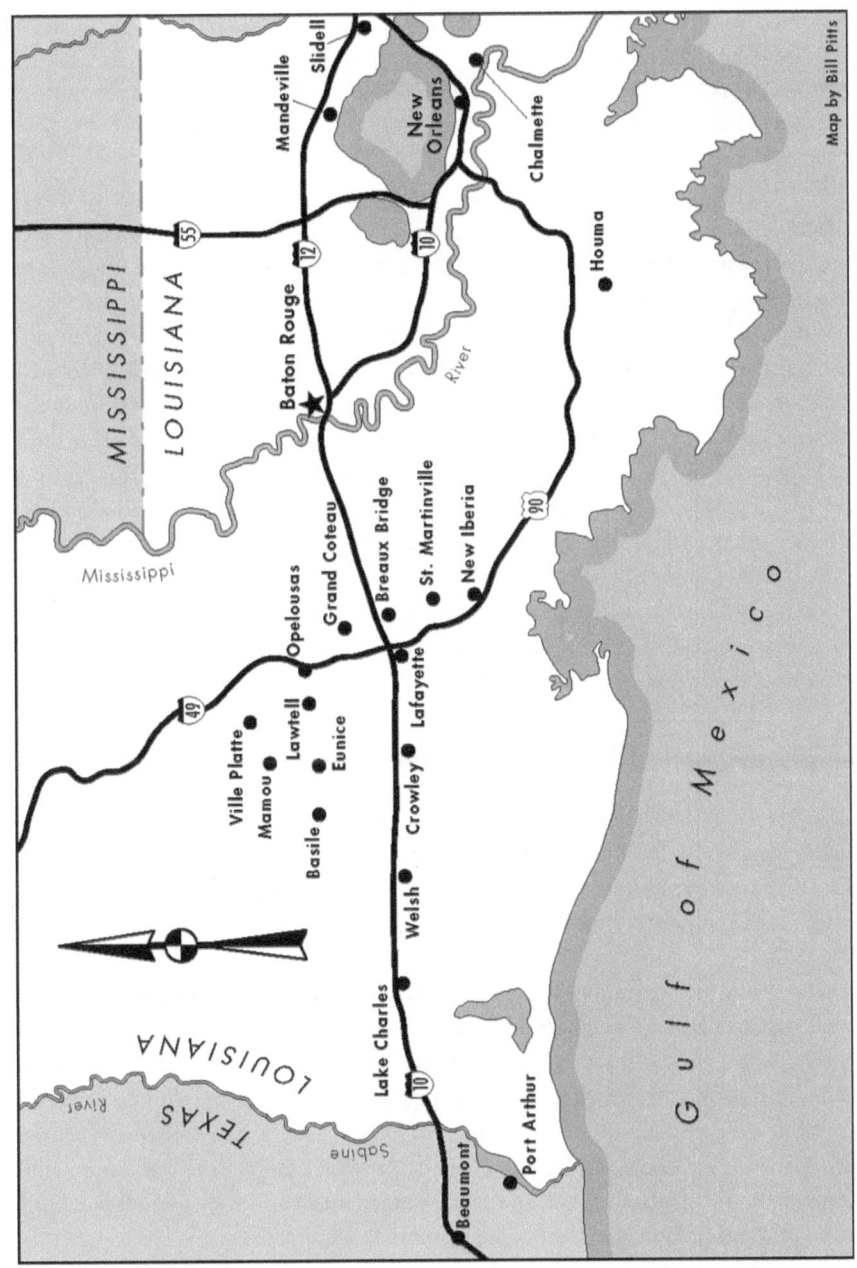

pull, like in G and if you push it's in C, and that's the way it is. And you usually end the dance pressing in, so no matter what key it's in, it's going to end in C. So if the song's in G, it's going to be the four. And that's what happened, that's the only reason, it's not like any kind of musical reason.[14]

The point of ethnography remains, as Gupta and Ferguson have put it, "diversifying and making more complex our understanding of various places, people, and predicaments through an attentiveness to the different forms of knowledge available from different social and political locations." Mary Chapin Carpenter has done exactly this in "Down At The Twist And Shout." The songwriting and arranging communicate knowledge of Cajun culture at multiple levels of sophistication simultaneously. While the dance groove that the rhythm section establishes creates a moment-to-moment sense of a Cajun two-step, the song's form and arrangement do not. The sound of the accordion and fiddle evoke Cajun music, while the singer's English does not. These and other irresolvable conflicting tendencies in the song effectively iconify the sometimes conflicting, sometimes congruent motivations of the American and Louisiana French people who convene to dance to Cajun or zydeco music in Washington, D.C., in northern California, in Louisiana, and elsewhere. The song illuminates romanticized notions of Cajun culture and optimal experiences of dancing that go to the heart of why so many people take up Cajun and zydeco dancing as an avocation. Carpenter may never have waltzed a Cajun waltz at the time she wrote the song, but she had traveled, been exposed to images of Cajun culture in the media, and (one supposes) had experienced a "dance high" firsthand; for her this was enough. As Dean MacCannell points out in *The Tourist*, "the deep structure of modernity is a totalizing idea." From this same atmosphere of modernity that everyone breathes have Cajun dancers and the songwriter drawn their inspiration.[15]

This opening chapter touches on themes that are central to the book, including the wide dissemination of symbols of Cajun culture, tourism, and the meeting of cultural insiders and outsiders on the dance floor. But the book is about much more than abstract themes and trends; it centers around a vibrant Cajun and zydeco music and dance scene in the San Francisco Bay Area and nearby regions of northern California. Global and national trends provide a larger context, but equally important are historical events that concentrated interest in Cajun and Creole cultures in the Bay Area, and the people who made it happen.

The heart of this volume is devoted to particulars: the Creoles (as well as some Cajuns) who moved to California from Louisiana during and after World War II and the music they made in their new home; the folk revivalists who eventually

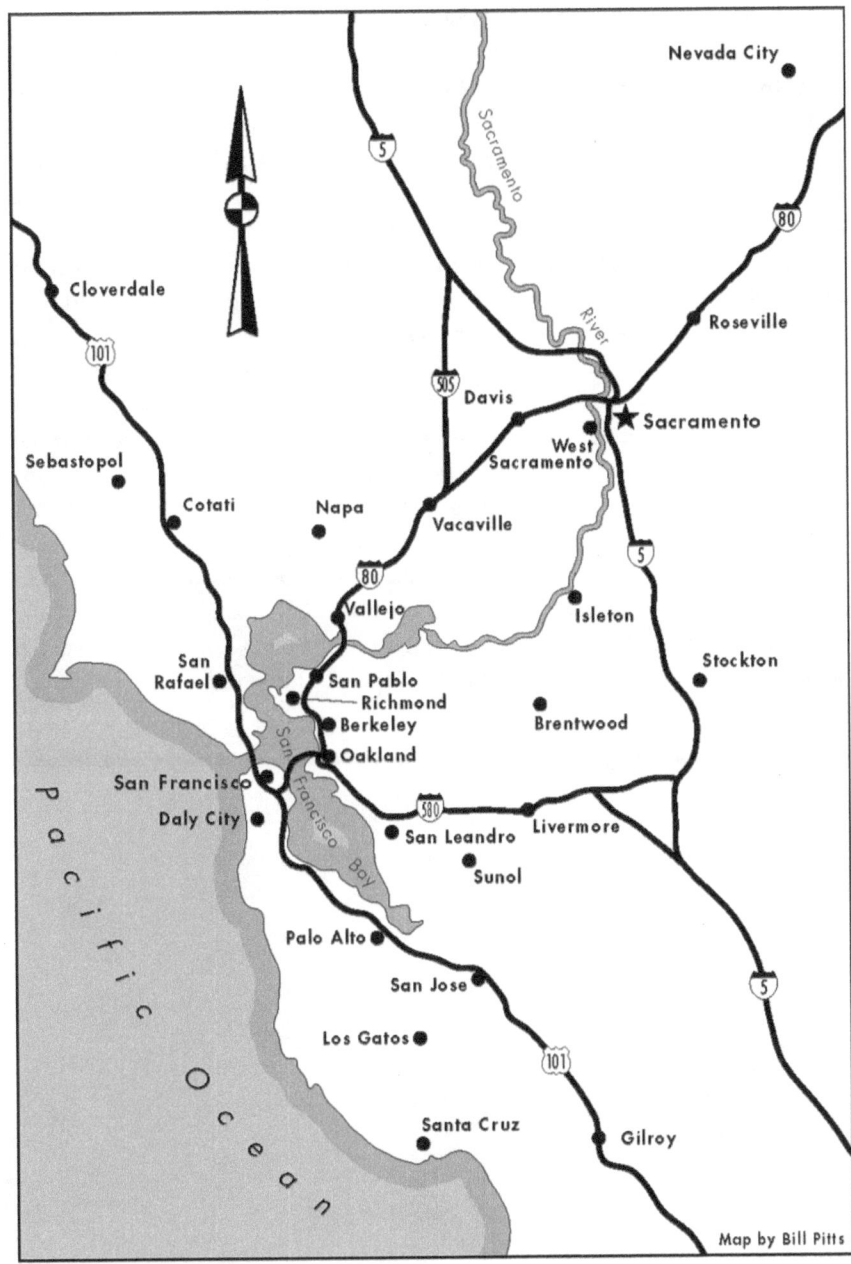

joined them on the dance floor and the bandstand; the careers of record producer Chris Strachwitz and filmmaker Les Blank, both of whom are based in the Bay Area; and the key role that accordionist Danny Poullard played as tradition bearer and mentor for a great many of the musicians who still play for dances today.

Within this loose narrative of the development of Cajun and zydeco music in northern California dwell larger questions: What underlying forces led to the twin births of an ethnic renaissance in francophone Louisiana and a discovery of Cajun and Creole music within the larger nationwide folk and blues revivals of the 1960s? How can Creole migration to California be understood in the context of general population resettlement patterns of the mid-twentieth century? How does the mediation of Cajun and zydeco music through concert tours, recordings, films, and cultural tourism serve to reinforce attendance at local live events? How does the scene sustain itself? These questions in turn flow from the most fundamental ethnographic question: What is going on here? This is the thought that struck me when I realized my mistake of thinking that "Down At The Twist And Shout" was inspired by what I was seeing in California. This is a question that you might ask yourself, as I did, the first time that you walk into a dance hall in Berkeley or Alameda or Brisbane or Sacramento to see couples fluidly waltzing and two-stepping to live Cajun and zydeco music emanating from the bandstand, not as a special occasion but as if this were the most normal thing in the world.

CHAPTER TWO

Identity Issues, Research Methods, and Ethnography

When approaching the music and dance of living ethnic groups actively appreciated by others, be it zydeco or Balkan music or salsa, it is difficult to escape a rhetorical opposition of insiders and outsiders. Indeed, the first chapter employs this opposition in describing the tableau of "Down At The Twist And Shout" (a band of insiders and a dance floor full of outsiders) and in analyzing the song's possible receptions using a range of perspectives from outside to inside Louisiana French culture. This prevalent habit of thinking in terms of insiders and outsiders has had a fundamental impact on the intertwined developments of Cajun and Creole ethnicity and the mass-mediated consumption of Cajun and Creole culture as we know them today. This chapter grapples with questions of identity as they apply to Cajun and Creole history, to the author and his research methods, and to how the book is written. In the course of the discussion, it should become clear what is meant by the book's subtitle, *Modern Pleasures in a Postmodern World*.

Modern Pleasures

The opposition of insider and outsider contains within it the seeds of two opposing views of identity. Identity definition revolves around the insider, who has something that the outsider does not have that involves belonging to a group. Whether that belonging is based on racial characteristics, or someplace where one was born and raised, or a language spoken, or a religion practiced, or some combination of these circumstances, such an identity is taken to be an essential, lifelong experience for those who belong to the group. The sentiment about rural living, "You can take the boy out of the country but you can't take the country out of the boy," exemplifies this essentialist view of identity, as does the notion of *roots* when we talk about "roots music," "I'm going back to my roots," and so on. Stuart Hall describes such a view of identity this way:

> [T]he language of identity has often been related to the search for a kind of authenticity to one's experience, something that tells me where I come from. The logic and language of identity is the logic of depth—in here, deep inside me, is my Self which I can reflect upon. It is an element of continuity. I think most of us do recognize that our identities have changed over time, but we have the hope or nostalgia that they change at the rate of a glacier. So, while we're not the fledglings that we were when we were one year old, we are the same sort of person.[1]

Hall's explanation of identity immediately brings in another problematic term, *authenticity*, that is integral to how many people talk about Cajun and Creole music. References to the authentic or to its correlates—*genuine, original, traditional, real,* or *heritage*—serve both as shorthand and as a power move. They are shorthand for an intellectual history that goes back over two hundred years to Herder, Rousseau, and others. The discourse around authenticity combines various ideas of what modernity has displaced—nature displaced by civilization, oral tradition by the printed word, innocence by constant reflection and alienation concerning our place in the world—and expresses a longing to recover what has been lost. Popular sentiments run parallel to intellectual history along these lines—for example, themes of loss and longing in the words sung in Cajun dance music. The etymology and semantic associations around the word *authenticity*—"one who acts with authority," "made by one's own hand," the determination of sacred relics or masterworks of art as genuine or spurious—resonate with power. To declare something authentic is to legitimate it, perhaps even to suggest that it has been touched either by God himself (in the case of sacred relics) or through the intermediary of inspired human genius. That genius has typically been traced to a great artist by name or to a folk community expressing its emotions in a "natural" (God-given) fashion.[2]

In her book on the scholarly and popular search for authenticity through folklore in German-speaking Europe and in the United States, Regina Bendix grants that "this search arises out of a profound human longing, be it religious-spiritual or existential," and yet if she had her way she would abolish the concept: "If this work assists in removing authenticity—in particular, its deceptive promises of transcendence—from the vocabulary of the emerging global script, its major purpose will have been served." Authenticity's deceptions have, for example, led folklorists at various times to (wittingly or unwittingly) aid political movements such as Nazism in Germany to justify their notions of racial or ethnic purity, and according to Bendix they have led the field of folkloristics itself to the brink of academic extinction in North America.[3]

Deception and confusion are built into the concept's multiple meanings, which often come into conflict in their application. One meaning of authenticity resides within the individual; this is what Stuart Hall uses when he describes identity in terms of "authenticity to one's experience." Other meanings of the word get applied to things or people external to oneself. Musical performances are often judged for authenticity based on the evaluator's comparison of the sounds heard with sounds imagined from a bygone era whose musical practices can, at best, only be intelligently guessed at—what the orchestra at Prince Esterházy's court sounded like in 1780 under Franz Joseph Haydn's direction, for example, or what Cajun dance music sounded like at the dawn of the twentieth century, when Dennis McGee was a boy. Musicians themselves are judged authentic or not, especially in relation to music from specific folk or ethnic communities, based primarily on circumstances of birth and enculturation. Folklore is often collected or appreciated according to its authenticity in terms of "salvage value," i.e., the extent to which it represents a marginal survival of an endangered or disappearing culture. As we have already seen in "Down At The Twist And Shout" and will continue to see throughout this book, all of these meanings of authenticity and more come into play with Louisiana French music both at "home" and in other locales such as California.[4]

The much-chronicled story of the *Grand Dérangement*, the 1755 British deportation of Acadians from Canada that caused thousands of refugees eventually to relocate to Louisiana, is an ethnohistory that typifies the notion of an essential identity. It also received an early popular culture treatment with the publication of Longfellow's long poem "Evangeline" in 1847. Cajun historian Carl Brasseaux has refined the notion of Cajun "roots" by clustering Cajun history into three phases: the Acadians coalesce in Canada in the seventeenth century and then regroup in Louisiana in the eighteenth century; the Acadians assimilate other groups and become the Cajuns in the nineteenth century; and the Cajuns slowly accede to Americanization in the twentieth century. Interest in genealogy among Cajuns has increased in recent years, as one may witness through publications and the establishment of the Acadian Memorial in St. Martinville, Louisiana, where the names of all of the documented original refugees from Acadia who settled in Louisiana are enshrined and which provides assistance to amateur genealogists. The Acadian Memorial also happens to be just down the street from the Evangeline Oak, a tourist site that commemorates a legendary tragic reunion between supposed real-life counterparts to Longfellow's Acadian lovers (event and persons apparently with no basis in fact).[5]

Group identity among Louisiana Creoles may be just as strongly held as the Cajuns', but the history and discourse surrounding them are much different. Rather than introducing the Creoles with a tale of origins, it is more common to begin with definitions of "what or who is a Creole?" because the definition is so contested. Dominguez cites seven different dictionary definitions of the proper noun *Creole* that are concerned with Louisiana, one of which is "loosely, anyone from Louisiana." Her research revealed multiple conflicting views of Creole identity among New Orleans residents. In the New Orleans white Creole conception she describes, there are whites (Americans, Creoles, Cajuns, Italians, Irish, Jews) and coloreds (mulattos or *gens de couleur*, and Negros); thus Creoles are not black and those of Afro-French descent are lumped with African Americans. One alternate conception maintains the white/colored dichotomy but divides the coloreds into Creole and black, thus claiming Creoles to be "colored." Yet another view is that there are white *and* colored Creoles, as well as white and colored non-Creoles.[6]

Outside of New Orleans, the rural version of this eternal terminological contention is hardly less profound:

> In South Louisiana today, French-speaking whites generally call themselves Cajuns, though some maintain the traditional distinction by calling themselves French Creoles. French-speaking blacks ordinarily call themselves Creoles. These distinctions are frequently overlooked by outsiders, who lump all groups together as "Cajuns."[7]

> When speaking French, many Cajuns do not refer to themselves as being "Français" or "Cajin," but rather as being "Créole." But when these same people speak English they refer to themselves as being simply "French." To a Cajun a "Français" is a person from France, and a "Cajin" is a Louisiana-Frenchman, and a "Creole" is a French-speaking black.[8]

Ben Sandmel summed it up best in his book on zydeco: "'Creole' is a highly controversial word in south Louisiana, involving a complex, biased web of racial and socioeconomic identities. . . . Many people who call themselves 'Creole,' by whatever definition, become livid when the name is used by others whom they consider inferior, unworthy usurpers."[9]

Evidently, summary attempts to identify Louisiana Creoles as a group of people are doomed to failure, or at least to interminable debate. In this book, "Creole" refers to the group of French-speaking blacks and mulattos of southwestern Louisiana most often associated with zydeco music and dancing, and from whom have come most of the musical innovators of the style.

The history of Creole identity starts with the French adoption of the Code Noir in Louisiana in 1724, which legally established a tripartite racial classification of white, free people of color, and slave. Over time, the numbers of the middle category swelled with black mistresses of white men and their mulatto children, beginning in New Orleans and then fanning out into frontier prairie regions to the west. This group, which also came to be named Creoles of Color, had the same rights as the whites under the law at the time, and thus established a group identity separate from the black slaves in order to maintain those rights. The Louisiana Purchase of 1803 marked the beginning of a "vigorous battle among Latin creoles, Americans, and foreign French for control of the society" in New Orleans, and the Americans gradually came to introduce their two-category, white/black, system of racial stratification. The institution of racial segregation in the 1879 version of the Louisiana State Constitution marked the evaporation of the rights and privileges enjoyed by upper-class free people of color through remnants of the Code Noir; they became subject to the same segregation laws as the freed slaves. "But despite the loss of status and property," James Dormon explains, "the Creoles maintained their sense of identity and belonging, their basic group identity, as well as their conviction of their own superiority over the mass of the black population.... With the advent of systematic Jim Crow segregation in the 1890s and the removal of all vestiges of their 'in-between' social status, the Creoles were left with nothing but their sense of group identity and a nostalgia for halcyon times."[10]

Why are the Creoles so often lumped with Cajuns? I would argue that an archetypal narrative of diaspora like the Jewish liberation from Egypt, refracted through the lenses of American and Acadian histories, means that the Cajuns more closely fit common notions of an ethnic group in the United States than do the Creoles. Both groups have persisted in Louisiana for over two hundred years, for much of their history as oppressed groups, so there is little differentiation on the basis of longevity or social status (although race, obviously, is a factor, and I do not mean to deny the presence of racism as a factor in the Creoles' invisibility and therefore in the conflation). The Cajuns are a more prototypical ethnic group precisely because they are a diaspora group, "scattered to the wind" by the British only later to regroup in Louisiana. Their story of "travel," while not integral to their religious beliefs, brings them one step closer to the narrative of a chosen people, and closer to the story of early immigrant settlements in North America.[11]

Most definitions of Creole, by contrast, even if they agree on nothing else, do agree that to be Creole means to have been born in Louisiana: i.e., as a group, the Creoles have never relocated. Although their ancestors came from Europe and Africa, the history of the Creoles proper begins in Louisiana, and except for the minority of them that migrated to California or elsewhere, it remains there. Add to this lack of movement the amount of energy that is inevitably spent in discussing the racial makeup of the Creole group, the conflicting applications of the concept of "Creole" in other parts of the world, and the confusion for most Americans that ensues when they are confronted with a group of African descent that holds itself distinct from African Americans, and one may see why Creole identity is such a difficult concept to grasp for most who have never lived in Louisiana.

However problematic has been the application of the terms "Cajun" and "Creole" and the confusion thereof, the fact remains that rural francophone Louisianans of all stripes have shared much in common: the French language (albeit with several highly localized subdialects), a region they called home, Catholicism, many folk beliefs and customs, and economic circumstances. With respect to one of the strongest ethnic markers, language, they shared the status of an oppressed linguistic minority. In the 1920s, state officials turned to the problem of formal education in rural southern Louisiana, where there was an illiteracy rate of over half the population. Many Cajuns, for example, were illiterate in French and did not speak English at all. The Louisiana state constitution was revised in 1921, in part to mandate English instruction and to forbid bilingual education, and Governor Huey Long followed with an English literacy campaign.[12] Dormon describes the impact of this policy:

> It was only a matter of time before the schools would do what no prior force had been able to accomplish: They would render the ethnic French monolingual population an object of derision and scorn, even among its own children. And with the penetration of urban bourgeois cultural imperatives ever deeper into the hinterland, all but the most totally isolated of the Cajun population was to be brought under its sway.... [Long's] programs... portended the end of a positive value attachment to the Cajun ethnic identity.[13]

Many Cajun and Creole children who grew up in the wake of the anti-French policy were disciplined for speaking French in school, even when it was the only language they knew. This push to Americanize Cajun schoolchildren intensified during World War II. As Dormon indicates, these children internalized prevailing attitudes about language: not only must they learn English to get ahead, but they must also hide their French-speaking skills or simply forget them altogether. Those who learned English and became bilingual were often literate in English but not in their native French, and generally avoided speaking French outside the home. Those who chose to leave French behind made sure that the next generation grew up speaking English, in order to avoid the problems in school that they themselves had experienced.[14]

As contact with the outside world grew, ethnic stereotypes associated with Cajuns and Creoles were not limited to illiteracy and language. Dormon indicates that many of the stereotypes about Cajuns were already in place during the first half of the nineteenth century: "material poverty combined with a certain lack of ambition and enterprise and an unwillingness to adopt the aggressively materialistic values of the Anglo-Americans"; "ignorant, uneducated, and without any inclination to formal education"; "hospitable to a fault, always ready to welcome visitors and offer them refreshment"; "a fun-loving people, given to such hedonistic pursuits as drinking, eating, dancing, and gambling"; "large, tightly knit families." These same themes appear a hundred years after Dormon's sources, sprinkled throughout *Louisiana: A Guide to the State*, published by the federal government's Work Projects Administration in 1941.[15]

The limited truth value and specificity of the stereotypes applied to Cajuns can be seen when one considers the larger discourse surrounding folk culture in America and Europe. An extreme example is German folklorist Hans Naumann, who in the 1920s developed his theory of *gesunkenes Kulturgut*, the highly questionable evolutionary notion that all creative artistic ideas originate in the high or elite culture and then "sink" to the level of folk culture. Among Naumann's characteristics of the "primitive" mental character of peasants were included several that other commentators have thought to apply to the Cajuns: laziness, hedonism, and a tendency to devote inordinate resources to festivities. The fact that Naumann, a European folklorist who had no contact with Cajun culture, expressed peasant stereotypes so closely associated with Cajuns only demonstrates the degree to which these ideas were already in the storehouse of Euro-American thought. They were then available for use whenever expediency called for them, such as during the campaign for linguistic assimilation.[16]

Where, then, are the pleasures to be taken in modern, essentialist views of identity? In the face of oppression, there are some rewards such as the sweetness of nostalgia and a sense of belonging that motivate many to cling to such an identity even as other options become available. Let us also consider Robert Cantwell's insight that, "In the modern world, the idea of folklife belongs to the romantic tradition and, like that tradition, is a response to, an instrument of, and a phenomenon of modernity." To maintain the notion of a permanent or continuing identity while living in modern society where ways of life change at an ever-accelerating rate, the idea of folklife must almost necessarily be invented to cope with the dislocations that ensue. As Bendix puts it, "The continued craving for experiences of unmediated genuineness seeks to cut through what Rousseau called 'the wound of reflection,' a reaction to modernization's demythologization, detraditionalization, and disenchantment." Self-awareness of dissatisfaction with one's life leads to an interest in folklife as potential salvation, which in turn leads back to a critique of the initial moment of self-awareness.[17]

Where Cantwell writes of folklife, Barbara Kirshenblatt-Gimblett similarly uses "heritage," which she defines as "a mode of cultural production that gives the disappearing and gone a second life as an exhibit of itself." "Heritage music" is "music that has been singled out for preservation, protection, enshrinement, and revival," as opposed to "music that is part and parcel of a way of life." When that way of life disappears or changes beyond recognition, the music it accompanied can either likewise disappear or gain "a second life as an exhibit of itself." The experience of heritage music is a modern pleasure in part because it remains a relatively fixed reference point with respect to the rapidly changing conditions of everyday life. It is reassuringly dependable. It also sets up socially approved channels for physical display and emotional expression. As much as Cajun and Creole musics are heritage musics (as they certainly are in California, and to some extent in Louisiana itself), and as much as people still find pleasure in them, they represent quintessentially modern pleasures for Cajuns, Creoles, and outsiders alike.[18]

Knowing some of the history of Cajun and Creole music gives us another perspective for understanding the identity formation of these two groups. The nascent music recording industry expanded its efforts in the 1920s into a wide array of ethnic and regional markets with an equally various offering of musical styles for every taste. This eclecticism sprang from a motivation distinct from those of the early folk song collectors. Industry leaders were in the business of selling phonograph equipment, and having recordings available of music that the customer wanted to hear helped to close the sale. Accordion-based Louisiana French dance music joined this mix when Columbia recorded Cajun musicians Joe and Cleoma Falcon in New Orleans in 1928. Amédé Ardoin, the influential Creole accordionist and singer, recorded there with Cajun fiddler Dennis McGee the following year. Cajun and Creole musicians recorded hundreds of sides in their first decade in the commercial recording industry.[19]

In 1934, John and Alan Lomax traveled to southern Louisiana for the Library of Congress and made field recordings of Cajun and Creole music that was not finding its way onto commercial discs. Some of these French songs subsequently were published in transcription in *Our Singing Country* and in the Library of Congress' *Folk Music of the United States* series of recorded albums. Irène Thérèse Whitfield, a Louisiana French woman who accompanied the Lomaxes on some of their song-hunting trips as well as doing her own field research, published her collection of folk song transcriptions in 1939, *Louisiana French Folk Songs*. The song-collecting from this period is inevitably permeated with romanticized notions of the folk, but at the same time it provides an invaluable record of the diversity of music-making in the region outside of what can be heard on commercial recordings of the same decade.[20]

The pairing of black accordionist Ardoin and white fiddler McGee around 1930 is thought by many to be a pivotal moment in Louisiana French music, for several reasons. Some point to the high quality of the music, the popularity of the performances, and the influence of Ardoin and other Creole musicians of that period on Cajun music. Others view the interracial collaboration as a road not taken, in that mixed-race bands would remain a rarity in Louisiana for decades to follow. Yet others point to the shared musical language between the two men as evidence that at one time, "it was all French music," with no arbitrary boundaries between black French music and white French music that developed later between zydeco and Cajun music.[21]

The story that "it was all French music" conjures up an appealing image, a sort of musical Eden before the fall into racial self-awareness that led people to cover themselves with the appropriate category. Yet one only need listen to the Lomax field recordings from 1934 to hear that there was already a variety of musical styles in this region, and some of the Creole selections have a heavy African influence (especially the *juré* selections) unlike any heard on the Cajun ones. At the same time, there *was* a style of dance music shared by blacks and whites in Evangeline Parish and surrounding prairies where the place names (Basile, Eunice, Lawtell, Opelousas, Mamou, Crowley, etc.) are commemorated in the repertoire (song titles and lyrics) and in the names of the bands that play it. The style and repertoire, once dubbed "the Basile complex" by Spitzer, was shared by Creole musicians Freeman and Canray Fontenot, Amédé and Bois Sec Ardoin, and Bébé and Éraste Carrière, as well as by Cajun musicians like Nathan Abshire and the Balfa brothers. This shared tradition now regarded as "Cajun music," and the creative contributions of Creoles to it, have been well documented and can be heard in Amédé Ardoin's recordings.[22]

The twentieth-century history of Cajun music, Creole music, and various mainstream American popular musical styles serves in part as a barometer of the vicissitudes of identity relations. From the early 1930s up through World War II, the interests of Cajun musicians seemed to follow the trend toward Americanization, especially in taking up popular styles of commercial country music of the day. Musicians such as the Hackberry Ramblers, Leo Soileau, Happy Fats, and Harry Choates left out the accordion from their ensembles and increasingly sang in English rather than French. This trend reversed after World War II with the accordion-based music of Iry LeJeune, whose followers moved Cajun dance music back to its French language and song repertoire but with amplification and steel guitars from country music added. Continuing the trend of reaction to Americanization, the custom of the rural *courir de Mardi Gras* was reintroduced in the 1950s in several communities that had discontinued it. Further descriptions of postwar trends in Louisiana French identities and music are laid out in opening sections of Chapters 4–8 in this book: the revaluation of Cajun and Creole ethnicities; the development of zydeco music out of older Creole styles and black popular music; the place of Louisiana French music and dancing within the mid-twentieth-century American folk revival; and the increased currency of Louisiana French music, dance, and food in American popular culture since the late 1970s. In music as in other cultural spheres, to lay claim publicly to one's own ethnicity within American society became, if not a modern pleasure, at least a modern comfort, or what Stuart Hall has termed a "counter-identity" against the forces of globalization.[23]

The 1990s saw a marked increase in the number of young musicians in Louisiana and east Texas who were interested in playing Cajun music and zydeco. While the music continues to change, thus far it has done so largely in a modernist, organic way: incrementally, with new elements incorporated so as to form a seamless whole. Several musicians have made what could be called postmodern experiments, in which other styles of music or songs from those styles are imported wholesale into the Louisiana French milieu and juxtaposed for effect, from the heavy rock of Wayne Toups to the hip hop elements used by up-and-coming zydeco musicians in their teens and twenties. Yet in a world of popular culture that so delights in pastiche, these experiments have thus far remained on the periphery of Louisiana French dance music. As vital as they are today, Cajun music and zydeco remain distinctively modern pleasures in a postmodern world.

A Postmodern World

A second view of identity is suggested by the image of the outsider, which may seem like no image at all since an outsider is defined negatively in terms of what one is not. But recall the floor full of dancers in Carpenter's song, who have escaped a "cold, cold rain" to warm up with a night of Cajun dancing. Who are these people? In the absence of other clues, we can speculate that they are non-Cajuns who appreciate Cajun culture and perhaps even enjoy an experience of role-playing for a night of dancing. As the evening unfolds song after song, they tell themselves stories and stories within stories that they are participating in a Cajun dance. Simon Frith points out that music is an eminently suitable vehicle to carry such storytelling: "Music, whether teenybop for young female fans or jazz or rap for African Americans or nineteenth century chamber music for German Jews in Israel, stands for, symbolizes *and* offers the immediate experience of collective identity. If narrative is the basis of music pleasure, to put this another way, it is also central to our sense of identity. Identity, that is to say, comes from the outside not the inside; it is something we put or try on, not something we reveal or discover."[24]

This constructivist view of identity, in contrast to the essentialist view described above in relation to the insider, suggests that identity is a matter of personal choice rather than personal discovery, subject to radical change rather than permanent or slowly evolving. The contrast between essentialist and constructivist views of identity points to another opposition that figures in the title of this book: modernity vs. postmodernity. "If the *modern* 'problem of identity' was how to construct an identity and keep it solid and stable," Zygmunt Bauman writes, "the *postmodern* 'problem of identity' is primarily how to avoid fixation and keep the options open."[25]

A major flaw in the essentialist view of identity is an insufficient acknowledgment of the role of outsiders in the definition of insider-ness. Membership in a group is characterized in part by who does *not* belong. Outsiders may form their own ideas (e.g., through stereotyping by other groups or in "mainstream" popular culture) of what it means to be an insider. Moreover, meanings undergo historical change as popular culture inevitably moves on and the relative political fortunes of insiders and outsiders shift. Such change, as that seen in the last century of Louisiana Cajun and Creole history, gives the lie to such notions as a fixed ethnic identity and an unchanging musical tradition.

In order even to think about one's own identity, one must have other identities against which to compare. This is true of insiders and outsiders alike and is what Bauman means when he says that the "problem of identity" was "born as a problem"—once the question of identity arises, the problem of competing identities (and how to maintain one's own identity in the face of them) comes right with it. Stuart Hall articulates the same notion using different language: "History changes your conception of yourself. Thus, another critical thing about identity is that it is partly the relationship between you and the Other. Only when there is an Other can you know who you are. To discover that fact is to discover and unlock the whole enormous history of nationalism and of racism."[26]

For insiders to a particular group, the Other may in certain situations be another identifiable group, or it may be outsiders as a general class. For outsiders, insiders to a group represent a particular instance of the Other. Obviously, in a multicultural society like the United States there are many Others, regardless of one's vantage point. Oppression, such as the racism to which Hall refers, arises when one group is able to maintain superior wealth, power, and prestige in part by identifying certain groups of Others in order to marginalize them economically and politically. Notions of the Other may take more benign forms, such as the economic and cultural stimuli that cultural tourism has brought to southwestern Louisiana beginning in the 1980s, but even this developed out of earlier periods of oppression in Cajun and Creole history.

When outsiders perform the cultural expression of an Other, there is ever a fine line between imitation as the sincerest form of flattery and keeping the Other in his or her place. It is up to the parties to each individual performance, performers and audience alike, to negotiate these meanings amongst themselves. More often than not in this book, I use the term *revivalist* to refer to an outsider who plays or dances to Louisiana French music, and I use the term advisedly. Certainly I do *not* mean that the music was dead and needed to be brought back to life. To the extent that the music at times needed to be awakened or enlivened (another sense of "revived") in people, partnerships of insiders and outsiders (Clifton Chenier and Chris Strachwitz, Dewey Balfa and Tracy Schwarz, Marc Savoy and Ann Allen Savoy) have indeed been key, but in those cases the cultural insiders could be said to have done as much or more of the work of reviving as their partners. But here I refer to outsiders as revivalists in the sense generally understood by those who administer government "folk arts" funding in the United States, as Jeff Todd Titon relates his experience in serving on a funding panel for the National Endowment for the Arts: "The NEA panel could identify revivalists easily enough: they had not grown up inside the family or community whose tradition they came later to practice; rather, to pick it up they had to cross ethnic, geographic, and class boundaries, or they learned it in some kind of institutional setting, and as often from other revivalists as from those with a birthright to the traditions they carried."[27]

The operative difference in the folk arts context is that "community members" are eligible for funding and "revivalists" are not, in most cases. While this practice may have the admirable goal of avoiding any possibility of cultural exploitation by outsiders at the taxpayers' expense, it also works to preserve the status of the "community" as a marginal Other, and it denies the contemporary reality of how musicians create music from everything they hear and how dancers express the music drawing on all of their bodily cultural experiences. The purpose of using *revivalist* as shorthand for cultural outsiders is not to reinscribe the folk arts meaning but to critique it, for this book shows the thoroughgoing extent of the partnership between insiders and outsiders in maintaining Louisiana French dance music, in California and more generally.

Returning once more to Mary Chapin Carpenter's image of a Cajun dance band playing for people who live and who are from somewhere else, an essential identity is as elusive for the Cajun musicians as it is for anyone else. Outsiders may rely on the fiction of stable identity for the Cajuns in order to act out their role-playing on the dance floor (the often-used phrase "dance scene" suggests a theatrical metaphor), but the Cajun musicians themselves have lives to live, places to go, business to conduct. They may engage in some "code-switching" to get themselves through their day, adopting other identities in order to simplify social interaction in situations off the musical stage. For example, they may wish to check into a hotel merely as weary travelers—no need to explain to the desk clerk that they are weary Cajun travelers. At one point, Beausoleil had (and may still have) in its boilerplate performance contract that they *not* be served Cajun food as part of the hospitality during their tour stop.[28]

So another way of looking at this dance floor vignette is that everyone is in the same boat when it comes to identity, insiders and outsiders alike. With the prototype of the vagabond, Bauman suggests that we are all postmodernists now:

> The early modern vagabond wandered through the settled places; he was a vagabond because in no place could he be settled as the other people had been. The settled were many, the vagabonds few. Post-modernity reversed the ratio. Now there are few "settled" places left. The "forever settled" residents wake up to find the places (places in the land, places in society and places in life), to which they "belong," no longer existing or no longer accommodating; neat streets turn mean, factories vanish together with jobs, skills no longer find buyers, knowledge turns into ignorance, professional experience becomes liability, secure networks of relations fall apart and foul the place with putrid waste. Now the vagabond is a vagabond not because of the reluctance or difficulty of settling down, but because of the scarcity of settled places. Now the odds are that the people he meets in his travels are other vagabonds.[29]

It is not difficult to see how the population of the San Francisco Bay Area, where most of the people one meets seem to be from somewhere else, fits this description. The thousands of Louisiana Creoles who have migrated to California since the 1940s for military-related jobs and economic opportunities of all kinds were joined by hundreds of thousands of others. Those who were born and raised in the Bay Area have had to deal with the same problems as the newcomers: homeless people on the streets, military base closings, economic upturns and downturns, old manufacturing and now new information economy jobs going overseas.

But what of Louisiana? Surely the people whose families have lived there for generations do not feel like strangers in their own home state? Here is what Cajun historian Shane Bernard has to say about the uptick in interest in Cajun culture since the 1980s:

The wild demand for south Louisiana cuisine heralded into existence a national Cajun craze. Beginning around 1980, this culinary phenomenon introduced the region's delicacies to the world, but it also led to a rash of fake Cajun food products in grocery stores and restaurants. Meanwhile, the media presented Cajun stereotypes in movies and on television, depicting them as backward swamp dwellers. The nation's infatuation with Cajun culture, real or otherwise, also created a tourism boom that economically benefited Acadiana while disrupting its remaining folk rituals. The ethnic group's dependency on tourism increased during the devastating oil glut of the 1980s, which caused a mass exodus from south Louisiana. Exiles boosted the ongoing craze by introducing others to their culture, but they also exposed themselves to influences that further eroded the traditional way of life. Cajuns who remained at home fared little better, as demonstrated by the proliferation of strip malls, fast food restaurants, and other trappings of mainstream society.[30]

While this testimony is ripe for cross-examination with respect to unreconstructed notions of fake versus authentic and "the traditional way of life" in opposition to "trappings of mainstream society," it does handily give a name for and some reasons why "Cajun" became a household word across the country in the 1980s. It also bears witness to the alienation that many feel in Louisiana. Not only have more Cajuns left their home state to seek their economic fortunes elsewhere—in Atlanta, Los Angeles, and Washington, D.C., for example—but those who stayed put may be feeling like vagabonds in their home environment. Cajun and Creole families who want to bring their children to a dance have become fellow travelers, mixing it up with the tourists at dance-hall restaurants designed originally for visitors from outside the region. Of course, tourists also visit many of the adults-only bars and nightclubs in the region that hold Cajun or zydeco dances, so there is considerable contact between tourists and locals. Likewise, Louisiana Creole families in northern California, who as a group brought zydeco and Cajun music to the state, nowadays can count on seeing outsiders at whatever dances they attend, whether located at a church, a festival, or a bar.[31]

In addition to the "backward swamp dweller" image that Bernard decries, media stereotypes of Cajuns and Creoles often seek to affix static essences. Journalists' descriptions of the home of Cajun music and dance tend to reinforce the notion that although life may be changing in Louisiana, their culture gives the Cajuns something to hold onto and stabilizes their identity as a group. In *The Virgin Directory of World Music* Andy Kershaw wrote, "For anyone with an appetite for romantic rural Americana Louisiana is a paradise. . . . In a community where [Cajuns] are still playing, enjoying, recording and buying a style of music that has remained virtually unchanged since it was first recorded in the late 1920s, the tremors of Beatlemania, it seems, are just being felt." The pigeonhole for Cajun culture in the popular imagination could hardly be stated more clearly. The characterization of Cajun music as "virtually unchanged" since the 1920s, while wildly inaccurate, reinforces the romantic notion of Cajun Country (the Louisiana Office of Tourism's moniker for the region of Louisiana that contains the highest concentration of Cajuns) as a bastion of authenticity. The emphasis on timelessness echoes now-discredited folkloristic theories of community authorship of folk culture, in which the contributions of creative individuals (and hence the possibility of culture change) are denied in favor of a "singing, dancing throng" that conducts itself according to unwavering laws of folkness tied to natural cycles. As an antidote to such idealizations of Cajun or Creole identity, we might consider the possibility that sweeping change has been as much a part of life in rural Louisiana for the past fifty years as it has been in big cities such as San Francisco or New Orleans. The civil rights movement, ups and downs in the oil industry, environmental problems like the receding coastline, hurricanes Katrina and Rita in 2005, and global agribusiness have all made their mark.[32]

The Researcher's Identity and Its Relevance

Over the years, social and cultural anthropologists have reported on the cultures they study according to various intellectual preoccupations: social functions, structural patterns, cognitive categories, symbolic analyses, or ethnicity, to name a few examples. Through these ever-changing schools of thought, there was a consistent reliance on data collection through participant observation in the field and an implicit understanding that the researcher's personal experiences and relationships with informants, while important, were largely irrelevant to the research findings and unnecessary to report. Ethnomusicology, the subspecialty in which I received my graduate academic training, shared most of these same methods and blind spots. Since the 1980s, when criticism of anthropological writing grew to challenge the epistemological foundations of the discipline, there has been a recognition that relationships between researchers and the people they study are indeed crucial for a proper critical reading of the findings presented. What is the identity of the researcher and what are the power relations between this identity and the group of people under study? What linguistic and cultural barriers might exist that could hinder understanding? Are the group members that participated in the study representative of the group?[33]

Into the discussion of researcher–subject relations is often brought the opposition of outsider versus insider. In the early days of anthropology, the status of the researcher as an outsider to the culture being studied was a given. Confronted with unfamiliar languages, customs, and worldviews, the anthropologist would somehow make sense of a foreign culture in a remote location and translate fragments of it into terms that a European or North American audience could understand. In the transition to a postcolonial world where these remote locations themselves were attaining nationhood, the training of native or indigenous anthropologists became increasingly common. The presence of researchers who studied their own culture invigorated the debate over the relative merits of outsider versus insider perspectives on a culture.

In ongoing reflections on insiderness on the part of "native" anthropologists, it became clear that insider versus outsider status was not an either/or proposition, but rather one of degree along many possible dimensions such as race, class, and gender. A classic example in the ethnomusicological literature is Mellonee Burnim's report on her gospel music research with two black Pentecostal churches in Indiana. As an African American woman who could sing and play familiar gospel songs on the piano in an appropriate style, Burnim found herself welcomed as insider. On the other hand, there were moments in her research when she was reminded that she was also an outsider in terms of social class (her status as a university researcher) and religious denomination (a Methodist working among Pentecostals).[34]

There is another distinction to keep in mind when discussing the roles of insider and outsider with respect to ethnic groups and their cultural practices: belonging versus understanding. The point for the anthropologist or ethnomusicologist is not to become a member of the group, but to develop a sufficient amount of knowledge and empathy so as to be able to explain and interpret the culture accurately in presentation of the research results, be they oral or written. The same is true of many (not all) amateur enthusiasts who not only enjoy the music but also actively seek to learn more about the culture from which it came. One can belong to an ethnic group by ancestry but lack understanding if raised outside the group's cultural environment. Conversely, one can steep oneself in another culture through acquired knowledge and experience and achieve much understanding without belonging to a group or desiring to belong. Often enough, the desires for understanding of the Other and for merging with the Other appear together in the same individual, as in Stivale's notion of "becoming-Cajun," but such a pairing is not inevitable.[35]

In order to evaluate the information and points of view presented in this book, the reader must be able to consider the source. To this end, I provide below some autobiographical details relevant to the study at hand. Not infrequently, when I tell someone that I am an ethnomusicologist specializing in the study of Cajun and Creole music, I am asked if I myself am Cajun or from Louisiana. That this question even arises with any regularity raises some interesting questions about public perceptions of anthropology and of Cajun culture. First, is the notion of a "native anthropologist" who studies his or her own culture perhaps more accepted as commonplace than heretofore? On the other hand, what is it about Louisiana French culture that would lead the questioner to assume that it would hold less interest for outsiders than for insiders? Is it because Cajuns and Creoles, whose group identities sprang from American soil, are somehow not exotic enough to fit the traditional notion of an anthropological Other? As Jacques Henry and Sara Le Menestrel point out in their volume on doing field research in Louisiana, "the Louisiana field does not fall neatly in world system categories: it is both center and periphery, elite and exploited, powerful and disenfranchised." Why would a researcher knowingly take up such a mixed bag unless he had a personal connection to Louisiana French culture?[36]

I was born in 1960 in the state of Ohio and was raised there by parents of western European descent, mostly Dutch and German stock several generations removed from the immigrant experience. Culturally speaking, the western half of Ohio where I lived can be considered on the eastern edge of the midwestern United States. In terms of musical background, my parents both sang in the church choir and had taken voice lessons as young adults, and we had a piano in our home. I started studying piano at age seven, the double bass at age ten, and singing at age fifteen. All of this training centered around Western art music and its written tradition.

In college in Boston, I developed a listening interest in the blues thanks to a knowledgeable fraternity brother from North Carolina and a predisposition for blues-based rock from bands like Led Zeppelin and Lynyrd Skynyrd. The blues hobby grew and took the form of collecting LPs and attending as many live blues performances as I could. At Nightstage, a club in Cambridge that I frequented for blues and jazz shows, one night in the mid-1980s was advertised something called "zydeco" from a touring group named Queen Ida and the Bon Temps Zydeco Band. Out of curiosity for what blues in French might sound like, I went to hear them and liked the music immediately. I was aware that the music was from Louisiana but had no idea then that Queen Ida herself was based in California.

Coming to study Cajun music and zydeco, from the perspective of class, ethnicity, and music culture I was clearly an outsider: a middle-class Anglophone American from a northern state, not a fluent French speaker, unfamiliar with Louisiana dialects, and unrehearsed in any oral musical tradition except for singing in some choral groups where arrangements were taught by ear. However, even in such a clear-cut case of outsiderness there were mitigating factors. Simply having lived my entire life in the United States and being immersed in its popular culture left me less of an outsider in some ways than a researcher from France who speaks French but does not speak a Cajun or Creole dialect. With respect to musical performance, I was accustomed to singing in French and would need only to accommodate changes in diction and singing style. Ear training in music theory allowed me to pick up chord changes and musical forms quickly without the aid of notation, which was all I needed to be able to play simple bass lines in Cajun music. My prior musical training also helped me come up more quickly to an intermediate level of skill on the Cajun accordion. These mitigating factors helped me to participate in the field in ways that brought me closer to understanding insider perspectives on how the music is made.[37]

From another standpoint, I am not an outsider at all but rather belong to the group of people with whom I worked for this project. This is a study of the people who play and dance to Cajun music and zydeco *in California*, which itself is a heterogeneous group consisting of Creoles, Cajuns, and a significant proportion of people like me or the subject of Mary Chapin Carpenter's song (probably more than half of the regular participants) who had no connection to Louisiana French culture prior to a chance encounter that led to a sustained involvement. The particular qualities of such a motley collection of individuals tied together by the practice of certain cultural activities—referred to in the literature alternately as a "folk group," "affinity group," or "community of practice"—are a major focus of this book. Even as an insider to such a group, of course, my experience is still only partially representative. For example, a female researcher in my shoes would have had different kinds of firsthand experiences on the dance floor and probably also in learning the accordion. The autobiographical sketch I have provided here can be compared with those of others, profiled in chapters 6 and 7, who came to the music by some route other than ancestry.[38]

I left New England in 1990 to study ethnomusicology at the University of California, Berkeley. My research on Louisiana French music began almost before I knew that it was research, in the fall of 1992 when I attended my first dance class and dance at Ashkenaz Music and Dance Cafe in Berkeley. By January 1993 I was taking Cajun dance classes every week in Berkeley and starting to think about dissertation topics. Over that summer I was introduced to two Cajun women, Freida Fusilier and Jolene Adams, who were the mainstays of a history and research committee for one of the local Cajun and zydeco clubs that had formed, the West Coast Cajun and Zydeco Music and Dance Association (WCCZMDA). They accepted my volunteer services to assist them, mostly through proofreading and fact checking, with what became their self-published history, *Hé, Là-Bas! A History of Louisiana Cajun and Zydeco Music in California*. Through working with them and the material that went into the book, I met a number of Louisiana French people in the area and was given much information on the scene right from the start. It was during work on this history that I initially settled on Cajun music as a topic.[39]

I took dance classes through most of 1994 and augmented my researcher role by videotaping an awards dance put on by the WCCZMDA and writing a newsletter article on it. More newsletter articles followed, in which I interviewed musicians for the dual purpose of writing short profiles and of obtaining oral histories for a longer project. Once it became clear that funds for a year of field research in Louisiana were not forthcoming, I refocused my efforts on a dissertation based on the northern California scene. A small grant in early 1995 from U.C. Berkeley allowed me to purchase an accordion made in Louisiana and avail myself of Danny Poullard's offer of instruction. A few short trips to southwest Louisiana helped to ground what I was learning about the place from books and from people who had lived or visited there.

Learning to play the music myself proved beneficial to the research in a number of ways. I gained some knowledge of how the music works from a musician's perspective, and the challenges that outsiders face in learning how to play and sing it. As a classically trained musician, I found learning by ear somewhat challenging. I would rely at times on my musical training to mentally transcribe and analyze what I heard, in terms of musical form and melodic analysis, to help myself understand the musical ideas underlying all of the glorious ornamentation in Cajun music. I was made aware by the people who taught me and those with whom I learned that this was not the typical path of beginning Cajun accordion players, most of whom play by ear and do not read music at all. I got to know some of the other musicians who were learning at the same time I was, through playing music with them at Poullard's. First as a bass player and later also as an accordionist, I learned enough to sit in for three songs or a set at a public dance when invited, which allowed a firsthand look at a dance from the musicians' perspective on stage. I have also taken turns playing jam sessions in public and at house parties. I did not push my musical participation further than this, as I did not want to compete with the musicians in the scene for work.

Overall, I found that participating as a musician in the scene was crucial to developing relationships that made my field research possible. While the roles of dancer and newsletter contributor were important, it was not until I picked up someone's bass at a house party and started playing along that I was seen as someone who could contribute something of real value. In her research in gospel music, Burnim found that "the cultural insider who conducts field research is commonly viewed as a potential contributor to the group, rather than an exploiter." I found in my case that even though I did not belong to a relevant ethnic group, the ability to play the music helped me (as it did for Burnim) gain the access I needed to people and places in the field. It would not have worked, for example, for me to have returned to Poullard's garage week after week with my tape recorder just to listen to others play, without also practicing the tunes he gave me and showing him the progress I had made.[40]

Ethnographic Presentation

The "field" of the field research for this book is part globalized popular culture—like the first chapter's case study—but mostly the Cajun music and zydeco activity in northern California. This study therefore does not fit the classic anthropological model, in which I would have lived in southern Louisiana for a year and worked with musicians and dancers there for my research; neither does it belong with more contemporary studies of transnational cultural phenomena, since migration of the cultural actors has largely taken place within the boundaries of the United States. Moreover, the field cannot be said to be simply wherever the Cajuns and Creoles are, because the active involvement of others in Cajun music and zydeco is part of the study as well.[41]

The approach to this work has been inspired by the rethinking of anthropological practice by James Clifford and others, in which the location of fieldwork is no longer the prototypical "tent in the village," nor are the outsider/insider distinctions between researchers and subjects predetermined. As Clifford points out, "Ethnography is no longer a normative practice of outsiders visiting or studying insiders. . . . How identities are negotiated relationally, in determined historical contexts, is thus a process constituting both the subjects and objects of ethnography." Locating the field and identifying the players and their roles in an ethnography can no longer be taken for granted but rather must be worked out in every case.[42]

The bulk of the book dedicated to research findings (ch. 4–8) weaves together historical information from documents and secondary sources along with interview material from participants. One objective is to piece together the development of Cajun music and zydeco in northern California, a history that begins with migration from Louisiana in the 1940s and that turns with Queen Ida's ascendance in the late 1970s and increasing involvement from folk revivalists and others. The other main objective is to introduce the reader to a wide range of the backgrounds and personalities that comprise the scene through the medium of extensive quotes from taped interviews. Material from these interviews contributes to the historical facet of this project, but it also conveys the variety of perspectives that can coexist within one social milieu.

In reading the interview material, it is useful to keep in mind Jeff Todd Titon's distinction between story and history. There are differences in goals and methods between someone's life story told with minimal prompting and presented in "unadulterated" fashion, and a personal or oral history in which the interviewer asks the subject a series of questions for the purpose of discovering knowledge about the past and in which the results are highly edited for the most effective presentation of the knowledge obtained. The interviews and how they are presented here combine these two approaches. From the life story side, I tried as much as possible to take a nondirective approach to interviewing. If the conversation drifted away from music and dance, I would steer it back, and I would ask questions for clarification. The best interview results came when I spoke the bare minimum and let the person talk about what was important to them.[43]

However, I also was interested in piecing together a history of the scene from oral sources, and so I did not "stay out of the way" in an interview as much as one might for a life story. I asked everyone how and when they became involved in the Cajun and zydeco scene in northern California and about the developments they have witnessed in it since they started. With the Louisiana immigrants, I made sure that they talked about their experiences growing up with respect to language, music, and dance as well as the circumstances of their migration to California and discovery of the network of Louisiana French transplants. With the folk revivalists and other outsiders, I elicited information on their early enculturation in music and dance of whatever style, how they first became aware of Louisiana French culture, and what drew them to it.

In editing the interviews, I have elided certain locutions such as false starts and verbal tics such as "you know" unless they contribute some extra meaning or emphasis to the passage being quoted. I have also used standard spelling of words that may not have been pronounced using standard diction; for example, if an interviewee said "goin'," in most instances I have replaced it with "going" except where I thought such a change would blunt the impact of what the person was expressing. I have not, however, made any changes to syntax (word order), and I have attempted to provide at least one or two lengthy quotes from each interview so that the reader can get a glimpse of the personalities involved, not only the where and when. So, by some standards, the voices of the participants are distorted but they are there.

In an attempt to preserve the integrity of each person's story, each chapter containing interview material follows the same three-part structure: first, historical context from Louisiana and at the national level; second, individual profiles; third, commentary on the individual profiles combined with historical background on the dance scene in northern California. Someone interested primarily in the individual profiles could read just the middle section of each chapter, while a reader seeking an overall historical trajectory might elect to skip the individual profiles and only read the first sections (for a national perspective) or the last (for a local history). An individual profile in this book should not be regarded as a verified, factual account; rather it is, as best I can translate it to the printed page, that person's representation of his or her own life. Where an individual's account of events diverges from others' accounts or from documented sources, I attempt to reconcile the discrepancies at the end of the chapter or in a footnote.

Chapters 4, 5, and 8 present profiles of people born and raised in Louisiana or east Texas who then moved to California as adults. Chapters 6 and 7 focus on revivalist musicians and dancers. That said, the reader will find much to learn about the revivalist activities in the chapters devoted to Louisiana French participants, and likewise there is additional insight to be gained on some of the Louisiana French musicians and dancers in the chapters about the revivalists. The fact that I could not separate the stories of these two groups, even if I tried, is a testament to their interconnectedness in the scene.

For those who grew up in southern Louisiana or east Texas, one distinctive theme is childhood enculturation: to what were they exposed during their formative years that bears on their participation in the dance scene? To put it another way, what cultural capital did they acquire as a result of their early regional and home environments? Bourdieu explains this perspective: "Cultural capital can be acquired, to a varying extent, depending on the period, the society, and the social class, in the absence of any deliberate inculcation, and therefore quite unconsciously. It always remains marked by its earliest conditions of acquisition which, through the more or less visible marks they leave (such as the pronunciations characteristic of a class or region), help to determine its distinctive value." For the revivalists, there is some coverage of childhood experiences with music and dance, out of a general interest in developmental psychology perspectives on music and dance. In all of the individual profiles, insiders and outsiders alike, I try to present sufficient context from the individual's life so that the reader can gain some appreciation of what music means in that person's life and how it is used. In editing these interviews for publication, I took some of my sensibility from ethnographic work—such as Crafts, Cavicchi, and Keil's *My Music* and Tia DeNora's *Music in Everyday Life*—where there is an attempt to make up for a lack, in DeNora's words, of work "on how real people press music into action in particular social spaces and temporal settings" both as a "technology of the self" and as a means of social ordering. Even though the focus on Louisiana French music was understood in all of the interviews here, those interviewed could not help but talk about their other musical interests and about how Louisiana French music fit within their musical universes and within their lives as a whole.[44]

For all the rich detail that interviewees provided on what the music meant to them as individuals, they seldom lost sight of the character of Cajun music and zydeco as *social* dance music. As the focus of this book is on the entire scene and how it has come together (rather than on a few star individuals), a central concern is to understand the kinds of interaction that make up the whole social and cultural context. To that end, the interviews go into a level of detail of who met whom, and who learned from whom, usually reserved for biographies of pop music celebrities. The attempt here is not to make the interviewees and their associates celebrities—although I believe that some of the people profiled in this book are worthy of mention in any thoroughgoing history of Louisiana French music, and I have used individuals' real names with their blessing and on the assumption that the publicity could only aid their musical endeavors. Rather, the hope is that by following the intricacies of who knew whom and the nature of those relationships, we can gain a clearer picture of how this particular social network of Louisiana émigrés and cultural revivalists coalesced to form the scene as constituted at the time of this writing, decades after its outlines first appeared. To help understand the unfolding of this history, we must move beyond cultural capital and dichotomies of ethnics vs. revivalists to consider social capital (the leverage to get things done emergent in social networks), and how everyone involved in the scene has contributed to it.

CHAPTER THREE

Music, Dance, and Social Capital

Un bal de maison: A House Dance[1]

In mid-December 1995 I received an invitation from Josephine, a dancer I knew, to a birthday party at Harry's place, a generously sized farmhouse in Sonoma County, California. The party would start at 2:00 PM on December 30 and food would be provided, so "just come." I forgot to find out whose birthday it was, and repeated attempts to phone Josephine the night before and that morning failed because the line was always busy.

By the time my girlfriend and I show up with a bottle of wine, people have already started eating. I had been to this house once before for a larger, outdoor party and had met our host, a Cajun man in his sixties, at another event, but he can't place my face. He just waves good-naturedly and tells us to have a good time, not just sit around (meaning, be sure to dance), and to get some food. Two or three of Harry's adult children are also at this party.

On the way in, we also greet Josephine; I ask her whose birthday it is, she says it is a December birthday party for herself, Harry, and a name or two that I do not recognize. "What do you think, I would invite you to someone else's party?" Josephine and her husband Hank are retirees in their sixties, retired, and live in Stockton, some 120 miles from Sonoma County. Around this time they could be seen frequently at dances all over the Bay Area. The blanket recognition of birthdays of all born in a given month is not unusual. One custom of a few years' standing is the June Birthday Party, an open-invitation picnic and outdoor dance in Berkeley's Tilden Park, organized by a dancer whose birthday falls in that month. At some public dances, birthday celebrants for the current month may be called out onto the dance floor so that all may sing "Happy Birthday" led by the band.

Someone tells us that the food is in the garage. On our way there I am hailed by Peggy, whom I introduce to my girlfriend. Peggy and her husband Joe are avid dancers (currently taking tango lessons), but she has also decided to try her hand at playing the bass so that she can participate in Cajun jam sessions. Since she has seen me playing the bass at sessions in the past, she is eager to tell me that she has rented an upright bass and to inform me of the progress she has made in practicing thus far. A bass player in one of the local Cajun bands has made up an instruction book for her on how to play Cajun bass. She and Joe have tickets to see Beausoleil perform in Davis this evening. She hands me a business card that has their names, home address, and phone, with a silhouette of a dancing couple.

A buffet is laid out on a table in the middle of a three-car garage with door closed: white rolls, roasted chicken, white rice, gravy, beans or black-eyed peas, candied carrots, yams, cooked cabbage, potato salad. Bottles of wine with clear plastic cups are on the table, beer and soda outside on the driveway in coolers. Disposable plates and utensils are set out. People sit on various folding and patio chairs up against the wall in the garage, in the house around the kitchen counter (women, mostly), and around the dining room table.

Sue and I get our food, find seats at the dining room table, and join the conversation. We introduce ourselves to Alida, one of Harry's daughters, and her husband Vin. Alida and her siblings are all from Lake Charles; they moved from there when she was twelve and she still speaks with a Cajun accent. She and Vin were last there seventeen years ago, his only trip there, and he says he will never go back. Sue mentions our plans to visit Louisiana in March. Alida indicates that Leticia, also seated at the table, is an expert on where to go.

Speaking of her travels to Louisiana, Leticia tells a story of going to the Offshore Lounge in Lawtell with Cheryl and Bobby, a couple from Louisiana who married and settled in California. They had a hard time finding the rural zydeco club, and when they finally got there Cheryl did not want to go in, but finally relented while saying that her Cajun daddy was turning over in his grave. Leticia then tells of a dancers' directory she saw on sale in Louisiana, with home addresses, phone numbers, and occupations for purposes of getting out party invitations and for business networking. She thinks it would be a good idea to have such a directory here in California. "How many people here would buy one?" she asks. No one answers. Louie turns to Leticia and says, "You make the best gumbo!"

The conversation turns to occupations: Vin installs tile floors, Cynthia's a textile designer, and her companion Louie is starting a career in therapeutic massage after studying at the National Holistic Institute in Emeryville. Louie says he is from New Iberia, Louisiana, originally; moved to Texas when he was thirteen; spent a long time in South America with his former wife, who was a banker; then moved to California by way of Miami. He gives us an extended description of his new massage business, equipped with a van for house calls. The sales pitch is interrupted when someone comes in to announce that dancing has begun in the garage. Louie immediately says, "Let's go!"

In the garage, the food table has been pushed aside to make way for dancing. Against the closed garage door the musicians sit or stand and play. Walter is playing his Acadiana brand diatonic button accordion (made in Louisiana), Jim is on guitar, and Frisco Freddie is on rubboard playing with plastic knives. This is the first time I have seen Jim, an accomplished dancer, on guitar. Walter plays "J'ai passé devant ta porte," "Eunice Two-Step," and another half dozen or so tunes from the standard Cajun repertoire.

Elsewhere in the garage out of the way of the dancers, Bobby and Harry are talking with three or four other men about someplace where the women were good-looking. "Jolies femmes!" Bobby says, "Harry, do you remember?" Harry replies something like yeah, they looked like if you would just touch them, they would melt.

There is a lag of twenty or thirty minutes until André Thierry, a junior in high school from a Creole family in Richmond, brings in his Cajun brand accordion and starts to play. At first it is just he and Freddie, then someone talks Jim into getting out his guitar again. "I just play by ear," Jim says, which explains the occasional chord clashes as he works out the patterns to each song. I try to follow André's fingers, with little success. He throws in some fast triplet interpolations from time to time, especially on endings, but otherwise does not vary much from one chorus to the next. He gets around the button board and does not play just in one "pocket." At one point, Cheryl and I waltz by and she says to him, "You look so bored!" He is playing slouched down in his chair, no facial expression, legs akimbo. He makes a slightly more animated face in response for a few seconds, then returns to the adolescent mask.

At one point when the dancing seems to be in full swing, I count approximately thirty-five people in the garage; I would guess total attendance at this party is around fifty. The turnout of musicians is a little slim; it is an unusual case in that there is no singing to be heard. Attendance is roughly balanced between Louisiana French people (either Cajun or Creole) and those not from Louisiana. Of those named above, the Louisiana French contingent includes Harry (the host), Alida, Cheryl, Bobby, Louie, and André. Those not from Louisiana families include Josephine (the party cohostess who invited us), Hank, Peggy, Joe, Leticia, Vin, Cynthia, Walter, Jim, Freddie, and Sue and me.

The Creative Power of Social Capital and Music

The *bal de maison* (house dance) was a foundational custom in the development of zydeco music in Louisiana, and so it was also in northern California. Dances held in Catholic parish social halls were another. Fifty years or more prior to the event just described, immigrant Louisiana Creole families were inviting each other to house dances in and around San Francisco. In her autobiographical cookbook, Queen Ida supports the idea that Louisiana French music in California began in Creoles' homes. Some time after her family's arrival in 1947, she met accordionist John Semien, and through him the family entered a network of Creoles in San Francisco among whom music was an integral part of socializing: "The parties went from house to house, because we had started reaching out to the Texas and Louisiana people of our Creole background, people who knew about the music. In those days, if you played zydeco for anybody else, they thought you were crazy." Certain core elements of the house dance custom, as described in eyewitness accounts, have survived in the contemporary California version: the focus on food (usually potluck), availability of alcohol, clearing of the house's largest room or outdoor space for dancing, and live music. The importance of socializing was heightened at the California house parties of newly arriving Creoles in the 1940s, since they did not necessarily live in proximity to one another and had need of a social network to help get themselves established in a new environment.[2]

In the 1990s sociologist Robert Putnam popularized the notion of social capital, the idea that the connectivity inherent in social networks can itself be a productive force. To illustrate, he notes that "civic virtue is most powerful when embedded in a dense network of reciprocal social relations. A society of many virtuous but isolated individuals is not necessarily rich in social capital." The density required for a network to acquire social capital requires sustained and frequent social interaction, whether based on family ties, interlocking business relationships, community work, or leisure interests. With frequent interaction comes trust, a necessary prerequisite for social capital. One form of trust is "generalized reciprocity," whereby I give you something now, not in direct exchange for something but with the expectation that you will be similarly generous to me at some future time. The hospitality involved in organizing a house party is a good example of generalized reciprocity.[3]

What kinds of social interaction count in building social capital? Putnam makes a playful yet telling distinction, borrowed from Yiddish, between *machers* (roughly, those who get things done) and *schmoozers* (those who "hang out"):

> *Machers* follow current events, attend church and club meetings, volunteer, give to charity, work on community projects, give blood, read the newspaper, give speeches, follow politics, and frequent local meetings.... *Schmoozers* have an active social life, but by contrast to *machers*, their engagement is less organized and purposeful, more spontaneous and flexible. They give dinner parties, hang out with friends, play cards, frequent bars and night spots, hold barbecues, visit relatives, and send greeting cards.[4]

In the above vignette, Leticia's unpopular idea to create a dancer's directory illustrates well the difference between mach-ing and schmoozing. In what was clearly a macher's impulse, she thought it might help to formalize the informal social contacts she had made by making and publishing a list. The lack of response suggests that such formality is irrelevant or even runs counter to how this network functions. Peggy's business card also suggests a macher's approach to schmoozing, containing as it did no advertisement of services offered, only a way to get in touch with them and a reminder of their love for dancing.

In raising the distinction between those who get things done and those who socialize for the sake of socializing, Putnam maintains that *both* are important in the creation of social capital. In this light, we can see more clearly the customs of the house party and the church social hall dance as key components in the building of a Cajun and zydeco scene in California. While the scene has grown greatly thanks to the machers who have organized public events, started social clubs, and disseminated information through telephone hotlines, calendars, newsletters, and websites, the scene would not exist at all without an infrastructure of social capital created by decades of schmoozing.

For Putnam, the most important distinction in social capital is that between bonding and bridging:

> Some forms of social capital are, by choice or necessity, inward looking and tend to reinforce exclusive identities and homogeneous groups. Examples of bonding social capital include ethnic fraternal organizations, church-based women's groups, and fashionable country clubs. Other networks are outward looking and encompass people across diverse social cleavages. Examples of bridging social capital include the civil rights movement, many youth service groups, and ecumenical religious organizations.

He goes on to suggest that *bonding* allows individuals to get by (for example, mutual aid provided within ethnic networks) while *bridging* allows them to get ahead, such as through business contacts.[5]

How can the concept of social capital help us to understand the development of the dance scene? Social capital is comprised of access to social networks plus the resources to be mobilized, be they economic, political, intellectual, or cultural. Some actors will have direct access to more resources than others, or to resources of different kinds. Trust between actors in the social networks should be added to this equation as a necessary prerequisite. Ties between actors in a network vary in strength (that is, some immigrants were more connected than others). In the early days of Louisiana French dances in California, the social networks involved consisted mostly of Creole families, friends from "back home," and Catholic parishes where Creole families worshipped. The resources at hand lay in the cultural capital possessed by the immigrants—their knowledge of the Louisiana French language, music, dancing, and other customs—as well as other kinds of capital that they possessed (such as homes where house dances could be held) or to which they had access through other networks (church parish halls).[6]

Trust between individuals began at a high level because they were related by blood, had known each other already "back home," or had mutual acquaintances from there. For social capital to be present, at least one person must recognize that these networks and resources have the potential to be used to some end; thus an element of individual creativity is also involved. Bourdieu explains:

> The reproduction of social capital presupposes an unceasing effort of sociability, a continuous series of exchanges in which recognition is endlessly affirmed and reaffirmed. This work, which implies expenditure of time and energy and so, directly or indirectly, of economic capital, is not profitable or even conceivable unless one invests in it a specific competence (knowledge of genealogical relationships and of real connections and *skill at using them*, etc.) and an acquired disposition to acquire and maintain this competence, which are themselves integral parts of this capital.[7]

Once certain individuals recognized that the ingredients were there to recreate the sorts of events (the house party, the church hall dance) that they enjoyed back home, the social capital (i.e., the potential for concerted action) was in place to continue those traditions in California. Unlike the party described above, in the early years house dances were primarily for people who had first experienced the music and dance while growing up in Louisiana or east Texas. In other words, the dance scene in California began with a reserve of bonding social capital from the immigrant Creole community.

Creoles' encounters with others interested in their music presented opportunities for both cooperation and competition as the pool of event venues and musicians increased. The folk and blues revivals of the 1960s marked the beginning of contact with other social networks outside of the immediate ethnic and religious spheres. Bridging social capital formed when it was no longer, in reference to Queen Ida's earlier comment, "crazy" to present Cajun and zydeco to the general Bay Area public, rather it was (at least marginally) commercially viable. Interest grew from national figures who brought attention to Cajun and Creole music, such as the New Lost City Ramblers, filmmaker Les Blank, and music entrepreneur Chris Strachwitz of Arhoolie Records, the last two of whom happened to live in the Bay Area. Starting in the 1980s, the cultural tourism industry in Louisiana grew as the state developed itself as a destination to experience Louisiana French culture. This increased exposure of the culture led to gradual inclusion of more and more outsiders in the network of dancers and musicians. Louisiana French musicians, including California-based ones like Queen Ida, acquired new roles and status as public performers as they performed for the first time in venues such as folk and blues festivals and recorded on labels outside of the regional Louisiana market.[8]

As musicians and event organizers made these crosscutting social connections, social capital of the bridging variety, they began to think in terms of getting ahead, not just getting by. Ideals of success turned to the recording contract or a large festival modeled after others such as the New Orleans Jazz and Heritage Festival. Over the four decades that followed, many attempts were made in northern California to tap local Louisiana French music into a wider audience and bigger profits. Among these ventures, long-term successes were exceedingly rare; Cajun music and zydeco and associated dancing have remained a minor niche market. In the attempt to reach large numbers of people, however, some were reached and have come to form their own social network of dancers and musicians that overlaps and interacts with the already existing immigrant network. Some who initially may have been attracted to Louisiana French music as a way to get ahead have since found it a pleasant way to get by, the satisfaction of "gumbo in the bowl right now," as musician Billy Wilson once put it. In other words, bridging social capital is not exclusively about getting ahead.[9]

In terms that Mary McNab Dart has used to describe the development of contra dance choreography, the context for the music shifted from a "community dance," where members of an immigrant community who had many sorts of ties to each other came together to hold a dance, to a "dance community," where "the dance provides the major focus for the participants' relationship with one another." In the process, the music and dance became media for bridging ethnic, racial, and socioeconomic differences among participants of various backgrounds. As suggested above, the new social network has patterned some of its forms of interaction from the older, established network of Creoles at the same time that it exhibits many differences.[10]

Having social capital is not the same thing as using it, or using it well. In studies of social capital, "using it" usually refers to the exercise of political influence or the rendering of civic service, although social capital that formed for one set of purposes (e.g., a church congregation) can be turned to other purposes (community organizing). In the dance scene context, we can say that social capital is being used to support public cultural expression, an aspect of civil society that is often overlooked. The notion of civil society, which springs from a need to explain social organization that owes its existence neither to the market nor to the state, is most often associated with relationships between people and their government, either in the vein of political organizing and advocacy or along the lines of civic groups that provide social services alongside government agencies. The dance scene is an articulation of civil society in the form of support for community folk arts, something that the federal government supports in modest ways and the California state government almost not at all. In recent years, private nonprofit organizations have been established, such as the Ashkenaz Music and Dance Community Center and the now-defunct California Friends of Louisiana French Music, that allow individuals to make charitable contributions that directly or indirectly support Cajun music and zydeco in northern California. However, this is not a major source of support for the dance scene. Mostly, it seems to sustain itself by bringing together what Mark Slobin calls "those two collective components of micromusics, commerce and enthusiasm": a combination of private enterprise; volunteers who contribute time, expertise, and in-kind resources; and cultural reinforcements on various levels (as described in chapter 2) that motivate both immigrants and others to continue making Louisiana French music and to patronize dance events. Events open to the general public are one frequent by-product of this complex ecology. These events in turn serve to maintain cultural capital (in this case, music and dance know-how), occasionally to enhance economic or political capital, to strengthen existing ties in the social network and across networks, and to create new ties among existing and new social actors in the network.[11]

A few observers of the northern California dance scene have suggested to me that there is much more dance activity there than in Los Angeles, which saw a similar migration of Louisiana Creoles starting in the 1940s. While there were house and church dances in Los Angeles as there were around San Francisco, as well as some interest among folk revivalists, the contention (which I have yet to verify firsthand) is that the bridging process never happened to a significant extent, and therefore the frequency of dances and public support for them is not up to the same level. Whether or not this portrayal of Los Angeles is accurate, the very perception reinforces the notion that

> ... social capital is necessarily a local phenomenon because it is defined by connections among people who know one another. Even when we talk about social capital in national or regional organizations (United Parcel Service or the Texas Industrial Foundations, for example), we are really talking about a network or accumulation of mainly local connections. The Internet and the World Wide Web, though much in the news as technology that would transform community and relationship, play a surprisingly small role.[12]

The growth of the dance scene in northern California was not the inevitable result of global cultural and economic trends, but rather a creative response by resourceful participants to these global trends and to local conditions.

In the historical trajectory of the dance scene, the process of bridging was well advanced by 1995 when the house dance at Harry's was held. Crosscutting social ties between Louisiana natives and nonnatives are evidenced in conversation. Alida, who maintains strong ties to Louisiana, has married Vin, who has visited the state once and never wants to go back. She points to Leticia, a nonnative, as a resource for where we should go on our tourists' visit. Leticia, as a white out-of-state tourist, can visit a Creole zydeco club in Louisiana without fear of local censure for crossing racial lines still strongly felt by those who lived under Jim Crow laws. What is more, she is able to cajole Cheryl, who grew up in southern Louisiana in those days and would not have set foot in such a club then, to come with her. Louie from New Iberia, already a cosmopolitan given his string of previous addresses, by completing a program at the National Holistic Institute has ventured into an endeavor resonant in associations to California and the human potential movement. On the other hand, Louie also demonstrates social capital in its bonding mode, where there is more to social networking than simply having a specific purpose in mind such as finding a job. When word came that the dancing had started, he practically interrupted in mid-sentence the description of his new massage business to lead the way from the dining room to the garage dance floor.[13]

Social capital is proving to be a useful conceptual lens through which to view the development of a sustainable local music and dance scene, where government support and any kind of centralized direction are lacking, where the marshalling of resources has grown initially from a set of overlapping networks of Creole families in northern California, their relatives in southern California and Louisiana, and the Catholic church. The resources at hand include cultural knowledge as well as volunteer efforts to organize events and physical locations to host them. Later, a group of outsider-enthusiasts attracted to the music and dance enlarges the audience and brings other resources with them. Trust among individuals—developed in this dense social network through frequent face-to-face interaction—facilitates cooperation. We can see and hear the creative power of social capital through the dancing and music that are both its end product and vehicles for its own perpetuation.

CHAPTER FOUR

Wartime and Postwar Creole Migration to California

The next five chapters present a history of how the local scene developed in the context of concurrent events in Louisiana and in the rest of the country. As noted in the previous chapter, the various social sub-networks that comprise the current Cajun and zydeco dance scene in northern California did not all come together at once. The chapters are organized chronologically according to when specific sub-networks joined the scene, beginning with the Creoles in the 1940s to 1960s (chs. 4 and 5), revivalist musicians beginning in the late 1960s (ch. 6), revivalist dancers in the early 1980s (ch. 7), and other Louisiana immigrants in the mid-1980s (ch. 8). Of course, this chronology is only generally descriptive and is not meant to ignore the reality that individuals from all groups are constantly entering and leaving the scene.

Revaluation of Cajun and Creole Ethnicities Following World War II

Chapter 2 describes the formation and history of Cajuns and Creoles as ethnic groups up to the 1930s, when as linguistic minorities in Louisiana they were under pressure to assimilate by the state government at the same time that they were being depicted as quaint, colorful natives by the press. Negative views of Cajun ethnic identity both from within and without continued through the 1960s and beyond, but a reversal in this trend had already begun forming during World War II. True, the push toward Americanization of Cajuns was more intense than ever during wartime as Cajun soldiers had to fit themselves socially into the military, civilians were asked to rally around the war effort at home, many families relocated for wartime employment at factories in New Orleans or Texas or as far away as California, and schools redoubled their efforts in English-only instruction. Yet this was not, to borrow a proverb, just a case of "the nail that sticks up shall get hammered down." In coming out of isolation Cajuns and Creoles gained greater perspective on who they were, and the outlines of those ethnicities as we know them today gained definition. Some Cajun GIs who served in France were able to use their French language skills to tactical advantage, and some were recognized for outstanding bravery. The homesickness of these soldiers has been credited as the reason for the popularity of Iry LeJeune, who brought back the accordion and an unapologetically Cajun style and language in his singing to great regional success from the late 1940s. In the early 1950s, Cajun "cultural activists" started incorporating traditional Cajun Mardi Gras observances into the formation of a modern Cajun identity.[1]

The creation of a more positively defined Cajun ethnicity gained momentum during the 1960s, when it became part of a wider "new ethnicity" movement that appeared across the United States in conjunction with the civil rights movement:

> The great civil rights revolution of black Americans patently anticipated the rise of ethnic awareness, and indeed, contributed in some ironic ways to the rise of the "new ethnicity." Ethnic awareness on the part of white ethnic groups developed in part out of a sense of resentment at the achievements (both political and cultural) of the blacks, and the determination to assert "white ethnic power" was at least in part a response to the "black power" movement of the period. The achievement of white "ethnic power" required the reestablishment of a sense of ethnic identity and unity, hence the fevered search for ethnic "roots."[2]

The formation in 1968 of the Council for the Development of French in Louisiana (CODOFIL), was a symptom of the "new ethnicity," although again the schools became a battleground, this time between the teachers of standard International French that the elite-sponsored agency brought from Europe and the Cajun- and Creole-French–speaking populations, who resented the implication that their spoken dialects were inferior. CODOFIL has had some positive effect in promoting Cajun ethnic identity through the French language and cultural festivals, and more recently has accorded greater respect to local French dialects. Still, the amount of French-speaking that takes place in public is rare in daily life outside of the milieux of cultural events and French-language radio programs. The story of the early CODOFIL attempts to import instructors to teach the correct French still resonates with Louisiana French people in California, who take a dim view of self-styled experts who appear to be lecturing them on their own culture.[3]

As Cajun ethnicity came to be seen in a more positive light, the image of the Cajun who works hard and plays hard became an available role model for all seeking cathartic release in a leisure activity. Prior to the new ethnicity period, the

Cajun penchant for celebration carried a negative connotation in conjunction with another perceived Cajun trait, the "disregard for the Anglo-American work ethic and materialist orientation." In the 1960s, as countercultural currents were calling into question the values of this work ethic and materialism, the abilities to express one's feelings and to have a good time became seen as enviable qualities. In his assessment of swamp pop's most important musical traits, Bernard echoes the received wisdom that Louisiana French people are particularly expressive by focusing on "intensely emotional lyrics and vocal deliveries—a characteristic . . . borrowed from traditional Cajun and black Creole music." The value placed on emotional expression in Louisiana French music fits well the profile of an "authenticity of emotionality" that Timothy Taylor identifies as part of the discourse about world music, which is usually associated either with spiritual or with joyful and celebratory expression. Some writers have sought to deconstruct the *bon temps* stereotype in order to capture the human suffering that the music also expresses.[4]

Although the 1960s civil rights movement brought blacks and Creoles closer together under a common political cause, the Creoles have maintained their distinct group identity up to the present through the primordial ties of family, religion, and homeland. So that they might also benefit, Creoles in Louisiana have formed their own cultural organizations in response to tourist interest in Cajun culture, particularly Creole, Inc., its festival spinoffs, and *Creole Magazine*.[5]

"Queen Ida" Guillory[6]

Ida Guillory (née Lewis) was born in 1929 to Ben Lewis and Elvina Broussard Lewis, in Lake Charles, Louisiana, the fourth of seven children. Her father worked as a sharecropper and also sold vegetables that he raised on the family farm; he played the harmonica for his own amusement. Ida had two uncles who played the accordion and another who played the violin, and they would visit her family's home in warm weather and play music on the porch. She rarely heard women sing except in church. Her mother would tell the children stories containing morals for proper behavior. Two of her favorites were "Monsieur Barbe-Bleue" and "Rosa Majeur," the latter of which her brother Al later used in writing a song.

Until she began attending a one-room schoolhouse that served the local community's Creole and black children, Ida spoke only French ("our Creole patois") and had very little exposure to English. She explains that it was when she first went to school and discovered that not everyone spoke French that she became aware of her family's ethnic identity as Creoles. She defines Creoles as "originally French and Spanish, migrating directly from Europe (not from Canada) about 300 years ago. Then, of course, the Creole group was broadened by mixing with all the other Louisiana nationalities: Native American (my own lineage is part Cherokee), West Indian, African, German, etc., no one is sure what the mixture is." Her description of the adjustment of having to speak only English at school when she had previously only spoken French is not unusual for Louisiana French people of her generation:

> I can remember starting school feeling very excited—"I'm big enough to go to school!" The letdown came when I discovered that it was very difficult to communicate with the teacher: she's telling me something in English and I'm telling her something in French, and we're not understanding each other at all. I kept trying to tell her, in French, "I don't speak English." Some of the older children translated, and told me that she said I had to speak English in school. I told them to tell her I would, as soon as I could learn the language.
>
> I went through that for a couple of weeks, and suddenly the English just came. You keep hearing the same things over and over, and somehow it all gets locked in. Suddenly you're saying, "I'm going," "I went," "I will go." It's the way a baby learns to speak. The teacher didn't want us to revert to French. In fact, we got spanked if she caught us; she actually slapped our hands. She felt that we *could* speak English, and so we should.

When Ida was in the second grade, her family moved some sixty-five miles to Beaumont, Texas, so that her father could help his brother farm there and earn more money than he was able to do around Lake Charles. Life there was less isolated; the family acquired a radio, the schools were larger, and her father eventually hired additional men as farm laborers, a mixture of blacks, Creoles, whites, and Mexicans. The women and girls in her family cooked for the workers as well as for the family. There were fewer Creoles around Beaumont than in Lake Charles, but plenty enough to carry on social functions with music and dancing. Sometimes her parents would attend a Saturday night dance at a public dance hall and bring their children, who would go to sleep in the children's room while the adults danced late into the night. More common were house parties where guests would dance to live acoustic music in a cleared-out living room. She learned how to dance by watching the adults and dancing with her sister. There were also church hall dances, but the music for those was usually rhythm and blues or country and western, not Cajun or zydeco.

Ida's family moved to San Francisco in 1947 at the suggestion of her married sister whose husband was stationed at Treasure Island. They paid cash for a house in the Bernal Heights district, where their neighbors were mostly white and Chicano, and her father found work as a meat cutter. Ida was eighteen at the time and in her senior year in high school. There she made a key acquaintance with another girl whose family had migrated from Louisiana. Through her new friend, Ida and her family met accordionist John Semien and became introduced to the network of Creoles who gave house parties for each other that featured music and dancing.

Dance hall events in postwar San Francisco grew out of the house party circuit.

> They would ask John Semien (who was still the only Louisiana accordionist we knew here) if he could play on a particular date. Then my dad and some of his friends from Louisiana would put up the money to rent a small hall, and they spread the word around. They asked people who came to the dances to chip in to pay for the hall rent and the music, and to bring their own bottles... friends would call out, "Oh, come over to my table and have a drink with me." It was a time for visiting, for dancing, and for just having a good time together.

Ida's father and friends also started a membership social club that put on dances, for which attendees would dress up and parents would encourage Creole teenagers to court each other.

Ida's musical tastes as a teenager did not include much zydeco. She listened frequently to country music on the radio, and she liked to listen to blues when she could find it. While most of her friends listened to rhythm and blues, she was buying recordings of pop singers like Perry Como and Andy Williams. Her mother Elvina, on the other hand, was determined to maintain the presence of French music in the house. Visiting Louisiana twice a year, she would bring back recordings of Cajun music. One day she took this a step further by purchasing a musical instrument for her children.

> In 1948, my mom brought an accordion home for the boys. It was the first one we ever had. "I brought this accordion here because this music is dying," she said. "I don't think you should let it die, because we've been carrying it on through my two brothers all this time. I want you boys to keep this music alive, keep it in the family, keep it going." I had no interest at that time in playing, because girls were not allowed. The accordion was not a very ladylike instrument. And when you were told what was right, what was wrong, you didn't have to make a decision, it was made for you and you just followed through.

Of the boys in the family, Ida's youngest brother Al was the one who took most to the accordion and taught himself to play with some help from Albert and Wilson

Perkins, distant relatives on his father's side who lived in Los Angeles and visited San Francisco occasionally. Watching Al learn, Ida thought she could do it too, and when no one else was around she would play around with it.[7]

A couple of years later, Ida and Ray Guillory were married and moved into a house in San Francisco (also in Bernal Heights) that her parents helped her buy. They bought a piano and Ida started lessons but soon quit. The couple began throwing house parties in their own basement, inviting mostly friends of their own generation from Louisiana. When she visited her parents' house, she would pick up the accordion and pick out some melodies—only now for her mother to hear. She found that her mother did not disapprove and her father was actually enthusiastic, so she continued.

It was not until the youngest of her three children was in school, however, that Ida's involvement in music really increased. Her brother Al had his own band that played "mainly Latin and rock," and since he had little use for his accordion she asked to borrow it and starting practicing in earnest. She found some inspiration in the music of Clifton Chenier (whose records she first heard in the late 1950s), adapting some of his piano accordion numbers on her triple-row button accordion. Her husband Ray had become friends with John Semien and other members of the Opelousas Playboys, and Ray made sure to tell his musician friends that Ida knew some songs on the accordion. After being asked on numerous occasions to play a number with the guys, she eventually consented at a small house party and received enough encouragement to want to do it again. She started sitting in with the band more often.

> One of the reasons they wanted me to sit in was that a woman accordion player was such a novelty. Every time I played one or two songs with the Playboys at those dances, the area in front of the stage would fill up with men. It was "Whoa, there's a woman playing this stuff." They had probably never seen a woman play before. I had no desire, no need, to become a musician. I was very satisfied with my life. But for some reason, after I conquered those two or three songs, I wanted to expand my repertoire.

She continued through the early 1970s to make guest appearances with Semien's band. She also started sitting in at selected clubs with her brother Al's band, which had begun to incorporate zydeco into its repertoire as the music's public exposure increased. When local Creole musician George Broussard organized a Mardi Gras masquerade dance in 1975 that he advertised in newspapers, he invited both of these bands to play, and Ida as well. At the dance, Broussard introduced her set by proclaiming her "Queen of the Zydeco Accordion and Queen of Zydeco

Queen Ida at a San Francisco church hall, circa 1978–79. Photo by Gary Canaparo.

Music." She played her few songs and thought nothing more of it until two weeks later when her picture appeared with the caption "Queen Ida" in a feature article of the Sunday magazine of the San Francisco *Chronicle*, one of the city's major daily newspapers. Journalist Peter Levine had attended the dance, taken photos, and written an article on Louisiana French culture and the immigrants who were continuing its traditions in the Bay Area. In it, he described the music and the musicians who played it, including nineteen-year-old Mark St. Mary, "Little John Semien" and the Opelousas Playboys, and a female musician named Queen Ida. Thus did Ida acquire her stage name.[8]

From there a musical career unfolded with startling rapidity for this forty-six-year-old mother of three with five songs in her active repertoire and no band of her own. After the newspaper article she received numerous calls for bookings that she soon turned over to brother Al, who was experienced in the music business. She began rehearsing with her brother's band and when she had learned enough repertoire to play an entire engagement, he changed the name of the group from The Barbary Coast Band to Queen Ida and the Bon Temps Zydeco Band. In 1976, the year after her unsought initial publicity, she appeared before thousands of people at the Bay Area Blues Festival and cut her first album with GNP/Crescendo Records, a

Los Angeles jazz label. She started using an agent in 1978, who among other things booked her on a tour of the West Coast funded by the National Endowment for the Arts. She played her first European tour in 1979 and continued to tour there twice a year for several years. In 1980, she received her first Grammy nomination for the album *Queen Ida in New Orleans*. Queen Ida and the Bon Temps Zydeco Band received a Grammy Award in 1982 for Best Ethnic/Folk Recording Album for *On Tour*. She was nominated twice thereafter, in 1984 and 1986.[9]

Her husband Ray retired and became her road manager in 1986, by which time she was on the road approximately half the year. A second brother, Willie, joined her band during the first European tour in 1979 and played the rubboard with them for nine years. When he left, her eldest son Myrick stepped in. She played in Japan, and in 1989 took part in a State Department–sponsored tour of Africa. In the 1990s she went gradually into a state of semi-retirement and both her son Myrick "Freeze" Guillory and her brother Al (recording under the name Al Rapone) released their own recordings. As of 2007, she could still be seen playing occasional events in the Bay Area or coming to hear other musicians and visiting with friends and family.

John Semien

A key early figure in the musical life of the immigrant Louisiana French community in northern California was accordionist John Semien, who played at dances that Ida Guillory attended when her family first moved to San Francisco and who stepped aside years later to let her play a few numbers with his band. As described by Ida and others, Semien was one of very few Louisiana French accordionists to supply live music for house parties in the Bay Area from the 1940s to the 1970s. For many house parties, recorded music was played when live musicians were not available.

Semien passed away in the early 1980s, but a biographical sketch of sorts can be pieced together with remembrances from people who knew him, an interview that Freida Fusilier did with John's younger brother Joe in 1993, and other sources. Joe was born in October of 1923 in Lebeau, Louisiana, to "Sidney" Louis Simien and Alice Carrière Simien, and the family later moved to Lawtell. Many of John and Joe's relations, including their parents, grandparents, and uncles, played music. Two accordions were kept in the kitchen for anyone to try; Joe and his older brothers John and Holland all learned to play the accordion in this home environment. By the time Joe moved to Los Angeles in 1947, the family had lost touch with John, who had moved from Louisiana to Arizona to California.

Joe recounts that with great effort, he tracked John down in the fields of Tulare, California. Surprisingly, John had stuck to the familiar, despite having traveled across the country. He was still doing the back-breaking work of farming, and still playing and singing the old French music. Joe recalls that unlike John, most people from back home were dropping the harsh work they had done on their Louisiana farms. They were also dropping their French language and music once they moved to the city. "Some people thought John was crazy!" says Joe.[10]

Although by some accounts Joe and John were not close, when Joe demonstrated interest in playing the accordion again, John bought him one. While John played for house dances in the Bay Area off and on in the 1940s and 1950s, it was not until 1964 that he formed a regular band, thanks to the organizing energy of drummer George Broussard who had moved out from Basile and Lake Charles, Louisiana. The Opelousas Playboys played their first gig at a 1964 fundraiser for All Hallows Parochial School in San Francisco with Semien on accordion, Broussard on drums, and Ben Guillory on fiddle.[11]

The Opelousas Playboys played around San Francisco for over ten years at church dances and house parties, as well as occasional other engagements such as the 1969 Berkeley Folk Festival. Ralph Gleason, a nationally known music critic who wrote for the San Francisco *Chronicle*, reviewed that festival and made comment both on Cajun fiddler Doug Kershaw, who had appeared on a televised variety show hosted by country superstar Johnny Cash the previous summer, and on the Opelousas Playboys, for whom he uses the faulty ethnic term "black Cajun" and to whom he misleadingly refers as a band "from Louisiana."

> [Kershaw] has the magic. It is undefinable but obvious when you see it and from the moment Kershaw steps on the stage you know he has it. He sings well in a strong, full voice, and plays the guitar nicely but it is his work with the fiddle that turns you on. When he plays it he dances like a swampland snake, all rubber legs and shifting hips and swirling hair. He gets a wild, excited sound to the violin and the combination is very effective....
>
> The Opelousas Playboys, a black Cajun band from Louisiana (turning out not to be quite that black) did its set with charm. Both the Playboys and Kershaw performed "Jambalaya" (that Hank Williams hit) and "Cotton Fields at Home" (Odetta's early contribution to contemporary folk music). It made an interesting contrast, the simplicity of the Playboys against the effective staginess of Kershaw.[12]

At some point in the early to mid-1970s, Semien returned to Louisiana to record an album using the facilities of La Louisianne Records. A few people in

Figure 1. Song titles as printed on *John Semien and His Opelousas Playboys* (La Louisianne LLC-509)

SIDE ONE	SIDE TWO
1. EUNICE TWO STEP	1. THE MARAQUIN
2. GRAND BASILE	2. THE LENOIR TWO STEP
3. LAFAYETTE TWO STEP	3. 99 YEAR WALTZ
4. TETE CA NAÍ	4. BERNADINE
5. JOLE BLON	5. LA VALSE DE SOMDI SOIR
6. FI FI FONCHEAUX	6. ROZA

the Bay Area still possess this recording. The album was titled simply *John Semien and His Opelousas Playboys* and featured John Semien on accordion and vocals. The Opelousas Playboys in this case were not his California bandmates but rather Louisiana musicians Calvin Carriere on violin, Nolan Cormier on guitar, and Ray LeJeune on drums and vocals. The songs that he chose to record (see fig. 1 for song titles as they appeared) were taken from the standard Louisiana French dance hall repertoire. Judging from this recording, Semien's music was of the older prairie Creole style, described in chapter 2, that sounds less like the R&B–influenced zydeco of Clifton Chenier and more like Cajun music with its use of the button accordion, the fiddle, high-pitched vocals in French, and mix of waltzes and two-

John Semien at Canaparo home in Sunol, California, 1979. Photo by Gary Canaparo.

steps. This style of Creole music was not unusual around Lawtell, where Semien grew up. Danny Poullard would continue in this style after Semien was gone.[13]

At the time when Semien was letting Queen Ida sit in with the Opelousas Playboys, a band named the Louisiana Playboys was forming that eventually included all of Semien's former bandmates. The following chapter contains more details on this transition; suffice it here to say that from the mid-1970s to his death in the early 1980s, John Semien continued to play music but more sporadically and infrequently. His major contribution to northern California Creole music was in the thirty years prior, when he provided community entertainment to generations of Louisiana French immigrants to northern California, gave Ida Guillory a chance to play accordion with a group of experienced musicians, and passed on his musical knowledge to Danny Poullard and to Ida's brother Al Rapone.[14]

George Broussard

Drummer, percussionist, and singer George Broussard was another central actor in the Creole community, most noted for his abilities to bring people together and organize events. He was born in 1934 in Basile, Louisiana, to Marius and Laura Ballard Broussard. His father and several of his father's siblings played accordion, one of whom was Elvina, mother of Queen Ida. George married Mary Guillory and lived in Lake Charles, Louisiana, then moved to California in the late 1950s in search of better economic opportunities. He would find work as a welder.[15]

George described his musical development this way:

> I grew up in a little place they had, they called Basile, Louisiana, where they had a lot of Cajun music being played, time I was a teenager. But I wasn't too interested in Cajun music at the time, my biggest thing I wanted to be a rock and roll star. And my job was, I was a drummer, and I was hooked up with a little band we called the House Rocker[s], and we played rock music. Then when I left Louisiana to come to California to work and try to make a better living for my family, I guess by being homesick, I started thinking more and more about Cajun music. Because my father was an accordion player, his brother played accordion. He had a couple of sisters who played a little accordion also. And it was like something that I was used to hearing but I wasn't very interested in it until I came to California. So then I went on and bought a set of drum and met up with a guy named John Semien, and John had been playing in different little bars and places like that. And after we met up with John, we formed a band that we called the Opelousas Playboy. And we started off by playing church hall event, and then it growed out of the church hall into the club and places

like down at Fisherman Wharf they had this Longshoremen Hall, we performed there several time.[16]

Other key musicians he tapped for the Opelousas Playboys were fiddler Ben Guillory (his wife's uncle) and Junior Felton, an African American blues guitarist from Slidell, Louisiana, who previously was unfamiliar with the Louisiana French repertoire. George became well known for organizing church dances and house parties in San Francisco. He knew many musicians and had several family members in the area: brother Calvin, sister Mary, and then Ida and her siblings were all his first cousins. He also helped others with their church dances on the other side of the bay.[17]

In an interview in the mid-1990s when he was no longer playing regularly with a band, George gave an overview of the musical evolution of Louisiana French music in California and in Louisiana, beginning with the 1970s when the Louisiana Playboys (with Danny Poullard) formed and started getting more gigs outside of the Creole network.

> And then we start performing at places like Ashkenaz, the Chez Panisse and places like that, where the music became very popular with some of the people that used to follow us. And it grew to the point to where now there's several band in the Bay Area that's performing such as Queen Ida, and Andrew Carriere. Then you also have Danny Poullard and the California Cajun Orchestra. But we actually started off Danny Poullard with the Louisiana Playboy, after Little John passed away and it became the Louisiana Playboy with Danny Poullard on the accordion and Ben Guillory, because he was like the godfather on the fiddle. And I believe that carried on until even today, which is a little different today, you have what they call the zydeco, more or less. And the new zydeco, so, they kind of took away from the fiddle that was in the band, but the younger generation today, you have to give them more or less what they want to hear. And this is what's happening right now, but we still like the old singing, the old accordion with the fiddle in there, and that's what makes the traditional Cajun music.[18]

As for many who saw him, Clifton Chenier stands alone as a performer and musical innovator for George, who attended Clifton's performances both in Louisiana and California. George also made a clear distinction between zydeco, the music that Chenier is often credited with inventing, and what George and Danny would call "traditional Cajun music," the older style and repertoire of Louisiana French dance music played by both Cajuns and Creoles in the prairie region of southwestern Louisiana.

George Broussard (right) at his place of business, with friends. Photo by Gary Canaparo.

Clifton Chenier was the most influence and best of them all when it came to what's considered to be the zydeco. And zydeco is sort of a mixed version of traditional Cajun and sort of mix of the blues and mixed with singing in Cajun French. And when I was a youngster in Louisiana that was more an upbeat type of music for me and I would go listen to Clifton Chenier every other weekend at this little club right outside Basile, this guy named Freeman Fontenot. So I'm pretty familiar with Clif, when I was a teenager, and then I became even more interested in his music after I moved to California, because Big Pete was one of the first person to bring Clifton to the Bay Area and perform. And I was one of the first person who was able to get the church hall, as far as the church hall event is concerned, and book Clifton. And it was something that people didn't want to believe because the place was jam-packed and they had never anyone who had played the zydeco, I don't believe, any better than Clifton did. And until the day he died, I guess you could say he still is the King. You had others that came along, like Rockin' Sidney, Boozoo Chavis, and Beau Jocque and on down the line. But Clif stood alone as far zydeco music went. . . .

What really was the difference between the type of music Clifton played and some people don't really understand that. Clifton and the zydeco was the black version of our own creative music. And what the traditional Cajun music was something black musicians, there was a very few that played tradition, except for Amédé Ardoin, Alphonse Bois Sec [Ardoin], and a few others, like Bébé Carrière, people like him. It was a few, and the rest of them that played zydeco, that was sort of what you call the version of our own music that we had created, the zydeco.[19]

Ray Stevens[20]

Ray Stevens was one of the few who had immigrated to California in the 1940s who was still attending public dances during my field research in the 1990s. He found work in wartime Oakland, settled there, and has been an observant eyewitness to sweeping changes in American society as a whole as well as the Louisiana French dance scene in northern California over more than fifty years. His profile is the first of many in this book taken primarily from interviews with the author.

Ray was born in 1925 "in a rice field between North Lacassine and Welsh, Louisiana," into a French-speaking sharecropping family with nine brothers and one sister. His Protestant father and Catholic mother raised their family in the Catholic church. The social conflict surrounding the Louisiana term "Creole" was evident in our taped interview. "You're looking at a so-called Creole. In my opinion, there's no such thing as that." Yet he showed me baptismal certificates from his mother's side of the family from Our Lady of the Sacred Heart in Church Point, Louisiana, including one for his grandmother, Alicia Leger (born in 1872), who spoke only French. He told me that Alicia's parents were Genevieve Valerie, a slave at the time of Emancipation, and the man who had owned her. "Genevieve Valerie, which she was my great-grandmother, my grandmother's mother, she was African but she was in the position of Sally Hemings. You ever heard of Sally Hemings? And Jefferson, our great president? That's what she was. She had the white babies in the back house. That's who my grandmother was. See, I know who I am. If you know what you're looking at, when a Cajun look at me, a Cajun see the European in me. They know what to look for."

Ray's parents spoke only French to each other at home. Although he only attended his one-room school through the third grade, he remembers the stigma that was placed on speaking French. From then on, he was self-educated and developed an interest in reading history.

> Oh, when I come along, it wasn't nice for you to speak French. They were trying to kill the language. The Cajuns and the blacks, which I call Creoles, I'm supposed to be Creole... the Cajuns and the African Americans was just discriminated against, and the area where I grew up at, I'm not going to speak for the whole state of Louisiana, my own people, small community where I grew up at. In that little community, you

only had three white people. That's three different white people. Italian hadn't got white yet, the Jews hadn't got white yet. Not yet. You had the Dutch, the Germans, and the English. They threw the Cajuns in the swamp, and the Africans right there with 'em. But the Indians was already there. So they all come together. Now when you see, when you look at the musicians that play right here in the Bay Area, I won't name them because they can give their own description of theirs. Take a good look at 'em and then get a picture of the Coushatta Indians and other tribes in that area, and see if you don't see a resemblance.

Ray remembers Creole dances as a child in Louisiana at the church social hall and in people's homes. There were no musicians in his family, but he had one brother who was an exceptional dancer.

>Ray: What they did, they played the music in the church. You'll notice how, when you go to these dances you very seldom, in over thirty years here I've never seen a crime, not openly. You notice how you see very little violence? When I was a kid, growing up, if I want to do something bad, and you've got it here too, there was my mother—at the dance—there was me, one generation. My mother and father, two generations. My grandmother and grandfather, three generations. And in some cases, the great-grandmother or great-grandfather. Four generations, all at that dance. And if I get ready to do something ugly, I got to deal with all that, all of that gonna be kicking some asses if I do something ugly in front of my grandmother! Especially my daddy's mother. So that's why the children act nice. Very nice! And the old priest [was] there, and a nun was there too.
>
> Author: Were they dancing too?
>
> Ray: Yeah, the nuns danced and the priest too. They drinking too. Yeah, he'd drink a little sip. [laughs]
>
> Author: So did the church get a little, did they charge for entrance?
>
> Ray: Chicken, give 'em a chicken.
>
> Author: For the musicians? So nothing for the church then? It was just a place to have it?
>
> Ray: That's all. We didn't have no money. When Amédé Ardoin played, about 1930, about '35, '36, he played at a house. Remember we did it at a house, in a living room. Now his pay, they'd go out in the yard to give him a chicken, he'd take that home. He was paid.

During wartime Ray joined the navy early (lying about his age), but found that he did not like the regimented nature of military life. He ended up associating with a group of rebellious black soldiers who received a "special order discharge," "about a hundred and fifty of us, to not cause more trouble." After his discharge, he no longer desired to live at home, and in 1944 he took a train to California with fifty dollars in his pocket. He knew only one person there, but had no trouble finding work at the Naval Air Center in Alameda and the Naval Supply Center in Oakland. "At one time, Naval Supply was the anchor for Oakland. Naval Supply was quoted as being a city within a city. It was a beautiful place to work in spite of all the problems. We had our own library, our own theater, police department, traffic officer. We had everything, right there on the base."

After the war, Ray sought to buy his first home in the East Bay.

> Bob Alva, real estate man, taught me what was going on here, he taught me that in 1946. I was gonna buy a house [by] David E. Bohannon, which was building San Leandro at the time, and I wanted to buy one of the houses in San Leandro for six thousand dollars. And I went into Bob's office and asked him to buy a house. He says, you can't buy that. He says, but I'll show you one. He said, buy that one now. So what happened is that Bob sold me a little house in West Oakland. . . . A thousand dollars, forty dollars a month, a dollar down, a dollar when he could catch you. Couldn't get no bank financing. Went to Bank of America, said we don't loan you all the money, we don't make no money off y'all. No problem. You didn't hurt my feelings, you made me smarter. Bob showed me how to do other financing. . . . The only thing you had was West Oakland. The iron curtain was Martin Luther King [then Grove Street], that was the iron curtain for blacks.

From Ray's point of view, the racism he found in California was no more or less than in Louisiana.

> I traveled America. I've never been to no foreign country. Racism is all over America. California, Arizona, Mississippi. It's all the same. One just acted different. You can't fool me with that. You come to California expecting you're free? And the newspaper, the Lake Charles *American Press*, it says no Negroes and a few other n-words allowed in this neighborhood. Over here, it just said "restricted," that's the reason I didn't know I couldn't buy to begin with. See, if they'd have said "No colored" I could understand that. I'd have never went there and asked that day. I waste my time, I didn't understand that.

Through that one acquaintance that he knew from back home in Louisiana, it was not long before Ray was getting invited to house parties where zydeco dancing took place. He remembers going to one in Richmond where John Semien was playing. At other times, dancing was done to recorded music. "We'd all get together, make a big gumbo on the weekend, play the music on an old piece of jukebox and dance to the zydeco. That was back in the forties, late forties and fifties." Ray spent practically all of his time in the East Bay; he did not go over to San Francisco for any of the church dances or house parties over there. He did not attend church himself. He did have to cut back on dancing when he was raising a daughter and running a liquor store full-time. Otherwise, he has been attending dances all along, and has been visiting Louisiana yearly or more often to see family. He first saw Clifton Chenier at a night club/motel in Lake Charles that his brother ran, called Steve's Drive-In. In more recent years he has attended zydeco festivals such as the one in Plaisance.

When I asked him if the music was called zydeco when he first settled in California, he responded, "It was always zydeco! The only thing changed is the people playing the music." He has followed the music as it has changed, and he appreciates the newer styles. "Beau Jocque and Keith Frank, to me, they brought zydeco at another level. Zydeco got to move on." He does not see dance style in terms of progression, however, rather as individual expression. "Zydeco is something like everybody have their own step. And they craft it so unique, they wanna put it where no one can copy. When you see Ray Stevens dancing, he dancing his own way." At the same time, he has definite ideas of what is and what is not zydeco dancing. In California, he does not see that much of what he would call zydeco style.

> They don't know how to do no zydeco here, they're just doing a combination of country and western. And a combination of swing. Very few people on the floor do zydeco. If you wanna see a person doing zydeco, you look at Welda and Virginia. And there's a Thibodeaux girl, she's married to somebody else. There, you're seeing zydeco. Watch them. You gonna see that little.... That's zydeco. Not all that [arm-twirling stuff]. Zydeco don't do that. You don't see that in Louisiana *at all*. Nothing wrong with it, now. I'm only telling you when you go there, and you go to the little bitty clubs where the zydeco is done, it's a crafted step. Always together. And that girl will wrap herself around that man like they's one.

Occasionally, couples have come to Ray to show them how to dance.

> Sometimes you'll see me with the men come with their wives. They don't know how to dance and they want to learn. So I take the man and the wife and myself, that's three people. I don't teach the dancing, I can teach anybody as far as the zydeco thing, the basic foundation, all you need to know in three minutes. And the rest will take care of itself. It's only two steps. All I do is use my rhythm to show 'em how to balance their rhythm, you see. The bane, the problem with the people that teach

zydeco is how to do someone else's step. Let 'em dance to their own damn rhythm. Not to mine or somebody else's. She'll develop her own rhythm. Everybody's born with their own rhythm, in my opinion.

Ray exhibits an independent, inquisitive mind in a number of ways. At home, he enjoys listening to country music. "It's just like blues, jazz, some of it's very spiritual, to me. It delivers a message." He brought photos to show me of an indigenous peoples' festival in Berkeley that he had attended, and talked at length about the beautiful cultures of and injustices suffered by Native Americans and Australian aboriginals. He also showed a photo of himself and some friends who had hired a sixty-foot sailboat to have a private zydeco party on San Francisco Bay. Although he is not one to join clubs, he has developed a group of friends who seek each other out whenever they come to dances.

> See, I have my own group that I hang out with. See, and that bunch, it's a group within a group. See you got a lot of people that come in that can't connect. If you don't form your own little group, get with your own group of people within that group, you might feel isolated. Because they can be a little messy here.... I don't want to belong to [clubs]. They'll see Ray Stevens with a lot of people around him, then they want to set a standard for me. You know the clubs have bylaws and stuff? I don't want that. I gotta be free, man. That's it.

Over the years Ray's social group has come to include a greater and greater percentage of people who are not from Louisiana.

> I don't know nobody from Louisiana at the dances, except [one couple]. The rest of 'em I don't mess with, because they ... do their thing and I do mine. That's it. I have my own circle of friends and we're very close. See, most people, if you never leave the dance floor, you'll never know the person. You can't get acquainted on the dance floor. That don't work. There is people I go dancing with, when we get through dancing, then we leave the dance floor and go have coffee like you and I are doing here now. You can know the person you're dancing with for two years, you'll know more about 'em, and you'll get more better acquainted with 'em in two hours at a coffee table than you will for two years on the dance floor. That's it, that's how you connect and bond.

One other thing that Ray likes to do at dances where musicians play for tips is to pass the tip jar for them. This custom is common at California dances where the guarantee and cover charge for the band are small or nonexistent.

You know, I worked in charity, I did five years with a community center. I know how to behave. I'm a master at it. I go into the crowd, they're already worked up. You don't con 'em out of anything. The zydeco people are very generous to the musicians. All you gotta do is get out there with a big jar, and I take the jar and work that whole crowd from front to back. [punctuates with finger on table] "Help the needy, not the greedy." Don't help me, I'm greedy. And they'll fill the jar up. One lady, "Are you doing that for yourself?" I say, "no ma'am, I'm too greedy. Help the zydeco, they starvin' like Marvin." Musicians don't make no money. No. I love to donate to 'em. I give very generously to musicians, because they're dedicated to what they're doing.

Black and Creole Migration from the South to California during and after World War II

In his book *Pioneer Urbanites*, Douglas Henry Daniels portrays blacks in San Francisco in the 1920s as a relatively small group who were largely satisfied with their living conditions and their standing within the community as a whole. Some families had already been there for two generations. The 1940s brought a great migration of blacks to California from the South—especially Texas, Arkansas, and Louisiana—for the wartime industries of building aircraft (in Los Angeles) and naval vessels (in and around San Francisco). The blacks already living in the Bay Area were overwhelmed by the newcomers in terms of sheer numbers, but there were also cultural differences with which to contend. One of Daniels's native black San Franciscan interviewees claimed that she could spot newcomers right away just by the manner in which they walked down the street, and that it could take up to nine years for such a person to become culturally acclimated. Another native black described his difficulty in becoming accepted socially by the newcomers, who ridiculed some of his favorite activities such as hiking and running long distances for exercise. Class differences became an issue between the established blacks and the newcomers. "Spitting in public, trying on new clothes when dressed in overalls, shooting birds from telephone wires, asking to rent garages for housing—all these highlighted variations in background and custom as well as the poverty that became increasingly apparent to older residents." Yet the longtime residents were forced by circumstances to accept the new immigrants and work with them to establish better conditions for all.[21]

Tens of thousands of blacks migrated from the South to northern California in the 1940s. Economic opportunity for wartime industrial laborers in cities such as San Francisco, Oakland, and Richmond compared favorably to earning

Figure 2. Summary of Wartime Black Population Growth in Bay Area Cities (census figures compiled in Broussard 1993:135–36)

City	Population Sector	From	To	Total Increase	Percentage Increase
San Francisco	all	1940	1945		30.4 %
	black	1940	1945	27,155	665.8 %
Oakland	black	1940	1945	37,327	341.1 %
Richmond	black	1940	1947	13,500	5,003.0 %
Los Angeles	black	1940	1946	69,322	108.7 %

potential at home, and a desire to leave behind the overt racism of Jim Crow laws was also a factor. Among this large influx were some indeterminate number of Louisiana Creoles who found themselves under the same new conditions as their fellow immigrants, and yet like the native black San Franciscans they considered themselves a group apart from the southern African Americans who comprised the majority of blacks in the Bay Area after World War II.[22]

Because many Creoles are light-skinned (some can pass for white, and more easily so where the law does not define race by bloodline), the value of applying what is known of the experience of black immigrants in California to that of Louisiana Creoles is limited. As Lena Pitre told Michael Tisserand, "You got people come here, want to pass for something else. . . . I'm going to tell you just like it is. They have a lot like that. They get in their minds that if they pass for something else, they get a better job. White, Mexican, everything they could pass for but black. I know where they come from, that's why I don't say anything." Nonetheless, to account for the migration of the many who did not pass for white, it seems reasonable to assume that they faced similar situations and hardships as the blacks via others' ascription of race to them, and thus the existing research on black migration from the South to California provides some helpful context for a discussion of Creole migration.[23]

Creoles and blacks came west together in the 1940s and greatly swelled the black populations of San Francisco, Sausalito, Oakland, and Richmond, responding to hiring demands in the shipbuilding yards. Figure 2 summarizes the massive influx of blacks into selected cities in the Bay Area during the war that dwarfed the existing black population, as well as in Los Angeles, which already had a substantial number of blacks. The Los Angeles Creole population has made itself felt in northern California in a number of ways, from the newspaper *Bayou Talk*, to the movement of immigrants up and down the coast, to interchanges among musicians.[24]

We can only approximate the number of Creoles that came with this wave of black migration. A breakdown of black migration by state of origin is equally elusive, but there are scattered indications that the proportion that came from Louisiana to the Bay Area is fairly large. One source states that Texas, Louisiana, and Oklahoma together contributed 51 percent of black immigrants during this period. After the war, when black in-migration continued, an Urban League official remarked that he found it "hard to believe that there are any Negros left in Texas and Louisiana." Although the percentage of Creoles in this influx of blacks from Louisiana was probably small, the sheer number of immigrants was large enough to imply that certainly hundreds, perhaps thousands of Creoles made their way from Louisiana to San Francisco, Oakland, and Richmond alone during World War II.[25]

Some of the black immigrants from Texas were Creoles. Francophone migration into Texas began in earnest at the beginning of this century, and by 1970 the state had some 85,000 U.S.-born French speakers, of whom over 20 percent were classified as black. For some like Ida Guillory and Danny Poullard, Texas was only an intermediate stop on the way to California. The tendency for migrating southern blacks to bring their families along was shared by Creoles such as Ida Guillory's family.[26]

In the wartime employment boom of the 1940s, California provided an escape valve for oppressive conditions in Louisiana and other southern states, as it had for a smaller number of blacks who had migrated there previously. One woman who moved to San Francisco from Texas during World War I felt "it was just like coming from hell to heaven." She marveled at how her children "could run up and down the streets and play and they wasn't called nigger and all this kind of stuff." For a man born in 1903 who was brought to California from Alabama as a child, the thrill of the freedom to sit anywhere on the train carrying him westward was an indelible memory. Douglas Henry Daniels concludes: "While they did not leave race discrimination, or even segregation, behind them, San Francisco–bound southerners managed to escape Jim Crow laws and humiliation. . . . Racism intensified as the number of white and Black southerners increased in the twentieth century, but compared to the rural, segregated, fundamentalist Protestant, tradition-bound south, San Francisco still symbolized freedom as much as Harlem or Chicago's South Side." Many Creoles have stated that they have found a greater tolerance for racial difference in the Bay Area than in Louisiana or Texas, where they too were relegated to "colored" schools and facilities under Jim Crow laws. Nicholas Spitzer, writing in the mid-1980s of California Creole immigrants, reports that he interviewed "several people who didn't return to Louisiana for up to 25 years because they had fled the regressive nature of the social order. Some individuals living on the West Coast have returned only after long term economic success."[27]

Comparisons to Jim Crow aside, the San Francisco Bay Area in the 1940s was hardly a utopia of equal opportunity. Historians support Ray Stevens's statement, "Racism is all over America. California, Arizona, Mississippi. It's all the same. One just acted different." Yet very few blacks moved back to the South after their wartime jobs ended, and in the postwar period black migration to California continued despite discriminatory practices by employers, labor unions, and in the housing market that belied the Bay Area's liberal reputation.[28]

One prominent form of discrimination in the postwar Bay Area was residential segregation. This segregation was based not only on informal practices by landlords, but also by restrictive covenants placed on the sale of property which stipulated by race who could purchase or occupy a home. The original covenant on the author's current home, in a neighborhood of Oakland developed in the early 1940s, contains a stipulation no longer in effect stating that "No lot shall be used or occupied by any person or persons othan [sic] the Caucasian Race. Provided, however, that the employment by the owner or occupant of said property of persons other than the Caucasian race as servants shall not be construed as a violation of said condition." Such covenants, which had the sanction of the federal government in the name of preserving property values, played a key role in the postwar economic development of San Leandro, the city bordering Oakland to the south where Ray Stevens was denied the opportunity to buy a home.[29]

In the San Francisco of the 1940s and 1950s, blacks were essentially limited to three neighborhoods (which were still predominantly white). One was the Western Addition, bordered by Presidio and St. Joseph's Ave. on the west, Gough on the east, California St. on the north, and Golden Gate Ave. on the south. A second was the Fillmore district; the third was Hunter's Point. Ida Guillory's family settled in the late 1940s in Bernal Heights, "a mixed neighborhood, mostly white and Mexican" not strictly in any of the three districts just mentioned but not far from Hunter's Point. Although the NAACP successfully challenged discriminatory policies in San Francisco public housing in 1952, *de facto* discrimination by individual property owners remained legal until the California legislature passed its Fair Housing Act in 1963.[30]

Patterns of segregation notwithstanding, Creole community-building in the San Francisco Bay Area owed much more to the Catholic church and their own social networking than to any particular pattern of residential settlement. With the great migration of blacks into the Bay Area starting in the 1940s, the Creoles were a small minority within a minority. The extremely tight housing market for blacks within the restricted areas limited their choice of housing to the extent that the formation of Creole residential neighborhoods would not have been feasible. In the absence of one or more identifiably Creole neighborhoods within San Francisco or Oakland or Richmond, Catholicism still socially differentiated the Creoles from their largely Protestant African American neighbors. As blacks from the South migrated to the Bay Area in great numbers (to certain parts of San Francisco, for example), the Catholic parishes already in existence in those areas saw increased attendance not from a representative cross-section of the southern states, but from the region in the South where the most Catholics lived: southern Louisiana.[31]

In addition to their role as meeting grounds for Louisiana French immigrants, at some point Catholic parishes also became places to hold dances. The earliest reports of these are in the early 1960s in San Francisco and Los Angeles. The churches provided a more spacious dance floor and venue for local musicians such as John Semien and his Opelousas Playboys in the 1960s and early 1970s and, later in that decade, the Louisiana Playboys with Danny Poullard on accordion. Drummer George Broussard has been credited with popularizing the idea of using such dances in northern California to benefit the church. Due to a restructuring of the local diocese, All Hallows (where Queen Ida made her public debut) is no longer an active parish, but church dances are still occasionally held at other local parishes such as St. Francis of Assisi in East Palo Alto and St. Mark's in Richmond.[32]

Seminal zydeco figure Clifton Chenier also performed at church dances in the Bay Area during the years he recorded with El Cerrito–based Arhoolie Records, playing several times at All Hallows to "increasingly gigantic crowds." Arhoolie record producer Chris Strachwitz credits priests at three different California parishes—All Hallows in San Francisco, St. Mark's in Richmond, and a third in Los Angeles—with the idea of bringing the popular Chenier out to California to play a series of church dances in order to maintain some kind of notion of Creole community in California through the music. Chenier recorded a live album for Arhoolie at St. Mark's in 1971.[33]

The Catholic church halls have been a vital component in the development of the northern California dance scene, not only as a gathering place for the Louisiana French who moved there but also as a semi-public space where venturesome folk revivalist dancers and musicians could come and experience a glimpse of Louisiana lifestyle on California soil. The church halls served as an important site of enclavement for the Creole community, but at the same time the dances were open to all—even if only a few events over the years were widely publicized. Outsiders did indeed start attending the church dances on a regular basis in the early 1980s, as detailed in chapter 7.

While it helps to understand overall patterns of black migration and residential segregation mid-century in the Bay Area, as well as the general parameters of the Creole migration experience within that context, the individual profiles above provide a personal glimpse of what it was like for someone with a Louisiana Creole background to relocate to northern California at that time. Looking back at those profiles we might ask ourselves, what did the Louisiana immigrants bring with them in terms of culture, experience, and worldview, and what did they do in their new environment with what they brought?

Ida Guillory and Ray Stevens both migrated from California to Louisiana as young adults, during or shortly after World War II. They were both raised in Creole French-speaking families and encountered the same ban on speaking French in school that Cajuns faced in that era; the corporal punishment that Ida reports was practiced in some French-speaking districts and not in others. Both made connections to the network of Louisiana French immigrants shortly after arriving in their new home, and were able to purchase homes and thrive economically. Ray maintained personal contact with friends and relatives in Louisiana with frequent trips; Ida's mother performed this same function within her family.[34]

Ida's and Ray's stories also exhibit many differences. Ida moved with her nuclear family, then married within the Creole community and started a family of her own. Ray moved to California on his own and, while he enjoys zydeco dancing and socializing at the dances, his connection to the Creole community appears not as strong. These are but two of thousands of ways that individual Creoles negotiated the transition from Louisiana or east Texas to California in those immediate postwar years.

Queen Ida and Ray Stevens both expressed strong ideas about the nature of Creole identity as a mixture of African, European, and Native American peoples, while they differ in the details of which European and Native American groups are mentioned, thus reflecting the diversity of views on Creole identity discussed in chapter 2. It is notable that both stressed the Native American contributions to Creole bloodlines. One reason for this may be the connection in the popular imagination between indigenous groups and the land on which they lived, which in turn resonates with the usage of the word "Creole" to mean "local, homegrown, not imported." At the same time that they give clearly defined views of Creole group identity, both Queen Ida and Ray Stevens point to the socially constructed, contingent quality of this identity. To give a name to it responds to the need of others to delineate cultural differences. Ida says, "It was only when we started going to school, where we spoke French but many of the other kids spoke English, that I learned we were Creole." Ray Stevens says, "You're looking at a so-called Creole. In my opinion, there's no such thing as that." For Ray, the contested nature of Creole identity is a personal experience. He uses phrases like "so-called Creole" and "I'm supposed to be a Creole" to hold himself at arm's length from the fray. By some definitions he is a Creole, by virtue of the fact that he was born in southwestern Louisiana into a family of French-speaking blacks that had been there for generations; by other definitions he is not. As he made clear with the baptismal certificates that he showed me, he is not descended from free people of color. This group of African descent, whose descendants are sometimes known as Creoles of Color, consisted of slaves who were freed by their masters during antebellum times, who often were offspring of black mothers and their white owners and allowed to inherit property under Louisiana law. Ray's grandmother was born too late to fall into this category. As of the mid-twentieth century when Ray left Louisiana for California, there were still status differences between Creoles of Color and descendants of emancipated slaves. At social functions around that time, this boundary was sometimes marked by skin tone. Spitzer describes the use of a "'paper bag test,' which has been reported to me by informants in New Orleans as well as in the rural communities of St. Landry Parish. This involved the comparison of a person of questionable phenotype as to skin tone with a paper bag. If he was the shade of the bag or lighter, he could enter the club or other social function." Those with darker skin were turned away.[35]

All of the individuals profiled in this chapter had a strong appreciation for country music, a style normally associated with southern whites but available to all in the form of radio broadcasts and recordings and with a rich history across the state of Louisiana, from north to south. Photographer Gary Canaparo has one portrait of the Louisiana Playboys that he shot in the basement at George Broussard's house, showing a large poster of Charley Pride displayed prominently on the wall behind them. Gary remembers: "DeMarco's [in] Brisbane was a place where John [Semien] played and I guess Ullus [Gobart] would go up to Brisbane and dance. We're talking about country, they all had a country western kind of interest that they felt comfortable with. George in particular with Charley Pride because he was country western but also he was a black guy who was making it pretty big in country western. So it was interesting that Ullus and John Semien and George and most of those guys, country western was another kind of music that they all enjoyed."[36]

From a young age, Ida learned that "the accordion was not a very lady-like instrument," and that although a woman might play an accordion around the house for her own amusement (as her mother did), she would never play it in front of other people either at home or in public. Part of what paved the way for Ida in overcoming this gender bias was the support of her husband, whose musician friends invited her to sit in, and her brothers (and later her son) who not only supported her musically but who also lent respectability to Ida's public appearances simply with their presence on the bandstand. Ida herself points to Cleoma Falcon, a Cajun woman who performed and recorded with her husband Joe Falcon in the late 1920s, as one woman who had taken this route before her.[37]

The ingredients to Queen Ida's success are varied, and many opinions have been offered. First, by her own account, her acceptance as a musician within the California Creole community happened over a period of time prior to her first public appearances as she accumulated acceptance (either explicit or tacit) of her efforts by her parents, her husband, fellow musicians, and dancers. A woman in a man's position fronting a band, she presented a singularly unthreatening figure as a housewife who had already raised her children and who had the support of her family. After she was led to form her own band following the initial "Queen Ida" publicity, her brother Al Lewis (later known as Al Rapone) became a welcome and necessary business partner and musical director for her band, producing her recordings and writing himself or co-writing with Ida most of her songs. Al's musical polish contributed to the band's popularity outside of the Creole community, as did the choices that he and Ida made in creating their music outside of the usual mold: the Latin influences, the rewriting and singing of song lyrics in both French and English, and the use of nontraditional instruments.

Last but hardly least in this list of reasons for Queen Ida's success is her ability to establish audience rapport. She carries herself with great poise and in her comments to the audience between songs she exudes the persona of a warm, gracious, inviting host. Once in the late 1990s at the Stern Grove Festival, an annual outdoor series in San Francisco's Sigmund Stern Grove, Ida appeared with her band without her accordion as she was recovering from a shoulder injury. Her band, including her son Myrick on accordion, played behind her while she stood in front with just a microphone, her modest singing voice, and her between-song patter. Sitting in the audience, I expected a subdued reaction from the crowd but instead experienced an unusually strong response culminating in a noisy standing ovation at the end of the set. If ever a musician could be said to have played the audience like a musical instrument, she did that day.

Both Queen Ida and George Broussard exhibit a heritage orientation to their music, up to a point. Ida's mother brought back the accordion from Louisiana for her sons to play because she felt "the music was dying." George says he got "homesick" for Louisiana French music once he'd moved to California; nostalgia for family life back home led him to seek out music that he had previously avoided as not hip. Yet his homesickness did not lead him to seek out only Cajun or Creole music; with the Louisiana Playboys he also lobbied to include some Charley Pride songs in their repertoire. Queen Ida obligingly took up the mantle of spokeswoman for Louisiana French music and culture, but she also mixed more diverse influences in her band's music than have many zydeco bands since.

CHAPTER FIVE

Further Creole Migration and Bridging to Other Social Networks

Creole migration to California continued well beyond the wartime and immediate postwar periods of the 1940s. Although the wartime boom in jobs came to an end, military bases continued to operate and serve as stimuli to the local economy and as destinations for servicemen and their families. Social inequality in the South and differential economic opportunities still made California look attractive as a place to live, and the foothold that Creoles had gained in the Bay Area during World War II eased the way for friends and relatives to follow. Most of the Louisiana French people active in the northern California music and dance scene in the 1990s grew up in Louisiana or Texas and migrated between 1960 and the mid-1970s, when Queen Ida became a public figure. From 1960 to 1975, Louisiana French musicians in both the South and in California started making their presence felt to Bay Area residents Chris Strachwitz of Arhoolie Records and documentary filmmaker Les Blank, whose influence on the music has been significant both locally in northern California and in Louisiana itself. Their involvement in the Bay Area scene represents early and important local connections made between Creoles and others with an interest in their music and culture.

Postwar Trends in Louisiana French Music

The recording industry underwent a period of lowered production during World War II and largely ignored Cajun music, and national labels mostly did not pick it up again after the war was over. A number of small labels in Texas and Louisiana sprouted up in response to the local demand for regional music, including Fais Do Do (1946); O.T. (1949); Goldband (1949); Khoury (1950); Swallow (1958); La Louisianne (1959), at whose studios John Semien recorded his album; and Lanor (1960). Houston-based Gold Star released the hit version of "Jolie Blonde" (which they spelled "Jole Blon") in 1946, performed by the hillbilly-influenced fiddler Harry Choates with a band that included piano and no accordion. Iry LeJeune followed on another (short-lived) Houston label in 1948 with "Love Bridge Waltz/Evangeline Special," and his success paved the way for accordionists to find work again. LeJeune, who drew heavily from the recorded repertoire of Creole musician Amédé Ardoin and who died at twenty-seven in a car crash in 1955, along with Ardoin is one of the most storied figures in Louisiana French music. Although venerated for his accordion skills, it is LeJeune's singing that draws the strongest superlatives from writers—that it can "bite and burn and blister the heart" and "encompassed all the pain, loneliness, and hardship of the isolated prairie farmers." Aside from the compelling qualities of his recordings, Ann Savoy's 1984 songbook transcribed nearly twenty LeJeune songs and made his repertoire a touchstone among revivalists. Accordionists Lawrence Walker and Nathan Abshire, both of whom had started performing careers before the Western swing craze pushed them out in the late 1930s, came back to record again and play for dances following LeJeune's success. The plaintively styled, blues-inflected French singing of these men effectively reestablished French as the language of choice in Cajun dance hall music. Aldus Roger and the Lafayette Playboys came to the forefront in the 1950s and hosted their own television show on KLFY in Lafayette from 1955 to 1970. Roger, who played accordion and had other band members do the singing, developed a reputation for superb musicianship, inspiring critics to write comments like: "set the standard for the modern traditional Cajun dancehall band"; "No one plays an accordion with better timing and with more perfection"; "With a smooth, precise style, the band was highly danceable, emphasizing professionalism and good musicianship over performance tricks."[1]

Just as the accordion was making its resurgence in Cajun music in the late 1940s, members of the Balfa family formed their own band in 1948 to play in clubs around Mamou, and early on were best known as the band that played behind accordionist Nathan Abshire. Then folklorist Ralph Rinzler called Dewey Balfa to be a substitute guitar player for a Cajun trio at the Newport Folk Festival in Rhode Island in 1964. Never before having traveled outside the region to play his music, Balfa was energized by the audience response at the festival to promote Cajun music more actively back home, where it was still looked down upon as low-class "chanky-chank" music. He persuaded reluctant record man Floyd Soileau, who did not think that the Balfas' acoustic sound would sell, to record them, and Swallow Records released *The Balfa Brothers Play Traditional Cajun Music* in 1965. Creole musicians Bois Sec Ardoin and Canray Fontenot performed at Newport in 1966 and the Balfa Brothers themselves did so in 1967. The Louisiana French answer to the Newport Folk Festival debuted in 1974, a "Tribute to Cajun Music" that was the precursor to what has become known as Festivals Acadiens in Lafayette, Louisiana. Dewey was involved in this and other efforts to educate young and old about Cajun music. In 1979, Dewey's brothers Will and Rodney were killed in a car accident but he carried on his work as a cultural representative until his passing in 1992.[2]

While the fiddle sound predominated in the Balfa band, they did play and record with various accordionists, including Allie Young, Nathan Abshire, and later in their career with a younger musician named Marc Savoy. A young college graduate in chemical engineering in 1965, rather than going to work for industry Savoy started his own business making button accordions and operating a music store near Eunice. His instruments were double the price of the competition, but he established a reputation for quality that sustained a demand for his work. While he was not the first Louisiana-based accordion builder, his was a notable early example that many others later followed and collectively developed into a cottage industry with dozens of makers. Also known as a virtuoso performer, Savoy has frequently recorded and performed at festivals. He met a young guitarist and singer from Virginia named Ann Allen (who had majored in French in college) at the 1975 National Folk Festival in Washington, D.C., and they were married the following year.[3]

One of the first Cajun musicians to begin his career in the ferment of the renaissance efforts of the Balfas and others was Michael Doucet. Born in 1951, Doucet grew up around Lafayette in the 1950s and 1960s hearing a variety of Cajun music, jazz, and popular music; as a youth he played trumpet in the school band and folk rock guitar in a band that played in clubs. He and his boyhood friend Ralph Richard (now known as Zachary Richard) first tried playing Cajun music together shortly before Michael decided to take up the fiddle. Doucet had an epiphany meeting folk revivalist musicians in France that was not unlike that of Dewey Balfa at Newport, in that it involved the appreciation that outsiders exhibited for Cajun music:

> I had a chance to meet some people who influenced me very much ... people who had accepted Cajun music as the new folk music, something really beautiful. Whenever I had dealt with Cajun music before, it had always related to older people and how things were. Here were serious musicians in their twenties playing and relating to Cajun music in terms of what it could be. In Louisiana, around that time, Cajun music was being displaced by Cajun country sounds which didn't ring true. I couldn't identify with them. In France, I saw eight fiddlers playing "Jolie blonde" the old way,

accompanied by a hurdy-gurdy and all sorts of different sounds. I began to understand what we had and what we stood for. What we really had here in Louisiana was underneath the surface.[4]

Doucet took care first to learn playing technique with a violin teacher and a sampling of other styles of music. The next year (1975) he received a Folk Arts Apprenticeship from the National Endowment for the Arts to study Cajun fiddling. He visited with several older fiddlers, including Varise Connor, Dewey Balfa, Creole fiddler Canray Fontenot, and an octogenarian Dennis McGee (1893–1989). "Dennis McGee really did it for me. I had never met such a dynamic person. And his songs were so old. Anything after 1940 was a new song to him. Those experiences really helped me musically, culturally, historically, linguistically (Dennis never speaks to me in English). I gave up graduate school in English to come and do my own version of graduate work in Cajun French language and music here [in Louisiana]." At that time, Doucet was playing in two different bands, Coteau and Beausoleil. In 1976 Beausoleil played at the National Folk Festival in Washington, at President Jimmy Carter's inauguration festivities, and at a festival in Paris commemorating the American bicentennial, and released its first record (on Pathé Marconi, in France), but it was the more experimental Coteau that was popular with a young audience back home. When Coteau broke up in 1977, Michael (with his guitarist brother David Doucet) refocused his energies on Beausoleil and on working with Dewey Balfa to bring Cajun music into public school classrooms. Beausoleil would go on to become the highly successful touring and recording band acknowledged by Mary Chapin Carpenter in "Down At The Twist And Shout" (see Chapter 1), and they collected their own Grammy Award for Best Traditional Folk Album in 1997.[5]

While the retrenchment of Cajun musical identity continued into the 1960s and beyond, other Cajun musicians continued a closer association with American popular music trends. As Doucet indicates, some continued to follow country music, covering Nashville hits with straight translations into French and writing original compositions in like musical style. Both Cajun and Creole musicians experimented with rhythm and blues and early rock 'n' roll, sometimes adopting both language and instrumentation of these styles that were sweeping the country and sometimes throwing in a French lyric or an accordion fill, in a variant that British record collector and author John Broven dubbed "swamp pop."[6]

Creole musician accordionist and singer Clifton Chenier (1925–1987) took a set of influences similar to those in swamp pop, added jump blues à la Louis Jordan and urban blues in the Chicago mold, and with his piano accordion established a new style of Creole music called zydeco. He had his first hit single with the Los

Angeles label Specialty in 1955 ("Ay-Tete-Fee"), after which he toured the country in efforts to establish himself as a rhythm and blues artist. Lowell Fulson, a blues guitarist who began his career in Oakland, California, toured with Chenier for a year and taught him a few things about stagecraft. However, follow-up success eluded Clifton until he connected with Chris Strachwitz of Arhoolie Records a decade later. Several recordings followed, as did tours to Europe and a 1973 documentary profile by California filmmaker Les Blank, *Hot Pepper*. According to Chenier, he started wearing a crown onstage and billing himself "The King of Zydeco" after winning a 1971 accordion contest in Europe. Producer Strachwitz relates,

> [H]e became the biggest name in the zydeco field. But Clifton was never really satisfied; he always thought that he should be as big as Ray Charles or Fats Domino, he was disappointed because I never got him a real hit. And in a way he was right. He told me several times, "I should be making the kind of money B.B. King is making." And I would agree, I think in the right hands perhaps he could have been a superstar. But thinking back, I think I probably documented him better than anyone else would have done, because I encouraged him to do what I heard him do best.[7]

After 1975, Chenier went on to record with other labels and received belated Grammy recognition for Best Ethnic or Traditional Folk Recording of 1983, a year after Queen Ida received her award.[8]

By the 1960s, Creole music (in the form of zydeco) and Cajun music were more racially marked than in the period when Ardoin and McGee recorded, with musical traits more clearly indicating a black/white boundary. Perhaps not so coincidentally, this was also the period when the civil rights movement and judicial decisions were bringing an end to segregation of the races by law in the South. In place of clear legal distinctions came clearer musical distinctions to preserve the social status quo, while at the same time these ethnic groups and others were jockeying for new positions in the political hierarchy. Zydeco songs may not be replete with references to political struggle, but the existence of an identifiably black style of Louisiana French dance music was consonant with the black pride movement of the 1960s and yet retained for Creoles their own modes of expressive culture. During the same decade, Cajuns responded to changing social trends by participating in the "new ethnicity" movement (as already mentioned) that led to the self-conscious Cajun pride of musicians like Zachary Richard and Michael Doucet in the 1970s and to the formation of the Cajun French Music Association in the 1980s. After Clifton Chenier's death in 1987, the reemergence of Boozoo Chavis and his button accordion music took zydeco away from a heavy emphasis on urban twelve-bar blues into a new synthesis of rural Creole and contemporary popular music.[9]

Danny Poullard[10]

Danny Poullard (1938–2001) is a pivotal figure in the history of Louisiana French music in California, as a performer and as a teacher and inspiration to other musicians who are still playing today. Danny was born into a large family of four brothers and six sisters on January 10, 1938, to John and Dorence ("Dorsina") Poullard in the hamlet of Ritchie, near Eunice, Louisiana. French was his first language; he did not learn English until he started school. His father was a sharecropper there and played accordion before Danny was born. John Poullard gave up playing after he was mistaken for someone else and shot in the back one night coming home from playing a dance, which caused him to be hospitalized for a long period. Danny rarely saw his father play music while growing up—only when John sat in with Canray Fontenot out at Freeman Fontenot's place in Basile. Danny had other relatives around Eunice who played music, and he enjoyed going to dances. He expressed interest in learning to play the accordion when he was ten or so, but his father forbade it because of the shooting incident. Around 1951, when Danny was thirteen his family moved to Beaumont, Texas, where his father found iron work and later a position with the county government. French language and music were much less prevalent in his new home, although there was a radio program of French music out of Port Arthur every Saturday. Danny was more interested in popular music at that time, and he started teaching himself piano and organ on instruments at his school and church.[11]

The size of his family, combined with friction between him and his father, caused Danny to decide to drop out of school and join the army. He served for two years, including a tour of duty in Europe where he found his French to be rusty yet useable. With his brown skin and straight hair, he encountered antagonism from both white and black soldiers in his unit and found a social niche among his Native American and Mexican American comrades. He earned his high school diploma while in the service, was discharged in 1958, and returned to Beaumont. There he worked as a delivery driver and waited for a job in the oil refineries to come open, but after three more years in Texas he was ready for a change of scenery. With a sister already living in Los Angeles, California seemed like a good choice.[12]

When Danny traveled to California in 1961, he first looked for work in Los Angeles but found nothing satisfactory. He was offered a job in San Diego but decided he did not want to live there, so he went up to the San Francisco Bay Area to visit other relatives and there he stayed, eventually landing a civilian job as a butcher on the Presidio military base. Not long after arriving in San Francisco, he found himself immersed in the network of Creoles who were already living there, including many people he had known as a child growing up near Eunice whom he had not seen since then. At a dance at All Hallows Church, he heard and met accordionist John Semien, whom he had heard play years before in Louisiana. Danny and John became friends and through John he met a number of other Louisiana French musicians living in the Bay Area.[13]

In his new home, Danny surrounded himself with music. He learned how to play guitar and experimented with the harmonica. John Semien was single and would want to play music whenever anyone came to visit him, which gave Danny a chance to play guitar with other people. In 1969, the same year that he married his wife Ruby, Danny started learning the accordion. Semien had an extra instrument that he would let Danny play when he came to visit, and he would show him a couple of tunes to try. Danny bought his first single-row button accordion for twenty-five dollars on Columbus Avenue (in San Francisco's North Beach neighborhood) and started learning how to play in earnest. He learned a couple of tunes and Ullus Gobart, a fiddler and legendary dancer, encouraged him to get a better instrument. This soon became necessary after Danny went to play his tunes for Semien; John tried the "baby" accordion himself and blew out the reeds. Danny then bought himself a Hohner brand accordion, learned additional tunes, and Semien showed him some more. Tisserand relates the story of how Danny played as little as possible in his lessons so as to elicit the maximum from his teacher without threatening him. When John finally asked Danny to show him what he had learned, he played so well that John grew angry and refused to teach anymore.[14]

In what must have been the early 1970s, John Semien acted on an opportunity to record an album in Louisiana. This experience left him dissatisfied with his band back in California, and the Opelousas Playboys fractured after his return. The other men in the band then came after Poullard to learn more accordion so that they could form a new band; fiddler Ben Guillory would drive up from Palo Alto four times a week to practice with him. Soon the remaining Opelousas Playboys reformed as the Louisiana Playboys with Danny on accordion. The band started out playing the same types of gigs that they had with Semien, mainly house parties and church dances.[15]

As it became apparent to Danny that he had the ability and the opportunity to play the accordion, something he had wanted as a child and had been denied, he redoubled his efforts to learn the instrument as if in an attempt to make up for lost time. When Will Spires asked Danny how his father felt since he had started playing Cajun music, he responded this way: "He was real glad after I came out here, and he saw I was still interested, and interested enough to get an accordion and fool around. But he realized, and I think he was sorry, that he had made a mistake when he denied me of getting one at the age that I should have gotten one. Because I'm sure I'd have been probably a hell of a lot better than I am now if I'd

Ben Guillory, Danny Poullard, and Charlie St. Mary performing in the Brazil Room, Tilden Park, 1976. Photo by Gary Canaparo.

have learned how to play then, at that time." Nonetheless, with constant practice and the availability of jamming partners he was able to make great progress. His musical point of departure was the prairie Creole style that John Semien played and that developed in the same area of southwestern Louisiana where Poullard was from, near Eunice. Not surprisingly, this was the style of music that Danny's father had played before Danny was born. Several years after he had forbidden his son to learn the accordion, John Poullard started playing music again and sharing what he knew with Danny during brief visits, and with Danny's brother Edward. Edward was fourteen years younger than Danny, still lived in Beaumont, and had much greater access to their father. Ed picked up the guitar in high school and accompanied John Poullard but did not think of learning the accordion until he visited Danny one time in California and witnessed his painstaking learning process.

> Although I couldn't play either, on the accordion, when he would try to learn how to play a song, I could tell him, "No, that's not right. I've been playing with Daddy, and I know how it's supposed to sound." [laughs] ... You know, he was on the West Coast, and I was on the Gulf Coast.... I was there at home. When my dad played the accordion, I was right there watching him, or listening or playing the guitar with

him.... When I realized I could do that—that I had absorbed those old songs from Daddy—from talking with Danny, I said, "Hell, I ought to try to learn play too."

Danny would then get further instruction from Ed by long-distance telephone, the two brothers actually playing for each other over the phone. Ed went on to play the fiddle later, after a workplace injury forced him to take a break from the accordion.[16]

Even with these renewed family connections to enhance his music-making, Danny still did most of his learning from recordings. Cajun accordionists Nathan Abshire and Aldus Roger were two of his favorites, and he had videotapes of Roger playing on Louisiana television so that he could watch as well as listen. One day in the garage of his home in Fairfield, where a couple of us had come to play music on a weeknight, I found him listening to a recording of Aldus Roger's "Lafayette Two-Step" and playing along with the recording as he had done when he was first learning the song. He stopped playing when the vocalist started singing and explained as the recording continued: "Hear that? That's how I learned, doing that. Repetitive, over and over and over, one song like that. I can play every damn thing on that tape, Aldus Roger, note for note. [laughs] Because I spent many, many nights, boy. Every night, until two or three o'clock in the morning, and I had to go to work, get up at six o'clock, you know?" He would also go to watch visiting accordionists such as Marc Savoy whenever he could, with the intent of studying what they were doing on the instrument and how they rendered a particular melody. With recordings, he would put them on tape and slow them to half speed (resulting in the same key an octave lower) so that he could learn them, as he says, "note for note," and then play along with them at full speed. He practiced while looking at himself in the mirror, so that he could reinforce the music he was hearing with a visual image of what it looks like to play it. This in turn trained his eye to the point where he became adept at picking up what other players were doing just by watching them. Finally, he strengthened his playing by frequently playing with other people, at a time when most other musicians from Louisiana played guitar or fiddle or both.[17]

By coincidence or not, as Danny's confidence in his accordion playing grew, the Louisiana Playboys started getting work outside of Creole community events. Arhoolie Records producer Chris Strachwitz, based nearby in El Cerrito and Berkeley, by this time was already familiar with local Louisiana French music-making, and he hosted a regular radio program on KPFA in Berkeley. Danny identified a Thanksgiving Day in the early to mid-1970s as the beginning of the transition of the music from the Catholic church to venues for the general public. Strachwitz had heard of the Louisiana Playboys and had invited them to play on his KPFA radio program on Thanksgiving. Les Blank was there at the station watching them,

Jam session at Gobart residence with Charlie St. Mary, Louis Semien, Danny Poullard, Ernest Leday, and Ullus Gobart, circa 1978–79. Photo by Gary Canaparo.

and subsequently got them invited to play for parties, weddings, and art events from Sonoma County to Monterey. In 1977, Blank arranged for Alice Waters to invite the Louisiana Playboys to play in Berkeley on Bastille Day, in the middle of a "garlic festival" she was having at her famed restaurant Chez Panisse. Blank recorded this event for posterity in *Garlic Is As Good As Ten Mothers*, showing the band (Poullard, Junior Felton, Ben Guillory, and Charlie St. Mary) playing in the middle of the dining room. At another moment in this film, Danny is shown playing music with Dewey and Rodney Balfa. At this point in time, it is difficult to say just how frequent these gigs were for the Louisiana Playboys in comparison to playing for the Creole community, but they represent the beginnings of a bridging between the ethnic community and others in the region who were showing an interest in Louisiana French culture. In this bridging process, cultural misunderstandings were bound to occur. In 1976, the same year that Queen Ida cut her first album, the Louisiana Playboys played the first Cajun or zydeco music heard within the walls of Ashkenaz, a folk dance club then only three years old but destined to become a Berkeley cultural institution. The Ashkenaz calendar advertised that "the Louisiana Playboys will perform Louisiana Cajun Music Friday Night Oct. 15th 8:30–9:30. They will then play for an Old Time Square Dance called by Bob Black." It is not known whether or not the square dance went off as planned, but it is safe to say that the old-time music used for square dances was not in the Playboys' repertoire.[18]

Personnel in the Louisiana Playboys varied over time. Fiddler Ben Guillory passed away in 1978. On November 3 of that year in her second appearance at Ashkenaz, Queen Ida played a benefit dance to help defray the family's medical expenses. Tensions among the remaining Louisiana Playboys surfaced that continued to simmer for the remaining five or so years of the band's existence; guitarist Junior Felton wanted to play rock and roll, while George Broussard preferred country music. Meanwhile, Poullard continued to work on his accordion playing and repertoire. Danny saw Junior's and George's tastes for American popular music as "getting off the bandwagon," as he put it, of keeping Louisiana French music alive. Each of the men wanted to lead the band in his own direction.[19]

While the Louisiana Playboys were still together, Poullard found another performance outlet through his connections with folk revival musicians in the Bay Area. Around 1982, he began sitting in with the Bay Area–based Blue Flame String Band, including Eric and Suzy Thompson. The band's repertoire included old-time, bluegrass, blues, jug band, and Cajun music, and they had already done some recording with Cajun musician Marc Savoy. From this band, guitarist Alan Senauke would occasionally fill in on guitar with the Louisiana Playboys. Poullard appeared with Blue Flame at sit-down folk music venues such as the Freight and Salvage Coffeehouse in Berkeley, and they also played a few dances at Ashkenaz.[20]

In addition to playing with local bands, Poullard had occasional opportunities to play with touring musicians from Louisiana. In the late 1970s, he was invited to play accordion with Cajun fiddler Dewey Balfa at a festival in Marin County. He subsequently played with Balfa on several other occasions, such as when Balfa was in residence as visiting faculty at California State University–Fresno in the spring of 1987. In early 1983—before he ever brought his band Beausoleil to the West Coast—fiddler Michael Doucet visited Chris Strachwitz's KPFA radio show in Berkeley and performed live with Poullard on accordion and Alan Senauke on guitar, then packed the Freight and Salvage Coffeehouse that evening. Strachwitz later released the live radio performance on his Arhoolie label.[21]

By 1985, Poullard's collaboration with the Blue Flame String Band on a portion of their repertoire had led to the formation of the California Cajun Orchestra, which played exclusively Cajun dance music and which showcased Danny's accordion playing and repertoire. The California Cajun Orchestra recorded two albums on Arhoolie Records and received recognition in Louisiana. He also appeared with members of this band in another Les Blank film, *J'ai Été Au Bal* (1989). While personnel in the band changed over the years, the core trio remained with Danny on accordion, Suzy Thompson on fiddle, and Eric Thompson on guitar. Together they played monthly Saturday night dances at Ashkenaz in Berkeley for over a decade. A full biography of the band appears in chapter 6, in the profile of the Thompsons, but the importance of this band to Danny's musical career should be noted here. He was proud of its accomplishments and of its place as the premier Cajun band in the region. By the 1990s the other members of the Louisiana Playboys were no longer musically active in the Cajun and zydeco scene. When Danny was not playing with the California Cajun Orchestra, he would play dances with a band he simply called Danny and Friends, a shifting lineup of local musicians most of whom also played in the growing number of other bands in the area.

The number of bands in northern California was growing in part due to all of the musicians who were learning Cajun music from Danny. The first to get some accordion tips from him (in the mid-1970s) was Mark St. Mary, a Creole musician who eventually took a different direction with a bluesy piano accordion style that more closely resembles Clifton Chenier's zydeco than the old-school stylings of Semien and Poullard. In the 1980s came students, first Gerard Landry and then Bill Wilson, who would go on to start their own bands with the foundation of button accordion skills that Danny had given them. Several more would follow in the 1990s. His reputation as a transmitter of musical tradition to other musicians became another point of pride with Danny. It began with his enthusiasm for informal music-making, which did not stop when he began fronting his own band and was not limited to his fellow Louisiana expatriates. Just as he learned by playing with others, others began learning by playing with him. His willingness to play with others of varying skill levels at informal gatherings, as evidenced by numerous stories in this book from musicians who came into playing Cajun or zydeco music through Poullard, marked the beginning of his master-teacher phase. If someone had an instrument, he would encourage him or her to get it out or bring it next time even if the person had never played Cajun music before. Having people over to his house on a regular basis to make music became part of this pattern.

Significant in Poullard's teaching is the fact that he literally gave it away. He did not charge for lessons, or for taping material, or for anything else with the exception of the stipends he received from summer camps. Poullard would work with anyone serious about learning and making at least some progress. If he perceived someone not to be serious, he felt free to disinvite him or her at any time (although he seldom did so) since he had not incurred any obligation by accepting payment.

In fact, Poullard did not teach a great number of lessons to individuals, although he would arrange times for them upon request. What happened during one-on-one time, as he called it, varied quite a bit. In any given lesson, a student might have done one or more of the following: tape Danny playing solo to take home and learn new repertoire, videotape him so as to be able to study his fingers, listen to recordings together and comment on them, play an accompanying instrument while he played accordion, play accordion while he played guitar or fiddle, or play accordion together. If he heard something he did not like from a student he said something, but he never insisted on a single right way to play a particular tune. Rather, following his own practice of never playing anything quite the same way twice, there seemed to be a range of acceptable variations for each tune. Learning from recordings was encouraged, in fact he rather expected that most of his students would learn mostly as he did, working alone with a mirror and recordings. Music notation and tablature were never used. Students arriving with instruction method in hand were told to "get rid of that damn book!" It was acceptable, however, for students who sang to refer to written song lyrics.

At the weekly group music-making sessions that I attended between 1995 and 2000, attendance varied widely, from one to ten or more. The types of teacher–student interaction that happened in one-on-one sessions also took place in the group. Sociomusical dynamics that accrued in the group setting were sometimes competitive but more often cooperative. When everyone in the circle was playing music together, some accordionist kicked off the tune and led the group. Leadership did not alternate every song; rather, one person played for a while and then ceded leadership to someone else. Danny often played accordion for a while, taking requests for particular tunes. If there were several musicians present, beginners would usually remain the aural background, either listening to or accompanying the more advanced players. During a song, multiple soloists could take a turn, including a second accordionist. Singing was encouraged but not required.

Danny's stature as the acknowledged leader of the session as a whole seemed to limit competition from taking over the proceedings. Danny did not often have to assert his authority, but he would if he perceived the need. For example, if someone tried to lead off a song or supply an accompaniment from outside of the Louisiana French traditions, he would stop everything and remind them that this was a Cajun music workshop. Cooperation was more the norm at these weekly sessions. While a song was in progress, for example, some might exchange information about how the chord changes fit into the song. Between numbers, there were generally two or three conversations going on at once, some about music, some not. Musical knowledge in this context flowed not only from Poullard directly, but also from the more experienced students to the less experienced, and instruction thus became a group activity. The more experienced students (and Danny himself) also got something from playing with the less experienced, especially the opportunity to switch instruments and play something that they would not normally play in public.

Eventually, Danny was able to claim to have taught a great number of musicians who went on to form their own bands, and he became more of a national figure in the 1990s as a result of his appearances at summer workshops like the Festival of American Fiddle Tunes in Port Townsend, Washington, and the Augusta Heritage Center in Elkins, West Virginia. At Augusta, where he first appeared in 1994, teaching the advanced Cajun accordion workshop became his specialty. Students from around the country came to study there, and when those from California who attended the workshop saw the respect that Danny was getting from the other students and teachers, his stock rose back home in California as well.

These festivals provided rendezvous points for him and his brother Edward, as well as platforms for them to perform together. Eventually, the Poullard brothers found D'Jalma Garnier to complete a performing trio. Garnier, who like Ed Poullard had gotten grants to study Creole fiddling with Canray Fontenot, was a jazz guitarist from a musical Creole family but was born and raised in Minnesota, and he shared the Poullards' heritage orientation to Creole music. While he played with the Poullards, Garnier was also playing fiddle with Filé, a Louisiana-based band with a contemporary electric sound that blended Cajun and Creole music in original ways. Poullard, Poullard, and Garnier recorded an eponymous album of acoustic music in the older Creole style of Bois Sec Ardoin and Canray Fontenot where each man's musical contribution can be clearly heard. Perhaps the most compelling tracks are the few that features Edward's French vocals, such as "Bee de la Manche" and Canray's "Les Barres de la Prison." On the instrumental selections Danny's accordion rings out, and on two of the tracks he plays rhythm guitar behind twin fiddles. The album was released in 2001, just a few weeks before his death from a heart attack.[22]

Betty Leblanc[23]

Dancer Betty Leblanc came out to southern California from Louisiana around the same time that Poullard did, in 1960, but unlike him she settled there for a dozen years before relocating to northern California. Betty was born to Caris and Eutah Zeno Leblanc and raised in Lafayette, Louisiana, in a family with four sisters and two brothers. Her first language was French, but she started learning English even before she was old enough to go to school:

> That [French] was my first language. I learned English, and the way I learned it, I used to climb a tree when I was a little girl, my neighbor.... We were living in the country part of Lafayette, and when we moved to the city, there was a older lady that

was in the back of our house, and she would speak in English to her husband. And whatever she would say to her husband, I would mock her. And she thought I was being funny. I didn't know how to speak English, and I was just saying everything she'd say. And I'd say it out loud but she could hear me, and she got offended. And she went over to my mother and my father and she said, your little girl is being very sassy. She's mocking me, everything I'm saying. And I went up to her and I said, no *tante*, I'm not being sassy, I just want to learn what you're saying. You know, but I said it in French, and my sister interpreted to her. And so she said, oh I didn't know that. So she took a book and she started teaching me.

As a girl Betty had the nickname "la Rougette" (little redhead), and remembers a Cajun band that used to rehearse in her neighborhood near downtown Lafayette on Thursday evenings. Hearing the music made on a screened-in porch, she was able to practice the dance steps she had learned at dances attended with her parents. She can recall dance halls where Clifton Chenier and Rockin' Dopsie played zydeco when she was young, such as Roger's Night Club on the way to Breaux Bridge from Lafayette and Man-Roy, which was in Breaux Bridge. Of Man-Roy she remembers:

> The place was a big, big hall ... they had benches all the way around. And that's where all the parents would sit, especially the mothers. Because that's how they would sit to watch their daughter. And the fathers used to be outside, smoking their cigarettes or drinking their beer, and the mothers used to be inside the place. Because you would never go to a dance without being escorted, you know, by parents. We were all young, you know, we were dancing zydeco. And I danced with the finest dancers that I could ever remember back home.

Betty's father, a laborer, also gave her dance lessons in the backyard using a piece of plywood for a dance floor. She and two of her sisters all became marching band majorettes and their father taught them some special steps in the backyard dance studio and also helped them with their baton work:

> We had a big large plywood, just like a dance floor, you know. And we would be outside at night and it would be dark at night. And he would have a big old barrel with fire, because it would be cold. And we would take our baton sticks and he'd light a torch and he'd throw it to us. And we had to better catch it so we wouldn't get burned, you know. And he taught us how to turn those batons, how to work with that, and how to put original steps down. And it was my sister Eva, and it was me, and then it was my baby sister, Gloria, after me. And we all three of us, when

we danced in the band, and we would go down in New Orleans, Canal Street, and when the Leblanc girls was coming, you please believe me, everybody would get excited about watching our steps. Because we had some beautiful steps. I know you commented me about my steps, about my dancing, but it's not nothing that I learned from other people. I learned that from my father. And my mother was an excellent waltzer. She was a great dancer, you know, and she would dance, everybody would just look at her.

Betty moved to southern California in 1960s first as a young single woman and then married her childhood sweetheart, who was serving in the military. She relates that Clifton Chenier, a family friend through her mother's brother, Weston, played at her wedding reception at Roger's Night Club. The couple returned to southern California to live for six years until they moved to the Bay Area in 1972, where her in-laws lived. Betty was already active at house dances in southern California, and she was able to participate even more in northern California right away because her husband's parents belonged to the Bon Ami club, which would hire John Semien to play for dances.

Ullus Gobart, Danny Poullard, and Charlie St. Mary performing at All Hallows Church in San Francisco, circa 1977–78. Photo by Gary Canaparo.

At the dances Betty met other Louisiana French people who gave her a hand off the dance floor as well. She danced with Ullus Gobart. "When Ullus was in the dance, every lady in that place would stand in line to dance with him, because he was that good. He had his style, you know? A woman would feel great dancing with him." Ullus and his wife Wilma helped with babysitting Betty's daughter for many years, in addition to hosting many of the house parties that she attended at their home in Daly City. Betty danced with fiddler Ben Guillory when he was not playing on the bandstand. She describes how Ben and his wife unofficially adopted Betty soon after she arrived in northern California: "They knew my parents was away and I didn't have any family here. So they called themselves my parents. Watching, you know, keeping an eye on me. And I used to feel like I was going at home when I would go to their house. I was part of them. Their kids, everybody in the family knew that I was a part of them. They never treated me like I wasn't a part of them. Every year around New Year's, Pasi used to make persimmon cake. She'd make a cake for every one of her kids and she had one for me too." Another of Betty's favorite dance partners was Charlie St. Mary, who would later play rubboard with the Louisiana Playboys and the California Cajun Orchestra. With Charlie, she won some zydeco dance contests sponsored by St. Michael's Church in San Francisco.

Betty has maintained her ties with Louisiana over the years. She made frequent trips back to visit her siblings and her mother, who lived into her nineties. She would meet musicians traveling from Louisiana when they played in northern California, and then see them play again "back home" when she visited her mother and sisters. She would sometimes plan her visits to coincide with music festivals such as Festivals Acadiens in Lafayette. She happened to be in Louisiana at the times when musicians Rockin' Sidney Simien and Beau Jocque died, and she made it a point to attend their funerals out of respect for these musicians. In her travels she got to know zydeco musicians such as Thomas Fields, Lil Malcolm, Nathan Williams, Boozoo Chavis, and Keith Frank, as well as Cajun accordionist Sheryl Cormier.

Eventually Betty's sociability and enthusiasm for zydeco music led her to organize the return of Louisiana French dances to Demarco's 23 Club in Brisbane, California, just south of San Francisco, where they had been previously booked by others. In recent years she has held dances there once or twice a month on Sunday afternoons. The club allows attendees to bring food for a potluck supper and makes its money at the bar; Betty and her fellow volunteers collect a cover charge and pass a tip jar, all of which goes to the musicians. The Sunday afternoon potluck is an institution that Betty recalls from her childhood. She thinks of moving

DeMarco's 23 Club in Brisbane, California, 1997. Photo by the author.

back to Louisiana one day, but in the meantime she still organizes dances at the 23 Club. "It had to take me to leave there to find out what I missed, and oh, did I miss a lot. But it's not too late to pick up the pieces. And I salute Louisiana, because I'm proud to say that I'm from there. I thank all and each every band that ever played zydeco and Cajun. I thank each and every one of them for doing that, and keep up the good work. From the Zydeco Lady, Betty Leblanc!"

Olivia Guillory[24]

Olivia Guillory was born in Lafayette, Louisiana, into a family of four daughters. Her childhood nickname Tee, a form of the French word for "small" which some still call her, was given to her by her grandmother. Her natural father, a harmonica player, passed away when she was very young, and her mother's side of the family was the strongest force in her childhood. Olivia's maternal grandparents were sharecroppers who eventually bought the land on which they raised crops, livestock, and fifteen children. Her memories of the farm include traditional *boucherie* get-togethers, where all in attendance would be sent home with cuts of meat from a butchering, and back-porch music-making by some of her relatives, including a great-uncle who played the accordion.

Olivia spoke Creole as a child, but early on was sent to live with relatives in New Jersey for more than a year. When she returned to Louisiana she was an English speaker, and never quite regained her first language completely. Most of her childhood years in Louisiana were spent in Basile. There were no musicians in her immediate household, but she started dancing at age five or six, both at home to zydeco recordings and out at public dances. She remembers:

> There was a little club in Basile where we used to go pay fifty cents at the door and Mom would be working at the hamburger joint around the corner, so she always knew where we were, so we were allowed to go. And Clifton Chenier was about the only one that played zydeco, and also the Ardoin family, so we used to go to their dances. We called them the "French la-la's" at that time. They focused on fiddles and playing accordion, and the sound didn't have that rhythmatic boost like most of the zydeco bands have right now. The music was mostly like the mellow stuff and people had fun. People brought all their kids, and you'd see women on the wall, sitting down on these benches, sort of like pews, on the side of the walls. Women were also visible with their babies and they breast-fed them right at the dances 'cause it was like a family thing, like a fais-do-do.

While they were in Basile, her mother Lena began seeing a man named Houston Pitre. Houston eventually decided to go to California in search of job opportunities in construction. He found work and asked Lena to come out to California and marry him. He had to ask her twice; in 1966 she agreed and Olivia found herself a teenage resident of Richmond.[25]

After staying in housing owned by her stepfather's relatives, the family moved into their own home in Richmond in 1969. This house and this family have been very important to the history of zydeco music on the West Coast due to the tradition of zydeco benefit dances at St. Mark's in Richmond, which were started by David Pitre, a boyhood friend but no relation to Olivia's stepdad Houston. Clifton Chenier first played at St. Mark's in the late 1960s. Visits by Chenier and other Louisiana musicians would be occasions for jamming in the garage behind Houston and Lena's home and parties with dancing in their backyard attended by family and friends.[26]

When I interviewed Olivia at the family home in 1995, she showed me the bedroom where visiting musicians slept. The dresser top was adorned with framed photos, including a black and white promotional photo of John Delafose and one of her son André in the form of a clock. The stereo cabinet in the living room was full of zydeco recordings, from vintage eight-tracks by Chenier and Buckwheat Zydeco to then-current releases by Beau Jocque and Keith Frank. "Dad would like a lot of people around, so he would invite a lot of people that would come.... All the time, every weekend there was something going on here, because these people liked to dance. And if there wasn't a band here, they'd have a party, they'd turn up the music, put on Clifton's album on the stereo, and they would dance.... So we got a lot of dancing here at home."

After David Pitre died, Houston and Lena took over organizing the dances at St. Mark's. In the mid-1980s Olivia took over the booking responsibilities. In addition to local bands, she booked several musicians from Louisiana including zydeco accordionist John Delafose (her mainstay attraction until his death in 1993), John's son Geno Delafose, JoJo Reed, and Beau Jocque.

In the 1980s Olivia was raising a family, including son André Thierry (born in 1979) and two younger daughters Julie Ann and Chasya, whose early childhoods were surrounded by music and dancing and punctuated by visits from Clifton Chenier, John Delafose, and other musicians from Louisiana. André showed an interest in music, especially the accordion, and received his first button accordion as a gift from local musician Billy Wilson.

She credits joining the gospel choir at St. Mark's (she was one of its four founding members in the late 1980s) as the experience that brought her out of her shyness: "I was able to focus and actually look at people in front of me." She then put these newfound social skills to use, giving her first public zydeco dance lesson in 1988 and a few years later playing rubboard in her son André's band when he was a young teenager. As the St. Mark's choir became better known, they were asked to sing at other Catholic parishes and at churches in other denominations as well, and Olivia finally had to tell her choir director that she could no longer sustain the time commitment. From the gospel choir Olivia learned an alternative "Happy Birthday" song, a completely different composition from the standard, which Zydeco Magic would play at shows upon request.

Freed of her choir obligations, Olivia the single mother had more time to spend with her children. Her stepfather Houston passed away in the early 1990s and the backyard jam sessions and parties became a thing of the past. "When I slowed down, I think that's when André started really getting into the music. I spent more time with him, like buying tapes and traveling to Louisiana; he came with me twice." Prior to that time, when musicians like Geno Delafose and JoJo Reed would come and rehearse in the Pitres' garage, "André was watching, just watching. I never knew he would pick up the music at all." All of the music in his childhood environment—his father's amateur musical activities, the visitors from Louisiana and the house parties—eventually had their effect.

André Thierry now has his own career with a band that he still calls Zydeco Magic, the name he has used since he started fronting his own band at age twelve or thirteen. André reportedly served as his own musical director from early on, while Olivia acted as the band's manager, taught dance lessons at many of the gigs, played rubboard, and helped with the vocals onstage. She also made sure that André, who was in a gifted students program in high school, kept up with his schoolwork. She helped organize an all-youth zydeco band called the Creole Kids that played occasionally at community events, which included André, his sisters, and his cousin Jason Thierry. This lineup was in contrast to the Zydeco Magic band during André's youth, which relied on adult musicians who also played in other zydeco bands such as rubboardist and vocalist R. C. Carrier.

Of the dance teachers in the area who regularly offer Cajun or zydeco dance instruction to the public, Olivia has been the only one from Louisiana to do so. "When you're teaching you've got to have patience with those who do not understand a *thing* about the music." She says to beginners who get distracted by the up-and-down motion of the dancers or by rapid accordion playing: "We're going to get our *feet* moving in one direction. Don't worry about your upper body, get your feet moving. Listen to either the drum beat, or the bass beat." She found a huge improvement in the dancers in the Bay Area from 1985 to 1995: "These dancers have come a long way, they've got good dancers out here."

Like many people, Olivia has her ideas about what is traditional, what is creative, and what is going too far on the dance floor. "What I hate is when you get out there and you're doing something that really doesn't originate with the music. . . . But if you see people doing the basics, and adding to it, and they're having fun, go for it! I love to see 'em have fun. . . . You get a basic and you do your own style, and it's a style that you really don't see in Louisiana, so you're saying that the West Coast has their own zydeco style of dancing, their own way. And it's good to see them do that."

Along with Queen Ida's, Olivia's family stands out as one of the few where the California-born children have remained actively involved in the Louisiana French culture of their parents beyond attendance at an occasional church dance. The extraordinary environment of seeing their mother and grandmother produce dances at their church and of having visiting musicians from Louisiana like Clifton Chenier and John Delafose stay and rehearse in their home obviously was a factor. André could have left his playing days behind him after graduating from high school, but instead he has continued to develop a career as a zydeco musician. His technique on the accordion was already close to extraordinary when Danny Poullard put together a scholarship for him to study at the Augusta Heritage Center in West Virginia, a summer folk music festival where Poullard taught. André's subsequent return there as a staff musician strengthened his network of contacts outside of California to the point where he was able to tour the East Coast from a second base in Houston, Texas. A few years later, André's sister Chasya Thierry also received a scholarship to attend the Augusta Heritage Center to study zydeco accordion.

Andrew Carrière[27]

Unlike the other people profiled in this chapter who relocated to the West Coast in their early twenties or younger, Andrew Carrière was a married man in his mid-thirties when he moved to California in 1971. Andrew was born outside of Crowley, Louisiana, in 1937 into a noted family of musicians. His father, fiddler Joseph "Bébé" Carrière, and uncle, accordionist Éraste "Dolon" Carrière, played house dances when they were young and then formed a group called the Lawtell Playboys that included Dolon's son Calvin on fiddle and daughter Beatrice on guitar. This group played for dancing in clubs until their old-time style of Creole music went out of fashion, some time after which Calvin picked up the Lawtell Playboys name and started a more modern-sounding zydeco band with accordionist Delton Broussard. Later in life, the Carrière Brothers received recognition outside of Louisiana at folk festivals and with a handful of recordings on the Maison de Soul, Rounder, and Arhoolie labels.[28]

As a child, Andrew was surrounded by music, although he did not become a musician himself until decades later. His family moved from Crowley to Lawtell shortly after he was born and worked at sharecropping. He remembers being at house dances when he was small where his father played the fiddle and his Uncle Dolon took turns on accordion with an uncle from his mother's side of the family, Tee Gilles. "I used to sit around there when they had the house dances. When they get too crowded, I had to go back in the back room. But I'd watch them play that accordion. I'd sit right close until they make me leave, you know, every now and then I'd touch the button . . . I loved the sound, I always did love the sound of that accordion. But they wouldn't give me the chance [to play it]."

English was Andrew's first language; his parents only spoke French when they did not want their children to understand what they were saying. This parental communication strategy stopped working after they employed Andrew's maternal grandmother as a babysitter. "As I grow older, you know, my grandmother, she couldn't speak English," Andrew explains. "So I had to learn what she was talking about or either get whipped. I picked up French real good." Once it became clear that Andrew knew French too, his parents spoke it with him and never discouraged him from speaking it.

Andrew attended school in Lawtell as a youngster, but as the oldest boy there was also economic pressure on him to work in the fields to help the family. He eventually dropped out of school. When he was fifteen his parents split up; his mother moved with her children to Lake Charles so they could get more education, while his father stayed behind in Lawtell. Andrew went to school up through ninth grade. He met his wife in Lake Charles, married at age twenty-one, and continued to work there at various jobs in shipping and construction. Although he had never danced at the house dances in Lawtell, Andrew started going to clubs in Lake Charles and heard some zydeco. He had a friend who had a club, Thibodeaux's Club, that had zydeco music, and he started dancing there. "Then in '71 my wife said, 'We gotta move up down the road, we gotta go to California.' She had two sisters out here and I moved out here in '71. I didn't really want to go, but I'm glad I did, because I'd have probably still been working out there with no benefit, no medical. You know, it's kinda hard, the economy, it's kinda down out there."

When they arrived, Andrew got a job with the Maryland submarine shipyard in Vallejo as welder's helper with no skills. He worked as a helper for five years and then accepted an offer to go to welding school. He went back to work in the same shipyard as a welder until 1990, when they started cutting back. They transferred him to Moffett Field near San Jose so he could get his twenty-five years and retire, and he worked there as a truck driver. Andrew took retirement reluctantly in 1995, only then to start working in construction on a part-time basis.

The way Andrew tells it, his childhood desire to play the accordion was reborn shortly after he arrived in California, seeing his cousin John Semien play the accordion.

> Because I didn't have no friends, I didn't know where to go, where's the Creole people. So I'd hang out with David Duhon a little bit, and he took me up to the St. Mary's, they was having a party out there. They was playing that music. So John, my cousin was on the accordion, Danny was on the guitar. So I started going to visit Danny down in San Francisco. I'd grab his accordion, play around with it. I said shit, I'm gonna learn how to play this thing. I came up with a song. Danny said it'd be kind of hard for you to learn, you're left-handed. I said, no I'll play around with it some more. So I got a tune going on, "J'ai passé," you know, "doon-doon-doon" [singing sol-fa-mi]. I said wait a minute, I'm getting something going there.

Not until almost twenty years later, however, did Andrew buy his first accordion. In the meantime, he started sitting in with the California Cajun Orchestra in the 1980s, playing triangle and taking some lead vocals in French. When the band went into the studio to record its first album on Arhoolie, Andrew was invited to lend his strong tenor voice on three tracks. He received positive feedback for his work on this album. When Andrew subsequently traveled to Louisiana, he heard these tracks being played on the radio.

Around the time that this album was released, Andrew bought his first accordion while on vacation in Louisiana. He purchased a number of recordings—some of his father's and uncle's recordings, Canray Fontenot and Bois Sec Ardoin, Iry LeJeune—and started learning the words to the songs and trying to play along with them on the accordion. He also managed to obtain a copy of the recording that John Semien made in Louisiana and learned from that. Once he had learned to play a few tunes, Danny Poullard would let him take a turn on accordion at California Cajun Orchestra gigs.

When Andrew was still first learning the accordion, he received a visit from Joe Semien, John Semien's younger brother who lived in southern California. Joe, who also did not pick up the accordion until he moved to California as an adult, expressed his dissatisfaction at seeing Andrew onstage playing the triangle. According to Andrew, Joe said something like, "Man, that don't run in our family, playing a piece of iron. Why don't you start learning the accordion real good?" This exchange strengthened Andrew's resolve to learn the accordion despite the fact that he started after his fiftieth birthday and had never played a musical instrument before, aside from the triangle. He kept on practicing, got some pointers from Danny Poullard, and formed his own band, Andrew Carrière and the Cajun Classics. Joining him on fiddle was John Rothfield, brother of Suzy Thompson. They played their first engagement in 1993 at Ashkenaz in Berkeley.[29]

Public acceptance for Andrew's band leadership was swift. Although there were some tense moments with the accordion early on, his strong singing and energetic stage presence would carry the day. Common notions of authenticity also worked to his advantage; his audience would and still does refer to him as "the real deal" in reference both to his cultural background and to the well-known older generation of musicians in his family. Opportunities arose: he occasionally played entire gigs with the California Cajun Orchestra when Danny Poullard was unavailable. One year during the annual Cajun festival at the Berkeley Farmer's Market, Andrew caught the attention of a television crew and ended up in a commercial for Pacific Bell's Yellow Pages.

Andrew's standing as a musician in the local scene has steadily increased. Since Danny Poullard's passing in 2001, Andrew's symbolic importance as a tradition bearer has grown. He occasionally appears with his own band but more often is a "special guest" with the Creole Belles, a band of women started by Delilah Lee Lewis, who learned to play Creole fiddle style in Louisiana and who is profiled in

Andrew Carrière performing at Ashkenaz in Berkeley, California, 2006. Photo by the author.

the following chapter. One of the many things that Delilah and her band appreciate about Andrew is his ability to make up new song lyrics on the spot; with his facility in French he is not limited to verses learned from a recording or a book. Furthermore, his command of the accordion has improved greatly. At an accordion master class hosted by the California Friends of Louisiana French Music circa 2005, Andrew gave an impressive solo display of Creole accordion playing in the Cajun-sounding style of players like his uncle Eraste Carrière, Bois Sec Ardoin, Danny Poullard, and John Semien.

The Contributions of Danny Poullard and Others

In part, this chapter is about the passing of the musical baton from the Creoles who arrived in northern California in the 1940s to those who came later. The handoff from John Semien to Danny Poullard was particularly crucial. Queen Ida's career took her out of town often enough that it was Poullard who was the one to play for the local church dances month in and month out from the late 1970s onward.

At this late date it is difficult to piece together what happened when Poullard first started playing accordion for dances. Peter Levine's 1975 San Francisco newspaper article, the same one that introduced Queen Ida to the general public, provides a snapshot of band personnel in flux. Ullus Gobart as fiddler is introduced as "the newest member of the Opelousas Playboys," John Semien's group. The Opelousas Playboys are described as having been "together as a group for only six months" evidently in that configuration, since the group in name, with many of the same members, had appeared in the Berkeley Folk Festival six years before. Fiddler Ben Guillory, who had left the Opelousas Playboys, also appears in Levine's portrait.

> Most of these people know each other. Practically all come from Louisiana. They have been guests in each other's homes and some have become in-laws through marriage. They are a tight-knit but friendly people. The mood at their dances is joyous; they have come to enjoy themselves.
> "We always get along, even when we're angry," says Ben Guillory, cousin of drummer George Broussard and leader of his own band, the Louisiana Playboys. "What's the use of crying, let's have a good time while we can."[30]

The Louisiana Playboys are already identified as a distinct band, with Ben Guillory as their leader. Levine's description of an ethnic enclave neatly encapsulates prototypes likely latent in readers' minds before they picked up the newspaper; there is little new information there. Ben Guillory's comments also make use of existing cultural tropes, sung for example by Clifton Chenier as "C'est pas la peine brailler" ("what's the use of crying") and "Laissez les bons temps rouler" ("let the good times roll"). The comment that "We always get along, even when we're angry," may have been in reference to Ben's former association with the Opelousas Playboys. The ties in his social network were sufficiently strong that he was not going to miss this event, despite whatever residual tensions existed among former bandmates.

Occasionally the question arises as to why Danny Poullard, a Creole musician, consciously chose to call most of the music he played "Cajun music" and use the word "Cajun" in the names of his bands. As I explained in a previous article: "While as an ethnic group, Creoles have been primarily associated with zydeco music, Danny was relatively free in California to follow his own preference for Cajun accordion playing, stemming from the older Creole 'French' style that his father played and that bears a closer resemblance to Cajun music than to zydeco. He was also a strict antiessentialist on the relationship between a musician's ethnic identity and his musical style, believing the two need not have anything to do with each other." Danny subscribed to the historical view that at one time "it was all French music" and believed that the style of music that today is called "Cajun music" was originally not the exclusive domain of ethnic Cajuns, nor should it be so today. He played Creole music and zydeco, too, but he kept coming back to "Cajun music," which he considered to be a designation of musical style only, not a declaration of ethnic cultural ownership. At the same time, he considered all of Louisiana French dance music a tradition worth preserving.[31]

This was a complex set of views for Danny to hold together, since he was divorcing arguments for the preservation of musical tradition and the maintenance of ethnic identity that usually go hand in hand. He was aware that others did not think this way, yet stubbornly stuck to his opinion that considerations of music should be colorblind with respect to race. He would go so far as to take exception to what others heard in his music. The following discussion from Eric and Suzy Thompson is representative of descriptions of Danny's playing style:

> Suzy: Danny Dannyizes the stuff. He does. Even though he thinks he's playing exactly like the record, he's not. He has his own way of ornamenting the stuff and there's kind of a rhythmic lift and lightness to it that is really unusual.
>
> Eric: Yeah, he plays Aldus Roger's stuff, but Aldus is way square. Aldus' playing is great but it's very regular.
>
> Suzy: Danny's playing has a certain syncopation to it, a little bit Caribbean or Creole sounding, and my theory is that it actually does have its roots in the Caribbean thing. I think that may be true, although we'll never know. And it's just so graceful, the way he plays.[32]

While I never got Danny's reaction to these specific comments, he did report to me receiving feedback similar to this at a festival in Rhode Island where he played and also participated in a panel discussion and musical demonstration with Cajun musicians. He mightily resisted any suggestion that when he played Cajun music, he "Creolized" it. He saw himself playing Cajun music the way it should be played; he was not trying to distort or subvert it. I think he also suspected that people were trying to bring race back into the discussion, even if benignly, by way of the cliché that black people have rhythm and that if he was playing Cajun music, it must therefore be more syncopated than when Cajuns played it (regardless of how he actually played). This is not to say, of course, that Danny's self-assessment is perfectly accurate and that there is not a grain of truth in the Thompsons' observations.

Recalling a time when Danny was in the hospital and his father John came out to visit and played a whole dance as Danny's substitute, Will Spires offers a perspective on what the father passed on to the son, musically:

> John was one of these old-time players that just stood up straight and held the accordion straight and didn't waste any motion at all. He didn't show you, he didn't try

and dance while he was singing or put anything into it. It was all about the music for him, and he did a wonderful job. Danny used to say, "Cajun music is relaxed music. It's got power, but it's relaxed music." And John exemplified that, he just had this wonderful relaxed style of playing that was still the most beautiful dance music you could ever want.[33]

In addition to the approach to rhythm that Will mentions, I would add that Danny took after his father in his no-frills manner of presentation. He was also taking after one of his main musical influences, Aldus Roger, in this regard. He would look up, establish eye contact with dancers and smile, but beyond that "it was all about the music." Despite his reserved manner on stage, Danny managed to affect a large number of musicians and dancers with his music.

Looking at a typical month in the northern California Cajun/zydeco dance calendar while Danny was active, one sees over forty events with live music supplied by some twenty different bands. Over half the events were played either by Danny himself or by musicians who credited Danny with teaching them. In some cases students took what they learned and found their own bandmates from elsewhere, and in other cases entire bands formed after studying with Poullard around the same time, such as Frog Legs (Maureen Karpan, Marty Jara, the late Ed Luckenbach) and Sauce Piquante (Blair Kilpatrick, Steve Tabak, and Robert Richard). Tabak and Kilpatrick (husband and wife) first met Danny at a summer camp (Augusta Heritage Center in West Virginia) while living in Chicago, then later moved to the Bay Area. They started hosting jam sessions at their home in Berkeley most weeks after Poullard passed away.

What did students get out of the lessons and workshops in Poullard's garage? Those who learn well by imitating and those with prior musical experience clearly learned the most and the most quickly; those without previous musical background or who require a lot of verbal explanation and analysis did not fare so well, although some of them did persevere. Those who came regularly received encouragement and subtle pressure to practice, massive exposure to the repertoire in ever-changing form, visual reinforcement of what they were hearing, tips on fingering and posture, opportunities to play multiple instruments, the calling out of serious mistakes, and social interaction with other musicians with whom one might later form a band. Many musicians with whom I spoke specifically mentioned the desire to absorb Danny's sophisticated sense of timing, both in terms of the syncopations he incorporated in his accordion style and also the sense of the dance groove that he injected into everything he played. The transmission of such intangibles is aided tremendously by repeated, face-to-face exposure. Accordion students in particular also received as much repertoire as they could handle in the form of audio and videotapes.

I believe there is a link between the proliferation of Cajun and zydeco dance music in northern California and Poullard's impulse to "give it away." His generosity extended not only to free lessons and workshops but, as many have pointed out, a reduction in employment opportunities for himself as a musician as more and more of his protégés formed their own bands and commanded lower fees for the same gigs. In an interview, he countered this interpretation. He saw himself as setting a different precedent from older musicians in Louisiana, who he said tend not to teach younger musicians because they feel threatened and don't want to lose what playing opportunities they have. When I asked him if he was still getting enough work, he said yes, that in years prior he couldn't take all the work that was being offered him, anyway.[34]

So what did Danny himself get out of all of this? Certainly there was the teacher's pride in seeing one's students do well, and the ability to claim credit and gain reputation for what his students accomplished. An additional return was through generalized reciprocity, a style of interaction that is the antithesis of the fee-for-service model. He often went to see his students perform, for example, and many times was invited to come and sit in with the band. This was not only a gesture of respect, but it also served to broaden his exposure to the public. He also enjoyed playing rhythm guitar and got hired by bands occasionally to fill in. When he needed someone to fill in one of his bands, he had plenty of people to call. The network of musicians he helped create provided support at times such as the loss of his father and the premature deaths of two of his most devoted students. The example of sharing that he set has in turn been emulated by some of those who worked with him, thereby establishing a positive feedback loop in which cultural transmission (of musical as well as other values) is fostered. The kind of social and musical interaction established within Poullard's garage thereby extended far beyond its walls.

Andrew Carrière was one of those who benefited from Poullard's generosity, and Andrew in return lent his strong singing voice from time to time. Bill Wilson, the bassist in the group at the time, told me:

> The best tunes on that album are the ones that he sings. Because then you've got everyone doing what they do best: Andrew singing, Danny playing the accordion, Charlie [St. Mary] playing the rubboard, me playing the bass, Sam [Siggins] playing the drums, Eric [Thompson] playing the guitar, Suzy [Thompson] playing the fiddle, and Kevin Wimmer playing the fiddle. That's a strong outfit right there. And those

three tunes that Andrew does—"Criminal Waltz," "Midland Two-Step," and "L'Anse a Paille"—those three tunes are just so cool.[35]

It is interesting to note that Danny and Andrew, in contrast to Queen Ida, Aldus Roger, and others, did not manage as youths to practice the accordion surreptitiously when others were not around. The story of the accordion in the house that the children are forbidden to touch is common enough among Cajun and Creole accordionists, many of whom would teach themselves to play on the sly and inevitably get caught by the authority figure. Consequences for getting caught varied. When Bois Sec Ardoin and Canray Fontenot were caught (by older brother and father, respectively), the confronter soon admitted that the child played better than he did and subsequently permitted use of the instrument. Nathan Abshire endured repeated whippings from his uncle for unauthorized use of the accordion until he was allowed to play the instrument. For whatever reason, as badly as they said they wanted to learn the accordion Danny and Andrew chose not to go behind the adults' backs and play it anyway when they were boys. In Danny's case, this may have been due to the strength of his father's conviction, born of a personal violent experience, that his children should not play music.[36]

Olivia Guillory credited David Pitre (also known as Davis Pitre, or "Big" Pete, or David Petri) as the first person to book zydeco dances at St. Mark's in Richmond. He also played some piano accordion (see photo). Some remember Arthur Arceneaux, who shuttled between Louisiana and California and was sometimes involved with Clifton Chenier's visits to the area. Then there was George Broussard, a frequent promoter of events in San Francisco and elsewhere (see ch. 4), as well as Houston and Lena Pitre and Olivia herself. Obviously, the Creole community was not without its own resources when it came to organizing events. This should not be forgotten even as we go on to consider the contributions of outsiders such as Chris Strachwitz, Les Blank, and others in later chapters to the further development of the scene.[37]

In reviewing Creole contributions to the local scene, a word should be said about the dancers, who are in danger of being overlooked in our attention to the music and musicians. Dancers are important to the scene not only as patrons of the musicians but as culture carriers themselves, who bring knowledge of dance steps and etiquette as well as advanced appreciation of the music to each event they attend. A newcomer to a church dance in the Bay Area is struck by the loose coordination on the dance floor as partners enjoy each other's company while avoiding collisions with other couples on the floor, the counterclockwise circulation of couples around the perimeter of the floor (especially on waltzes), and the spontaneous partitioning of the floor into couples and individual line dancers on some of

Junior Felton, Danny Poullard, Davis Pitre, and George Broussard performing at St. Benedict's church in Oakland, California, circa 1979–81. Photo by Gary Canaparo.

the slower duple-meter ("shuffle") songs. The presence and liveliness of the dancers encourages the musicians to greater efforts, as do verbal exchanges between bandstand and dance floor. Danny Poullard vastly preferred playing for a roomful of dancers over any other performance situation; he would sometimes refer to sit-down concerts as "playing for the funeral parlor." The basic dance steps for the waltz and two-step are simple and invite participation in the social dance, and also provide ample latitude for those who want to express themselves more creatively. Dancers like Ullus Gobart and Charlie St. Mary, who are mentioned several times in these chapters, developed their own style and were by all accounts fun to watch. Yet I have not heard anyone talk about influential dancers in Louisiana French music the way that they speak about influential musicians, with the possible exception of certain dance teachers. Perhaps this is a combination of the ethos of dancing, which values participation over virtuosity; the limited visibility that dancers have on the floor most of the time; and the extreme rarity of the opportunity to see this kind of dancing on stage. Much of a dancer's skill often cannot be seen except by the most keen observer, and can only be felt by the dancer's partner with whom he or she is in physical contact. For me as an outsider with a musician's understanding of the music through listening, to dance with Betty Leblanc was a revelation in

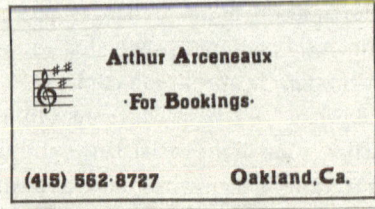

Business cards for musicians (John Semien, Louisiana Playboys) and promoters (Davis Pitre, Arthur Arceneaux). Courtesy of Gary Canaparo.

the rhythmic contours and feeling of the music, and likewise with Olivia Guillory and too many other dancers to name. Subtle points of style, like how to shift one's weight in time to the music while barely moving one's feet at all and how to subdivide musical time with the core of one's body (regardless of what the more visible extremities are doing), are difficult to explain verbally or to observe from a distance. The only way to learn these things is to dance with someone who has them until the fine points are absorbed. Once I internalized these "lessons" and danced with less experienced partners who had not, I realized the nature and extent of the generosity of those who had danced with me when I did not really know what I was doing. Multiply this type of experience by the number of newcomers to the scene who trickle into Eagles' Hall in Alameda and Ashkenaz every month, and one begins to appreciate the role of the relatively anonymous but vitally important experienced dancers and to understand the dance floor as parallel learning network for the transmission of culture.

The Local Influence of Chris Strachwitz and Les Blank

The careers of record producer Chris Strachwitz and filmmaker Les Blank are closely intertwined with the development of the Cajun music and zydeco scene in northern California. They produced several influential recordings and films that contributed to the heightened global interest in Cajun and Creole culture starting in the 1960s—pop culture commodities that would have reached northern California in any event, but they happened to live there and were among the earliest outsiders to exhibit an interest in the Creole presence in California. Their presence in the Bay Area had at least three kinds of beneficial effects on the local scene. First, they would occasionally bring the Louisiana musicians they worked with out to California. Second, they would throw parties where Louisiana French culture was featured in some way, or where they would hire local musicians to play. Third, they would use local musicians in their recordings and films, thus giving them greater exposure. For Creole musicians to connect with these men is a classic example of bridging social capital as a means of bringing in resources from other social networks.

In the same year that Queen Ida and her family arrived in San Francisco to stay (1947), teenager Chris Strachwitz immigrated with his family from lower Silesia (part of Germany through World War II, now in Poland) to the United States and landed in Reno, Nevada. His appetite for American popular music already whetted from listening to Armed Forces Radio in Germany and records that his mother had brought back from a previous trip to the States, Strachwitz soon began collecting 78 rpm recordings and expanding his listening horizons thanks to the diversity of radio broadcasts available around Santa Barbara, California, where he attended private school. While there he saw a film that showed New Orleans jazz musicians in performance, which developed his interest in African American music even further. In high school he already was thinking about making his own records, and when he came to northern California in the early 1950s to attend Berkeley he became acquainted with Oakland blues record producer Bob Geddins.[38]

Geddins, an African American man who grew up near Waco, Texas, had migrated to southern California in 1933 and opened a record shop there a few years later as a side business. His mother later moved to Oakland, and when he went to visit her in 1943 and saw the concentration of southern blacks living in West Oakland, he perceived a business opportunity that compelled him to move his family to northern California. In an interview, Geddins related to journalist Lee Hildebrand:

> I never seen so many people in all my life. The streets was so crowded you couldn't hardly walk down the street unless you bumped into somebody. There were people from everywhere—Louisiana, Alabama, Georgia, Mississippi, Texas, Oklahoma, Tennessee!
>
> I said to myself, "This could be a record heaven," because there was no blues records to be heard here in the Bay Area. You could hear some blues in Los Angeles, but here there was nothing. There were thousands and thousands of people working in the shipyards, and they were still calling for more.[39]

Geddins went on to produce and write songs for hundreds of records, a few of which became national hits for artists such as Lowell Fulson, Jimmy McCracklin, and Sugar Pie DeSanto. Fulson came from living in Oklahoma and Texas to work in the Bay Area's naval shipyards in 1943, and Geddins helped him make his first recording in 1946. Fulson would go on to record hits with Geddins and other producers, and toured briefly with Clifton Chenier in the 1950s. Geddins was in the middle of this productive career when Chris Strachwitz began visiting him and experiencing firsthand the richness of black culture from the American South, which had transplanted itself so dramatically to the Bay Area in such a short period of time. Strachwitz has claimed that Geddins, "more than anyone else, showed me how to make recordings," and that association was the first among many that Strachwitz would form with people who had the willingness and the ability to help him achieve his goal of becoming a record producer.[40]

Strachwitz finished his studies at Berkeley in the late 1950s and went to work as a schoolteacher in nearby Los Gatos while operating a side business buying and selling 78 rpm records. At Berkeley he had met blues writer Sam Charters, who played in a New Orleans jazz group that performed locally. Following a tip from Charters, who knew that Strachwitz wanted to meet blues musician Lightnin' Hopkins, he made a short trip to Texas in 1959 where he met in Houston with folklorist Robert Burton "Mack" McCormick (who was later credited with inventing the English spelling of the word *zydeco*). McCormick was able to make Strachwitz's introduction to Hopkins and other musicians. In 1960 Strachwitz made field recordings on his first long trip to the South, for the first time saw Cajun music performed live (by Aldus Roger), and issued his first release on the Arhoolie label, an album from African American guitarist and singer Mance

Lipscomb with notes by Mack McCormick. Other releases from rural blues musicians, mostly playing acoustic instruments and recorded with a single microphone, followed soon thereafter. From the beginning, Strachwitz exhibited a somewhat curatorial bent, selecting music to record that interested him the most rather than that which he thought would make him the most money.[41]

> My main aim was to document the best authentic down home blues singers and try to sell the albums to a new, mainly young white "folk music" audience which was increasing here in the USA, as well as in Europe, Australia, and Japan. I also tried to reach our black audiences with this magnificent historic music by releasing 45 rpm singles and searching for distributors to reach that market. However many seemed dubious as to the merits of this "low class" genre, considered by many at that time as backwards or even "Uncle Tom."[42]

Before he lost his teaching job in 1962 and moved to Berkeley to try his hand at the music business full-time, a young Eric Thompson, who had already started collecting 78 rpm records himself, visited the budding record producer at his home. "I collected a little bit then. Strachwitz lived in Los Gatos at that point, and he taught German, and he had started Arhoolie, he had like four records. He had the Mance [Lipscomb] album and a few more. He lived in a house that was about the size of this room, and all there was was seventy-eights, and a little place to eat and a bed. I mean, it just was aisles of seventy-eights."[43]

It was not long before Arhoolie's offerings diversified from the blues genre to other "vernacular musics," a term later suggested to Strachwitz by folklorist Archie Green for characterizing his eclectic interests in music. By 1961 he was making field recordings of Creole musicians in Houston and Lake Charles, and in 1963 he recorded and released an album of Cajun music by the Hackberry Ramblers, making use of Eddie Shuler's Goldband recording studio in Louisiana. In 1964 he first heard and met Clifton Chenier through Lightnin' Hopkins, who was related to Chenier by marriage. Chenier had already had an active career as an R&B artist in the 1950s, touring the South with a full band, but when Strachwitz saw him in a small Houston club, he was singing his blues all in French and playing his accordion with only a drummer backing him up. They found a recording studio in Houston and recorded a few songs that year; in 1965 Chenier recorded a whole album of material for Strachwitz in Houston, released as *Louisiana Blues and Zydeco*. Chenier recorded several albums with Arhoolie over the ensuing decade, ending in 1975 with *Bogalusa Boogie*.[44]

As a collector of 78 rpm commercial recordings, Strachwitz amassed a personal library of thousands of performances, most notably Mexican border styles, blues, and Cajun and zydeco, and from these (and the holdings of some his fellow 78 rpm collectors) issued numerous invaluable historical recorded anthologies on the Old Timey label, which he started in 1962, as well as on Arhoolie. These low-volume, specialty issues fueled revivalist impulses in Louisiana French music as well as other genres, whenever musicians have looked for songs to add to their repertoire. Arhoolie Records would probably not have been a viable business in the long term without cross-subsidies from the publishing rights to certain songs that he had been the first to record, such as "I Feel Like I'm Fixin' to Die Rag" by Country Joe and the Fish, which later appeared in the film and soundtrack of *Woodstock*, and "Mercury Boogie" by K. C. Douglas and Bob Geddins, covered as "Mercury Blues" by country artist Alan Jackson.[45]

Although he has produced new recordings and compilations of historical recordings in several genres and focused much of his resources on Mexican and Mexican American music, Strachwitz has remained a force in both historical and contemporary recordings of Cajun and Creole music up to the present. Floyd Soileau, one of the most successful Louisiana-based record producers, has credited Strachwitz with significant achievements in "rediscovering" older Cajun and Creole musicians and recording them, such as Joe Falcon. Other older musicians with whom he worked could not be considered rediscovered; rather, Strachwitz produced their only or some of their few commercially available recordings: Wade Frugé, Austin Pitre, Cheese Read, Octa Clark, Bois Sec Ardoin and Canray Fontenot, Bébé and Eraste Carrière, and several others. He also worked with a few younger musicians besides Chenier, particularly Marc Savoy and Michael Doucet. Strachwitz collaborated with Les Blank and Maureen Gosling to produce the quintessential film documentary on Louisiana French music, *J'ai Été au Bal*, released in 1989. In 1995, the Arhoolie Foundation was founded for the purpose of "documentation, dissemination, and presentation of authentic traditional and regional vernacular musics." The foundation's first major project was to accept the donation of Strachwitz's collection of Mexican and Mexican American recordings (78 and 45 rpm singles, and 33 rpm LPs) numbering in the tens of thousands, to catalog and digitize this collection, and to make it available for use online within the library system at the University of California, Los Angeles. Among the foundation's other projects are a few relating to Cajun and Creole music, including a short documentary film on the Cajun *boucherie* (a community event centered around animal slaughter and butchering), digitization of folklorist Harry Oster's field recordings, and support for short films made by musician Wilson Savoy, son of Marc and Ann Savoy.[46]

The fact that Strachwitz has been based in Berkeley and El Cerrito, California, for his entire career has had a significant impact on the reception of Louisiana

French music in the Bay Area. In addition to the field trips he made to Louisiana and Texas during Arhoolie's early years, he was also bringing musicians out to California to play at folk and blues festivals in Berkeley and San Francisco. When Clifton Chenier would come out to California to play for church dances in Los Angeles and San Francisco, Strachwitz would help him book additional shows at folk clubs on his off nights. He advertised one of Chenier's church dances in the San Francisco *Chronicle*, after which he received a call from a church member asking that he please not advertise the dances publicly anymore, because the publicity just attracted hippies who liked to jump around rather than dance properly. He would also help with booking for Cajun musicians like Savoy and the Balfa Brothers who came out without the benefit of the church dance circuit. Local musicians could purchase and learn from the wide variety of Cajun and zydeco recordings (not just those on the Arhoolie label) made available through his retail outlet in El Cerrito, Down Home Music, opened in 1976. Strachwitz had the additional forum of radio at his disposal, through a radio program he hosted twice a month on KPFA-FM in Berkeley from 1965 to 1995. As noted above in the profile of Danny Poullard, an appearance on Strachwitz's show led to further opportunities for the Louisiana Playboys. Clips of Strachwitz's interactions with musicians on the air can be heard on some Arhoolie recordings, such as the Poullard-Doucet-Senauke recording and an interview with Clifton Chenier. Arhoolie provided other local stimuli for musical activity through events open to the public such as record release events and anniversary parties. Notable celebrations were mounted for Arhoolie's twenty-fifth (1985), thirty-fifth (1995), and fortieth (2000) anniversaries.[47]

As Strachwitz has strengthened the Bay Area's connection to Louisiana culture in the sphere of musical recording, so Berkeley-based filmmaker Les Blank has done in the field of documentary film. In addition, the two men have a long association with each other stretching back at least as far as 1970, when Blank shot *Spend It All* (the first of his many films on Cajun culture), and Strachwitz served as one of his advisors.

Les Blank grew up in Tampa, Florida, attended high school in the Northeast, studied literature and theater at Tulane University in New Orleans, and attended graduate school in film at the University of Southern California. Around the time that he left film school, he made a short film on jazz musician Dizzy Gillespie (1964), then spent a few years freelancing in Los Angeles, during which time he also made a documentary on the 1960s counterculture of love-ins and flower children, *God Respects Us When We Work, But He Loves Us When We Dance* (1968). With *The Blues Accordin' to Lightnin' Hopkins* (1969), a thirty-one-minute film featuring the Texas guitarist, he found his directorial voice: making largely unnarrated, artistic documentaries featuring marginal individuals and minority ethnic groups. Anthropologist Margaret Hollenbach has written that, as "A white Anglo-Saxon Protestant, Blank finds the ethnicity of other peoples more satisfying than the ethnicity he got."[48]

Blank himself elaborated in a 1986 television interview:

> Ever since I was a little kid growing up in Tampa, Florida, where we had Cubans and black people in large numbers, and their ethnicity was clearly defined, I was taught at a very early age about racism. But the more I was told these people were beneath me and that I should stay away from them, or that they were dirty or ignorant or trashy, the more curious I became. The part of town where I lived in was right near their part of town, so I spent a lot of time doing my own research and finding out that these people, very often, had better attributes than my own family. They were warmer, they were more kind and caring among their own family members. Their music was certainly good. At my household, we had no music. Their food was always strange and interesting. And I just kept this interest as I got older and older, and then when the time came to make films, I couldn't do fiction films like I had originally planned, without a great deal of fortune and effort. I started doing documentaries on something that I had some concern for, which was the ethnic minority groups, and their music and culture. And also these were films I could make a small living [on] by selling them to libraries and schools.[49]

Well over half of more than thirty films he made between 1964 and 1995 feature music or musicians as the primary subject matter. The overlap in Blank's musical interests with Strachwitz's is remarkable, from Lightnin' Hopkins and Mance Lipscomb to Clifton Chenier, Marc and Ann Savoy, and Mexican American music. With at least three films (*Chulas Fronteras*, *Del Mero Corazon*, and *J'ai Été Au Bal*) Strachwitz assumed the role of producer or cocreator. With the help of Strachwitz, Blank has made at least six films that directly deal with Louisiana French music and culture and that show several prominent Cajun and Creole musicians in performance: *Spend It All* (1971) with the Balfa Brothers, Nathan Abshire, and Marc Savoy; *Hot Pepper* (1973) with Clifton and Cleveland Chenier; *Dry Wood* (1973) with Bois Sec Ardoin, his sons, and Canray Fontenot; *J'ai Été au Bal* (1989), a documentary based on Ann Savoy's history of Cajun music (Savoy 1984) that is longer (eighty-four minutes) and uses more voiceover narration than much of his work; *Yum! Yum! Yum!* (1990) on Cajun and Creole cooking with Queen Ida, Marc Savoy, and chef Paul Prudhomme; and *Marc and Ann* (1991) with Marc and Ann Savoy. Drawing from his own experiences as a Mardi Gras reveler as a college student at Tulane, he also made *Always for Pleasure* (1978), a portrayal of street celebrations in New Orleans. Blank's films got to be well known locally by the mid-1970s via screenings at the Telegraph Repertory Cinema in Berkeley.[50]

It is evident from the résumés of Strachwitz and Blank that these are two highly accomplished individuals who have received commensurate recognition for their work. In 2000 Strachwitz received a National Heritage Award from the National Endowment for the Arts, the first time this prestigious award from the U.S. government had been given to someone other than a creative artist. Blank received a lifetime achievement award in independent filmmaking from the American Film Institute and has had two of his films (*Chulas Fronteras* and *Garlic Is As Good As Ten Mothers*) named to the Library of Congress National Film Registry. Neither seems to have been hampered by a tendency toward unreconstructed romanticism in his work; each has continued to celebrate the ethnic heritages of others as a critique of modern life, steadfastly ignoring postmodern trends in popular culture and academia.

While he has grappled with the term *folk*, Strachwitz apparently has no need to deconstruct a concept like *authentic* and applies it frequently; he knows it when he sees it. In describing his initial impulse to record Lightnin' Hopkins live, playing electric guitar with a drummer in a Texas juke joint (not unlike his first encounter with Clifton Chenier five years later, in Houston), Elijah Wald comments that Strachwitz's aesthetic was distinctive.

> [T]hat feeling, that the way to record roots artists was on their home turf, doing their regular thing, would drive much of Arhoolie's future. It was a point of view that was quite unusual among the jazz and blues record collectors with whom Chris had spent much of his time. When Charters or McCormick had recorded Hopkins, they gave him an acoustic guitar and tried to capture the oldest, most traditional parts of his repertoire. This was standard folkloric procedure, to mine living artists for buried veins of old folk traditions, but it could not have been further from Chris's attitude. He did not care whether Lightnin' was a living link to Blind Lemon Jefferson (whose songs he had never heard at that time); he just knew that this was the hottest, most viscerally thrilling art he had ever encountered, and he wanted to capture that magic on disc so that other people would realize how great it was.[51]

Nevertheless, there has evidently been some congruence among his notion of the authentic, that of the folk revival audience of the 1960s that he succeeded in reaching, and that of the panel that awarded him the National Heritage Fellowship. The criteria for the latter continue to be "authenticity, excellence, and significance within the particular artistic tradition." Emblematic of his mission is his description of trying to reach the black record market by seeking distribution channels to an audience that he knew to consider the music obsolete. Whether it has been with the blues, with Cajun music, or with Mexican American music, Strachwitz seems to set himself the task of preserving styles of music from people who would rather forget about them in their quest for upward mobility. In Blank's *Spend It All*, Dewey Balfa expresses similar regret about how the old Cajun way of neighbors helping each other is being lost as individuals strive to make their own way in cash-based economies: "And as the years went, started getting more modern, and bettering yourself in life, and you do that by the mighty green dollar, and you got to run at it to get it." Shot through the work of Strachwitz and Blank are the ideals of salvage folklore (documenting a culture before it disappears) and ideas about how the quality of life is now inferior to what it once was, "declensionist narratives" about the loss of community. These conceptual foundations for authenticity and the study of folklore, regardless of the critiques leveled at them by German *Volkskunde* scholars in the 1960s and American scholars a little later, clearly lie close to the heart of the life's work of these two men.[52]

Cajun and Creole cultures conveniently provided rich subject matter for Blank, with his fondness for "warmer," more expressive culture and his preoccupations with music and food. His affinity for the "bons temps" aesthetic is already clear in the choice of title for his first portrayal of Cajun culture, *Spend It All*, taken from this exchange between the off-camera interviewer and a Cajun man about the horse-racing "business":

> Interviewer: Oh, so you just do it for the fun of it, uh?
> Cajun man: For the fun of it, mostly.
> Interviewer: That's like Cajun life in general, isn't it?
> Cajun man: Well, most of it. Work like hell to make some money, then spend it all having a good time. [laughter from friends nearby] That's Cajun, boy.

At other times, his films indulge in a fascination with exotic strangeness, as when another Cajun man in the same film pulls his own tooth at a picnic without anesthetic in a macho display of pain tolerance.

A recurring theme in Blank's work is the notion that modern American society has lost track of what is truly valuable, that other cultures (or Euro-American culture in past times) have successfully preserved these values, and that he and his compatriots would do well to emulate them. In his tribute *Gap-Toothed Women*, a young Indian woman says, "I asked my mom, and she said that half of Indian women have gapped teeth. *Why are they doing the film?*" (Emphasized text is also displayed on screen.) Lloyd John Harris, a self-styled garlic fanatic who plays a pivotal role in *Garlic Is As Good As Ten Mothers*, begins by saying,

> In Europe, they laugh at Americans who are into garlic because they've been into garlic for thousands of years. You know, it's the American Puritan Anglo thing that

has held garlic addiction down until very recently. And now all of the old structures that have held America together are falling apart politically, religious-wise, in every category, everything is falling apart, and people are looking to the old ways, the traditional folk, basic historical roots of what it is to be a human being, and garlic figures very substantially in that. Garlic is one of *the* foods, *the* nourishments, *the* medicines, that has been at the very foundations of civilization.

Blank's films avoid preachiness through subtlety and humor; for this speech Harris is shown wearing a preposterously large chef's hat in the shape of a head of garlic.

About Blank's *Garlic*, one critic gushes that "in time, personal funding, sweat, and psychic involvement, it is his *Apocalypse Now*.... The film is many films in one. It is the *Citizen Kane* of food films, substituting 'clove' for 'rosebud'..." Superlatives aside, Blank's *Garlic* is still certainly about more than food or a healthy diet. Garlic becomes a symbol of an agrarian utopia, the wisdom of the folk, of people like the black and Cuban families on the other side of the proverbial tracks in the Tampa of Blank's youth whose music was "good," whose food was "always strange and interesting," and whose families were "warmer, more kind and caring." In the world of this film, there are two kinds of people: those who eat garlic (and consequently are healthier, happier, and know how to have a good time) and those who do not (the uptight, the WASPish, those who have forgotten the important things in life in an effort to get ahead in modern industrial society). Over a scene of pigs being fed garlic, a disembodied woman's voice says, "I think if we plumb deeply here, we would discover the garlic secrets, as to why it appeals to people who are really passionate about life, and not imprinted with too much civilized behavior." Immediately thereafter, Alice Waters discusses garlic's "very special, enticing properties" in a flirtatious tone as the camera zooms on a poster for her garlic festival at Chez Panisse, adorned with the figure of a nude woman reclining in the out of doors holding a set of panpipes, an icon for pastoral bliss. As the camera lingers on this image, the Cajun music starts and the film is on to footage of the festival inside the restaurant. On the side of garlic we find Waters (chef of her Provençal restaurant), Cajuns, Andalucian gypsies, belly dancers, Mexicans and Mexican Americans, an Italian American farmer cooking squid at the Gilroy garlic festival (plugging garlic as "the Italian marijuana"), a Chinese American chef in San Francisco, an African American barbeque proprietor in Oakland, and a gentleman organic farmer in Marin County "with Ph.D. in Shakespeare." In the anti-garlic camp we find a hapless Irish American woman whose mother would not let her cook with garlic for four days prior to having guests over for fear of making them sick from the smell in the kitchen, the faceless "American Puritan Anglos" invoked by Harris, vampires, and . . . Chris Strachwitz! He is shown, unidentified, in a brief sequence in which he converses with a man at a party who, judging from what he says, is probably a musician. Strachwitz, or the character he plays, comes across as a reluctant convert to garlic at best.[53]

> Musician: How about the cloves of garlic in the sausage you ate last night? When we came over here last night, we ate the sausage . . .
> Strachwitz: Well I'm used to old Pollock sausage.
> Musician: And it's got lots of garlic in it, right?
> Strachwitz: Yeah . . .
> Musician: Well I mean then, what are you talking about, you don't like garlic?
> Strachwitz: Well, I like it if I don't know it's in there!
> Musician: And the food would not have tasted the same without that garlic.
> Strachwitz: I know it wouldn't have smelled the same!
> Musician: No, man, garlic provides the bass note. Garlic provides the bass note. It's like, in a chord, you've got to have that good, solid bottom? Garlic provides that bottom.

Blank places Strachwitz (and, presumably, himself) among the urbanites who "'discovered' and craved the rural folk's peace of soul" just as students of folklore in Germany had done a century before, forever admiring the folk and forever apart from them.[54]

CHAPTER SIX

Folk Revival Connection

The Musicians

While the American folk music revival of the 1950s and 1960s has not by any means been the only source of outsider interest in Louisiana French music and culture, it has certainly been an important one. Well before the 1980s Cajun craze, folk revivalist interest in Cajun music in the United States and France helped to energize musicians in Louisiana such as the Balfas, Marc and Ann Savoy, and Michael Doucet, as mentioned in the last chapter. In this chapter we will see how some revivalists from a hotbed of old-time country music and bluegrass activity in northern California found their way to Louisiana French music.

Revivalist musicians and dancers are distinct groups that have quite different histories of involvement in Cajun and Creole music. Revivalist musicians in the Bay Area first started playing Cajun music in the 1960s in contexts that were typical for "folk music" at that time: jam sessions, coffeehouses, and festivals where most of the patrons were seated and if there was dancing it was mostly of an individual, free-form variety rather than partner dancing. Meanwhile, revivalist dancers in the 1960s and '70s continued in the vein (begun decades earlier) of international folk dancing to recorded music in a variety of European peasant styles, and in the Bay Area they did not pay attention to Cajun music or zydeco until Ashkenaz started to feature the Louisiana Playboys and Queen Ida occasionally in the late 1970s. In her history of the Balkan music and dance scene in America, Mirjana Laušević traced its development through the international folk dancing movement to a more recently freestanding scene where live music has been added. In the Cajun scene, by contrast, it was the revivalist musicians (especially fiddlers) who were attracted first and the dancers later. The musicians began with interests in music of the American South, especially old-time music and the blues, to which Louisiana French music is closely related and which was sometimes included in print and recorded folk anthologies of the period; folk dancers, on the other hand, were more focused on dances of European origin, and with these and American genres that *were* done by dancers at that time (squares, contras, clogging) we can only surmise that Louisiana French dancing fell outside the folk paradigm because it usually involves dancing an entire number with a single partner. Because the revivalist musicians and dancers followed identifiably separate paths, a chapter is devoted to each; the musicians will be treated in this chapter and the dancers in the next.[1]

Louisiana French Music within a National Folk Revival

In the larger scheme of things, Louisiana French music occupied an inconspicuous corner of the postwar folk music revival. An early example was Harry Smith's *Anthology of American Folk Music* for Folkways in 1952, in which Cajun music made an appearance (five out of eighty-four selections). Cantwell opines that, coming as it did during the period when McCarthyism had put leftist folk revivalists such as the Weavers into retreat, the anthology provided for "the politically more innocent folk revival of the next decade a cultural text that would become its enabling document, its musical constitution." He makes a forceful case for the canon-making impact that the three-album release had in the beginning of the era of long-playing recordings:

> The Folkways Anthology in effect legitimized its material, investing it with the cultural authority both of its advanced technology and its rarefied sociopolitical connections. What had been, to the people who originally recorded it, essentially the music of the poor, the isolated, and the uneducated, the Anthology reframed as a kind of avant-garde art . . . a kind of mystical ethnography, converting a commercial music fashioned in the twenties out of various cultural emplacements and historical displacements into the "folk" music of the revival.

This influential electroacoustic text was based not on earlier field recordings but on the commercial releases of "ethnic and regional record markets" of the 1920s and 1930s, of which Cajun and Creole musicians produced a distinguished share. More important for Louisiana French music than the actual recordings chosen for the anthology was the general flurry of collecting, recording, and performing activity that the anthology inspired. Folklorist Harry Oster made many field recordings in the late 1950s around Mamou and from them released *Folksongs of the Louisiana Acadians* in 1959. Folk music enthusiasts, Strachwitz among them, collected early commercial recordings, reissued them in further anthologies, sought out the musicians, by then advanced in age, who had played on the recordings as well as younger musicians from the same communities, and put on concerts featuring both themselves and the musicians that they had "rediscovered," in musical styles ranging from blues to white Appalachian to Cajun.[2]

Interactions between the new ethnicity movement and the folk revival in popular culture were crucial to the fortunes of Cajun and Creole music. The Newport Folk Festival started in 1959 as an outgrowth of the Newport Jazz Festival. Although the relative amount of attention given to Cajun music over the years at the Newport Folk Festival was small, the impact on the reception of Cajun music both on folk revival audiences and on Cajuns themselves was large. Numerous sources have recounted the appearances on the Newport stage for the first time in 1964 by Dewey Balfa and other Cajun musicians, and Balfa's subsequent campaign for the reacceptance of Cajun music in his home state. Influential friends he met at the festival who would help him in his new mission included folklorist Ralph Rinzler and musician Tracy Schwarz of the New Lost City Ramblers. Drawing on his own experience from working at Newport, impresario George Wein went on to start the New Orleans Jazz and Heritage Festival (known simply as Jazz Fest) in 1970 and included Cajun music in the program from its inception. Jazz Fest and Festivals Acadiens have in turn provided not only popular destinations for tourists from California and elsewhere, but also models for Louisiana music events in California.[3]

The Balfa-Rinzler-Schwarz connection made at Newport led to an important precedent in folk revival performance of Cajun music. In 1966 Folkways released the New Lost City Ramblers' *Remembrance of Things to Come*, an album with one Cajun song on it, "Parlez Nous à Boire." The Balfa Brothers had themselves recorded and released this song the previous year on *The Balfa Brothers Play Traditional Cajun Music*, but the Ramblers' liner notes indicate that they had learned the song from a field recording that Ralph Rinzler had made of the Balfas, also in 1965. The Balfas' studio recording is already a "folk" departure from contemporary Cajun music of the time, with its use of twin fiddles and all-acoustic instrumentation. If anything, the New Lost City Ramblers' version is even more rustic in its spareness. Where the Balfas use a rhythm guitar, twin fiddles, a triangle, and two-part vocal harmony, the Ramblers employ just the two fiddles, triangle, and a single voice. Although it was just one song on one album, the New Lost City Ramblers' recording of "Parlez Nous à Boire" appears, judging from the musicians profiled below, to have had a disproportionate influence in introducing the folk revival audience to Cajun music and to the Balfa Brothers. Mike Seeger, who provided the French vocals and lead fiddle on the Ramblers' recording, would go on to champion Cajun music by organizing nationwide tours for Cajun musicians such as the Balfa Brothers and Dennis McGee. Tracy Schwarz, the second fiddle on this recording, later became quite active in Cajun music, appearing on later albums with Dewey Balfa, recording his own albums of Cajun music (recognized in 1997 by the Cajun French Music Association), and collaborating in the production of instructional materials for Cajun fiddle (with Dewey Balfa) and Cajun accordion (with Marc Savoy).⁴

With Dewey Balfa, Schwarz helped to establish a Cajun/Creole week at the Augusta Heritage Festival in Elkins, West Virginia, starting in 1986. His teaching strongly advocates for a cultural authenticity of sound and of practice emblematic of a folk revivalist aesthetic:

> "I've always thought that if you play Cajun music, you should want to do it justice.... No caricatures or anything of that sort. Play the music like they play it there. There's a reason why they play it that way, and [then] they just ignore the fact that you're not Cajun. It takes longer because you're not Cajun, it takes longer to get these Cajun sounds, but it's really worth it. You really get something of value. Otherwise, I think you're just a dilettante."⁵

Of course, there have been and still are not one but many folk revivalist aesthetics and divergent personal opinions about individual artists. The writer of a 1965 record review in the San Francisco *Chronicle*, who raved about a new Arhoolie recording by blues musician Mississippi Fred McDowell, had only this to say about the Hackberry Ramblers release on the same label: "This is bluegrass with a French accent, and a little of it goes an awfully long way." Berkeley Folk Festival organizer Barry Olivier notes how his own tastes and those of festivalgoers changed over time:

> The [Berkeley] Festivals began as an expression of our feelings about folk music. We loved the best of the music and wanted to define what was folk music and, by exclusion, what was not. We were concerned about a *product* of the folk music process: the finished, traditional, pure, real, good, old folk songs. With popularizers all about—the Kingston Trio and its school—we had almost a religious fervor in laying out what we considered to be real folk music, so it would be fully appreciated and so that people wouldn't waste their time and energy with the watered-down, "impure" stuff.
>
> As the years passed, more and more of the *process* of folk music became important to us—particularly due to the topical and fine contemporary songs generated in the sixties as an expression of social protest and comment. The experimental, ever-

changing nature of this process was producing some beautiful results which couldn't be denied. Then Pete Seeger in 1963 brought many beautiful contemporary songs to us from his own pen, and from Bob Dylan, Tom Paxton, and others. That was an important turning point in our consciousness and I could feel a change in people's feelings after that Festival.[6]

In his comments Olivier identifies three sorts of affinity for "folk music" in the early 1960s: a textual orientation toward the purest "old" songs that traces back to nineteenth century folklore scholarship on English balladry by James Lowell and Francis Child; an ahistorical attraction to the polished commercial recordings of folk song arrangements such as the Kingston Trio's "Tom Dooley"; and an appreciation for contemporary songwriting where there is no pretending that a song was composed by an anonymous folk. These correspond to Ellen Stekert's categories of imitators, utilizers, and "new aesthetic," respectively, in her analysis of aesthetic controversies in the urban folksong movement. In tracing the evolution of his attention from product to process, Olivier also points to the location of authenticity in performance rather than in the text, an intellectual trend within revivalist circles that would be taken up by academic folklorists in the 1970s. The increased value placed on process and performance opened up an aesthetic space in which Cajun and Creole music could be appreciated by outsiders without first having to be "cleaned up" or reinterpreted. This is the space where Chris Strachwitz has operated since his early fascination in the 1950s with, as he puts it, "records of unadulterated, authentic, low-down country blues" and other "authentic, regional or traditional musics" whose recordings were "very raw, rootsy and unpolished but full of spirits and emotions."[7]

The comments of Ken Keppeler, a fiddler and accordionist who plays Cajun music and zydeco and who grew up in East Los Angeles, where he heard a lot of Mexican and country music, articulate the preference for the unpolished a little further:

> I started going out to see musicians, bluegrass at the Ash Grove in L.A. They booked Bukka White, the first time Doc Watson was on tour he went there. It was a big influence on me seeing traditional musicians. I was never into the likes of Joan Baez and all that stuff, because I heard all these other people and there's a certain rawness and honesty that touched something in my own experience, because I was so close to other traditions, living where I did. There's something that you can hear. This is not just somebody looking at a book and playing. There's a feeling about traditional musicians, that comes from human beings' experience. I was very attracted to that.

Our family was sort of lower, lower middle-class. My father had quite a class-consciousness. He identified very closely with the people where we lived and from that I've always thought of music as the expression of the people as part of a community.[8]

The musical and social values of the American folk revival of the 1960s survive at the time of this writing to greater and lesser degrees in other forms and under other names such as world music, roots, Americana, and so on. These values have been institutionalized at the national level at the Smithsonian Institution with its Folklife Festival and its purchase and operation of Folkways Records, and by the Folk and Traditional Arts program at the National Endowment for the Arts. The profile of Cajun and Creole music within the larger discussion of national heritage in the United States, while not precisely measurable, appears to have grown over the past four decades. Since 1982 the NEA's National Heritage Fellowship, one of the few direct grants available to individuals, has been awarded to eleven Cajun and Creole artists (see fig. 3), including ten musicians (and not counting Strachwitz's award in 2000 as record producer). When I nominated Danny Poullard for the award in 1997 and approached those well placed to write letters of recommendation, one person actually refused on the grounds that enough Cajuns and Creoles had won the award already. I did not agree with this reasoning and nominated him anyway. In accordance with the agency's policy, the nomination lapsed when Poullard passed away.

Figure 3. Cajun and Creole National Heritage Fellowship Winners, 1982–2006 (www.nea.gov/honors/heritage/allheritage.html, 14 January 2007. New Orleans awardees not shown.)

Awardee	Year Awarded	Description
Dewey Balfa	1982	Cajun fiddler
Clifton Chenier	1984	Creole Accordionist
Alfonse "Bois Sec" Ardoin	1986	African American Creole Accordionist
Canray Fontenot	1986	African American Creole Fiddler
Marc Savoy	1992	Cajun Accordion Maker/Musician
Inez Catalon	1993	French Creole Singer
D. L. Menard	1994	Cajun Musician/Songwriter
Gladys Clark	1997	Cajun Spinner & Weaver
Wilson "Boozoo" Chavis	2001	Creole Zydeco Accordionist
Luderin Darbone/Edwin Duhon	2002	Cajun fiddler and accordionist
Michael Doucet	2005	Cajun fiddler, composer, and band leader

The four individuals profiled in this chapter were initially part of the network of folk revival musicians in northern California, to which Strachwitz and Blank were also connected. They first learned of Louisiana French music via folk revival sources—Will Spires at the Berkeley Folk Festival; Eric Thompson from recordings that Strachwitz shared with him; Suzy Rothfield Thompson from the New Lost City Ramblers; Delilah Lee Lewis from Suzy—and therefore the folk revival became their initial frame of reference for Cajun and Creole music and the conduit through which they were able to make contact with musicians from Louisiana.

It should be noted that Will, Eric, Suzy, and Delilah went to Louisiana to learn directly from musicians prior to the significant enhancement of tourism amenities in southern Louisiana outside of New Orleans that started in the 1980s. Of that time Barry Jean Ancelet wrote, "Visiting south Louisiana has traditionally been a bit like a safari. There have not been many orientation points for visitors, so they have to make their own way most of the time. Consequently they often leave the area feeling frustrated and disappointed because they didn't see what they wanted to see or hear what they wanted to hear." Suzy Thompson corroborates this from the visitor's perspective:

> When we first started going down there in the late seventies, there really were very, very few young people who were interested [in Cajun music]. Michael and David Doucet, Beausoleil had already started, so maybe ten young people, probably fewer, were interested in it. And there were not a lot of people coming from out of town to come look for it either. And most of the middle-aged people we talked to about it, I think they thought "Why do you want to go listen to that chanky-chank music for?" It was kind of low-class. But at that time, as the oil industry was really booming there, people were seeing that as their economic salvation. And then in subsequent years, the bottom fell out of the oil thing, and they started figuring out about their nice renewable resource of tourism and their culture....
>
> When we first started going there, there was only two ways you could hear music, and they pretty much involved having somebody take you somewhere. I mean, you couldn't really do it on your own. You could have someone take you to visit someone at their home, which we did a lot. Or you could go to the clubs. Some of the clubs you *might* be able to find, like you could find Fred's Lounge [in Mamou], you could find the Blue Goose in Eunice. But some of the places like Snook's, which was near Mamou, if you didn't have really good directions, or preferably somebody driving with you, you would *never* find them. And the dances only happened on Saturday nights, there just wasn't a lot of events. And now with these restaurants where you can even go with your children, you can go dancing every night of the week.[9]

Will Spires[10]

Will Spires was born in 1943 in La Jolla, California, into an artistic family and was raised in the Los Angeles area. His father pursued acting, appearing on local stages in an amateur or semiprofessional capacity. Will's mother was trained as a classical pianist, did some music teaching, and became "deeply involved with folk music back in the postwar folksong revival," according to Will. "I grew up with lots of folk music records in the house and had folk music played and sung at me probably from shortly after conception. They didn't do anything like Cajun music then, around me. But there was a sense of continuity with the folk music scene in Los Angeles. I started playing in 1958 or '59, I started playing instruments... guitar and mandolin." His mother showed him his first guitar chords, but he learned more guitar from a family friend from Oklahoma named John Cleator. Very near to the same time that he took up playing music, in tenth grade, he decided to drop out of high school ("it was just not for me") and starting taking classes at junior colleges such as Los Angeles City College, where he gravitated toward the subjects of anthropology, history, and literature. He never took a music class, but played with others in string bands.

Will first encountered Cajun music in his early twenties.

> At Barry Olivier's Berkeley Folk Festival, I heard for the first time the Hackberry Ramblers with Luderin Darbone. And they were out here playing Cajun music and I was very much entranced by what they were doing. Luderin Darbone especially made playing the fiddle look simple and elegant and was playing this extremely beautiful music. I was not already fiddling, so I got my fiddle that day. A friend of mine in Berkeley, Charles Perry, who's a food reviewer for the LA *Times* now, used to be part of the old time music scene in Berkeley. And he handed a $25 instrument over to me and I started at that time. So it was really Cajun music that first made me want to learn to play fiddle.[11]

At first Will was unable to find Cajun music to work on or musicians with whom to play, so he played old-time music on his new fiddle. Then in 1966, he heard the New Lost City Ramblers' recording of "Parlez Nous à Boire" and got a copy of *The Balfa Brothers Play Traditional Cajun Music*. These recordings, along with what few others and French transcriptions he could find, became Will's study guide. By the late 1960s he had learned to play and sing several Cajun songs. He also continued to play old-time music; for example, he met Eric Thompson during this time and they played together in a Berkeley-based old-time group, the New Tranquility String Band.[12]

"Eric was the first person I knew out here that had listened to Cajun music very much, although he wasn't playing it much at that time. But he had 2 or 3 LPs of Cajun music and a few 45s too. And Eric has a wonderful music education and very broad tastes. And we'd listen to it over at his place and when I was in a band with Eric, briefly in the late sixties, we worked several Cajun tunes into the band." In the early seventies, Will corresponded directly with Mike Seeger and Tracy Schwarz of the New Lost City Ramblers, who sent him recordings of Dennis McGee and transcriptions of Balfa Brothers recordings.

In 1974 Will toured the coffeehouse-and-campus circuit as accompanist for Kenny Hall, a nationally known blind mandolinist from Fresno. At the Caffè Lena coffeehouse in Saratoga Springs, New York, Will finally got to meet the Balfa Brothers.

> Will and Rodney and Dewey were all there. Will Bolfa had a Steiner model violin with a lion's head carved on the scroll, a popular old German style of ornamenting violins. I had one just like it, and we both had the same name, Will. So that was my icebreaker, that's how I started the conversation. I said my name's Will too and I have a fiddle just like that one. He said really, let me see it. So I took it out. He said, can you play it. I said yeah, a little bit, you know. So I played something for him.... I played one of their tunes, right off the record, I don't remember which one it was. I think it was "T'es petite mais t'es mignonne." But Will just started looking at me, and I was really nervous and I was playing it as well as I could and I had it tuned down low like they had their violins tuned and everything. And he was smiling, and when I finished playing he just looked over my shoulder and jerked his head and I turned around and Rodney and Dewey and Allie Young were all standing there behind me. They heard me playing, they came up to say, what the hell's all this? And they all shook my hand and we went downstairs and drank beer and played my music. So I definitely felt prepared after that evening, let's see that was 1974. So that was like ten years after I first heard Cajun music. I had prepared myself to meet those people if I ever ran into them. And I still learned more that night watching and actually doing it, than I had ever thought of picking up off records.

In 1975 Mike Seeger organized a tour of older folk musicians that included the Cajun twin fiddle duo of Dennis McGee and Sady Courville. When the tour came to Zellerbach Auditorium on the U.C. Berkeley campus, Will made sure he was in the audience. "[T]hey came here and then they went down to play at Lou Curtis's festival in San Diego. And I met them here and followed them straight down there for that. And I could *not* be pried loose from Dennis McGee. I just thought he was fabulous, and he had an entirely different style from Dewey. And he was very gregarious and very outgoing and great company."

Will followed up on these acquaintances by arranging his first trip to Louisiana in the next year, 1976. He packed his fiddle and tape recorder and took the bus to Louisiana, where Marc Savoy had graciously offered him a place to stay in Eunice as well as occasional use of a car. During this visit, he spent time with several musicians including Dewey Balfa, Marc Savoy, Dennis McGee, Wade Frugé, Bois Sec Ardoin, and Canray Fontenot. His lessons were not confined to musical ones.

> I was performing music professionally in those days, Irish music, old-time music, Cajun music. But Louisiana was the first territory I ventured onto outside of my home to learn from the old guys. And you know, you learn a lot about yourself when you do something like that.... I think one of the main things you learn doing fieldwork or traveling in musical circles, I think you learn manners as much as anything else. Many attitudes down there were repulsive to me. There was a tremendous amount of racism in that part of Louisiana, however much some people may try to whitewash it and paint southwestern Louisiana as a more tolerant situation than the rest of the South. You couldn't prove it by me. And I found it, for a person of my background, pretty hard to be around that sometimes. In a situation like that, that far away from home and in a situation of different values, there's no point in opening your mouth unless you think it might do some good. And I wouldn't say that I compromised my own attitudes down there. A lot of the people I was around certainly had attitudes very different from mine, and I think they might have modified them to some extent when people from California were there. Because they know that certain language or attitudes are not going to go over. But we did discuss things frankly, many times. I found people trying to be tolerant and I found people down there who had been raised with less tolerant attitudes, and I think, well perhaps I don't know everything. Some of my white Cajun friends wrestled with that quite a bit. Even the most tolerant person had to examine themselves as they met people from other parts of the country. Some musicians with whom I worked were openly racist. But I had to think about that too, that I can't just reject someone as a friend or a teacher or a musical influence because I don't admire everything about them or share every idea that they happen to have. Many of them helped to destroy Fascism in Europe in World War II by serving in the military. And you have to give credit where credit is due, balance these things out. I guess the trip was an eye opener for me, and with more open eyes, I saw that racism and racialism were alive and well in my own California, too.

Figure 4. Partial listing of repertoire collected from Dennis McGee by Will Spires

Contradanse Anglais	Big Joe	Valse a Theophile Young
Valse de Couteaux des Lauriers	Brayais Pour Ma Patate	Valse a Desvilliers
	Reel de la Pont du Bois	Turkeys in the Straw
Valse a Ma Carreau	Valse a Tante Helene	Wang Wang Blues
Arkansas Traveler	Reel de Berzas	Gambling Man
Marche a Napoleon Bonaparte	Pa Janvier	Casey Jones

Will first met local Bay Area Creole musicians through the Balfa Brothers. The Balfas came through Berkeley, had a group dinner at Chez Panisse restaurant, and invited some of their California friends to join them, including Will and Danny Poullard. Shortly thereafter, Danny called Will to invite him to his house in San Francisco to play music. After Ben Guillory passed away, Will would occasionally sit in with the Louisiana Playboys on fiddle. On subsequent trips to Louisiana, Will also made the acquaintance of Danny's father, John Poullard, and visited the Poullard home in Beaumont, Texas.

In 1979 Will was awarded a folk apprenticeship from the National Endowment for the Arts to study fiddling with Dennis McGee in Louisiana. His project had two emphases: to record as much of McGee's unique older repertoire as possible, and to learn how to play some of these songs himself. Will estimates that he recorded some 125 of McGee's tunes, among which Dennis employed six different violin tunings. Many of these songs Dennis had not played in years, sometimes decades. According to Will, many of them Dennis never played in public because no one else, not even his old playing partner Sady Courville, knew them well enough to play along. A partial listing of the songs that Will collected from Dennis (see fig. 4) shows the diversity of his repertoire, in terms of the French dance tunes seldom heard now (reels, contradanse, and some of the waltz titles) and the items from other sources (e.g., "Turkey in the Straw," "Arkansas Traveler," etc.).

> Dennis was a person of very strong opinions about music. He was so disgusted to what happened to Cajun music down there in the fifties, that he knocked off of it entirely. I can't remember him saying particularly what he didn't like, but he just thought it was a long way from what he had tried to keep alive. And he believed what he had, his old tunes, were special. He said to me one time, he said, "You know, I quit playing my violin for twenty years. I didn't touch my violin for twenty years, I just played a little bit of accordion. But I always kept those old tunes in my heart, because I knew some day somebody would want those old tunes...."

You know how musicians use kinesthetic memory a great deal to remember music. He'd play one tune. I'd say, where'd you learn that? He'd say, I learned that over there from so and so. And he'd just have his head cocked over to one side and he'd be twitching his fingers and moving his fingers around, trying to find the shape of some tune in his head. And he'd sit there looking at his fingers and say, "I got one comin' in, Will!" And then he'd play something that nobody had heard down there for ages, you know? Beautiful material. And he had a phenomenal memory for those distant events, but he couldn't tell you what he had for breakfast that morning. But he performed astonishing feats of memory, and he was a very patient teacher. And when I learned a tune right, he was very eager to take me around to some of his old-time friends down there and say, "Look, play that for him!" And they'd say, "pretty good." And he'd say, somebody came down here and wanted to learn to do that.

Back in California, Will remained active in Cajun music circles, playing mostly at informal settings like jam sessions at Danny Poullard's and house parties. At one point he worked up a few tunes on the accordion and played alongside guitarist Frannie Leopold and Eric and Suzy Thompson in a band that called itself Les Blues de Bayou. The band was not long-lived but did play at some outdoor arts festivals and at the Freight and Salvage Coffeehouse in Berkeley. He learned a great deal from revivalists Ken Keppeler and Jeanie McLerie and also kept in touch with

Will Spires and Dennis McGee. Photo by Delilah Lee Lewis.

his musician friends from Louisiana and assisted them however he could when they came out on tour to California. From Dewey Balfa in particular he received much support in return.

> [T]he most important people I learned from as far as fiddle was concerned, were Dewey and Dennis, and after that Wade Frugé and Canray. I think my own playing is a synthesis of what I admired in their playing. I remember Dewey telling me one time, "When I first met you, you sounded like me or Will. And then after you'd been coming down here a little bit, I could hear a lot of influence from Dennis and Wade come into your playing. And now you sound like Will Spires." You know, I really appreciated that.... And Dewey often very generously gave me a lot of face when he'd have me come up and play with him in Louisiana or here in California, saying "this is our ambassador from California. This is an adopted Cajun and anywhere you go in California, anybody who knows our music will know Will Spires." That was true fifteen years ago [circa 1982]; it's not true now. Dewey always spoke of me and Tracy [Schwarz] as adopted Cajuns. They were very concerned that we understand that they regarded our efforts highly. Because they knew that would make us feel good and they knew that would make us keep playing the music.

The mid-1980s marked another turning point for Will, when he decided that he could no longer sustain his folk musician's lifestyle. "[I] went back to college seriously here when I was forty-one. And at that point I was going for degrees and trying to leave any kind of professional music behind and make some part of my living teaching." After receiving a B.A. in anthropology and M.A. in history from Sonoma State University, he remained in Sonoma County to teach courses in folklore, anthropology, and history at Santa Rosa Junior College and did some work in field archaeology. He also has done anthropological research and fieldwork with an indigenous group in northern Mexico, the Tarahumara, who make and play their own violins. He regards his days as a gigging musician as largely behind him, but he still plays for his own enjoyment and uses music in his teaching. Playing music when he likes allows him to follow his own musical aesthetics.

> I think that the Cajun music scene here in California, for my tastes, is a long way away from the kind of music that got its hooks into me, in terms of the acoustic two-fiddle style and pre-war low-impact aerobics. I liked the old stuff better, and I don't think that's really hung on out here in that way. And what's out here now is great, but when I play with friends now, when I play with my partner Lisa Pesce who plays beautiful old-time fiddle of all kinds, [when] I play with Delilah [Lee Lewis] or when I play for the dances up at Lark in the Morning, at Sweet's Mill, [California

festivals] where I go, we like to play the older-time stuff. Tuned down, two fiddles, C accordion, and singing in back of those dense fiddle overtones that you get with two low-tuned violins and a C accordion. I mean, that's the most beautiful sound for me. That's what I like.

At this writing, Will is still teaching at Santa Rosa Junior College and playing music at summer music festivals. He also has in mind to publish something from all of the work he did with Dennis McGee many years ago. Summing it up, he says: "These experiences, unimaginable to me when I started out, were among the richest of my life. I hope always to keep what I have learned of this music alive as a token payment of gratitude to my Cajun and Creole friends."

Eric and Suzy Thompson[13]

Eric Thompson was born in 1946 in Stockton, California, and raised in Oakland and Palo Alto. His father worked as a certified public accountant and his mother as a junior high school counselor; neither were musicians and their music listening habits did not have a strong impact on Eric. Music first really got his attention while he was a high school student in Palo Alto.

[T]he first musics I got really interested in, when I was about fourteen, I was kind of aware of the Kingston Trio and then almost immediately I found more interesting folk music. A friend of mine in high school had liberal parents and had Pete Seeger records, and then we discovered the New Lost City Ramblers and bluegrass. And I got right on it and got a good guitar. That was 1962, my last year of high school. By then, they were bringing bluegrass bands out to L.A. so there was a lot of interesting stuff going on at that point.

He started by learning rhythm guitar from New Lost City Ramblers records. He collected other recordings as well, "anything I could get my hands on. Haskell McCormick, Hoyt Skoggins, Bill Monroe, Reno and Smiley, Osborne Brothers, Flatt and Scruggs. The first lead guitar player who influenced me a lot before I discovered Doc Watson, was Don Reno. Also Jesse McReynolds."[14]

Eric finished high school early, at age sixteen, and concentrated intensely on music for the next four years. After high school, "I went to Berkeley ostensibly to go to college, except all I did was go to the guitar stores. I flunked out after a year, and then I went back to Palo Alto and played music." There he played in one of his first bands, the Black Mountain Boys, with Jerry Garcia. After just four years of playing the guitar, he left for New York for a few months and there he met mandolin player David Grisman, who was then a college student at New York University. With Eric flat-picking lead on his guitar, they formed the New York Ramblers, a bluegrass band that won a "world championship cup" at the 1964 Union Grove, North Carolina, Old-Time Fiddler's Convention. When Eric returned to California at the end of that year he played some with Mother McCree's Uptown Jug Champions, which included Garcia and other future members of the Grateful Dead.[15]

In 1966 Eric went back to school at the University of California, Berkeley, where he earned a B.A. in art history "because there wasn't anything in the Music Department that pertained to what I was interested in." During his academic studies, he continued pursuing his musical ones with a wide-ranging curiosity. The discographical liner notes that the New Lost City Ramblers put out with their records fascinated him. He first learned about Cajun music in the early sixties from record collectors Chris Strachwitz and his friend Bob Pinson; Strachwitz and Pinson had collected some 78 rpm records of Cajun fiddler Harry Choates that captured Eric's attention. When he heard the Kershaw Brothers' hits "Louisiana Man" and "Diggy Liggy Lo" on the radio, he could recognize them as Cajun music.

He first started playing Cajun music with Will Spires while still at Berkeley in the late sixties. The two of them lived in a house full of musicians on Colby Street in North Oakland, played in The New Tranquility String Band, and together explored the music of Harry Choates, the Balfa Brothers, and Bois Sec Ardoin. After graduating from Berkeley, Eric married musician Sue Rosenberg and the two of them formed an Irish band with Jeremy Kammerer, Sue Draheim, and Jody Stecher. In the early 1970s, Eric and Sue moved to live on the Preston Ranch property near the town of Cloverdale, in rural northern Sonoma County, California. Two or three years later accordionist John Paul, who had also lived in the Colby Street house and played some Cajun music with Will Spires, moved into another house on the Preston Ranch property with Suzy Rothfield.[16]

Suzy describes the Preston experience:

> It was owned by this very old doctor, Dr. Lee, and it had been a spiritual community in the late 1800s, run by Madame Preston. And a lot of the old buildings were still there. Now eventually, after we were no longer living there, a fire swept through there and burned everything up. But there was an old graveyard, and there were old houses and buildings in various states of repair and disrepair. Anyway, the people who were living there, I think all of them were in some way or another involved in the

Renaissance Faires, either as musicians, as dancers, as garbage men, as caterers, craftspeople, guards.

Suzy Rothfield Thompson was born and raised in Mount Vernon, New York, in a family with one sister and two brothers. Her mother was a medical doctor and her father, who also received a medical degree, was a research scientist. With four children, the Rothfields thought of having a string quartet in the house, so Suzy and her sister Jane studied violin, John the viola, and Larry the cello. While Suzy does not remember that they played together very much as a quartet ("a little bit when I was in high school"), three of the four have continued with music as adults. "John eventually got into playing Indian music and studied for a long time with Ali Akhbar Khan and played some kind of old-time music too, and then hooked up with Andrew Carrière and played with Andrew a lot."

Although all of her early violin training was in classical music, Suzy's mother brought an interest in other styles of music to the household.

> My mother played some. She played piano a little bit, she played violin a little bit. She actually got me started playing guitar. She wasn't a professional musician or anything, but she was involved in a Bohemian scene when she was in college [Bard College] and there were people who played guitar. Plus her parents were leftists; she was a red diaper baby. So there was folk music attached with that whole scene too. My mom's family had ... poets and musicians and theater people and my father's family, I don't think there was any music in that family at all.... And then I guess when I was nine or ten I started learning to play guitar. We went someplace and there was some girl who was a few years older who I really admired who played the guitar, and so I wanted to play the guitar. So they got me a guitar and my mother taught me a few chords.

With the handful of chords that she had learned, Suzy spent hours playing along with a recorded album by Peter, Paul, and Mary until she had taught herself all but one of the songs on it. Suzy's folk music education continued perhaps three years later.

> In junior high, I went up to this place in Vermont called Trailside, which was a ski camp in the winter and in the summer it was a wilderness travel camp kind of thing that was run by a guy named Mike Cohen, who was the brother of John Cohen of the New Lost City Ramblers. And Mike also was a musician, he had played in the Shanty Boys.... They had a lot of music there, and that was the first place that I tried

playing anything other than classical music on the violin. And it was also the first place that I heard Cajun music. Because he had his brother's New Lost City Ramblers records around and they had "Parlez Nous à Boire" on there.

In the middle of her high school years, Suzy's family moved to Connecticut. She applied to Yale and was admitted, and in the spring she visited California for the first time, thanks to a summer friend who lived in Berkeley. "I just flipped out. I couldn't believe how beautiful it was." She deferred her Yale enrollment, moved to Boston for a few months, then returned to Berkeley. "And I crashed in Dan and Rod's dorm room right up over there at Dwight and College [in Berkeley] for the first six months and played on the street. And of course I never did go to Yale. I came out here for a year and then I went to UC for about a year and a half, and then I dropped out to live with my boyfriend and be a hippie."

Some time later, Suzy and her boyfriend moved north to the aforementioned Preston Ranch where Will Spires was also living. There, she learned her first Cajun music on the fiddle from Will, who had already been playing it for ten years or so by that point. She did not have a phonograph at that time, or a tape recorder, so she did all her learning in face-to-face sessions with Will, playing along and learning the tunes. The next formative experience she had was at a 1976 San Diego folk festival, the same one where Will had seen Dennis McGee and Sady Courville perform a year earlier.

> Every year we would all go to this folk festival that they used to have in San Diego. And in those years, Mike Seeger would bring around a tour every year with a variety of incredible performers. One year he'd bring Dennis and Sady, and Lydia Mendoza, and John Jackson. And then the next year he'd bring Lily Mae Ledford and the Balfa Brothers and Elizabeth Cotten. Just incredible performers. And I was in England the year that Dennis and Sady came, so I didn't meet them that time. I heard tapes of them. But at that point I really couldn't appreciate what they were doing, it just sounded too funky to me. But when I heard the Balfa Brothers, I just completely flipped out. At that time, we didn't know about the existence of the Creoles here at all, we didn't know about Danny, Queen Ida.... And we certainly weren't aware that it was a dance music. So we just sat there, and I just cried through their whole set. I was really just emotionally overwhelmed by their music, for some reason that I never will understand.
>
> I have a good tape [of that set in San Diego] from the board. And I listen to it pretty frequently. It's a very interesting thing to deconstruct, because what it really shows you is the genius of Dewey Balfa, not just as a musician, but in the way that

he presented the music to people and made it accessible to people like us... the little raps that he did in between the songs. He laid it all out there, exactly what we should listen to. He mentions Dennis McGee. He mentions Canray Fontenot. They did a pretty wide variety of stuff, including a bunch of stuff without accordion. Marc Savoy was the second fiddle player. Allie Young was the accordion player. They're just playing all acoustic, there's no pickups, there's no drums, just into microphones, and it sounds to die for. And Rodney is singing his heart out, and it is really amazing music. Also Dewey's delivery, when you listen to it, it sounds like he's talking directly to you, the listener, even though there's a couple of thousand people in there.

Many of Suzy's friends who were at that concert with her were musicians with whom she was already playing Cajun music or with whom she would play it in the future: Will Spires, Eric Thompson, Jeanie McLerie, and Frannie Leopold. A couple of years after this concert, Jeanie McLerie went to live in Louisiana, staying on the property of Marc and Ann Savoy in Eunice. Soon thereafter, Eric and Suzy and Frannie all went together on their first trip to Louisiana to visit Jeanie. Just as Eric had done in a previous trip to Ireland, they visited older traditional musicians to play with them in their homes and learn some of their music, a pattern which would repeat on several return trips over the years in which they would visit many musicians including Dennis McGee, Dewey Balfa, Wade Frugé, Cheese Read, and D. L. Menard.

For the next two years Suzy played in an all-woman string band called Any Old Time. The group appeared in local venues such as Paul's Saloon in San Francisco and the Freight and Salvage Coffeehouse in Berkeley. They played a variety of acoustic music, including Cajun tunes, old-time string band music, and jug band blues. Their 1978 Arhoolie LP included "Ma Cher Bebe Creole" and "Valse de Orphelin" with Suzy (listed then as Susie Rothfield) and Sue Draheim on twin fiddles and Suzy on vocals. Meanwhile, Eric was completing his first album as a solo recording artist, *Eric Thompson's Bluegrass Guitar*, backed up by bluegrass stars David Grisman and Tony Rice. Around the time that album came out (1979), Suzy and Eric moved to Ithaca, New York, to form the Backwoods Band with Mac Benford, a banjo player who had played with Eric and Will Spires in Dr. Humbead's New Tranquility String Band in the sixties. The Backwoods Band recorded an album for Rounder before the year was out and toured extensively for the next two years. They played some Cajun songs with that band but did not record them.[17]

It was not until they moved to the state of New York that Suzy and Eric met Danny Poullard in California at Will Spires' place, during a winter break from touring. The Backwoods Band's touring schedule also allowed for side trips to

Louisiana, when Suzy and Eric would stay in the apartment above Marc Savoy's music store in Eunice for short periods of time.

The year 1981 was eventful for the Thompsons both personally and musically. Suzy received a folk apprenticeship fellowship from the National Endowment for the Arts to study fiddle with Dewey Balfa, just as Will Spires had done with Dennis McGee two years before. Before traveling to Louisiana to spend time with Balfa and others, she and Eric were married in California. Meanwhile, the Backwoods Band was breaking up. In Ithaca, Suzy and Eric had become friends with guitarist Alan Senauke, who had been editor for *Sing Out!* magazine in the 1970s. With Kate Brislin, one of Suzy's bandmates from Any Old Time, they formed the Blue Flame String Band and in very short order booked a tour, played their first date on the *Prairie Home Companion* radio show in Minnesota, and recorded an album for Flying Fish. By some coincidence, Marc and Ann Savoy were recording an album in the same Bay Records studio in Alameda, California, so Marc played accordion for the Cajun selections on the Blue Flame String Band's album. Blue Flame, in return, played on several cuts of the Savoy-Doucet LP entitled *Les Harias*. The Thompsons moved back to California in 1982. The band continued to tour for another couple of years, while also performing on their home turf. The band made its debut at Ashkenaz, the Berkeley folk dancing venue, in January 1983 with its music billed as "Old Timey, Cajun, Bluegrass, Blues, Jug Band."[18]

Eventually Brislin dropped out of the Blue Flame String Band and the band started finding more work close to home. Since the band already played some Cajun music and the Thompsons had been introduced to Danny Poullard, they started inviting him to sit in with them for the Cajun numbers. Playing with Danny in turn spurred them to expand their Cajun repertoire so they could play for dances at Ashkenaz and elsewhere. The Ashkenaz calendar billings for the band over the next two years suggest a gradual metamorphosis from the Blue Flame String Band

Figure 5. Dates of appearances at Ashkenaz for the Blue Flame String Band as it becomes the California Cajun Orchestra

January 9, 1983	Blue Flame String Band
May 26, 1983	Blue Flame Band with Danny Poullard
January 26, 1984	Blue Flame Band with Danny Poullard
March 9, 1984	Zydeco Express with Al Rapone* +
	Blue Flame Cajun Orchestra with Danny Poullard
March 2, 1985	The California Cajun Orchestra

*brother of Queen Ida. See Chapter 4.

to the California Cajun Orchestra (see fig. 5). As the California Cajun Orchestra, they would have two more Ashkenaz appearances in 1985, four in 1986, six in 1987, and twelve in 1988. They would continue to appear monthly on Saturday nights at Ashkenaz until shortly before Poullard's death in 2001.

The premise of the California Cajun Orchestra (CCO) constituted a departure for Eric and Suzy from the kinds of groups in which they have performed both before and since. Rather than their usual eclectic mix, they were playing one kind of music and their clientele consisted of dancers rather than listeners. Suzy described the change in 1997, when CCO was still active:

> One reason why we ended up just playing Cajun music, it's easy to describe, it's easy to sell, it's easy to market. Cajun music also is what our friend Bob Brozman calls a service gig, where you're providing a service. People can dance to it. You don't really have to listen to it, you can just dance to it or socialize to it or whatever. Before that, the bands that I played in were listening bands. This was the first time I ever played in a band that was a dance band. Other bands I played in sometimes would play for square dances or something, but we were not a dance band. This is a dance band....
> We don't play other kinds of music in the California Cajun Orchestra; we don't even play the other kinds of Cajun music that we like to play. It's become a real conscious thing to have it just be a showcase for Danny and to do what Danny wants.

New sets of expectations from Danny and the dancers also meant a shift from the acoustic string band format to an electric Cajun dance band instrumentation: accordion, fiddle, electric guitar (a new departure for Eric), electric bass, and drums. After trying various bass players and drummers, they settled on drummer Sam Siggins, a veteran local country musician, and bassist Bill Wilson, an experienced blues and country musician. They would supplement this core unit when they could with some favorite musical associates. Fiddler Kevin Wimmer, a musician originally from New York who had previously apprenticed himself to Dewey Balfa, added a lush two-fiddle sound and an occasional vocal to the band when he wasn't playing bluegrass with the Good Ol' Persons. Charlie St. Mary (noted in ch. 5 by Betty LeBlanc, for his dancing) provided an additional Creole dimension to the band with his *frottoir* playing and bluesy vocals.

The California Cajun Orchestra's performance venues were not limited to folk revivalist settings like Ashkenaz. Because Poullard and St. Mary were in the band, there was also demand from the Creole community for their services. They played often at church dances, mainly at St. Mark's in Richmond, St. Francis of Assisi in East Palo Alto, and occasionally at All Hallows in San Francisco and other parishes. Poullard's precarious health during the band's early years did not hold them back but rather gave extra urgency to their time together, according to Suzy: "Danny was having a *lot* of heart trouble, and I think it gave us all—the rest of the people playing with him—just a sense that we'd better play as much as we can with this guy because he might not be around forever. And I think it gave Danny a certain impetus to do a lot of playing, too." Thus the band gigged frequently when Danny's health permitted, and they also found their way to the recording studio.

Members of CCO appeared on an album that Eric and Suzy recorded under their own names that consisted of two-thirds blues and one-third Louisiana music, released by Arhoolie in 1989. That same year, producers Les Blank, Chris Strachwitz, and Maureen Gosling finished the film documentary *J'ai Été au Bal*. Suzy appears in that film in footage shot in their home in California, playing music with D.L. Menard and with Danny Poullard, and also in a "bonus track" on the DVD release of the film, playing and singing "Grand Mamou" with Queen Ida, Danny Poullard, and George Broussard.[19]

Following these projects in the late 1980s, Suzy pursued and procured funding from the California Arts Council for CCO to record an entire album on its own for Arhoolie, released in 1991 as *Not Lonesome Anymore*. The repertoire consisted mostly of electric Cajun dance hall standards, albeit some heard less often than others—for example, some tunes that Danny learned from his father and from John Semien. Vocals on the album alternate among Danny Poullard, Suzy Thompson, Charlie St. Mary, and Andrew Carrière; the overall aural portrait is of a balanced ensemble whose central "voices" are heard in the instrumental solos: Danny's accordion, Suzy's fiddle, and Eric's guitar. Also integral throughout are Charlie St. Mary's "hollers," yelled and spoken commentary not unlike those of many rubboard players in many zydeco bands yet with his own style.[20]

Perhaps surprisingly, the album started receiving radio airplay in Louisiana after Strachwitz sent out the release to his usual mailing list of radio stations. Awareness there led in 1993 to some rare recognition for a Cajun band not based in Louisiana or Texas: the first-ever "Le Cajun" award to an out-of-state band from the Cajun French Music Association, followed by an invitation to play at Festivals Acadiens in Lafayette, the largest festival of the year devoted primarily to Cajun and Creole French music. With financial help from Strachwitz, they were able to bring most of the band out, including Poullard, Wimmer, St. Mary, and Sam Siggins on bass. Danny's brother Edward came over from Beaumont, Texas, to fill in on drums. While in Louisiana for the festival, they also appeared on the *Rendezvous des Cajuns* live radio broadcast from the Liberty Theater in Eunice, near where Poullard was born. Suzy says, "The thing I remember about being at the Liberty Theater is that we were playing 'Not Lonesome Anymore' and we looked out and Aldus Roger was dancing. That was a huge thrill to see him dancing to us playing his tune."[21]

CCO made a second album with Arhoolie in 1995, again with partial funding from the California Arts Council. While many of the tracks are electric dance hall standards akin to the first album's offerings, a significant part of this album consists of instrumental numbers with acoustic instrumentation—just accordion, two fiddles, and acoustic guitar. Most of the tunes that received this old-time treatment were tunes without names that Danny had learned from his father, for which they invented names: "Ashkenaz Special," "Danse à Dorence," "Yoval Two-Step," and "John Poullard Two-Step," after the Berkeley dance hall, Danny's mother, his father's cousin, and his father, respectively.[22]

After this album the band's personnel saw some turnover, but Danny, Eric, and Suzy remained the core of the group and even made some appearances as the California Cajun Trio. Occasionally when Poullard was traveling, they would appear with Andrew Carrière on accordion. The band continued to perform until Poullard passed away in 2001, although not as often as in its early years. In late 1996, Ashkenaz club owner David Nadel was shot and killed in his club by a patron he had ejected earlier in the evening. Suzy Thompson became part of a group that formed a nonprofit organization to purchase the building from Nadel's family and to operate the club in the spirit that Nadel had started it, as a venue welcoming to all ages and all cultures.

> I was listening to the radio.... They were talking about art, and what is the purpose of art? And it just seems so obvious to me that art is about—and this is true of "low" art and "high" art—is that it's about transcendence, and transcending where you are and where you come from. And that's what I always felt was such a magical thing about the CCO, in our strongest years. Especially, I'd look out there at the floor at Ashkenaz and there would be every kind of person, and people that in the normal way of things would never have wanted to even be in the same room with each other because of their differences in background, race, politics, sexuality, you name it. And then they would all be dancing together. And I know that's kind of an idealistic way to look at it, but there is a core of truth there, too. And that's why Ashkenaz was so important to me.[23]

The group succeeded in its goal; Suzy served on the initial board of directors, helped to raise funds for the down payment on the building, assisted with its applications to become a nonprofit, and wrote grant applications for the organization. Once

California Cajun Orchestra publicity shot. Top row: Eric Thompson and Sam Siggins; middle row: Charlie St. Mary, Danny Poullard, and Suzy Thompson; bottom: Billy Wilson. Photo by Irene Young.

reopened some ten months later, the club initially had fewer nights of Cajun music per month than previously, but eventually resumed a similar rotation.

As their time commitments for CCO decreased, the Thompsons focused on other projects in and out of Cajun music. A few years before, Suzy had begun studying accordion with Danny. Not long thereafter they formed a Cajun band in which they could play other Cajun music and on different instruments from what they played in CCO. They named the band the Aux Cajunals in ironic celebration of its infrequent appearances. Its core personnel has consisted of Suzy Thompson on accordion and fiddle, Eric Thompson and Agi Ban on fiddle, and their former Blue Flame bandmate Alan Senauke on guitar. Early on, the band focused on an old-time acoustic sound with no other instruments and some three-fiddle arrangements. In recent years, they have added an upright bass, drums, and Mayne Smith's steel guitar to fill out the lineup for dances. Outside of Cajun music, the Thompsons have continued their other musical interests and developed new ones. Suzy has recorded a couple of albums under her own name; she has spearheaded an old-time music convention in Berkeley, and they have taught workshops at numerous festivals and camps.[24]

Delilah Lee Lewis[25]

Delilah Lee Lewis was born in 1952 in Porterville, California, in the foothills of the Sierra Nevada mountain range. All four of her grandparents were immigrants from Russia and Poland. Of her immediate family (her parents, a half-brother eighteen years older, and a half-sister seven years older), none played music or were particularly interested in it. What family connection there was to music was through her maternal grandfather, whom she continued to see frequently after her family moved to Fresno when she was in the second grade.

> My grandfather came to Ellis Island, went to Hartford, Connecticut, and then they ended up in L.A. He drove a covered wagon north from L.A. and stopped in Porterville, it reminded him of Russia where he was from, and he settled there. My grandfather, my mother's father, forced all my aunts and uncles and my mother to take violin lessons when they were young, and I think that was in the back of my mind. None of them ever really learned to play, they hated it, and they were forced to take these lessons and they didn't want to do it. When my grandfather died and we were cleaning out their house in Porterville, in the garage there was this really old, rat-eaten violin, I mean it was just trash. And so I never forgot that. They died when I was in the seventh grade. But I was pretty close with my grandparents and stayed with them a lot. They didn't even read or write English and they were pretty cool people and a big influence in my life.

Delilah made a few attempts to play music in high school, on guitar and organ, but gave up on it as she began married life right upon graduation. "I didn't think that I could ever play music, and I didn't think I could ever sing, and I just completely gave up on ever playing music." A year after they wed, the couple moved to the Bay Area with plans that he would attend law school and she would start nursing school at Merritt College, a community college in Oakland. They found themselves in an apartment across the hall from Mayne Smith, a professional dobro and pedal steel player who had been married to someone they knew in Fresno. "We became very good friends with Mayne, and when our front doors were open it was kind of like one big apartment. He had music parties all the time, and I guess I was just fascinated by these folk musicians sitting around playing fiddles and guitars and banjos and dobros and singing. They were very good musicians. They'd do country and swing, and they wrote songs, Mayne Smith and Mitch Greenhill." Delilah's role at these parties remained as attentive listener for a few years as she worked her way through school. Smith's new partner Leslie was the ex-wife of Stuart Brotman, another professional musician who would later become part of the klezmer band Brave Old World. It was at a party that Brotman attended in their apartment building, when Delilah was twenty-six and in her last year of nursing school, that finally changed her relationship to music.

> Stuart remained friends with Leslie, and happened to be at a party at Mayne's. And Stuart, I guess he was just watching me watch everybody, I don't even remember why, but he started questioning me about what kind of instrument I would want to play if I could play music. He just started talking to me and said, "What instrument would you like to play if you could play?" And I said, "Well, I can't play anything, so just forget it, you know?" And he said, "Well, what if you could, what would you want to play?" And I said, "Well it's just a moot point, Stuart, because I can't. I just can't carry a tune, I can't sing, I can't play, I just don't have it." And he persisted for about twenty minutes straight, over and over, he just would not let up on me. And he said, "I just want to know if you could, I know you can't, but if you could, what would it be, what instrument would it be?" I said, "Violin." "Well, finally," he said. "I just happen to have one out in my truck." He plays every instrument. He's a master, genius musician, a very elevated person. And so he went downstairs and he got it out of his truck and he gave me a five-minute lesson and he said, "You're great, you know, you're a natural, you can do this." And I thought, my God, I actually can do what he's saying to do, it didn't sound all that bad, you know? Just hit one string at a time, just use the whole bow, and then hit the next one, and do that with all four of them, and then try and hit two at a time. And he said, well I know where you can buy one. I bought this fiddle for twenty-five bucks, and I was completely convinced that I was never going to learn how to play this and I was also never going to take a lesson because I knew I would never learn how to play it.

Despite her pessimism about her own musical abilities, she threw herself into playing the instrument almost immediately, playing along with her husband's record collection.

> I always loved country music, being from Porterville and growing up near Bakersfield and hearing that stuff.... The way I learned how to play was, I started playing along

> with records which were mostly blues and jazz and country, just trying to scratch along. I kept hitting notes that sounded pretty good with it, kind of accidentally. I felt like I was playing the violin even though I sounded horrible. I just became obsessed with it. And I wasn't very happy being married anymore. We were childhood sweethearts, and had never been with anybody else. I just put myself into this fiddle. I wouldn't do anything for years, all I would do was play the fiddle.

Within a few months Delilah met a fellow nurse at Kaiser Hospital in Oakland, Karen Monson, who had studied classical violin in the past but had not played for ten years. Leslie Brotman recommended Suzy Rothfield to them as a fiddle teacher.

> When we first went, Suzy asked, what do you guys want to learn? And I said, I don't know, I didn't really want to play bluegrass or Irish music. I told her I was into blues and jazz and country and that's really what I usually listened to and she said what about Cajun music, and I said what is that? And she said, that's people from the southwestern part of Louisiana which I didn't even know. Never even heard of Cajuns before. Karen had heard, on KPFA, some Cajun music and so we said, all right, that would be fine, because they played twin fiddles in Cajun music, and there's two of us, so she could teach Karen the more difficult parts and me (the supposedly) simpler seconding parts, and after about six lessons we knew six songs.

In 1979 Karen and her boyfriend decided to take a vacation trip to Louisiana, and Delilah and her husband joined them. Suzy referred them to Jeanie McLerie, who was working in Marc Savoy's music store at the time. Jeanie told them about a festival that was happening in Mamou in May, where they met Canray Fontenot and Bois Sec Ardoin.

The next year Suzy moved to New York and sent Delilah and Karen to Will Spires, "because he was really the only other person around who was qualified to teach it." Will not only taught them many more tunes, he also taught Delilah more about seconding and how the two-note "chords" that she was playing on her fiddle fit with the melody. He also introduced the two fiddle students to Danny Poullard, who then became a frequent playing companion. Poullard gave her a few tips, too, such as to play on the lower strings when seconding behind the accordion, then to switch to the higher strings when it was her turn to play the melody. But mostly Danny taught Delilah and Karen by demonstrating the melodies with his accordion and with sheer repetition.

> I would say, I don't know that, and he'd say, just play along. I knew about ten tunes. He wouldn't call before he came over, he'd just come. I mean, it's rude in Louisiana,

if you have to call somebody and say, CAN I come over, they're not a real friend. So he would just drop in wherever I lived, and we would just play for hours. I mean, I really played on the average of ten hours a day on my days off, when I wasn't working. All weekend, we would just play all afternoon and until two or three in the morning. And Danny would just stay there and play and play and he taught us how to play. Karen and I played our first gig with Danny's band, The Louisiana Playboys.

Although Poullard was a far more advanced musician at that point, the encouragement that he gave worked in both directions when it came to singing. "We were both really insecure about singing, but if there was nobody else to sing either he or I would have to do it."

The rest of 1980 saw a turning point in Delilah's life, in the form of summer music sojourn to Sweet's Mill, a music camp up in the Fresno foothills, followed by the breakup of her marriage. "Two hundred musicians just playing music for two weeks, it blew my mind completely. And I thought, this is what I want to do. The fiddle just took over my life." While at Sweet's Mill she met Jemmy and Evo Bluestein, musician sons of folklorist Gene Bluestein and residents of Fresno whom she had never met in the years that she grew up there. Then in October she and Karen returned to Louisiana, just the two of them this time, bringing some of Poullard's accordions to Marc Savoy for tuning. They also briefly became a part of Dewey Balfa's ongoing campaign to promote Cajun music. "We pull up in front of Balfa Furniture Store, and Dewey, he called the newspaper to come over and take our picture and interview us and put us in the paper the next day. Two traveling nurses from California, and we're sitting there on stools playing fiddles."

After another year back in Oakland of living on her own, Delilah sublet her apartment for two months starting in November 1981 so she could spend a longer time in Louisiana. She had lined up a temporary nursing job at the local hospital in Eunice, and got her Louisiana license as a registered nurse so she could live and work there to support herself for that period. Will Spires drove with her that time and reintroduced her to Marc Savoy once they arrived. Marc, much to her surprise, offered her a place to stay in the apartment above their music store, which she gratefully accepted. What were to be two months stretched to six months and then, with a change in employment, to some two and half years.

> I hadn't been a nurse very long at all, but I guess I was a San Francisco bigwig there. So, I got offered a job as director of nursing in this nursing home in Crowley, which was twenty miles away. They had heard about me working in the local hospital in downtown Eunice, someone from California. The administrator wanted to hire me, but the head guy—he was the head of fifty nursing homes in Louisiana—he didn't think I should get the job at first, because I wasn't wearing makeup, and I drove a

van, and I didn't live there in Crowley. He was very suspicious of all that. And he wanted me to move to Crowley so I'd be right there in that little town so everybody could keep their eye on me. I wasn't moving [from Eunice], and he finally agreed to let me take the job because the administrator really wanted me.

In conjunction with her nursing duties, Delilah devoted some attention to the home's activity program.

The activity program is an important part of a nursing home. The residents need stimulation and fun and the families wanted to come when we'd have live music. We had an activity coordinator, a young guy, Patrick Menard, whose father was Nathan Menard, a pretty well-known accordion player there. And [Patrick] did all kinds of activities with them. But for special occasions, I would always get musicians to come and play, and they loved it. A lot of them grew up with Dennis McGee, everybody spoke French, and they mostly all knew Cajun music from when they were kids, the old people especially. When there wasn't live music, I had the tapes turned up loud while I was working. The residents were mostly hard of hearing and we were all very happy.

Will Spires, Delilah Lewis, Dennis McGee, and Tracy Schwarz performing in nursing home in Crowley, Louisiana, circa 1982–84. Photo courtesy of Delilah Lee Lewis.

In addition to Dennis McGee, she brought many other musicians in to play for the residents, including Nathan Menard, Aldus Roger, Lionel Leleux, John Vidrine, Wade Frugé, Danny and Edward Poullard, and David Doucet.

Outside of work, she spent as much time playing and hearing music as she could. While this was the reason that she had moved to Louisiana and it gave a useful focus to her social life, it made for some awkward moments for a single woman in her late twenties from out of state as she made new acquaintances.

> I was somewhat of an anomaly when I first came, people couldn't understand why I was there. They'd say, "Well, why did you come here," and I would say, "Because of the music," and they said, "Your husband works offshore, right?" Seven on, seven off, all the offshore [oil industry] guys. And I said, "No, that's not why I came here." "Oh, you're looking for a husband, offshore." I said, "No, I'm not looking for a husband offshore." [laughs] They could not get that I had just come there for the music. That's why they call it [the music] chanky-chank, kids would make fun of the music. Kids didn't even like Cajun music, they thought it was passé. Now it's so different, there are so many tourists and it's just become so popular but back then it wasn't like that at all. They really weren't used to anybody coming.

However, any discomfort she felt was overruled by her excitement at the chance to spend time with musicians she admired.

> I thought, what am I doing in California? This is the place to be. These people are all the people I have records of, and I can go to their house, they're begging me to come visit. You know, they were as honored to have me there as I was to be there. That's the way they made me feel....
>
> So I would make my rounds.... Wade Frugé always had high blood pressure and Bois Sec always had high blood pressure. Dennis was pretty healthy, really, he was way older than all of them, but he was in pretty good shape. So I would check their blood pressures, and then we'd play music and have some coffee or sometimes drink whiskey and hang out. Every weekend, you know, I would go to one or the other and there was always something going on, parties and anniversaries.

Although there was less tourism in southwestern Louisiana in the early 1980s than there is today, there was still a steady trickle of outsiders, even international visitors, to the Savoy Music Center in Eunice due to Marc's reputation as an accordion builder. Part of Delilah's role as resident above the store became tour guide, taking Savoy's guests along on outings to dance halls and visits to musicians' homes. In addition to entertaining guests, Delilah was able to participate in the Saturday morning Cajun music jam sessions at Savoy's store, not only playing music but cooking gumbo and sauce piquante together with the other musicians in the kitchen of her apartment above the store. She became close friends with Ann Savoy and accompanied her on some of the interviews with musicians that she did in the research for her book, *Cajun Music: A Reflection of a People.*

> Ann taught me how to sing many of the songs I sing as well as how to play bar chords on the guitar. We played together all the time and called our group, "The Fabulous Marc Savoy and the Eunice Party Dolls." We played at house parties, fish fries, trailer parks, benefits, churches, and camps on the bayou. She taught me how to develop black and white photos in her darkroom. We had a membership at the local gym and went to aerobic classes together. I was on the board of directors and was secretary and treasurer of S.P.E.C.I.A.L. (Society for the Preservation of Ethnic Culture in Acadian Louisiana), and worked on the opening of the Liberty Theater.

Along with the fond memories she has of her time living in Louisiana, Delilah openly recalls some of the social anxieties. Like the tourists who would come in greater numbers later, Delilah found that while local whites almost never frequented the black clubs, it was generally acceptable for white visitors from elsewhere to attend them. She perceived this formula to be complicated by the fact that she lived locally, yet she persisted in attending both white and black clubs. Her Jewish identity in a place where she knew few if any other Jews also occasioned some decision-making on her part.

> They didn't assume I was Jewish and I didn't hide that I was but I also didn't announce it. I just didn't talk much about religion or politics really. But that was a trip when Dennis found out one day... I was more worried about them finding out I went to the black clubs. I was very paranoid about people in Crowley, where I worked, finding out that I went to a black club, because it just would have been disastrous. I don't know whether they would have fired me or what. I just don't know what would have happened but I feared it wouldn't have been good. Fortunately, no one traveled from Crowley to Eunice, because you might as well be going from here to some other state....
>
> I just went basically to those two clubs [Richard's and Slim's] because I felt safe there. They knew I lived at Savoy Music, they knew I was a musician, and I just hung out with the families of the people who were playing there. And that's where I learned how to dance, at those black clubs, that was the fun part of my life. The black dances were so great because, as opposed to the white dance clubs where everybody would be in couples and I would hardly get asked to dance, at the black dance hall, everybody switched dance partners and that was what was done.

Canray Fontenot, Delilah Lee Lewis, and Bois Sec Ardoin. Photo courtesy of Delilah Lee Lewis.

She took some teasing from white friends who knew of her enthusiasm for Creole music. Ann Savoy nicknamed her "Z.Z.", "like Z.Z. Hill, just a bunch of black guys named Z.Z., musicians I think." Nonetheless, she spent time with Creole and Cajun musicians alike.

The Creole musicians Canray Fontenot and Alphonse "Bois Sec" Ardoin were on her regular rotation of musicians to visit, and she would be invited to family dances at son Morris Ardoin's place. From Fontenot she learned songs like "Bernadette" and a different way of seconding that involves just two chord positions for the left hand, simple in conception yet physically challenging in execution. Canray and Bois Sec were cultural icons in Louisiana, and they were also personal icons for her and for Danny Poullard and his brother Edward. The three of them would delight in trying to sound as much as possible like these older musicians.

A second Creole accordion/fiddle duo with whom she spent time was the Carrière brothers, Bébé and Eraste (father and uncle of Andrew Carrière, respectively).

> I had this old scratchy tape from Jeanie [McLerie] and Ken [Keppeler]. I thought it was really old, something from the thirties, forties, or something like that. I thought they were dead and when Michael [Doucet] told me that they were alive, I just couldn't believe it. He said they live right there in Lawtell. And I just went there with my fiddle by myself, and they took me over to Eraste's house, which was right across

the street and then we got in the car and drove way out into the country to Bébé's, and they set up their little amps in the house, and chickens were crowing. I told them, I'm not coming back until I learn "Madame Faielle" and "Blue Runner." And I think that's what impressed them, because I did. I went home and I learned them and I came back. And I played them and they were just so tickled that I did that. And so when I play those now with Andrew it's really fun, because he can sing them exactly like his dad. I met Andrew several years later, when Danny took me to a party at his and Annette's house in Oakland.

As he was for several musicians toward the end of his life, Cajun fiddler Dennis McGee was a central figure for Delilah. Other visiting female musicians had caused some dissension in the McGee household, and so she received some advance advice on how to introduce herself.

Will [Spires] told me, when you go there, you take her a big bouquet of flowers and you talk to Gladys, Dennis's wife. And boy, that was the best advice anybody ever gave me. Because I befriended her, and I was in like Flynn. She wanted me to move in with them several times. They were old and I was a nurse, so she loved me. It was

Delilah Lee Lewis and Bébé Carrière. Photo by Ann Savoy.

great. I used to go there every week, or as much as I could, and have coffee and play....

He said, "*Chère*, how long have you been playing?" And I said, "About three years." He said, "I played better than that after three months." He told me that. Oh, I learned a bunch of Dennis tunes. And I used to second him, I mostly just played second fiddle behind him for hours. Yeah, I learned a lot from Dennis. I really have a style, most of how I play is kind of a combination of Dennis and Canray Fontenot and Wade Frugé.

She received more explicit musical instruction from Frugé, as well as a cultural education.

He was a wonderful old guy and a *great* fiddler as well as being the most openly prejudiced person I met down there. I spent a lot of time with Wade, at his house and at the store. His wife Evelyn would make great coffee and we'd play.... Wade could actually teach. I mean, he could slow it down a little bit and go over and over it, and try and get rid of my "Yankee stroke," which he used to call my bowing.

He was a really great teacher but the guy was terribly prejudiced.... I would just tease him and laugh it off, but it was hard. The interesting thing was that to me, Wade's style of playing was very black and bluesy sounding. He learned from black fiddlers, talked about learning from an old one-armed black fiddler that used to strap the bow onto the stump, on the street corner. He learned this song that we just recorded, Wade's "Samedi Apres-midi." We call it "Wade's Shuffle" but it's a total blues thing. Wade played more black style than, you know, just about anybody down there, short of Canray. And so I loved his style. I loved the way he plays and I loved Wade.

When she lived in Louisiana she did not play in public much except for Thursday nights at Mulate's in Breaux Bridge, where she would sit in with Beausoleil, Michael Doucet's band, on a semi-regular basis. She felt more comfortable in the role of student, visiting with musicians in private settings. Other musicians whom Delilah visited, albeit less often, included Cajun fiddlers Dewey Balfa, Varise Connor, Lionel Leleux, Shelton Manuel and Raymond François. François introduced her to Cheese Read and accordionist Nathan Abshire.

In general, she found that the high level of hospitality in Louisiana and the willingness of musicians there to play with her allowed her musicianship to develop in ways that she felt never would have happened in California. She credits not only the individual musicians but also an ethos of community participation that she perceives to be a part of Louisiana French culture.

It's very close-knit, and music is just a huge, huge part of it all. You know, the reason I moved there, and I'll tell you the truth, Mark, was because I didn't feel all that accepted in the musical community here in California. It was probably due to my insecurity and the fact that I didn't think I was gonna be able to really learn to play.... But in Louisiana these guys ... just couldn't have cared less how bad I was, they didn't really seem to care if I could tune. They weren't always in tune either, they didn't care. They were just there to have a good time. I felt like I had come home....

It's just so much warmth in the homes in Louisiana. Like Bois Sec's house and Marceline, there are so many kids and their families, and music is such a part of their life as it wasn't a part of my life. One of the first questions you asked me, did I come from a musical family? Zero. They did not care. I had to force my sister to listen to me play. She'd go, "Oh God, get out of here. That is horrible, scratchy, what is that, Cajun? What is that? Why are you playing that?" They just couldn't figure it out, they didn't understand it or seem to appreciate it. So it's amazing, I have a whole different life than my family. I love them dearly and over the years they've come to love my music and we're much closer now. They just came to a gig that I did and I played a demo tape for my mom, and she said, "Honey that is so good, you have gotten so much better." I was thrilled, you know, she's eighty. So it really meant a lot for me to go to a culture in which music was such a major part of everyday life. I was very happy there. It was really nice to be able to give something back to the community in the nursing home.... I felt really good about it because it was a fifty-seven-bed nursing home and had twenty-five vacancies when I came, and we had a waiting list of twenty when I left....

It almost killed me leaving, I tell you. It was really hard leaving, but it was time for me to go.... It's a really great culture, and the food is incredible, but it was not a very healthy place for me. I drank way too much and the pesticides were really frightening on that Crowley Road. It's just surrounded by giant fields and the crop dusters would come, spraying, and they'd get to the road and would stop for a second while crossing the road and then they would just start up again, spraying the poison. I would just hold my breath and drive, because I didn't have air conditioning, and hope for the best.

Shortly after returning to California in 1984, she traveled to Europe for a year by herself, taking the opportunity to visit with many of the international travelers she had met at Savoy Music Center.

Upon returning home in 1986, she took a job as an emergency room nurse in Fresno and helped her mother look after her ailing father. Delilah also remained active musically. She renewed acquaintance with the Bluestein brothers, whom she had met at the Sweet's Mill music camp a few years before, and started her first band with them. The band was named ZZ and the Bad Boys, using the nickname she had acquired in Louisiana, and included not only Jemmy and Evo Bluestein and their father Gene on drums but also multi-instrumentalist Bill Wilson from the Bay Area on bass.

In 1989 she taught Cajun fiddle at Lark in the Morning, another summer music camp in California, where she met her future second husband, Sean. Her father passed away the same summer. The couple wed a few months later. Delilah and Sean spent their first year of marriage living in San Francisco, during which time she played Cajun music with Wilson in a lineup named Bayou Pon Pon. After that, she and her husband bought property and moved two counties north, near Santa Rosa. She dropped out of the music scene for a few years, only playing occasionally up in the wine country with another band, the Cajun Coyotes.

In 1998 Delilah and her husband separated; she moved back to San Francisco and started playing music again in earnest. She formed an all-female band with guitarist Karen Leigh, bassist and fiddler Karen Heil, and accordionist Maureen Karpan. "We named the band the Creole Belles because I play a lot of Creole music. I play not just Creole music, but that's my big love. Dennis is my other big love, but it's hard to play too many Dennis tunes in a big dance situation. They're more fiddle tunes, they're not really accordion tunes. . . . We found this old sheet music, the Creole Belles, our poster. They were all white Creoles [on the original poster]." The design of the sheet music cover featured the faces of young women, four of which were replaced with photos of the band members. At the bottom, it read, "Creole Belles, Cajun old-time dance band." The band occasionally also uses a drummer and has joined the regular rotation of Cajun and zydeco bands that play for dances throughout the Bay Area. In recent years, Andrew Carrière has regularly appeared with them as a "special guest" on vocals, percussion, and accordion. The band's repertoire includes Carrière family tunes, Karen Heil and Delilah on double-fiddle numbers from McGee, songs from Canray Fontenot ("Bernadette"), Bois Sec Ardoin ("Petite ou la Grosse"), and Cajun dance hall standards that Maureen Karpan learned on accordion from Danny Poullard and others.[26]

In 2000, the year of our interview, Delilah's band had recently made a demo recording and she had served as a fiddle instructor that summer at the Port Townsend Festival of American Fiddle Tunes, where she served as Canray Fontenot's assistant some dozen years prior. She and partner, guitarist Karen Leigh, played concerts with Danny Poullard, and taught workshops in Creole fiddling. Her experience there represented a sort of culmination.

> We just made our first little demo CD about two weeks ago. I just never wanted to make recordings, I've never felt like I wanted to be in the festival circuit or try to promote myself, because I don't do it for that reason. I didn't get into it to make records and travel and be a big Cajun fiddle star. [laughs] The way I play is kind of

scratchy and rough. Going to Port Townsend this year was such a huge honor. I was up there with incredible virtuoso violin masters, very famous people. I was filling in for Edward [Poullard], trying to channel Canray, so to speak. Danny and Ed and I have been friends a long time, and they both told Warren that I was the only one who could play that style....

One of the biggest hits I taught there was "Bernadette," one of Canray's songs. And I wasn't even going to try and teach it, because it's so free-form, I mean I have no idea what order I play the parts in or anything. I tried to teach things that were a little more clear-cut, that I could do the same way twice. But when they heard me play that on the big stage in front of fifteen hundred people, the next day there were a whole bunch more people in my class. They wanted "Bernadette." I said "Well, OK, you're gonna get 'Bernadette' then." It was really fun. In my class I had a superior court judge, two physicians (family practice doctors in Seattle), and a world-famous astronomer. Amazing, all want to learn Cajun fiddle. But I was very proud of myself, I did a great job, because I could simplify it, even these doctors who play classical music and read music stayed in my class the whole week. They were there with their tape recorders every morning at nine o'clock.

Her experience at this festival was cause for much reflection. "The fiddle just took over my life. It reminds me of what Warren Argo said at Port Townsend... he was introducing us, he was talking about me and my past, and he said, 'I'm sure the fiddle just ruined her life.' And in a way, when I think about that, I was really going to go back to school... but I got my RN license and never went back. I was so into this music that I just wouldn't stop that."

Having lived in Louisiana, Delilah knows well the dilemma of someone who loves another culture but who can never really claim it for her own identity. Unlike some musicians and dancers in California who travel to Louisiana regularly, she has not visited much in the years since she moved back west, yet she remains grateful for her time there. "I have stayed in touch with my old friends there over the years even if I haven't been able to visit in person as much as I would have liked. Going back is always wonderful and very emotional for me.... I must honestly say it was one of the greatest experiences of my life and I feel very fortunate to have stayed as long as I did."

Louisiana French Music Meets the Bay Area Folk Music Scene

As we began to see in the last chapter in the interactions among Chris Strachwitz, Les Blank, musicians in Louisiana, and Creole musicians in the Bay Area, social capital accumulates in a network of people who in turn belong to other social networks. Will Spires goes on tour with Kenny Hall, another folk musician, and meets the Balfa brothers at a concert venue in the state of New York. He meets Dennis McGee at a concert produced by Mike Seeger, whom he already knew. A year later, Suzy Thompson undergoes her own conversion experience listening to Dewey Balfa at another Seeger-produced concert. All four of the musicians profiled (and Jeanie McLerie and Ken Keppeler before them) benefited from the generosity and hospitality of Marc and Ann Savoy, who were willing to provide a base of operations to many in pursuit of learning Cajun music and who already had a connection to California through Blank and Strachwitz. These musicians—the Balfas, the Savoys, McGee—were meanwhile actively involved in the Cajun music revival in their home state. Somewhat later New Yorker Kevin Wimmer apprentices himself to Dewey Balfa, moves to California and plays with the California Cajun Orchestra, then moves to Louisiana to play in Balfa Toujours with Balfa's daughter, Christine. These are just some of the interconnections between California and Louisiana facilitated by folk revival activities. It should also be said that Will, Eric, Suzy, and Delilah took their involvement a step further than the admiration-at-a-distance that a folk revival approach sometimes fosters. The local presence of Poullard and other Creole musicians gave them much more face-to-face time playing music than occasional visits to Louisiana alone would have afforded, and obviously Delilah's move to Louisiana provided even more opportunity for musical enculturation to take place.

One theme that runs through this chapter and the next are situations where whites who were not raised in the American South and who live in a politically liberal region of California visit Louisiana, where they must confront racial attitudes to which they are not accustomed. In the case of these four musicians, it was not the prospect of visiting Creole musicians or going to Creole clubs that gave them pause; it was the attitudes of whites toward Creoles and other groups (both Suzy and Delilah are Jewish) that presented the greater challenge. Will Spires articulates well the complexities involved. It is not an intention of this book to claim moral superiority for California when it comes to racism; the reader who has that impression should review chapter 4. Racism is more difficult to perceive when one lives with it daily; one reason that these musicians noticed racism when they traveled to Louisiana was because it took an unaccustomed shape and therefore caught their attention. The California folk revivalist musicians' liberal ideas about race came from a complex of countercultural currents that either emanated from or found immediate favor in the San Francisco Bay Area in the 1960s: Berkeley's Free Speech Movement, Viet Nam war protests, the civil rights movement, California cuisine, and hippie subculture. It was from this environment that the

California musicians profiled in this chapter ventured in Louisiana French music, and also *into* this environment certain Creoles ventured—the Opelousas Playboys, the Louisiana Playboys, and Clifton Chenier himself—in search of a larger audience for their music.

While Berkeley made its reputation as a cauldron for political and cultural change in the 1960s, its lively folk music scene was already thriving in the 1950s when the university town was a much quieter, more conservative place. A case in point from that period was musician Barry Olivier, who first moved to Berkeley in 1947 as a teenager from rural Brentwood and was influenced by folk revivalists—Burl Ives, Carl Sandburg, John Jacob Niles, and others—that he saw perform on campus. In 1949, a small group of pacifists who had refused to fight in World War II went on the air in Berkeley with the first listener-supported FM radio in the country, KPFA. With the small FM market of listeners at that time and without the constraints of corporate sponsors or shareholders, the new radio station experimented with both public affairs and cultural programming. One such program debuted in 1952, a live midnight folk music program on Saturday nights, hosted by Berkeley High School student Barry Olivier and one of his classmates. KPFA continued with the *Midnight Special* program for several years after Olivier left it; circa 1961 future Grateful Dead members Phil Lesh and Jerry Garcia could be found performing on the show.[27]

When Olivier moved on from the *Midnight Special* program, he found a niche in organizing and presenting his fellow musicians starting in 1956: taping folk music shows for delayed broadcast; running folk music jam sessions at a restaurant on the north side of the Berkeley campus; and presenting folk music concerts on the campus itself in the summers. One of the musicians who participated in those north side sessions was Mayne Smith, later the neighbor of Delilah Lee Lewis whose music parties would get her started playing music, and even later a bandmate of Eric and Suzy Thompson in the Aux Cajunals. In 1958 the summer campus concerts grew into the Berkeley Folk Festival, which focused on "the finished, traditional, pure, real, good, old folk songs" in its first few years, inviting a mixture of folk revival musicians like Pete Seeger, the New Lost City Ramblers, and Joan Baez along with musicians from the communities whose music was being honored, such as Jesse Fuller, Roscoe Holcomb, and (through Chris Strachwitz) Mance Lipscomb. In keeping with the campus setting, the festival supplemented its schedule of performances with talks and panel discussions by a succession of scholars and public sector folklorists over the years, including members of the Lomax and Seeger families (musicologist/patriarch Charles Seeger appeared several times), Archie Green, D. K. Wilgus, and ballad scholar Bertrand Bronson. It was into this somewhat rarefied atmosphere that the Hackberry Ramblers traveled from Louisiana to make their appearance at the Berkeley Folk Festival in 1965, when Will Spires saw them. Olivier had already begun to depart a bit from his original programming idea of the "good, old folk songs"; certainly the Hackberry Ramblers had no hesitation in blending traditional and popular music, albeit popular music of an earlier era. He embraced this concept in a more contemporary way—after losing money on the 1965 festival and some stinging reviews by the San Francisco *Chronicle*'s Ralph Gleason—by inviting the Jefferson Airplane and Country Joe and the Fish the next year. In 1969, the year that the Opelousas Playboys and Doug Kershaw appeared, Kershaw had recently made an appearance on national television (Johnny Cash's summer variety show) and was recharting with "Diggy Liggy Lo," which had first hit the country singles charts in 1961. For personal reasons, Barry Olivier and his wife Helen decided to discontinue producing the Berkeley Folk Festival after 1970, and there were no attempts to continue it.[28]

Outside of the festival context, a great deal of everyday folk revival music-making went on in the region. The Colby Street house where Will Spires and Eric Thompson lived for a time was one center of such activity. Belly dancer Zahar Hayatti recalls her first impressions of this communal house of young musicians when she arrived from New York circa 1967:

> We parked on a quiet street with big, leafy trees, and walked toward this huge, three-storey house. The neighborhood was really peaceful and lovely, and there were flowers growing everywhere in everyone's front yards. I was thrilled to be out of the snow and into the warmth of California. "There are a few musicians on the top floor who play in the 'Cleanliness and Godliness Skiffle Band,'" remarked my host. "Some of them are also in 'Dr. Humbead's New Tranquillity String Band and Medicine Show.'" I really thought he was pulling my leg! We walked up the steps to the second floor and I heard the sounds of a button accordion coming from inside. "Who's that playing?" I asked cautiously. "Oh that's John Paul. He plays with the band 'The Golden Toad.'"

Hayatti reports that the tune Paul was playing was "Parlez Nous à Boire" (the Cajun song recorded not long before by the New Lost City Ramblers).[29]

In 1970 Mike Seeger recorded an anthology album for Folkways entitled *Berkeley Farms* featuring over twenty musicians, most of whom he had seen at the Freight and Salvage Coffeehouse (established 1968).

> The Bay Area (and Berkeley especially in the time this LP was assembled) is one in which the making of many kinds of informal music is important. In warmth, humor, and musicality it reminds me of the Galax, Virginia, area of years ago. And

during the hectic days of planning and recording the music it felt like a renascence of older music and life styles, brought up to date (and beyond). The excitement of it paralleled in my imagination those first days of recording of rural music by the commercial companies in the mountain south during the 1920's. We were fortunate in recording during a time of great musical ferment when most of the best musicians were in town playing in a variety of combinations.

In addition to these comments by Seeger himself, the album includes biographical descriptions of the musicians and various contexts for music-making in and around Berkeley at that time, including a Renaissance Faire, Irish dances in San Francisco, Sweet's Mill music camp, and the Berkeley Old Time Fiddler's Convention, a free event held as a sort of spoof of fiddling contests in the South: "First prize was 3 lbs. of rutabagas, second prize was 5 lbs. rutabagas.... One year a fourth prize was included because the judges felt that at least one prize should be awarded for quality. No one remembers who won it!" Among the musical performances on the recording is a rendition of "Bayou Pon Pon" by an assemblage named the Bayou Croakers, featuring Colby Street residents John Paul (accordion), Will Spires (melodeon, also known as button accordion), and Sue Draheim (fiddle). Spires and Eric Thompson appear together on "Sally in the Garden" along with others in the New Tranquility String Band, and Eric plays with the Spare Change Boys on "Policeman." Other musicians mentioned in this chapter that appear on the album include Mayne Smith, Mitch Greenhill, and Mac Benford.[30]

Several of the Colby Street musicians spent part of their time performing in Renaissance Pleasure Faires, reenactments of life and culture in Elizabethan England that were gaining in popularity at that time in California. A venue for such events was established in Marin County in 1967. Two years later a troupe of Renaissance Faire musicians, some from the Golden Toad ensemble in residence on Colby Street, came upon a property of ramshackle buildings one county north of the Renaissance Faire grounds, near the town of Cloverdale—the Preston Ranch described above by Suzy Thompson. The property had previously been a community formed around the presence of Emily Preston, a sort of mystical healer and spiritual leader who had a knack for gathering people and resources. In 1886 one of her followers had a church built for her outside of Cloverdale; soon thereafter came a one-room schoolhouse that her husband built and then taught at, a general store, a railroad depot, and a post office. Madame Preston, as she was known, lived there with a hundred or so people who were her spiritual followers and medical patients. Preston died in 1909 but vestiges of her community remained until the 1940s. The initial attraction for the musicians was the church building; although it was in disrepair one of their friends wanted to get married there, and it made a suitable facility for musical rehearsals. Eventually the music-loving owner agreed to rent the entire property to the group of Renaissance Faire performers and craftspeople. Where Colby Street had been a focal point of musical activity in the 1960s, Preston Ranch became the rural equivalent for many of the same musicians in the 1970s, including Lark in the Morning founder Mickie Zekley and Thompson bandmates Sue Draheim and Jeremy Kammerer.[31]

The musicians who lived at Preston Ranch in the 1970s had the time and freedom to try playing a wide variety of music. In addition to Will, Suzy, and Eric, another musician who visited the ranch to play Cajun music was fiddler Jeanie McLerie, who had moved to neighboring Mendocino County in 1974. Jeanie grew up in New Jersey and started playing music at age seven on the ukulele, then moved to the guitar. She first encountered Cajun music as a child, when she saw the film *Louisiana Story*. "Then I heard Harry Smith's *Anthology* in Paris, in 1963 (I was 20 and going to the Sorbonne) and I went wild over the Cajun French, and the raw innocence of the music. I knew then that someday I would spend time in Louisiana." Around that time she started making her living as a musician, playing on the streets of Paris. Shortly after college, she moved to London where she made her living playing music and started learning the fiddle. She married musician Sandy Darlington and they lived in Berkeley in the late 1960s, where she played a little Cajun music. After moving away from California for a couple of years, her marriage dissolved and she found herself at Sweet's Mill in 1974, where she met some new playing partners like Frannie Leopold, with whom she formed the Delta Sisters, and Irene Herrmann and Alice Gerrard, who with Jeanie formed the Harmony Sisters. She then lived in Mendocino through 1977, dropped in on Preston Ranch and "played a lot of Cajun music during this time" at the Renaissance Faires and elsewhere in the Bay Area, north to Oregon and south to San Diego. This period in her life drew to a close when she decided to move to Louisiana to brush up on her French and learn more Cajun music.[32]

Jeanie moved to Louisiana in January 1978, having been invited by Marc Savoy to stay with him and his new wife Ann in Eunice until she could establish herself. She started by working as an assistant in Marc's music store to earn her room and board. A month after she arrived there, she a met a musician named Ken Keppeler from southern California, who had been visiting Louisiana to play Cajun music periodically for the previous four years. Jeanie relates:

> Ken arrived there in early February for Mardi Gras, and we clicked right away. We played street music in New Orleans within three days of meeting each other and made $100, and then we started to play in Lafayette with Mike and David Doucet at the Red Dog Saloon and other places. We played in Germany and France that

summer with Mike and his friend Françoise Schaubert. We returned to Louisiana and lived behind Mark and Ann's house near Eunice in the Buvette, a little old house that had a wild history. We put in doors and windows, electricity, running water, and eventually a shower and a screened porch. We loved to visit all the old musicians like Dennis McGee, Canray Fontenot and Bois Sec [Ardoin], Lionel Leleux, Varise Connor, Freeman Fontenot, Raymond François, Will, Rodney, and Dewey Balfa, and many more.

During the time that she and Ken lived in Louisiana, she gave fiddle lessons to Dewey Balfa's daughter Christine, worked with Dewey in the Artists in the Schools program that he had established for Cajun musicians, played Cajun music regularly near Ville Platte in a band with Ken and local musician Maurice Berzas, and supported herself by working in a sewing factory and touring with the Harmony Sisters. During this time Dewey Balfa's brothers Rodney and Will were killed in a car accident. In 1980 she and Ken moved to New Mexico on the advice of Jeanie's doctor, who warned her that her allergies to mold and mildew were life-threatening

Jeanie McLerie and Ken Keppeler performing at Ashkenaz, Berkeley, California, 2006. Photo by the author.

in Louisiana's damp climate. They have lived there ever since, playing under the band name Bayou Seco, drawing on traditions of fiddle music and folk songs of the Southwest in addition to the Cajun music and old-time music they already knew to create their own "Chilegumbo" music.[33]

In the process of recalling their time in Louisiana, Ken Keppeler reflects on a lifetime of revivalist music-making:

> Living in Louisiana allowed us to know the context of the music and to live surrounded by it. We were able to know, even before Cajun music became a big fad, the people who lived their whole lives with Cajun music and culture as the background to all of their experiences, the musicians and dancers who never were well known and who played only at home and/or danced every weekend. None of us can ever know what it is like to be so deeply a part of a culture like that, no matter how often or how long we have played the music.... We modern folk musicians are like voyeurs, looking for a culture to be a part of. But by treating the cultures and the music of those cultures with absolute respect, we can pass on to others some of the depth of our experience and the joy that we have been given by those people. Our romantic visions are often belied by the actual hardships, closed-mindedness, racism, sexism, and other aspects of a long isolated society. We have had the opportunity to go far enough into them as people to see beyond that and to learn to appreciate them as human beings. Being from East LA, I should probably be playing some combination of Chicano, Mexican, and hillbilly music, as that is what I grew up with. But in the end, all the music expresses the same emotions and the same desires, and as musicians we are just looking for pathways for our own emotions and lives, to bring some joy to others and to give them glimpses of their own lives had they been raised in a different human culture. We can help them become themselves, but with different rhythms, languages and dances.[34]

In these comments, Keppeler addresses head-on the question of representation: who are we to be playing Cajun music? There is no one answer to this thorny question, and he does not speak for everyone mentioned in this chapter, but it is a question that revivalists of all musics must address. In the Balkan scene, Laušević found it not uncommon for American musicians who played Balkan music to "give concerts or lecture-demonstrations in schools, often unaware that they are not simply *presenting* their group's repertoire, but *representing* Balkan culture to people who know little, if anything, about it." She found a full range of revivalist responses to this issue, from unconcern to lifetime commitment and courageous performance under hostile circumstances; the same range can be found in the Cajun and zydeco scene. An egalitarian ideal of "everyone can perform" within one social network and the value of self-representation to another social network come into conflict when the two networks have significant interaction, as they have had in northern California. The "absolute respect" to which Keppeler refers mitigates the potential conflict through acts of good faith, including musical practice and performance, carried out over many years in the company of people whose music is being represented.[35]

CHAPTER SEVEN

Folk Revival Connection

The Dancers

While revivalist musicians and revivalist dancers came at different times and by different routes, both groups had accumulated strong cadres in northern California with well-developed social networks before the enthusiasms of a few of them turned to Louisiana French music. Just as the folk musicians who got interested in Cajun and Creole music early would go on to contribute musically to bands that play for dances, international folk dancing provided a pool of people who were curious about other cultures and welcomed the challenge of learning new dance steps and styles. A handful of these dancers became interested, then pulled in their other folk dancer friends. From club owner David Nadel's perspective, "Back in the Queen Ida days people didn't know how to do two-steps, waltzes, and shuffles. They did the old Berkeley jiggle-around step. Once dance teachers began to give lessons to the locals, Cajun-zydeco music found its sustaining power."[1]

Folk Dancing across the Nation and in California

Urban social reform movements within the United States that began in the nineteenth century led to, among other things, settlement houses and organized programs of recreation for urban workers. Urban church leaders and settlement workers saw dance halls—where young couples danced waltzes, two-steps, rag, and jazz steps unsupervised and switched partners often—as immoral and hoped to lure immigrants and their offspring away from them with folk dancing. Settlement houses offered a model of "mental integrity" for urban workers that included recreation and cultural activities such as ethnic music and dance. Educators used folk music as an Americanization tool with immigrant children by having them sing English words to "their" melodies and by having immigrants perform dances not only of their own culture but of their fellow immigrants from other lands, thereby promoting mutual respect among the various groups. Beginning in the early twentieth century, a sanitized version of folk music and dancing found its way into institutionalized physical and music education for public schools. Of Henry Ford, Robert Cantwell writes that out of "class anxiety and ethnocentrism" he "sought ... to museumize the preindustrial artisan economy that his own enterprise had done so much to abolish, even to the extent of installing it among his own workers with instruction in square dancing and vegetable gardening."[2]

International folk dancing came out of the dances prepared in the settlement houses and physical education programs, retaining dances from a wide variety of cultures while downplaying the values of moral and physical discipline in favor of fun and recreation. This form of folk dancing, a leisure activity for adults both foreign- and native-born, first took institutional form in the 1930s on college campuses and in projects of the federal Works Progress Administration. Dancing to piano accompaniment gave way to music provided by recordings, especially once recordings made especially for folk dancing were made in the 1940s. Song Chang formed a folk dance club in San Francisco in 1937, which received much public attention two years later when it performed at the San Francisco World's Fair on Treasure Island. Very soon thereafter, the membership of Chang's group swelled, other groups formed, and folk dancing was a popular activity in the Bay Area, with classes available every night of the week. The Folk Dance Federation of California, formed in the Bay Area in 1942, became important to folk dancers across the state and across the country for developing a notation system for dances, publishing numerous folk dance books, and generally standardizing an international folk dance repertoire for Americans. In addition to its popularity as a participatory activity, performance troupes of folk dancers such as Changs International Folk Dancers continued to prepare and give choreographed presentations of folk dance on stage.[3]

While international folk dancing was still in the process of becoming institutionalized, another trend developed which threatened its "forty dances, forty countries" model by focusing on the music and dance of a single region. Just as Shane Bernard describes a "Cajun craze" that appeared in the 1980s, Laušević writes of a "Balkan craze" that swept through the international folk dance scene in the 1950s. Also known as "kolomania" after the kolo, a line dance where a dancer holds hands with dancers on either side and dances in a procession that circles or snakes around the dance floor in step with the music, the Balkan craze was experienced across the country but with special intensity in California, where early kolo exhibitions and instruction were offered by U.S. Marines stationed in San Francisco during World War II. Evenings and weekends dedicated to kolo sprang up alongside international folk dancing events, with many dancers attending both types. Unlike their international folk dance counterparts, some kolo teachers did their own ethnographic research in the Balkans and brought back more dances to teach. This was approximately the state of affairs in '60s- and '70s-era folk dancing when some new folk dance troupes and coffeehouses came into being in the San Francisco Bay Area.[4]

The Westwind International Folk Ensemble, which began as a choral group and soon added a dance component, formed at the University of California, Los Angeles around 1960. Neal Sandler, one of the group's directors, moved to the Bay Area in 1966 and organized a similar group using the same name. A few years later Sandler started his own folk dance coffeehouse in San Francisco, the Mandala. One of the dancers in Sandler's Bay Area Westwind troupe was a U.C. Berkeley student and political activist from Los Angeles named David Nadel. Nadel also danced at the Aïtos Greek Taverna on San Pablo Avenue in Berkeley but wanted something more. He organized a collective to purchase a building up the street from Aïtos and started the Ashkenaz Music and Dance Café in 1973. For two decades after most folk dance coffeehouses had closed their doors, Nadel kept up his unique mix of radical leftist politics and a multicultural dance floor dedicated to peace and joy, thanks in large part to his work ethic that helped keep expenses down and his willingness to expand his programming beyond Balkan and international folk dancing. Cajun and zydeco dancing became an important ingredient in Nadel's transformation of Ashkenaz from a folk dance coffeehouse to a world music dance club.[5]

Gary and Maryanne Canaparo[6]

Gary and Maryanne Canaparo were a young married couple living in Livermore, California, in the mid-1970s when they first heard of Queen Ida and zydeco music. Maryanne was born in San Francisco and raised in Oakland; Gary was born and raised in Oakland. They have lived in California all of their lives except for a few years when Gary taught at Florida State University. Of music and dance during their formative years, they remember:

> Maryanne: I always loved to dance, in junior high and high school I went to all the school dances. I watched *Dance Party* faithfully! I played the violin for nine years and was in an orchestra (not fun music).
>
> Gary: I was not much into dancing as a kid but into radio and records. In grammar school I got busted for sneaking away from schoolyard during lunch to go to Red's Record Shop on Grove Street in Oakland. I remember it was a small one-

counter shop with a phonograph on the counter. I would bring my lunch and Red (I guess) and I would listen to her new records. I still have a Hank Ballard and the Midnighters record on the Federal label I got there.[7]

Queen Ida was the first Louisiana French music that either Gary or Maryanne ever heard. A friend, Will Gorman, saw Ida play at a club in Oakland and told them about her. The first time they saw Queen Ida play live she left an indelible impression in Gary's mind, as did Clifton Chenier later when Gary saw him play in California.

The first place we saw Ida was the West Dakota, an old night club on San Pablo [Avenue].... I remember the part that blew my mind was Queen Ida in a white dress and a little red accordion cranking out this music that I'd never heard come out of an accordion before. And then when you saw Clif... These guys all had these things they did. Clif came out with a suit and tie, and then he would turn the tie around behind so it wouldn't get in the way of his accordion. I mean, just crazy stuff like that, that's what legends are made out of.

Maryanne relates how their involvement with the Creole immigrants and their music started:

We started with the Louisiana Playboys, actually we started listening to Queen Ida. And then my sister wanted to get married at the Brazil Room at Tilden [Park], and she wanted to have Queen Ida. And she already was pretty expensive, so Chris Strachwitz told her to call the Louisiana Playboys, which at that time was George Broussard, Charlie St. Mary, Junior Felton, and Danny Poullard ... and Ben Guillory on violin. So she called them, they came and played, and Gary went with them after to Brennan's bar down in Berkeley, and they started up a conversation and we became family. We were included in weddings and birthday parties and barbecues.

After Gary befriended the musicians at the wedding, it was not long before George Broussard found out that he played the harmonica. While he was spending time with these musicians, he used the opportunity to take black and white photographs of them and their milieu, several of which are included in this book. At the time (circa 1977) Gary was working independently as a graphic designer, photographer, and teaching part-time when he could. Maryanne was working for the East Bay Regional Parks.

Author: So you mentioned something about, you played in John Semien's band?
Gary: Just to be able to go along and take pictures. George used to make you play.

Maryanne: Well, he would have a little blues section for Junior.

Author: Right, so he could wail on his blues guitar.

Maryanne: So Gary got pulled in on the blues part with the harmonica, because he doesn't play other instruments.

Gary: ... but it was a great way to get in there and just kind of hang around all the time.... What happened with John Semien, after Ben Guillory died [in 1978] they put together this kind of haphazard band and Danny would play bass. He didn't play any accordion at all and Junior would play blues. So John would play Cajun and zydeco. And then he started playing boogie woogie, one of his favorite things was to play boogie woogie on the accordion, not the piano accordion but the little one. And then he'd play "Me and Bobby McGee" and start doing things like that. And then Junior would do an intermission and that's when they'd throw me in there. But we were part of things anyway. George would do that. George pulled a lot of different people in. He wouldn't just keep it Creole, he would include anybody in the neighborhood at his get-togethers.

In their casual conversations with Gary and Maryanne, George Broussard and Danny Poullard would tell stories about what it was like growing up in segregated Louisiana. Humorous banter was a way they used to keep these serious subjects within view. "Danny would make fun of white people, we would make fun of Danny. Just low key, because we both had this inside view of what each other had to deal with," says Gary in describing the nature of their friendship. Danny might make a racially tinged joke when Gary and Maryanne would show up as the only non-Creoles at a church dance, and Gary in turn might kid Danny about the French beret he often wore when performing.

Gary experienced those early years of following the Louisiana French dance scene in the Bay Area, when they were following John Semien's band and the Louisiana Playboys, as the witnessing of a new cultural creation by his Creole friends. According to him, the emphasis on "codifying" and on heritage preservation mostly came later, even as these bands were already playing for functions outside the Creole community. One comment in particular from frottoirist Charlie St. Mary prior to a performance has lingered with him, as has the dance style of his family.

Gary: ... during those days we played, like, the psychiatrist's wedding ... different people were hearing it and we had a couple of friends who could get to people who would be interested in this music. So we got to play some places that were private parties but were just great to go with these guys. And you'd get to hang out and you'd hear what they were all about. And here they're going in to places, I don't think they had an idea what was going on. Neither group knew about the other

Charlie St. Mary at Canaparo residence, Sunol, California, circa 1979–80. Photo by Gary Canaparo.

group very well. And Charlie would always say, "tonight we're gonna do something we ain't never done before." And I think that really explains where they were at, I mean they were going to push the envelope. We're not just going to repeat what we did last time, we're going to cover some new territory. And I think that really explains, like Clifton and a lot of these guys, what they would do when they got out there and played together. Because all of it was basically blues. They were playing these old kind of traditional things, but one guy would do something a little bit different or they'd connect with the rubbing board player or something. So that would encourage people on the dance floor. Robbie [Robertson]'s a great guy for that, to start improvising. It's only been recently that you have these set steps. Because I remember the St. Marys...

Maryanne: We used to call them the peacocks.

Gary: They were like roosters, you know, and they had their own step. And according to George and Charlie, that was pretty true that the different families danced a certain way. They had kind of a unique characteristic to their families. It's been recently when "this is how you do this" and line dancing and stuff like that evolved. But these guys were just characters, so the people on the dance floor were doing the same thing the musicians were doing. They were all sort of pushing the envelope.

Maryanne: And the St. Marys were the ones who would always do that big slap with the...

Gary: Oh yeah, they started that one, at least they started it around here.

Author: The stomping. I associate that with Junior [St. Mary] for sure. With those red boots.
Maryanne: Exactly.
Gary: So that's really what made it fun to go out with these guys. Because there was that element that when, if you were close enough to the bandstand, you could tell when we were going into uncharted territory.

In following the musicians to their performances, the Canaparos would often find themselves at dances in church parish halls attended largely by Creole community members. There would usually be at least one or two dances to attend each month. The three locations they visited most frequently were St. Mark's in Richmond, St. Francis of Assisi in East Palo Alto, and All Hallows in San Francisco. In addition to John Semien or the Louisiana Playboys, they would see Queen Ida when she wasn't touring, or Clifton Chenier on his occasional visits, and after Chenier's health deteriorated John Delafose would be brought out from Louisiana to play. They learned how to dance by observing and dancing with their new friends. Maryanne found Ullus Gobart particularly helpful in this regard. "[T]his was before guys would come with their shirts and change shirts because of the sweat. He would just be a wet rag. You could wring out Ullus! [laughs] He'd sweat so much. But he actually is the one who taught me how to dance, and he was a fantastic dancer. He didn't explain anything, except one thing. He would say, just follow my shoulder, if you could just go with my shoulder, you'll be able to follow me. And I was able to do that, and from then on I was able to dance with almost anyone."

Gary and Maryanne found the house parties given by Louisiana French people to be as enjoyable and culturally educational as the church dances.

Maryanne: The Louisiana Playboys, they would practice in George's basement, rumpus room type thing. They'd have house parties all the time. And most of it was not practiced, it was just they got together and jammed.
Gary: The introduction for us for this music with these guys was that if you were going to get together, you were going to barbecue and then there would always be some music. And one wasn't more important than the other. It was just, that's how it went. . . . In George's basement, Queen Ida would play a couple of numbers, and Danny would play a number, and somebody else would play. And nobody sustained all night in those early days. Maybe Ida could have. . . . And it was pretty typical of a party where everybody would play.

In 1979 the Canaparos bought their own home in Sunol, a rural location in Alameda County south of Oakland. Very soon thereafter they started having house parties of their own, and found their Creole friends and acquaintances were glad to attend. Their own children were ages twelve and fifteen at the time, and guests would bring children as well.

> Gary: To them, it was like a piece of Louisiana, just out in the country [with] kids, barbecue, and just drive in with your car and get out.
> Maryanne: It was pot luck pretty much, we usually supplied mainly the meat and then people would bring side dishes.
> Gary: What they would do, they'd call up and say what are you doing? And we'd say, well nothing, come on over. So you'd stay on the phone and get as many people out here as you can. Sometimes you had ten people, sometimes you didn't have anybody, and it really didn't matter.

The couple had larger parties at their place once or twice a year that they planned in advance, where they would have musicians playing Louisiana French dance music in their backyard in an area they called "the beer garden." They might invite local musicians to play, or Charlie St. Mary might arrange to bring a friend from Lake Charles, Louisiana, accordionist Louis Semien, to visit and play for their party. Gary recalls how Charlie was a strong supporter of their efforts: "The parties would start typically about one o'clock, two o'clock starting to light the barbecue. They didn't eat until three. Charlie would be here at eleven. You'd just hope he could make it until one o'clock to light the fire, because he was partying. And he could do it, he had the bulk and he could drink like that. I really couldn't."

They weren't sure at first what their new neighbors would think of these outdoor parties.

> Maryanne: We'd obviously invite the neighbors, in that canyon.
> Gary: We never had anybody fight.
> Maryanne: But people would say, that know us now that didn't know us then, they'll say, "We would have done anything to be invited to your party. We would just drive by." Because they were fun, they were really a lot of fun.
> Gary: The other thing, Sunol was like Livermore, a little rednecky.
> Maryanne: Either real hippie or rednecky, [very little] in between.
> Gary: We moved in and we got along with both of them. But there were no blacks among them. All of a sudden, one day, or a couple of days a year there was a mixed crowd here. A real diverse group, the only blacks that area had ever saw. And there was never a problem with it. But the first couple of times, especially when we were new, we weren't quite sure what the deal was with that. And that was part of what we used to laugh about too, Danny and Charlie would sit out there and wave! [laughing] And if that car stops, run in the house!

The Canaparos' large parties became increasingly popular. The couple continued to host house parties through the 1980s and into the 1990s but eventually, Maryanne remembers, "it got spread out to all these people that just heard about it that we really didn't know. And it got so that it was a whole different feel." By the early 1990s, some of the close friends they had made in the Creole community were no longer able to attend due to either their own health problems or those of their parents. The parties were getting quite large, requiring them to rent portable toilet facilities. At their last house party in the mid-1990s, they estimate they had some three hundred guests, but they had had enough: these events at their house had become unmanageable, and not enough of their old friends were there anymore.

Maryanne's supervisor where she worked at the East Bay Regional Park District had attended some of the parties at her house. It so happened that around the time these parties were coming to a stop, her supervisor had the idea that she should organize a festival with a Cajun theme. Maryanne was working at Ardenwood Regional Park as their revenue operations manager. Her responsibilities included concession agreements, communications sites, special uses, park residences, and building rentals. Maryanne explains the genesis of the festival: "What happened was, Ardenwood Farm is such a money sink for the Park District. It's a farm that's set in the 1890s and it's basically for kids to learn the history part, a working museum. So the main focus is children's programming during the week, but on the weekends, it's as dead as a doornail. So they did a business plan nine years ago and they said, what can we do to bring in more people to see what's here? And so they decided to start doing special events, on a weekend." During a brainstorming session, her boss remembered the Canaparos' parties he had attended. "And so, how about a Cajun festival, Maryanne? Because they knew I had connections. Well, I said I'd love to do that, you know, because I know the people. And there was a Celtic festival we did, and we're doing Civil War days. But this was put on as one of the events that was going to happen, and so I just started doing it. The first one I did was all local bands, and then the second one, I started bringing Steve Riley and I brought in Boozoo [Chavis], and it started to get bigger."

The park provides a setting for the festival that reinforces nostalgia for simple rural living. Visitors drive a curving road through fields where nineteenth century farm equipment is being used to cultivate the land. Cars park on a grassy field near a gate where entrance fees are paid. From there, one can walk a quarter mile on a paved path to the festival area or take a steam train with open-air passenger cars, whose track runs right behind the stage area. Those who choose to walk can visit a restored farmhouse/museum along the way. Reaching the festival area, pedestrians encounter the food area first, where in early years Bobby Gradney (see ch. 8) had a

Louisiana Playboys performing at St. Francis of Assisi church, East Palo Alto, California, circa 1977–78. Photo by Gary Canaparo.

booth. Some booths feature food inspired by Louisiana cuisine, others do not. A local nonprofit club, the California Friends of Louisiana French Music, staffed a tent in past years that included educational displays about Cajun and Creole culture and items for sale to raise funds for the club. Nearer the stage, Gary Canaparo has a small photo gallery tent featuring his black and white photographs of Creole musicians in California from years gone by. The festival area is an open grassy field with very few trees; the only relief from the September sun is the tent covering the portable wooden dance floor and bandstand. Festivalgoers bring their own lawn chairs and blankets and sit in the sun on the grass adjacent to the dance floor.

The park district does not provide subsidies for musicians' travel or other expenses; the festival is expected to pay for itself. Maryanne has found that a one-day format works best, with attendance hovering around the 2,500 mark. "I'd like to get about three thousand, but I really don't like a whole lot more than that because what makes this one kind of neat is that it is small, and it does have a feel.... The first festival I did, it was [musician] Sam Siggins who got on the mic and said, 'This is just like a big one of Maryanne's parties!'" In recent years, she has tried to feature two generations of musicians from the same family: Chris and Black Ardoin; Keith and Preston Frank; "T" Broussard and his mother, Mary Jane; Tommy Michot and sons Louis and Andre; Nathan Williams and Nathan, Jr.

Paul Strogen[8]

Paul Strogen is from Batavia, New York, a town between Buffalo and Rochester in the Snow Belt. Growing up in the 1940s, he listened to the radio every night coming home from school, serial dramas like *Tom Mix* and *The Lone Ranger* that used classical music for musical themes. The Eastman School of Music was thirty miles away from his hometown, and they also broadcast on local radio. He started square dancing in high school, in physical education class. Now he does such things for pure enjoyment, but back then "it was a good way to meet girls." He would go to a town named Leroy on Saturday nights to a square dance at a school. The adult dances were at American Legion halls, VFW halls, and the like for weddings and other functions. He was introduced to a variety of ethnic music in this manner, especially Polish and Italian, which were the predominant ethnicities in the local population. He attended more Polish weddings than Italian ones; the Polish danced mostly polkas and waltzes, whereas the Italians did waltzes and tarantellas. He worked for an Italian American proprietor in a shoe repair store when he was in high school where some of the patrons would speak Italian. His own family was Slovak on his father's side, Dutch and English on his mother's.

Paul's early experiences with musical participation included some brief attempts at clarinet and piano. He took up the drums with a drum and bugle corps when he was around fourteen years old and did this for four or five years. Growing up he thought he would end up living in New York City, but after high school he went into the navy to get out on his own. He stayed in military service for eight and a half years, four of those years stationed in the San Francisco Bay Area, at Treasure Island, the site of the 1939 World's Fair that was converted thereafter to a Navy base. In San Francisco circa 1960, Coit Tower still dominated the skyline, and the romance of Herb Caen's writing about the city captured his imagination. Paul was "a party animal" who reveled in his new environment. He didn't do any dancing during his navy years except at parties. In 1965 he went back east to teach in some factory schools, then served in Viet Nam. While aboard ship, he listened to music on his record player in the radar room, something he said kept him "sane" and "connected."

Paul got out of the navy in December 1967 and started his first civilian job the next month, working in what is now called Silicon Valley. A year or two later, he started dancing in "a concerted, focused way." A friend of his from the navy had discovered the eastern European dance scene in the East Bay at Aïtos, a Greek taverna in Berkeley, and at International House on the U.C. Berkeley campus.

> I think the first night I got over here they were doing Turkish and Armenian at Aïtos, and there was a guy here from Turkey by the name of Bora Özkök. As I recall

he was an Olympic-class swimmer, going to the University here and teaching his native folk dances. And he was a really macho guy, big, muscular swimmer. And those Turkish dances can be really, really something. The music itself is really great, but you get a line of people with their hands intertwined, gripped together like that and rocking back and forth in unison. You're connected and it's a feeling that you have to really experience to feel the power of it, you know? A whole line of people moving together, just feeling this great, great motion and movement.

Paul also found Balkan music and dance to be "quite a challenge and very fulfilling." He enjoyed both the music and the people. They danced mostly to recordings back then, but occasionally they would get a live band as during the annual Kolo festival around Thanksgiving, when there would be three days of nonstop dancing from all different regions, mostly Eastern Europe.

The Balkan rhythms really caught me. You know, the Bulgarian nine sixteenths, thirteen sixteenths, seven sixteenths. And being a percussionist, well, this is really cool. And you can move your feet to it, too, and the dances themselves were challenging. Back in the early seventies, the teachers that were bringing dances back from Eastern Europe were choreographing them to make them interesting to folks back here. And they wouldn't be the same dance that was danced in the village there, they were more the choreographer's and it was for stage and performance, to give it a little more flash.

Soon he found other places to go folk dancing. Neil Sandler ran the Mandala in San Francisco, on 16th and Taraval. At Aïtos, the Sofios brothers reserved Friday and Saturday nights for Greek dancing; three other nights a week they would have Balkan dance or some other theme that fell under the rubric of international folk dancing at that time. "So that was one of the reasons David Nadel decided to open a place where we could dance Friday and Saturday nights. And he started Ashkenaz [in 1973]. It started as a co-op, originally. I remember there were little pottery things in the corners and all around. We had a really tiny little dance floor and all these little booths around or stalls where the people who belonged to the co-op did their arts and crafts." After a few years, Nadel bought out his partners in the cooperative and cleared out the arts and crafts booths to make way for a larger dance floor.

Paul continued to dance at all of these venues through the 1970s. He had his first experience as a dance performer with a small group from the Mandala that demonstrated Balkan dancing in nursing homes. After a divorce in 1982, he "branched out into some other kinds of dancing" and joined a Hungarian dance troupe. He discovered the Cajun and zydeco scene around 1984. His girlfriend had a friend whose husband worked with Danny Poullard at the Presidio.

> We got some of our folk dance friends together one night and we went down to East Palo Alto, to the church dance down there. And gosh we walked in there and we weren't sure that we were in the right place. We were the only whites there. There might have been another white couple there, that were familiar with the area and the scene. [Our friends] Steve and Nancy introduced us to Danny. So from there, we caught on. The music was great. We sat and watched a little bit to see what this was about, what they did. The waltzes were pretty easy to pick up, the two-steps didn't take too long. This one old fellow that was really great, his name was Earl Lundwall, and he was a folk dancer also. We all danced over at the Mandala and different places. But Earl had to have been [in his] late sixties, maybe seventies, and he loved to dance. So he would go out after we discovered this Cajun-zydeco scene, he'd go out and start rounding up all these gals he could, say "hey come out, you gotta come Cajun dancing." So he started gathering people from the folk dance community and getting them involved in this. So gradually we started to grow in terms of having more and more of the folk dancers and white dancers present in all the different dance scenes around.

As far as Paul remembers, this was the first time that folk dance regulars such as himself had been to dance at the St. Francis of Assisi parish in East Palo Alto, where they would return many times in the years to come, as well as to St. Mark's in Richmond and All Hallows in San Francisco.

The arrival of the folk dancers at the Creole church hall dances required an initial adjustment period for both groups. For the Creoles, the challenge was how to respond to the presence of these outsiders at their event; by all accounts the path they chose was gracious and unhesitating hospitality. For the folk dancers intent on learning the dance movements, there were other lessons to be learned about social comportment at a dance different from that to which they were accustomed. For example, the folk dancers would take to the dance floor as soon as they heard the music start, only then to notice that they were alone out there. Paul later discussed this with his friend Ron Rumney and relates:

> As I was talking to Ron, he was saying that there was sort of a little protocol there. The reason that they didn't kind of accept us right at first was we didn't conform to their protocol. Nobody got up and danced the first dance, and very few got up and danced the second dance. But usually by the third dance there was a guy by the name of Benny. Thin, wiry, he could have been ninety years old. I mean, he looked that old,

> but he was just a great dancer. He'd get out there, and there was another guy that I really tried to emulate, [who] since passed on. He waltzed so smoothly, just glided around the floor. And I just loved to sit back and watch him and say, I've got to perfect that waltz. That's just so cool....
>
> One of the things I noted initially was there were a lot more people sitting there chatting than were out dancing. You know, it's a social thing, which I now understand more. When I dance I tend to dance for me and for what it gives me, it keeps me alive and it feeds my soul. But I also now realize more that the connection to the people and the socializing is vitally important also.

He remembers that his friends Ron and Earl "were especially great mixers" at these dances and would sit down and talk to people. He also remembers that the adjustment period did not last long; within a year or so he and his girlfriend Stefanie entered a zydeco dance contest at one of the church dances and won it, much to their surprise.

By the early 1990s, Paul was devoting much time to Cajun and zydeco dancing as the number of events outside the Creole community grew—events such as Franklin Zawacki's Cajun festivals in northern and southern California. He made his first and only trip to Louisiana during this period, to attend Festivals Acadiens. There were frequent house parties to attend, some at the homes of Louisiana French people and some at the homes of others who, like Paul, had begun spending a lot of time following the music. He says, "The community was Creoles and the whites all mixed together and there wasn't a lot of separation as I recall. You know, we'd all go to the dances no matter where they were. Yeah, it was just a really good feeling." Eventually, he perceived a decline in the *gemütlichkeit* at Cajun and zydeco dances while his diverse interests in other styles of dancing were pulling him away.

> Paul: We've got all of these musicians in this area, so I look at that now and say, gosh, I don't think I could live anywhere else. Even in all my travels, I go places where they only have one dance a week. I sometimes go to two or three dances a night. Or go to something in the afternoon and hit two more dances in the evening. It's just great to have those choices. I feel very fortunate to be able to live here and experience this kind of thing. And it does distress me when I see stuff fall apart, splinter. Because I saw what happened to the Balkan scene.
>
> Author: I was going to say, doesn't that happen in other dance scenes too?
>
> Paul: Yeah, I guess it does. And it happens to dancers, too, I noticed. And it's happened to me a couple of times, and lots of all my other friends where they just, all

of a sudden they just go away. There's a point too, where you can burn yourself out on any one particular thing and you need the break.

He started spending more time with Cape Breton step dancing and traveled to Cape Breton three summers in a row to hear the music and to dance. He also became involved as a dancer in a demonstration troupe called the Jubilee American Dance Theater that performs a variety of folk dances, including Cajun dance. At the time of our interview (2000), Paul was spending relatively little time on Cajun and zydeco dancing, but he was still enjoying it and could reel off the names of several of his favorite bands or musicians, including Danny Poullard, Marc and Ann Savoy, and local favorites Gator Beat and fiddler Tom Rigney. Unlike the majority of the dancers in the Bay Area, Paul prefers Cajun music to zydeco, although he appreciates both. "I prefer Cajun music to zydeco, when I've got to make a choice there, but I can get really down and dirty zydeco, too. Just a different sense and feel to me. It's more of a really heavy pounding down, really powerful kind of dancing when I do zydeco. Whereas I might use the same footwork for Cajun but I'm up, lighter, more an 'up' feeling. Zydeco is more driving, it's just a continuous, repetitious kind of thing, too." When prompted to draw a connection between his small town upbringing and his current life, he is reluctant to do so.

> Paul: I don't generally think much about western New York anymore. I mean, I consider [the Bay Area] my home, you know I've been here more than I've been anywhere else. Although I'm thankful for having grown up there and what it did impart to me: growing up in a small town, for one, living on the edge of town with nothing but farm fields out there to go play in. You know, it was a great place to be as a kid, but not a place to be as an adult. Not much there.
> Author: Was that your model for a community, in any sense?
> Paul: Ah [dubious inflection, followed by a pause]. It probably was, yeah I think maybe around the Polish and the Italian community events and things like that. It's around music, it's around dance, it's around celebration. . . .
> I guess coming from a small town, I didn't think much about community then. I don't have any connection to my family back there anymore. My mother's side of the family, she was the youngest of eleven kids and the only girl, so I had like ten uncles. Most of them were in that town. And on my street where we lived in this little town of seventeen thousand, there were two uncles, one across the street and one two doors down, and they had five or six kids apiece. So I was constantly surrounded by all these relatives. And you couldn't get away with anything, they're going to tell your mother, right? [laughs] So when I got out of there I just left it all behind.

He is clear in his preference for the urban area where he can choose his own community rather than live in a community that is all-encompassing.

> I don't make a distinction or go looking for, are you a Cajun, or are you a Creole, or are you a Bulgarian, are you a this, are you a that, it doesn't matter to me. We're all enjoying and taking part in this community. That's probably one of the higher things on my list of priorities in terms of what it means to me, the dance and the music, is the community aspect of things. It keeps me alive, it keeps me sane, and it's a great place to get exercise and all these things that are beneficial. The people are supportive if you need support. It's just a great way to be in a large city that's not your home from the beginning. You find you make your own home place and this place [Ashkenaz] has been kind of a little bit of a home. I've spent I don't know how many years [laughs] of evenings here dancing. There's a ripple in the dance floor out here just where you come onto the floor from the left side of the stage there. And I think that's because that's where I dance, that's pretty much my corner when I'm here for a dance.

Ron Rumney[9]

Ron Rumney was born in San Diego in 1939; his father was also a California native, while his mother came from the state of Washington. Growing up, he was more interested in sports than in music or dance, although as a teenager in the 1950s he did enjoy rock and roll music. In high school, he played on the varsity basketball team and was not allowed to go to school dances because of a team curfew, but as dancing held no attraction for him, this was not a disappointment. He had a thirty-year career in secondary education teaching mathematics and biology. At the time of our interview in 2000, he was already retired.

Ron's interest in dancing appeared approximately halfway through his teaching career. "At age 40 I had a life change and started Greek dancing. And I met a Greek woman" named Anna Sofia, who taught classes in Greek dancing. He started folk dancing regularly at the Mandala in San Francisco, where there were Greek dance nights. He also frequented Ashkenaz during this period, when its programming still concentrated on various sorts of international folk dancing. It was in this context that in the early 1980s he first saw Louisiana French music and dance in person, at Ashkenaz. He remembers that Danny Poullard was playing that night, probably with the Louisiana Playboys, and that the folk dance regulars at that time were at a loss for how to dance to this music. Most were not even dancing in couples. "Most people didn't know what to do. So if they were a folk dancer, they would hambo, or when the waltzes came on they waltzed, you know, like a Viennese waltz. But there were some Cajuns there like Ullus [Gobart], and of course everybody stood around and watched him. It was amazing to watch him. And I think there were a couple of other Cajuns there who knew what they were doing. But most people were just kind of bumping and doing what we used to call the Berkeley jump-around [laughs]."[10]

After this first exposure to Cajun music at Ashkenaz, Ron started frequenting church benefit dances at St. Francis of Assisi in East Palo Alto with his friends Stephanie Arthur and Earl Lundwall. The Louisiana Playboys, Danny Poullard's group, were the usual band; on one occasion Myrick "Freeze" Guillory, Queen Ida's son, played instead. The admission charge would be around eight dollars; those involved with organizing the dance would also make and sell food dishes such as gumbo, red beans and rice, and boudin for approximately four dollars per serving, "home-cooked meals" that the parishioners would prepare or warm up in the parish hall kitchen. Alcoholic beverages were consumed. The men would wear suit and tie, the women party dresses. This manner of dress was more formal than was customary for the folk dancers, but they adapted. Ron remembers long rows of tables where people sat and visited, where he and his friends were also invited to sit, "and they accepted us right in. Personally for me at that time it was really wonderful because it was nice to be with people who wanted to talk to you and spend a few minutes with you and not rush off and do something. So it feels great." He wrote about his memories of these dances in the newsletter of the California Friends of Louisiana French Dance Music:

> It was just great. It was a family feeling, and people were there to meet their friends, eat/drink, and dance. I've never had more fun dancing. Most of the people were originally from Louisiana, and were great dancers, i.e., very little bumping into other dancers. I was really new to this kind of music, however many church dances later, I remember Benny saying, "Hey, Ron, you've got it." It was great, the zydeco style of always holding on to your partner with two hands. I call it the Clifton/John Delafose/Boozoo Chavis Era.[11]

From the beginning, he danced with both his folk dancing friends and with the church dance regulars. He and his friends learned the dance without a teacher, by observing and doing it. "I just asked somebody to dance, but I didn't really know what I was doing very well.... I was a pretty fast learner, and I really wanted to, and I had pretty good rhythm because I had danced for years and years, and I was an athlete before that. So I had always worked with my body. It just took me maybe four or five dances down there.... After a couple of months I became pretty good and then people would kind of look forward to dancing with me and then it was great." Returning to his home in San Francisco after these dances, Ron found that he could not go to sleep right away.

> I used to come home from those dances, take all my clothes off outside, leave my clothes outside all night, and go take a shower and wash my hair. Otherwise, ooh, your bed just stunk from this cigarette smoke. So I can imagine what my poor lungs were going through, you know? [laughs] ... The dances went longer then, they seemed to go until at least 1:30, and by the time we said good-bye to everybody, well that was two o'clock. An hour back, so you didn't get home until two-thirty, three o'clock. And you've got to go get your shower, and I was usually so hyper, all that music going through my brain that I'd sit down and read a book for another half-hour, and it was four o'clock before I got to bed.

Thus Cajun dancing became a new favorite of Ron's at a time when he was going out to dance many times each week to the various kinds of international folk dances prevalent at the time, including Greek, Balkan, and Israeli.

> One reason I don't really like Israeli dancing is they always have all this new stuff. It's like every week they've got a new dance coming out of there, and I don't like to go to learn all these different kinds of dances. Maybe that's why I love Cajun so much, because there's only two dances, two steps to it, but you could do it in your own style. But the Israeli music, every week they had eight different positions that you had to learn, and I don't care for that. It's not that it's complicated. What I love about dancing is that I can just get away from it all. And you're moving to this wonderful sound with a partner. I just love that, it's like you go into your other body, your other self. And if you're trying to learn something, you're not there, you're in the now and in the conscious and trying to learn something where once you learn it, then it's all unconscious. Dancing's all unconscious. I don't even have to think about it anymore if I don't want to, I just go do it.

He also found that he preferred the partner orientation in Cajun music, whereby one normally dances with a single partner for an entire song or two, in contrast to the group line dancing he did on Greek or Balkan nights and to the partner dances such as squares or contra where one switches partners several times within a single number. "That's probably another thing I really like about Cajun, is you go up and ask somebody to dance, and then you're dancing with *them*. It's not like, 'come and join our group.' I think it's a little more personable."

After the initial expedition to East Palo Alto by Ron, Stephanie, and Earl, the group of folk dancers that came expanded to four or five women and two or three men, including Paul Strogen. Growth in outsider interest did not stop there, however, as Earl continued to invite more people and Ron became concerned. "Earl would keep asking all these people to come down there. One thing I kept telling [him], 'Earl you gotta stop so many...' 'Ron, they're such wonderful people.' And I'd say, 'Well, it's going to change.' And it did."

Ron felt that the influx of outsiders eventually had a negative impact on the social atmosphere at these church dances. As the church dances became more popular with outsiders, however, the opportunities to dance to Cajun music and zydeco at other Bay Area venues multiplied. As he had watched Ullus Gobart dance that first night at Ashkenaz, now other dancers were watching him. "And then it seems like it started in the Bay Area again up in Ashkenaz. But then when we came up there, we were the old pros and everybody was standing around watching *us* trying to figure out what we were doing. So there must have been quite a time span between when I started going down to East Palo Alto and when Ashkenaz started having more [Cajun] dances. I would guess two or three or four years, maybe." Finding himself in this situation, he sought to emulate the social comportment of the man whose dancing he had first admired, Ullus Gobart. "He just flowed along, and he was having such a great time. There were a couple of things I really liked about him. He didn't want anybody to sit at any special table, he wanted to be with everybody. New people would come up, he'd show them how to dance. He'd always try to help a beginner. And that is what I still try to do."

As other kinds of folk dancing waned in popularity and the frequency of Cajun and zydeco dances increased, Ron found that Louisiana French dancing had become his favorite. He started traveling to Louisiana for Cajun and zydeco music festivals.

> Normally I would go with my friends, and we would just zoom everywhere, you've got to get to twenty things a day. And I realized, I don't like doing that. I'd rather go down and have a good breakfast and go visit something and go to a dance at night. Not go to twenty dances in one day. You were totally exhausted. But it was fun, because I was with all my friends, the first couple of times. Maybe six of us might share a car. Every night usually you'd go for dinner to a Cajun club, at Mulate's or Randol's, something like that. You'd have dinner, and then you'd dance. And the dances were usually over at eleven, eleven-thirty. And then we'd all get out and go to one of the black clubs. They wouldn't *start* until eleven or twelve. And we'd stay there until two or three or whatever it was in the morning....

So the last time, going into those clubs, I didn't feel all that comfortable, like I saw everything getting destroyed and I didn't want to be a part of it. So I thought, well I'm not going to go down anymore at festival time, I'm just going to go down during a regular time.

His ambivalence about cultural tourism has not been limited to his travels in Louisiana. The way he wrestles in the following conversation with the linguistic similarities between the words *diverseness* and *divisiveness* illustrates the conundrum well.

> Author: Earlier, when I was asking you about the different kinds of folk dancing you've done and what you liked about them, you talked a lot about the music. So that's one kind of answer. Other people sometimes answer about the culture, that there's really something about the culture they like, and the music happens to be part of that. So is there, do you have any feelings about the culture in general?
>
> Ron: Well sometimes, for me, it gets in the way a bit. Like when I go with Anna, she's the star of the Greek community, everybody knows Anna. And so when I'd go with Anna, I always felt like I could go there, but I knew if Anna wasn't there I wouldn't be welcome for ten minutes, because I wasn't a Greek, and the Greeks are very closed in. It was interesting to hear them talk and hear what they think and listen to this great music, but it was almost like a hindrance, in a way. If it weren't for Anna, I wouldn't be involved in it.
>
> Author: What about Cajun or Creole culture?
>
> Ron: Well, it's kind of the same way, I'm beginning to feel the same way. I'm not really accepted in certain groups just because of who I am, and so to me that kind of gets in the way. It's like a yin-yang because at the same time I really want that. You know, that was part of what I liked about Greek dancing was that I did like that diverseness, diversive, not divisiveness but diversity of the Greek community. I liked seeing that and being a part of it, but at the same time it kind of alienates me because I'm not a part of it. And I realize they don't want me to be a part of it.
>
> Author: Do you think you wanted to be a part of it initially?
>
> Ron: Oh, of course, absolutely.

According to Ron, he now likes Louisiana French music and culture without wanting to be a part of it.

Although Ron's interests in other kinds of folk dancing have not disappeared, his primary enthusiasm continues to be for Louisiana French dancing. He will occasionally go to polka parties in Sonoma County, where he now lives, and he still enjoys Greek dancing enough that he traveled to Greece not many years before our interview. He served for two years as the president of the California Friends of Louisiana French Music. When I asked how he decided which dance to attend when there were two or three happening on the same night (a frequent circumstance on Saturday nights), he responded thus: "I guess if I've got my choice between a mediocre Cajun band, let's say, and a good zydeco band, I'll go with the zydeco band. And the reverse. And if they're both good then I'd probably go with the zydeco, just because I know there's going to be more people there, because more people like zydeco, and more people mean more people to dance with."

As a parting comment in our interview, Ron stated that he felt "blessed" to have found Louisiana French music and dancing in California. "When I die, it will have been a great part of my life. Really glad that I've been a part of it. I hope to keep dancing for quite a while. In fact, my original idea a long time ago was to dance my ass off and hopefully die on the dance floor. [laughs] And pull me off and keep dancing!"

Dana DeSimone[12]

Dana DeSimone was born in San Francisco in 1953 and raised there by his parents, who met in the Bay Area during World War II after migrating westward separately. "I'm Irish and Italian. And my father was a laborer from outside of Buffalo, New York, and my mother is from Omaha, Nebraska." His mother's family was Protestant and his father's Catholic, and his immediate family, which included Dana and his two older siblings, never did settle on which church to attend. The DeSimone family lived in the Excelsior district of San Francisco, which Dana remembers at that time as a working-class neighborhood of various ethnicities, including Italian, Irish, Armenian, black, and Samoan. The family home was immediately adjacent to McLaren Park, a large municipal open space in the southeastern area of the city, "literally my backyard." On the other side of the park was the neighborhood of Visitacion Valley, the site of some housing projects where yet more migrating families lived, families from Mississippi, Louisiana, east Texas, and Oklahoma whose children Dana met in junior high and high school. Outside of school, "my father taught me how to gamble, how to play race horses, how to shoot craps, how to do just all sorts of stuff." Dana was a teenager during the height of the psychedelic era in San Francisco, and he remembers that while his peers shared an interest in experimenting with drugs, they did not take on some of the other accoutrements of hippie subculture. "College was kind of out, so they couldn't grow their hair long, because most of the guys I knew had to work after school at an auto shop, at the supermarket, or something like that."

No one on either side of Dana's family played any musical instruments or sang. He decided to take up the clarinet and played in marching and concert bands through most of high school. He remembers that his father and Italian uncles liked opera, although he himself never acquired a taste for it. "My mother would listen to a lot of country and western stuff, like Bob Wills and Merle Haggard, George Jones, Eddie Arnold, Marty Robbins, Ray Price. All them old guys. Dean Martin was a big hit in my family on both sides."

Dancing was not a popular pastime among his relatives, either; just one of his father's brothers was a dancer. He first discovered his own affinity for dancing in elementary school.

> Dana: When I was a kid, they used to have May Days, they used to dance around a Maypole. And they would have people who would teach dancing, and they would give you little instruments and you had to learn it. Our fifth-grade class had to do square dancing and we didn't quite get it. They [were] making us do some weird type of figures, like promenade-type figures with our partner.
>
> Author: Was this in a gym class?
>
> Dana: No, this was in just a regular fifth grade class. So I got some cute gal from Oklahoma who knew how to do this too. My mother had taught me, she didn't really dance but she knew a little about figures with her arms, so she could show me. So this little gal and I took first place in this thing and kind of liked it, actually. All of a sudden, at the early age of eleven or twelve, I said wow, this is cool.
>
> Author: You liked the recognition.
>
> Dana: Oh, sure. And then when I got into junior high school, we used to have junior high school dances a lot. And they had them after school, and you just go dance.
>
> Author: Was that partner dancing?
>
> Dana: No, this was more funk, James Brown was really big at that time. Sly Stone was really big, early Santana, some Motown. The beginnings of funk, back in 1966, '67. And you'd just watch gals dance and watch guys and if you were a fairly good dancer, you got some recognition, as you said.

His first encounter with Louisiana Creole culture was also during this time, through the French classes he took for six years through junior high and high school where he met some of the children of Louisiana immigrants.

> There were about four or five of them. There was a Leblanc, there was a Thibodeaux, there was a Bouchard. And a gal who I knew, her name was Daverné, last name. She and I spent six years together in the same homerooms, both junior high and high school, and her parents were from Lake Charles. So there were a bunch of these gals

who wanted to speak French because their grandparents did. And so every now and then, they'd come out from Lake Charles, and they'd be playing accordion, singing French songs. And I'm like, but you're black! I don't get this, you know? It took me a few years to figure this out.... Most of them played the piano-style accordion because they wanted to emulate Clifton Chenier, or they got the old three-row accordion, like Queen Ida plays the old Hohner.

He would forget about these encounters until many years later, when he discovered Cajun and zydeco dancing.

After high school, he enrolled at City College of San Francisco to study broadcasting, and he also served as news editor of the college's newspaper. His interest in dance was renewed after covering a school dance production for the newspaper. Shortly thereafter, he broke an ankle playing baseball and decided to take dance classes as part of his physical rehabilitation. At this community college he was able to learn a variety of folk dance styles, including Appalachian clogging, Balkan, and Greek.

> I just chose it by accident. I thought it was something else, and it just turned out this Greek lady taught Greek dancing and I just liked it. I said hell, I could live the life of Zorba the Greek, you know? That was in '74 and '75. And it turns out that a lady on my block was Greek, and so she turned me onto this stuff. I met my ex-wife, we got into dancing, Balkan dancing, every night of the week. I met David Nadel back in 1974. That's when I first went to Ashkenaz, late '74 or early '75. And there was a whole lot of people, like the Cajun scene we have now, the Balkan scene was almost as big as that and that would happen every night. And there was dancing in the City too. I'd go to Greek night clubs a lot, which is a whole other scene entirely. We're talking suits, money... these guys spent more money on their hair than I did in two weeks! There was a lot of different people there, I hung out with Greeks and Serbs, I mean real Greeks from Greece and real Serbs from Serbia, Croatians from Croatia. Oh God, we used to get drunk every night—cheese, bread, wine, ouzo, lamb—oh man, good stuff!

While reminiscing about dancing during his college days, Dana refers to how dancing saved his life. He explains:

> Essentially I was in a really bad spot, emotionally and stuff, and dancing just showed me the way I wanted to go. Because I was really unhappy, and just wasn't making any progress in hanging around with a lot of bachelor kind of guys who weren't going anywhere either. Man, we'd just sit and bitch about we ain't getting no women, and

then I found dancing and I'm thinking, Oh! This is where they are! [laughs] And it just saved my life and it really gave me an outlet and when it clicked everything felt right. It felt like this is my place to be in the world, you know, spiritually and emotionally and everything. It just did. That's why, when I'm not doing things like this, I don't function well in the world. I'm one of those type of people.

After he finished his radio training, he took a job at a station outside of the Bay Area, but by 1978 he had moved back. He worked for a short while as a janitor at the Mandala, the folk dance club in San Francisco, until he found a technical job working at a religious television station. Around this time he got married to a woman who shared his dancing interests and introduced him to some new ones, including salsa, country and western, and belly dancing. Hanging around the belly dance scene, he also learned how to play the drums that accompanied the dance (dumbek, tar, tambourine) and played with some Lebanese musicians in San Francisco clubs where belly dancers performed.

After he and his wife divorced in the early 1980s, Dana spent more time at clogging, one of his earlier dancing pastimes. He made several trips to southern Appalachia to learn the style and danced with a clogging performance group that rehearsed at City College, called the Cornmashers. His first experiences as a dance teacher were with the Cornmashers, as he would break down for the group some of the moves he had learned. He also achieved some recognition as a solo dancer, performing twice as a clogger at the San Francisco Ethnic Dance Festival. "We did a lot of festivals and a lot of drinking in those days. Just hung out with some old guys who made moonshine. I quit hanging out with the Balkan and the Greeks and then I just went to this, my real roots."

Also after his divorce, Dana traveled to New Orleans to "get lost" in Mardi Gras and heard a couple of Cajun bands on that trip. He had previously seen Clifton Chenier and Queen Ida at Ashkenaz and once happened across the Louisiana Playboys, playing outdoors at a Carnaval celebration in San Francisco. After seeing a Dewey Balfa concert in 1983, where he first met Danny Poullard, Dana started attending church dances at the suggestion of some of his folk-dancing acquaintances. He took a couple of classes with San Francisco State University dance professor Jerry Duke, but mostly tried to learn by watching, then tried teaching a little bit himself while he was still relatively new to the style. He soon stopped teaching when he realized he wasn't ready, "because my style was very clogging at the time." Seeing a video of himself dancing at Arhoolie Records' twenty-fifth anniversary party helped bring this home.

It was in the mid to late 1980s that Dana felt that he really caught on to Cajun and zydeco dancing—and that that style of dancing became more widely popular in the Bay Area. On the Cajun side, he discovered a style of dancing that featured a variety of arm moves from some dancers who moved from Louisiana to California.

> I remember seeing Cheryl [McBride] and Diana [Castillo] and Jim Belden. They all came from New Orleans, around '86, I guess—'86, '87, '88. But they came and all of sudden were doing all of this great one-step stuff. It's like, this is what I want to learn. Castillo and Belden looked great together. And then Cheryl and this guy Jeff were together and it looked just awesome. Awesome! And then they changed everything around. Four to six people, three or four couples changed the whole thing around. So a bunch of us learned it.

He had been watching some of the local Creole dancers all along. His memories of learning from these dancers are entwined with the music of John Delafose and the Eunice Playboys, a band he heard relatively often, between his travels to Louisiana and the band's tours to California. From Shirley St. Julien Robertson, wife of Robbie, he learned that what he was seeing were regional differences in dance styles from different areas within southwest Louisiana.

> I remember this guy Tony Royster, who was a great dancer. He was one of the guys I learned my style from. I started going to these church dances and I'd see guys like Robbie [Robertson], Lucky St. Mary were the two main guys I learned from, just by watching them. And they had two totally distinct styles. Robbie was Mister Smooth, everything is like gliding, man. He ain't gonna burst a sweat! And Lucky, man could he go! He and Tony had that Lake Charles kind of country style. More cowboy style, not anywhere close to the nouveau zydeco that you're seeing now. Fast! David Duhon has it, Junior St. Mary has it. Actually, the St. Marys, all of them dance the same way. They have this little gallop, every one of them, even the grandkids do it. It's kind of cool when you see the clans do that. It's very much a family thing. I learned from watching Junior and Della too. I can't quite get that gallop down. Lucky had it. He influenced me more, but he was big, wild moves. Chipso [Paul Ardoin] influenced me. So my main style that I really worked on was more the older style. Dancing to John Delafose, that country style. Faster, a little bit more vertical, weight-shifted time. Not so much bigger steps. They had the Prudhomme brothers play [guitar and bass], and John played the accordion. It was Tony [Delafose] playing drums and Geno rubbing the board. And then the bass player quit and Tony took over the bass and Geno went behind the drums and Germaine Jack came in. And that was the best Eunice Playboy band. Oh, Germaine is best rubboard player I have ever seen! But that style, that country kind of style, you're gonna get this little bit

more urgent when you're dancing. What Shirley calls prairie dancing, as opposed to where she's from (St. Martinville), where they've got more of the Afro-Caribbean style than Eunice and Opelousas.

Two events in Dana's life led to an even deeper involvement in Cajun and zydeco dancing. One was his decision to put aside his pursuit of clogging in 1988. The second was a workplace injury to his back in 1989 while working for the local telephone company, which led to a significant amount of time off work due to disability. He took advantage of the free time and disability compensation to engage in a period of extensive travel to and study in Louisiana, to experience as much Cajun music and zydeco and dancing as he could. "And went down a lot by myself, too, I didn't want to just always go down with California people. And I'd go down at different times of the year as opposed to festival times." Dana estimates that he traveled to Louisiana an average of three times a year, and one year he visited seven times. He would stay with a friend who had moved from California to Lafayette, Louisiana, and had a spare in-law unit for which Dana paid some rent when he stayed.

> Dana: The best time I probably had, not just the dancing but the whole Louisiana experience, was when I went down to Mardi Gras in Mamou. It was really weird, because it really made me realize, I am in the middle of almost a foreign country here. I am from the city of San Francisco and I'm partying with about two thousand drunk Cajuns here. That was the last time I drank, in 1992, it's been six and a half years since I've had a drop of alcohol. Some Napoleon brandy, Mardi Gras, boudin, crawfish étouffée, just wonderful stuff.
> The best time I had in Louisiana really, was in '94, when André [Thierry] played with Willis Prudhomme down there, after Plaisance. André played with Willis's old band at the front of Richard's Club, when they had their thing outside. Oh man! It was gorgeous, man, it was so beautiful. They had Beau Jocque, Boozoo, Willis Prudhomme, Keith Frank, John Delafose played. Roy Carrier. Five bucks! There's a little grassy area adjacent to the club, and right on the other side of the highway is the fields, and the railroad tracks there. The sun goes down, oh God it's gorgeous! It was one of the nicest times I had.
> Those two times actually symbolized, it wasn't just about the dancing. I mean it was a part of it, but it's the whole culture, it's the attitude. You know what I learned? I learned something, even though I can't keep it in my head, but when I go down there I realized no matter where you go, you're going to have a good time. I realized man, I'm killing myself, because this was in '93 when I kept doing a lot of stuff. And I finally said, that's it. I'm just going to go two or three places. I don't have to go eight or nine places the whole weekend, like a lot of people still do from here.

Author: So what is it about the culture that you like, do you think?

Dana: It's something I haven't learned, but I'm very envious of these people who just live and not worry about so much stuff. I mean, my Italian and Irish culture are worried about everything. I mean, everything. And to go to this culture where they don't worry about anything... I won't be totally that way, but somewhere in the middle would be nice. [laughs] And one thing I like about it, it's not just about dancing. I used to be this dance snob, thinking, "Aw, I only gotta dance." But I don't. It's, wow, kind of cool to go out to a fish fry, just hang out. They just live their life, and there's something to be said for it. The more I see in the Bay Area how my home area is changing, it's not looking too bad. I don't know if it's that I'm getting a little older, but I just like that as family, for the most part, they do things together. They just celebrate life down there a lot better. That's what I like.

Traveling to Louisiana as often as he did during this period and at times other than the peak festival periods, Dana did experience some discomfort around race relations. "Rural Louisiana's not the friendliest place sometimes, if it's not a festival time" he says, citing tense situations when he was the only white person in a rural zydeco club. He also had a falling out with some Cajun friends over dancing zydeco-style at a Cajun dance hall–restaurant, after which he turned more of his attention to zydeco clubs and festivals. At the Plaisance zydeco festival in 1995, the old baseball injury that had started him dancing over twenty years before flared up. He had to stop dancing for a while, and frequent dance trips to Louisiana became a thing of the past.

Meanwhile, in between trips to Louisiana, Dana had been gradually establishing himself as a dance teacher for Cajun and zydeco in the Bay Area. He was aware that others were already teaching or had taught Cajun and zydeco dancing before him, such as Diana Castillo, Irene Tenney, and Jerry Duke. He started out teaching for free in conjunction with individual dance events, especially for Billy Wilson's band, Motordude Zydeco. He often taught with female teaching partners, some of whom found him more teaching opportunities outside the context of dance events, teaching classes at college campuses, dance studios, and occasionally in corporate settings. Then he started teaching weekly classes with Peggy Shropshire, first at DeMarco's club in Brisbane, then at the South of Market Cultural Center in San Francisco, and finally settling on the East Bay as the best location to draw students, working out of a dance studio in West Berkeley approximately a mile from Ashkenaz. David Nadel added him to the rotation of teachers who would teach before-dance classes at Ashkenaz on Cajun nights, and for a while he rented the back studio at Ashkenaz and taught beginner classes there, too.

In 1995 Dana began producing dance events himself, on the East Bay island city of Alameda. Promoter Ray Jordan had started holding weekly Friday night dances at Eagles' Hall in Alameda in the fall of 1993, using Louisiana Ballroom as a brand name. Jordan taught dance classes and the band Motordude Zydeco provided live music each week. In the spring of 1995 Jordan moved his Louisiana Ballroom from the Eagles' Hall to the Elks' Lodge, also in Alameda. Some four months later, Dana held his first event at the Alameda Eagles' Hall, also on a Friday night and in direct competition with the Louisiana Ballroom at the Elks'. He explains: "The reason I started the Friday night things was that, when I started this, it was just Motordude Friday nights and CCO [California Cajun Orchestra] every once in a while on Saturday nights, that was it. And they got to be, you know, really tiring. Same old band, same old thing. Bunch of us asked to change it, and what you see now is what we tried to do. Now everybody's in the act."

At first he held Friday night dances at Eagles' once or twice a month, hiring the Zydeco Flames to play or bringing Kent Menard up from southern California. There was more competition on Friday nights with venues in other part of the Bay Area trying out Cajun dancing as an entertainment attraction. By the start of 1996, the Louisiana Ballroom was out of business and Friday night dances at the Alameda Eagles' Hall again became a weekly fixture. Dana alternated booking duties with Motordude Zydeco bandleader Billy Wilson; eventually Wilson relinquished this role, leaving Dana with weekly responsibility for producing Friday night dances. Louisiana Sue (see her profile in ch. 8) also got involved as a business partner, helping Dana book touring bands from Louisiana to play some of the Friday dances and at other times. When Sue's engagement at the Orleans Casino in Las Vegas ended, she started coming down to Alameda from Sacramento on Friday nights to work at the dances with Dana. Together Sue and Dana have also held occasional "dance camps," intensive weekends that combine dance workshops with evening dances open to the public.[13]

By 1998 when we had our full-length interview, Dana had left the phone company altogether and was deriving most of his income from dance-related activities. He teaches beginning dancers for an hour prior to the Friday night dances, some of whom then sign up to take the monthlong series of studio classes he still offers in Berkeley. Sometimes he is hired by individuals for lessons, such as couples about to be married. He quit working with a teaching partner for a while and developed his own ideas about teaching Cajun and zydeco dancing. He occasionally compares notes with other teachers such as Olivia Guillory (whose nickname, "Tee," he uses in the quote below).

> I really emphasize the beat a lot more. I emphasize that people have to be on the beat. My classes are longer now than they used to be. I can't even get going in an hour. Sometimes I get tired, but a good hour and a half to two hours is how I like to teach.

I get people who keep coming for months and sometimes for years, because they want to get it and they have more fun here in classes than they do at the dances. And I'm trying to teach them style, too, and that's a difficult thing to teach. I try to cater to a certain style but try to develop your own style within that. And I'm a little bit more technical than I used to be. I used to just do it. And now I have to figure out stuff and I've learned how to answer questions a lot more.

Tee just goes through it, she doesn't break it down. She slows it down, which is the way I like it to be done. It's the way I learned how to dance and do all kinds of dancing. You slow it down, you don't break it down. I mean, you can, but most people wind up breaking it down way too much and they suck all the life out of it. Because dancing's an expression at the time, and you're expressing yourself at the moment when you're hearing something, and it's a physical manifestation of sound. How you're feeling at that moment. That's what's supposed to be.

Dana has learned to address what he considers to be misguided ideas about the dance that his students pick up elsewhere.

> Dana: My style has changed because my dance style has changed. You know, I don't dance the way I used to.
> Author: Because of your injury?
> Dana: Partly. And partly I'm just growing, thank God. I'm not doing the same thing I was five years ago, which is a good sign. But my teaching style, it's changed a little bit. To give you a good example, I used to do slow, quick-quick and now I don't. I dance that way a lot of times, but I don't teach it that way. And people used to say, "Oh, you're teaching a Cajun two-step." Well, no. Because some people say a slow-quick-quick is a zydeco and a quick-quick-slow is a Cajun. And I'm like, really? Now I've done both ways, and I used to teach a slow first, that slow, quick-quick-slow, you open out a little bit. And then Tee taught me, she said, "Oh, you can do quick-quick-slow." I said, "Yeah, that's what I thought." So now I show both. Because as you know, once you're in the basic step, it just all depends on how you want to count it.
> Author: Right. Also, on some tunes it can change on you anyway [see ex. 2].
> Dana: Yes, that's right. Exactly right. I danced with a lady from D.C. a couple months ago. Could not start out with the quick-quick-slow. Couldn't start out.
> Author: So she wouldn't follow you
> Dana: No, she could not. But she kept saying she was an advanced dancer. And I'm saying girl, you can't be calling yourself that if you can't follow this. I mean, this is a basic move! She says, "Well, you're not doing it on the phrase." The phrase? What they're doing in zydeco now is they're choreographing phrases! It's amazing to me. People teach in phrases of four and eight. They start out at the beginning, they wait

until it comes around. You dance with somebody out here and they're saying, "What are you doing?" I'm just starting, let's just go! It's two beats, it's either you're on one side of it or you're on the other. And people are just amazed: "Do you teach that?" Well, yeah. Sometimes I'll dance to the phrase, sometimes I just want to dance. It's really that simple. You're having a crummy day, and you just need to dance. You ain't worried about your steps, you ain't worried about the count, you're just moving!

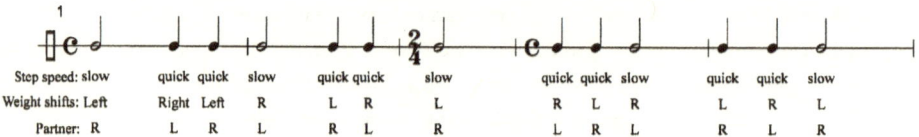

Example 2. How two-step pattern can change with respect to the downbeat

Louisiana French Dance Meets the Bay Area Folk Dance Scene

A festival poster from 1979 (see fig. 6) that Gary Canaparo saved illustrates the spirit of inclusiveness that he associated with George Broussard, only this festival was organized by Queen Ida's husband, Ray Guillory. The lineup of this festival weekend, held in the parish hall of St. Mark's Catholic Church in Richmond, includes several local Creole musicians and groups (David Petri, John Semien, Mark St. Mary, Queen Ida, the Louisiana Playboys), a couple of Louisiana French musicians from out of town (Edgar Leday from southern California and Louis Semien from Louisiana), local friends of the community (Will Spires on fiddle and Gary "L.C." Canaparo, sporting the stage name his Creole friends gave him), and a couple of acts specializing in other musical genres (blues pianist Mark Naftalin and an Italian American accordion duo). This poster provides a follow-up snapshot to Peter Levine's 1975 newspaper write-up of Queen Ida's debut. In 1979 Ida has her own band, has recorded two albums for GNP Crescendo, and in that same year plays her first European tour. John Semien is still performing (Cajun and country music) and the younger generation of performers (Mark St. Mary, the Louisiana Playboys) is carrying on. Outsiders from the international folk dance scene have yet to arrive.[14]

The decade of the 1980s, when folk dancers were discovering Cajun music and zydeco, was at the same time a period of decline for Balkan dancing in the Bay Area and for other varieties of international folk dancing. The Mandala in

FOLK REVIVAL CONNECTION: THE DANCERS

Figure 6. Poster for Cajun/Creole Festival at St. Mark's in Richmond, 1979

San Francisco closed and was replaced in the same location by a ballroom dance venue. Ashkenaz started shifting its programming toward a more contemporary mix of world music styles as early as 1979, when one handbill indicates a regular weekly schedule of 9:30 nightly shows preceded by dance classes at 8:00 PM: "Ethnojazz" on Monday night (preceded by salsa dance lessons), Balkan on Tuesdays, reggae on Wednesdays, Greek on Thursdays, square dancing or benefit events on Fridays, international folk dancing on Saturdays, and Israeli folk dancing on Sundays. Tuesday, Thursday, Saturday, and Sunday all used recorded music; the other nights were standing gigs for certain bands. There were exceptions to the regular schedule; Queen Ida played a handful of dates that year. Over time Nadel retained some European nights while moving largely to live music and music of Africa and the African diaspora: reggae, calypso, Brazilian samba, blues (with swing dancing), and New Orleans rhythm and blues. Cajun music and zydeco began to find their way into the rotation more often starting in 1981, when Queen Ida and the Louisiana Playboys played eight dates between them and Chenier himself made an appearance. In the latter half of the decade, the California Cajun Orchestra made increasingly frequent appearances at Ashkenaz, as did touring bands from Louisiana. The kinds of partner dancing that so concerned the settlement workers who laid the groundwork for international folk dancing eighty years prior were now helping keep Nadel in business.[15]

After years of featuring Cajun and zydeco sporadically on weekend nights, Nadel decided in 1989 to add Cajun dancing as a regular Tuesday night item once a month. This move would have wider ramifications for the northern California scene, as it opened up a space for less experienced musicians to play for dancers. Linda Schmidt, a dancer who went on to learn the bass guitar and play for several bands including Tee Fee, remembers it this way:

> I guess it was Danny [Poullard]'s idea to go to Ashkenaz during the week and have people sit in the middle of the floor, and just musicians play and people dance around them. And so it was me, and Gerard [Landry], and Billy [Wilson], and Lucky St. Mary on rubboard, and that was it. And we'd come and Billy would play guitar for a while and Gerard would play accordion, and then Billy would play accordion.... It was Danny's idea, but Danny didn't play. Billy decided to play. And so we would go there on a Tuesday night.... Gerard wanted to call it "Fifi Poncho" and we all decided we'd call it "Bayou Pon Pon" instead.[16]

At the beginning Bayou Pon Pon was not so much a band as it was a performance laboratory where Landry and Wilson, two of Poullard's earliest accordion students, could get some public exposure and other musicians like Schmidt, who was taking bass lessons from Wilson at the time, had a chance to play. Several other musicians got to play on Tuesday nights sooner or later, including Delilah Lewis on fiddle. Wilson, who around this time was playing bass with ZZ and the Bad Boys (Delilah's band in Fresno) and with the California Cajun Orchestra, also started his own zydeco lineup, named Motordude Zydeco after a Boozoo Chavis song. A number of changes later—Landry leaving to lead his own Cajun band, Lewis getting married and dropping out of the scene for a few years, the decision to move the band from the floor onto the stage with proper amplification—Bayou Pon Pon became a more conventional band, Billy Wilson's outlet for playing Cajun music when he wasn't playing zydeco with Motordude, with Schmidt on guitar and Agi Ban on fiddle. The significant point among the minutiae of these personnel changes is the very existence of the personnel and the number of dancers sufficient for Nadel to keep bringing Bayou Pon Pon back. No longer were Queen Ida, Danny Poullard, and touring bands the only games in town for the increasing number of dancers. Bass players were becoming accordion players, dancers were becoming bass players, new bands were forming, and Poullard's presence as a teacher was beginning to have an impact.

The dancers I interviewed exhibited a range of attitudes toward dance instruction. If there were any consensus, it might be that attempts to emulate Louisiana French partner dancing were preferable to the individualistic free-for-all that preceded them. Those interviewed for this chapter had to pick up the dance themselves or with minimal cues from their Creole partners; they did not take a class because, by and large, there were no classes to take in the early 1980s. For Gary Canaparo, this lack of formal dance instruction is as it should be. At one of my visits to his home, Gary returned to a comment that Charlie St. Mary had made, to the effect that "tonight we're going to do something we've never done before." He took this as an expression of the essence of zydeco that spoke to him more than any discussion of snap beans. I had thought it might have meant something more specific to a situation, like here we are, we sure have never played a wedding for a psychiatrist's daughter before. But Gary, perhaps with justification since he was there and knew the parties involved, took a more general meaning of social and music improvisation in the comment, that before outsiders came in and "codified" it the music and dance were more wide open and constantly being reinvented and personalized. Although I did not mention it at the time, the aesthetic he was outlining is summed up pretty well in this recorded exchange between Boozoo Chavis and a band member about how to play the next studio take:

> Boozoo: If it's wrong, do it wrong, you know, with me. Follow me. If I'm wrong, you wrong, too.

> Band member: Well, let's do it like we just done it.
> Boozoo: Yeah. But I don't know if we gonna do it like we just done it, but it gonna be done. You know, I can't promise you it gonna be like it was, but I can promise you it gonna be better![17]

Ron Rumney has no objection to dance instruction per se, as he certainly received plenty of it with international folk dancing. He does look for a minimum of complication, however, hence his nostalgia for "the zydeco style of always holding on to your partner with two hands," i.e., dancing waltzes and two-steps with one's partner in closed or semi-open position, without the twirling arm motions and turns seen in a style of Cajun dancing developed in Louisiana in the 1970s. This style is sufficiently controversial there that some refuse to give it a name, referring to it only as the "crippled chicken" step for its limping footwork. Proponents refer to it as the one-step or the Cajun jitterbug, although these names also refer to older steps. The newer style, with its many and varied moves adapted from swing dancing, lends itself to a dance class setting and became popular later once a few people like Diana Castillo brought it from New Orleans. Castillo, a swing dancer originally from Austin, Texas, became interested in Cajun and zydeco dancing and moved to New Orleans, where she learned the latest Cajun dance styles and taught dance classes for approximately five years before moving to California. Eventually she and Dana DeSimone separately started teaching series of classes in which the Cajun jitterbug figured prominently. There are several other teachers who teach single classes before events but who do not run series of dance classes outside of the dance venues themselves. As a dance teacher, DeSimone himself is obviously in favor of people attending dance classes, and yet would seem to be in sympathy with Canaparo's viewpoint in that he doesn't like to break down the parts of a dance or choreograph phrases for his students and thereby rob them of the potential for spontaneity.[18]

From a practical standpoint, dance instruction is perhaps the key to the subsistence economy of the northern California dance scene, because it constantly supplies new dancers that start coming to events as others lose interest and fall away. I signed up to take one of DeSimone's studio classes in 1994, perhaps a year after I first met him teaching a class at a dance. I had already taken a series of classes from Castillo, which were similarly organized, in 1993. Weekly classes were held in a rented space with a wooden dance floor and met at 7:00 or 7:30 on a weekday evening for an hour or an hour and a half. Students signed up and paid for a month of classes at a time, either individually or as couples, and the teacher would organize the month's worth of classes around a set of moves or steps geared to the advertised level of the class, usually beginner or intermediate. Classes were conducted to recorded music, although occasionally Dana hired an accordion-fiddle duo to play live for a Cajun class. Registration for the class was managed so that there were roughly an equal number of men and women; after I had attended as a paying customer for a few months, Dana called me back a couple of months to fill in as a male dancer for free to balance out the numbers. A full class consisted of approximately twenty dancers. Activities in class alternated among demonstration from the teacher(s), verbal explanation, and students dancing. Students switched partners every few minutes and no exceptions were made for married couples; the point was to have everyone learn how to dance with a variety of partners. Dance etiquette was also covered. Often on the night of a class, there would be a dance going on nearby in the East Bay, and many people from the class would head over to the dance after class. The social group of one's classmates that formed over a month or several months made for a conveniently nonthreatening initial set of dance partners to approach at an actual dance. Thus the studio classes served both to instruct in the coordinated movements of partner dancing and also to socialize dancers who were new to the Cajun and zydeco "scene" and, by Dana's estimate in half the cases, new to partner dancing altogether.

Anxieties about race relations expressed by the revivalist musicians in the previous chapter revolved chiefly around the attitudes of Cajuns in Louisiana toward blacks. An additional perspective appears here around a more personal concern for being "the only whites there," as Paul Strogen put it. This situation was commonplace for the Canaparos and the first folk dancers who attended the church dances in the Bay Area, but as Rumney observes, this has changed. Church dances are fewer and those that do happen get put on the dance calendar along with all of the other events, so non-Creole turnout tends to be more than a handful of dancers. It is still the case that white tourists who visit what Rumney refers to as "the black clubs" in Louisiana, such as Richard's Club or Slim's Y-Ki-Ki, outside of festival times may find themselves "the only whites there."

This observation of racial difference has the potential to signify several things simultaneously, of which I shall name three. First, a touristic sort of pride follows from having ventured into a cultural milieu unknown to one's fellows. Second is a concern that one has arrived at a party uninvited and may be unwelcome; of one night at Slim's, DeSimone recalls that "there was some white people there, so I didn't feel quite so rude about it." On the other hand, public clubs and church benefit dances do not operate by invitation only; who attends is a matter of custom and the degree of welcome for "visitors" (i.e., unknown faces) depends in no small part on how those visitors comport themselves. The Canaparos constantly reaffirmed their place in the social network through lively repartee, Gary's playing harmonica with the band, and eventually by throwing their own house parties. Ron

Rumney worried when his friend Earl started telling more folk dancers about the church dances, that these newcomers would jump up at the first dance (as was their custom) and otherwise ignore the finer social nuances that he had come to appreciate. Similarly, several dancers who have visited Louisiana during festival times have expressed concern about the possible negative impact of the heavy volume of guests on the clubs and communities that were not designed for that level of traffic, but in most cases this does not prevent them from returning for subsequent festivals. Finally, a third spin on being "the only whites there" is the concern (whether well-founded or not) for physical safety, for example in the predominantly black neighborhoods where St. Francis of Assisi, All Hallows, and St. Mark's are located. For this reason several white dancers voiced to me a greater willingness to attend dances at Ashkenaz or Alameda Eagles' Hall than at the churches.

A more diffuse but still identifiable theme among the revivalists, both dancers and musicians, is the first visit to Louisiana, which for most of them happened after they had already developed some kind of interest in Cajun or Creole culture. I have not quite found the intensity of feeling or mysticism that Laušević reports from some of her Balkan scene informants who speak of the Balkans as "sacred soil" and who wept or felt the urge to kiss the ground when they first arrived there, except perhaps for one dancer (not profiled here) who described a "spiritual mission" to visit Richard's Club in the daylight when no event was happening, an experience that reminded him of visiting ancient temples in India. For some, travel to Louisiana is an important part of their involvement in the music and culture, and something they do repeatedly. For others, it is something they do once or not at all. Paul Strogen told me that he did his "pilgrimage" once in the mid-1990s and that appeared to be sufficient for him. Frequently the impulse for dancers, as Ron and Dana describe, is to try to go to as many events in one weekend as is physically possible, without regard to the usual limits of human endurance. The excitement of seeing places that others have told them about, of hearing musicians live that they previously may have seen on tour or heard only through recordings, pushes them to do the maximum. That there is now so much to do and see in Louisiana around Cajun and zydeco dancing, to the point where standard routines and itineraries have developed, is an outgrowth of the 1980s Cajun craze which will be treated in more depth in the next chapter.[19]

CHAPTER EIGHT

Later Gulf Coast Arrivals

So far, in tracing the growth of the Cajun and zydeco scene in northern California we have seen a number of foundational elements: the history of ethnicities and musics in Louisiana, black migration in the 1940s to California, the growth of international folk dancing in that same decade, and folk and blues revivals that whetted outsiders' musical appetites for Cajun and zydeco in the 1960s. Of the historical changes, none was more profound than the civil rights movement, which not only changed the legal basis for race relations in the United States but also provided a positive identity model for other minority groups. The shift in dominant paradigm for the Americanization of immigrants from the "melting pot" model to multiculturalism opened up a space in the national discourse that Cajuns and Creoles could legitimately occupy without disappearing into larger wholes, and it marked a shift in the musical tastes and leisure interests with respect to revivalism. Generic interest in folk music and folk dancing began to splinter into what Neil Rosenberg calls named-system revivals, smaller affinity groups organized around specific cultures and practices, like Balkan dancing and Cajun music. The same conceptual shift would increase economic opportunities for cultural tourism to develop.[1]

Along with the sizable Creole migration to California, there have also been some Cajuns who have resettled there. In her master's thesis research on Cajun and Creole migration to California, Lisa Billeaudeau found that Creoles had compelling socioeconomic reasons to migrate that motivated entire families, while a Cajun's arrival in California was much more likely to be out of "personal choice." This ignores the fact that Creoles also acted out of choice, but it does point to an observation that Cajuns did not form significant social networks upon their arrival. As Louisiana Sue put it to me, in California, "if you meet a Cajun, he doesn't know where the other Cajuns are. But the Creoles know where [the other Creoles] are."[2]

Sacramento-based Freida Fusilier and Louisiana Sue (Susan Appe Ramon) collaborated prolifically in the mid-1990s on numerous presentations of Louisiana

French culture at festivals, fairs, and indoor dances. New Orleans native Ramon produced these events while Fusilier served as a spokeswoman and interpreter for Cajun culture, telling stories and singing songs on stage. Louisiana Sue was also joined by Russell Ardoin, son of musician Alphonse "Bois Sec" Ardoin, who served as a spokesman for Creole culture and emceed the zydeco acts. During this period of intensive public presentation, they exposed tens of thousands of Californians to Louisiana French culture firsthand. Ralph "Bobby" Gradney found a second career as a Cajun food caterer and restaurateur in part through operating a food booth at some of these festival events and fairs. Musician Richard Domingue and his band Gator Beat played at many of the same events. All four people profiled in this chapter have in common that they became active in the Louisiana French music scene in northern California in the late 1980s and 1990s, after the Creole community in and around San Francisco was already well established and outsiders like those described in chapters 6 and 7 had gotten involved. Once the Creole community network had grown and established a more public presence with the addition of some folk revivalists, these other Louisiana emigrants were able to learn of it and join it as well. They did so at the time of a dramatic increase of interest in Cajun music and zydeco in northern California. While most of this book deals with the earlier period of network formation, this final chapter gives more detail on the scene as it has, in a sense, expanded beyond its original Creole basis and taken on a life of its own.

The Rise of All Things Cajun in Popular Culture

Music and food were the elements of Louisiana French culture most readily commoditized in the Cajun craze of the 1980s and 1990s. Through the channels of the popular music and food industries, Cajun and Creole music and food traveled far and wide to reach and be appreciated in some fashion by many. Driven in turn by the popular interest in music and food, cultural tourism in francophone Louisiana was growing and increasing the demand for Cajun products still further as consumers became more familiar with other aspects of the culture and economic development of tourism became more sophisticated. Virtual tourism (in the form of record sales and the formation of small dance scenes in various urban areas across the country) and actual tourism grew together in a mutually positive feedback loop. Other commercial outlets for the Cajun craze included books (such as James Lee Burke's novels featuring Cajun detective Dave Robicheaux, the first of which appeared in 1987) and Hollywood films (such as *The Big Easy*, released the same year). We shall focus here on tourism and popular music.[3]

A particularly deep crisis in Louisiana oil production in the 1980s has in some quarters been credited with giving birth to the Cajun cultural tourism industry through economic necessity, although (as Bernard points out) the popularization of Cajun food outside the region shortly preceded the 1981 drop in oil prices that stayed in effect for five years. In order to exploit tourism as a resource, entrepreneurs had to devise new means of economic production to serve as front stages for the bulk of tourists to visit. Attempts at economic redevelopment in Louisiana through cultural tourism were successful. The 1980s saw an explosion of interest in Cajun and Creole culture and marked the beginning of music and dance tourism of the type that is prevalent today. Chef Paul Prudhomme, widely credited for popularizing Cajun and New Orleans cuisine, opened his restaurant K-Paul's Louisiana Kitchen in 1979 and published his first cookbook in 1984. Mulate's restaurant in Breaux Bridge and Prejean's in Lafayette opened in 1980, combining full-service restaurants with free live Cajun music and dance floors in an all-ages, tourist-friendly format that has spawned imitators within Acadiana. Of these establishments, Ancelet wrote that "some restaurants have begun programming Cajun music and zydeco regularly, providing not only a highly efficient cultural contact point for visitors, but also a place Cajun and Creole children can hear the music of their culture before they turn twenty-one." Frank Randol, the owner of a restaurant in Lafayette that opened in 1973 and added music and dancing in the mid-1980s, estimated in 1998 that his clientele was half tourists and half local customers. The 1984 Louisiana World's Fair and Exposition in New Orleans brought increasing media attention to Cajun music and culture, although the event itself lost money. Randol cites a 1989 "Cajun Fest" nationwide tour, which included a stop in northern California's Concord Pavilion, as the year of a crucial upturn in his business. These are just a few of the many events that could be cited from the decade when the popular fascination with Cajun culture went into full swing.[4]

Bernard chronicles this period with evident ambivalence, characterizing it as one of "exploitation and revitalization." On the side of revitalization, Bernard notes the changes in CODOFIL policy toward the encouragement of local French dialects, a Cajun literary movement, and participation in Acadian reunion events known as the Congrès Mondial. The controversial ethnic slur *coonass*, a term of uncertain origin against which CODOFIL leader James Domengeaux had campaigned in the 1970s, continued to be used as a badge of ethnic pride by some Cajuns, such as with bumper stickers that read *RCA—Registered Coonass*.[5]

All of the major types of tourism—environmental, historical, and cultural—flourish in Louisiana. Environmental tourism, which emphasizes the natural habitat, in southern Louisiana includes swamp boat tours and "man-land relationships" such as the Avery Island park and Tabasco Sauce factory. Historical tourist sites include the Evangeline park in St. Martinville and various restored plantation homes. Cultural tourism, focusing on a vanishing peasant culture such as portrayed in the Acadian Village and Vermilionville outdoor museums in Lafayette, permeates many of the festivals large and small held throughout Acadiana where music, dance, and food play a part. Of these three types, cultural tourism as it exists today in southwest Louisiana is the most recent development and most indicative of the wave of popular enthusiasm for Louisiana French music and dance, and it demands the most interaction between guests and hosts.[6]

Along with the civil rights and new ethnicity movements, in the ferment of the 1960s a lobby formed for a national park in Louisiana with an historical focus that would eventually succeed where a 1920s effort to establish an Evangeline National Park in St. Martinville had failed. The idea for the Jean Lafitte National Historical Park and Preserve originated as a 1966 proposal for a Louisiana state park. Subsequently, Congressman Hale Boggs brought a similar proposal to the U.S. Congress, for a national park in the Barataria marsh region south of New Orleans featuring the natural habitat and history surrounding the early-nineteenth-century pirate. One proposal recommended an "extended" option for the park that encompassed plantations and "Acadian towns and villages." The park was authorized in 1978 with three New Orleans–area sites only. Authorization came in 1988 for three additional Lafitte Park centers to interpret Cajun culture (the Acadian Cultural Center in Lafayette, the Wetlands Acadian Cultural Center in Thibodaux, and the Prairie Acadian Cultural Center in Eunice). Of these, the Eunice center is most significant to Cajun music, with its interpretive displays and programming at the Liberty Theater.[7]

The influence of Evangeline tourism and concomitant class associations is suggested in the use of the modifier "Acadian" to describe the Lafitte Park centers, and recognition of Creole culture has until recently had the appearance of an afterthought. The development of the Cane River Creole National Historical Park in Natchitoches, Louisiana, is fairly new, and its impact on cultural tourism remains to be seen. It was authorized in 1994 to "preserve significant landscapes, sites, and structures associated with the development of Creole culture." This occurred after the dissolution of many agreements between Jean Lafitte National Historical Park and Preserve and other ethnic groups (including Isleños, Germans, and Italians) to form cultural centers or museums.[8]

If the presence of tour buses in Acadiana is any indication, the level of tourism activity there has reached the "incipient mass tourism" stage, which is to imply a high impact on the host culture. (New Orleans, by contrast, had long since passed such a point.) At this volume of activity, "the local culture is probably at the 'Y' in the road, and should decide whether to (a) consciously control or even restrict tourism, to preserve their economic and cultural integrity; or (b) to encourage tourism as a desirable economic goal and restructure their culture to absorb it." "Cajun Country" has clearly taken the latter route and with it some predictable stresses. Bernard notes that "a subtle backlash developed against tourists, prompting a Cajun musician who benefited from tourism to complain nonetheless that south Louisiana 'wasn't intended to be a get-away for middle-class urbanites who want to escape the stress of a fast-lane life in the big city, and pretend that they are Cajun for a couple of weeks out of the year.'"[9]

Far from slowing down when they vacation in Louisiana, many dancer-tourists run themselves ragged trying to dance in as many clubs and to as many bands as possible in a compressed period of time. I was not immune to this syndrome myself in my first trips to Louisiana in the mid-1990s. By then, a calendar of regular weekly events had synchronized itself and the tourism infrastructure was in place to make it possible (if not advisable) to try to "do it all." Saturdays were the fullest, the morning with a jam session at Marc Savoy's music store in Eunice and a Cajun dance broadcast on the radio from Fred's Lounge in Mamou, the late afternoon with the *Rendezvous des Cajuns* radio show at the Liberty Theater in Eunice, and with Walter Mouton and the Scott Playboys playing at La Poussière in Breaux Bridge in the evening. All of this was potentially bookended en route from and to the airport by dances in New Orleans, a latecomer to Cajun and zydeco: a Thursday night zydeco at the Rock 'n' Bowl and a Sunday night Cajun dance at Tipitina's. The rest of the time could easily be filled by attending one or two dances a night at other clubs and visiting other attractions and restaurants during the day, even when a festival was not in progress.

In the sphere of American popular music, folk music had long since ceased to be a lucrative category by the 1980s. Queen Ida recalled that her model for commercial success with zydeco during this period was not folk music but rather Jamaican reggae. Paul Simon's 1986 smash hit *Graceland* album, taken up mostly with collaborations with South African musicians, also featured a zydeco track with Rockin' Dopsie. In that same year, Buckwheat Zydeco signed with Island Records, the label that had carried Bob Marley and other reggae stars and that would soon be absorbed into major recording label Polygram. In 1987, the first Festival Internationale de Louisiane was held in Lafayette, which celebrated francophone cultures from around the world, of course including Louisiana Cajun and Creole cultures. A decade later, organizers of this annual event claimed it to be "an artistic, cultural crossroads of the world music scene."[10]

Thus have Cajun music and zydeco come to be considered as part of "world music," a phrase that has been used as a marketing term for popular music only since 1987. To see how Louisiana French music fits into world music reveals much about how outsiders have viewed Cajuns and Creoles as the Other. Three popular-press overviews from the early years of the world music category, all organized geographically, included relatively lengthy treatments of Cajun and zydeco music under a "North America" heading. Although these texts may give the impression that Cajun and zydeco musics are firmly ensconced in the world beat marketplace, in fact they play a marginal role due to differential perceptions of exoticness. The collaboration between Rockin' Dopsie and Paul Simon on *Graceland*, "That Was Your Mother," was a cover of Clifton Chenier's "Josephine" (a song in Dopsie's repertoire) for which Simon received sole songwriting credit. The question arose, why did Dopsie or Chenier not receive credit on this track when South Africans were credited with cowriting other tracks on the album? According to Louise Meintjes, "[A]n answer to this lies in the more overt otherness of the African musicians' contribution than of the American minorities. The Africans' otherness marks their input much more clearly as their own." This placement of a Creole band along a continuum of otherness points to a somewhat peripheral position of Cajun and zydeco music in world music circles. Since the Best World Music Album category was added to the Grammy awards, for example, Louisiana French musicians have continued to be nominated, if they are nominated at all, in the Traditional Folk category. The perceived need in world music releases to have a curator such as Mickey Hart or David Byrne is largely absent in Cajun and zydeco music, presumably because the otherness of Cajuns and Creoles does not distance them from Americans "so far that to bring them back for consumption by westerners an intermediary is required," as Timothy Taylor has observed about cultural representation in the world music industry. Nor is it true that Cajuns and Creoles are always "categorized by their ethnicity rather than music," as witnessed by country singer Sammy Kershaw and blues guitarist Tab Benoit, whose recordings appear under country and blues headings, respectively.[11]

While perhaps marginalized with respect to world music, it has probably been of economic advantage to Cajun Country to be different but not too different. Older record labels that have survived from the commercial folk era (Arhoolie, Rounder) continue to promote "roots" styles including Louisiana French music. The perception of Cajuns as within the frame of a national "folk" made conceivable the Acadian Centers of the Jean Lafitte National Historical Park. As a relatively affordable domestic tourist destination, the geographic center of Louisiana French dance music was available to whet the appetites of dancers who formed their own scenes in cities such as Seattle, Minneapolis, Washington, D.C., and Atlanta, at times with the cooperation of Cajuns who had recently relocated from their depressed home region. While there were already dances happening in northern California when the Cajun craze started, the massive influx of new dancers (and not just from the network of revivalists already in existence) resulting therefrom dramatically changed the demographics and character of the scene by providing an increasing demand for live dance music and places to dance.[12]

Freida Fusilier[13]

Freida Fusilier was born in 1947 five miles outside of Ville Platte, Louisiana, near Plaisance on the Grand Prairie Road. She was the youngest in a family that included one brother (the eldest) and three sisters. Both of her parents spoke French. Following school policy common at that time, when her older siblings spoke French in school they received corporal punishment from the principal. The principal in this case happened to be their uncle, who was well regarded in the family and taught the kids to revere education. Her parents spoke English then to Freida to prepare her for school and spoke to each other and to the older siblings in French. One grandmother did not speak English although she understood a little of it, so Freida spoke French with her.

> The other grandmother spoke English well, but she always encouraged me to talk French, and I got her approval. She was a real matriarch. She was my father's mother and she wasn't a warm grandmother. She was really kind of stern, and I soon learned I got her affection and approval quickly by talking in French, so I did. And actually that grandmother had a big impact on my development. They lived on the adjacent farm, you know like Bruce Daigrepont has a song, "Nonc Willie"? He talks about a grocery store where people go in and they talk French. My grandfather had a grocery store. He had a card room. [Daigrepont] talks about the card room in the back of the grocery store. Our card room was a different building. So you see, there was a lot of action in French, and I followed my father around and all those men always talked French. And a lot of those old men didn't talk, didn't understand any English at all. And like he talks about, you see, they play cards and the winner would always give the kid money to buy something. And they'd talk to me in French.[14]

Her family's farm had some Creole tenants who also spoke French exclusively. So although French was not part of her schooling prior to college, she had plenty of opportunities to absorb the language.

As a girl Freida had no music lessons and never played a musical instrument. She did take some dance lessons in ballet, modern dance, and tap. Music heard around the house from the radio and phonograph included Elvis Presley, swamp pop, and early zydeco from Clifton Chenier ("we didn't know it was zydeco, we just thought it was black music"). As far as Cajun music was concerned, she followed the lead of her older siblings and did not pay much attention to it. At the time she thought Cajun music was for old people, but she did not dislike it. "At the street dances there would be a block for rock and roll, a block for black music, and a block for Cajun music. And that Cajun music would be real festive, it's just that's where the older people would be." At home, she did not watch Aldus Roger's Cajun music television program, but typically someone would be watching it, and so that was also part of the soundtrack of her childhood. At her grandfather's, she remembers that there would often be an accordion player around the card room or grocery store.

Freida began high school at a Catholic convent boarding school in Grand Coteau but spent the last two years in Mandeville, across Lake Pontchartrain from New Orleans, where she moved with her mother and attended public high school. "When I moved to the suburbs, to Mandeville, I noticed the American men were embarrassed to move gracefully. It took a while to process that, but those little macho Cajun boys were not embarrassed to dance and move gracefully. Somehow in the American culture, men don't have that permission." Attitudes toward dancing were not the only contrasts she noticed in her first experience living outside of the region that Cajuns tend to consider home. Insults to the family name were not uncommon; "I was not happy there at all."

Following high school Freida enrolled at the University of Southwestern Louisiana (USL), now known as the University of Louisiana at Lafayette. "I couldn't wait to get back to that part of the state." Having learned partner dancing from jitterbugging with her sisters, she gave Cajun dancing a try at USL. "Those Cajun boys danced so well that it wasn't difficult to follow them." In high school she had worked as an assistant to her brother-in-law in his dental office and was considering a career in medicine, perhaps as an oral surgeon or pediatrician. However, her brother-in-law sought to dissuade her from studying medicine because it was not a woman's field; "Women didn't have a lot of strength in their hands." He counseled her to be a dental hygienist instead. Dissatisfied with this advice, she hit upon a speech pathology major as a way to combine her interests in science and working with children.

At college, Freida found that the casual use of French among Cajuns was rare, used mostly in joking. She was sufficiently interested in the language to take some courses in the French department. A Paris-educated French professor was also from Ville Platte, and Freida knew his niece from elementary school. She often returned to Ville Platte by train on the weekends to visit her family, and when she and her professor encountered each other they would sit together and speak French. He pushed her to express herself in more than just "kitchen French." "He took me to a different conceptual level, and it was higher than in the classroom."

After finishing her bachelor's degree in 1969 she went straight on to graduate school in speech pathology at West Virginia University in Morgantown, West Virginia. She welcomed the opportunity to move away from Louisiana and found her new location an agreeable adventure in terms of weather, terrain, vegetation, and people. After finishing a two-year master's program, she worked in West Virginia for five more years before deciding to move to California. She had become bored with her work, and an overseas vacation served as an impetus to move on. "I went to the Middle East and I got back home on the East Coast and I was depressed. I don't belong in the American society. I just don't. When I leave and I come back I always get depressed. And I thought, I don't have to be here. And so then I thought I'd come here [California], and I think maybe the climate was more similar to the Middle East. So I was restless."

Freida took a job with Easter Seals and moved to Sacramento, knowing no one. For some years she followed her exotic fascination with Middle Eastern culture, taking belly dance classes and learning how to cook. She also traveled to the Caribbean, Mexico, South and Central America, Africa, Australia, and New Zealand. Except for visits to see her family in Louisiana, she did not maintain any relationship with Cajun culture until a boyfriend convinced her to see the film *Belizaire The Cajun* when it was first released (1986).

The real turning point, however, was approximately a year later when a friend asked her if she wanted to attend a performance given by Beausoleil in nearby Davis, California.

> Somebody said there's Cajun music at Davis, The Palms, do you want to go, that it was supposed to be good. They were talking about Beausoleil. I didn't know who that was, never heard of it. Then when they said "Doucet," they had my attention, because I thought, that's somebody from home. Well, look at what they do to the food here in California, and they charge you twenty dollars. These are the people who twenty years ago would have made fun of us. It's a terrible exploitation and that was where I was coming from, what they've done with the food, which is a mess. But I went because of that name....
>
> I sat there in the audience and I watched him and I listened to him talk in French and I thought: I just haven't used mine and I don't push it and I need to. And I thought I forgot, he got me remembering in there that when I left USL, I had a hard time leaving. I needed to leave because I needed an adventure and I needed to experience. And I also realized that women would never be treated right there. I just

wasn't going to have the life I wanted to have there.... They push you into [marriage], and you'll always be a second-rate professional.

At the same time, Freida had been pulled to stay in Louisiana because of her personal curiosity with history and tradition, in order to take part in "that cultural revolution that was going on down there" when she graduated from USL (1969). Watching Michael Doucet that night made her think that what he was doing was what she should be doing and should have been doing, even though she had never played music. Soon after that, she bought a couple of Beausoleil's albums.

In 1989 Freida relocated to Santa Cruz for what turned out to be only a few months. While there, however, she acquired her first Cajun accordion under multiple circumstances freighted with personal significance. At a social occasion there, she mentioned that her brother made accordions; the former carpenter had taken an interest in instrument-making after going through a divorce and taking up the accordion. He had wanted one when he was a child and had been given a violin instead, which he had not wanted to play. Upon hearing this, a friend immediately inquired as to why Freida did not have an accordion made by her own brother. Freida replied, "I don't have things just to have them," but soon afterwards changed her mind.

> So about a week later on my lunch break, I wrote my brother a note, saying I wanted an accordion, there was no hurry, I doubted if I would play anything on it, but I just thought it would be nice to have. And I enclosed a $100 check and said I don't know what it cost, but this is toward it, and I don't care if I don't get it for six months or a year or what. And that was at noon, and at 5:04 was the earthquake. But apparently my letter went out, because they didn't hear from us for a long time, from me for several days. But he had gotten the letter, and see he had a son die suddenly and a granddaughter die suddenly and he's sixteen years older than I am. And he got this letter apparently not knowing if I was alive or what. And so what happened is, the granddaughter who was ten had wanted one. And she was the only one in the family who wanted one, nobody else.... And she had wanted one because some of the kids at school had one, there was a little boy who had one. And she got hit by a truck when he was making it. She got hit by a truck and she flew, and he caught her. Anyhow, those were her bellows, and her reeds, and he didn't know what to do with them and he couldn't finish it and he couldn't play it and he couldn't sell it. So he put it in the back of the closet, but then when I said that, then he thought, well that's a good thing to do with it, is finish it and give it to Freida. And he called me when I finally had a phone, he called and said well you know, I'm finishing it and I'm putting

it in the mail and I'm using your hundred dollars to mail it, and I don't want any money for it because it was Danielle's. So that's how I got that.[15]

A month later she moved from Santa Cruz back to Sacramento. The accordion sat there for a couple of months before she picked it up and started trying to learn on her own using Larry Miller's instruction manual, but she couldn't get the timing right. Eventually she tracked down Danny Poullard for some accordion instruction, not through a personal Louisiana connection but through Chris Strachwitz's Down Home Music store in El Cerrito. Progress was slow since she had never played music before nor done much singing, and she was also learning to sing the Cajun French dance repertoire. Consequently, when she was called to play her first gig two and half years later, she hardly felt ready.[16]

For the 1992 Sacramento Jazz Jubilee, zydeco was included on the program and publicized, after which the organizers found themselves looking for a zydeco band at a point when all of the California Cajun and zydeco bands were already committed to other engagements and bringing a band from Louisiana was apparently out of the question. They called Freida after one of her coworkers in the Sacramento schools told a neighbor, one of the festival's board members, about her Cajun friend who was learning to play the accordion.

> And they had advertised in this huge schedule to a large population of people, and they didn't have it. And so I said, you know, you don't want me. I'm not a musician, I don't play on time, and I only have six songs. And she said, we'll give four hundred dollars to come and play your six songs for two hours. Talk to the people and there's this money. You need sound, we'll bring you sound. Danny [Poullard] said, that's good money, Freida. Nobody likes money better than me when it comes to spending.... And then on the other side of the coin, I said, you don't understand. This is my culture. This is not like a fad or something. This is serious. I understand your predicament, but.... And they kept calling me. And I kept saying to her, I have enough trouble with the bastardization of my culture already, you know, without me contributing to it. And she called at 9:30 on a Sunday morning, and it was like the fourth time she called. And I said I tell you what, I understand you're in dire straits. If I can get some decent musicians, like especially a very strong fiddler, you know some people to back me, and I'll talk a lot. I'll talk about the culture and I'll talk about the songs, he can do some solos. Well, I didn't even sing on time, you see. I'd never sung. I could not sing on time, and I didn't even know I wasn't singing on time. And she said OK. And I got Suzy's brother [fiddler John Rothfield, brother of Suzy Thompson] ... and we pulled it off. And I must have had forty of my friends there.

There were two or three hundred people there. And my friends all sat together and hollered, and I had all those little white-haired ladies lined up in the front there. So it went over fine, but I almost had a heart attack.

Freida was already acquainted with Louisiana Sue at the time of her appearance at the Sacramento Jazz Jubilee. Sue had established a public presence in the Sacramento area with, among other things, her own cooking show on local television and a regular "Bayou Report" on Louisiana French cultural events that she phoned in to community radio station KVMR in Nevada City. Sue had advised Freida to have someone record her performance at the Jazz Jubilee on videotape. After the festival, Freida could not bear to watch herself on the tape but did give it to Louisiana Sue, who requested to see it. At that time, Louisiana Sue and Russell Ardoin were looking to ramp up a business in musical event production, and in Freida's videotape Sue saw through the musical rough edges to an articulate spokesperson for Cajun culture who could help her with the kinds of events she wanted to present. She also asked Freida to give the "Bayou Report" on the radio in her place when she was out of town, which led to an opportunity to substitute for the DJ at the Nevada City radio station itself, and eventually to a regular weekly DJ slot for Freida on the *Bayou Country* radio program.

Louisiana Sue subsequently hired Freida to appear at the California State Fair and other outdoor fairs and events in northern California. Freida's performances grew from the model established in her first appearance at Sacramento Jazz Jubilee: some accordion playing and singing, some talking, and showcasing of other musicians and entire bands. As mistress of ceremonies, she focused her onstage patter toward the goal of interpreting Cajun culture for those unfamiliar with it, and employed such devices as delivering an opening statement in both French and English, translating songs before she sang them in French, and writing original stories for storytelling that foregrounded certain aspects of Cajun life. After extracting a commitment from Freida that she would continue to provide such performances, Louisiana Sue invested in the construction of a portable stage set that became known as the "Cajun Back Porch," which served as one of two or more stages at Louisiana Sue's festivals and at other outdoor events to which Sue was a subcontractor.

Outside of her work for Louisiana Sue, Freida continued to improve her musicianship and expand her repertoire of Cajun dance music to the point where she could form her own band, Miss Freida and the Cajun Fusiliers. By 1996 her band was playing once or twice a month at the Hot and Spicy Restaurant in Old Sacramento, once every couple of months at the Moose Lodge in West Sacramento,

Miss Freida and the Cajun Fusiliers, Big Easy Festival, Sparks, Nevada, 2006. Photo by Sally Thibodeaux.

and other engagements. She recorded an album with her band and self-produced the release, *I've Got a Sou in My Shoe*, which includes a handful of original compositions. She has since retired from performing but continues to make herself available as a resource, as she was through the 1990s, to singers and songwriters in other California bands in matters of Cajun French vocabulary, translation, and pronunciation.

Susan Appe Ramon ("Louisiana Sue")[17]

Susan Appe Ramon was born and raised in Chalmette, Louisiana, just outside of New Orleans, "where the Battle of New Orleans was fought." Her mother's side of the family (Gonzales) were "Isleños or what they call 'white Creoles,'" an ethnic group of "people that came from Spain, to Portugal through the Canary Islands, to St. Bernard Parish" in New Orleans on a ship called the *Sacramento*. She jokes that as an adult when she moved with her husband to Sacramento, California, her children thought that the coincidence had some meaning. Her father's side of the family (Appe) was a mixture of German and Cajun; "My great-grandmother was a Martin, and she lived in St. Martinville, and she married a German." She grew up hearing French and Spanish being spoken at home. Some aunts spoke one, some the other, but she claims that they all understood each other. As children she and her siblings understood their aunts somewhat, but she never became comfortable speaking these languages.[18]

When she was a child, her parents and their friends had a practice of regular Friday night house parties, rotated among homes, where seafood was served and dancing took place to recorded music. The seafood could be in the form of a gumbo, a fish fry, a "sack of oysters," or a crawfish or crab boil. She remembers the music played as mostly Fats Domino and other New Orleans music, some "Spanish music," and very little if any Cajun music or zydeco. The hosts would roll up the carpet in their living room and everyone would dance on the hardwood floor. Sue learned to dance with her father by standing on his feet and moving with him. The communal feeling that resulted from these regular events had the strength of blood ties: "Everybody in Louisiana's related. But they're not, you know, I grew up thinking that people were my aunts and uncles and they were just friends of my mom's and dad's." She did get the opportunity to hear "back-porch Cajun music" when visiting some of her actual relatives in St. Martinville.

While Sue never studied music formally or played an instrument, her mother paid for speech lessons to train her away from her New Orleans dialect, and she had plenty of performing experience as a pupil in a parochial school.

> I was in chorus, and we did plays. I was in theater. I've always been in production, I think, my entire life. But growing up Catholic, you do. We make our children perform. They call them bazaars or festivals or flings or whatever you're going to have, you know, your socials. The schools had them, the elementary schools had them, the high schools had them. I belonged to CYO, which is Catholic Youth Organization. You plan a big thing and they build a stage and all the schoolchildren have to perform.... I think we were in elementary school and raised [money] through little penny parties and little productions where they'd have on the weekend and things like that, fifty thousand dollars to put an organ in. The school was raising the money! And it wasn't just bingo, you had to do these things. I think in Louisiana, we all grew up that way.

She remembers a participatory ethic to these school productions; there were no stars and all the children were on stage, with extended family in the audience looking on. She says she did not know that "the rest of the world didn't do that" until she moved away from New Orleans.

Her father's business was M & M Amusements, a company that supplied music to jukeboxes in New Orleans. Sue would accompany him on his rounds, so she got to know where all the clubs were. When she was old enough to sneak out as a teenager, she knew where to go, and the club owners knew her as Freddie's daughter, so they let her in even though she was sixteen, under legal age.

Sue also started attending public dances in church social halls and VFW halls as a teenager. She attended public high school and then Louisiana State University in Baton Rouge for a year and a half, returned to New Orleans and took some community college courses. Around this time she saw her first live zydeco performance, Clifton Chenier at the New Orleans Jazz Festival. She loved the music and found Clifton "charismatic." Once back in New Orleans, Sue also met a young man from Chico, California, who had been living in Louisiana for just a year. They eventually married and moved to Concord, in the greater Bay Area.

Sue remembers her newlywed stay in California as a "cultural shock" that she wanted to end as soon as possible. When asked about what she found difficult about living in California, she explains:

> ... the detachment that people have from each other, and plus there was no family to draw on. There wasn't any big house parties, and I didn't know a lot of Louisiana people out here. You get singular, and you're not singular at home [in Louisiana]. Everybody knows who you are.... Now, some people moved out here [to California] for that reason, because nobody knows who you are and your business. Where everybody knows [you], I didn't have a name, I was either Freddy or Irene's daughter, or somebody's niece, that's the essence of who you were. Out here, I became no one. But then you turn into yourself. It has its good points and its bad points, but I hated it. I hated raising my children in that environment, because they had no sense of family. I think that's what it was. And it's not even the personalness between your brothers and your sisters. It's a collective feeling in Louisiana. Anybody who ever visits there knows exactly what I'm talking about. Just a whole different feeling in the South and in Louisiana in particular. We all tend to know one another and know about each other. You know, who's your *mama*? You know, who's *your* mama is real important, because that's who you were. I was Freddy and Irene's daughter. My uncle was a big politician, I was Henry's niece. That's who you were. Who's your mama? So the sense of that is what I missed.

Sue's first sojourn in California was brief. Within a year, her husband enlisted in the air force and was stationed in the South, first in Florida and then in Mobile, Alabama, "which was great" as far as Sue was concerned. In Mobile the couple started a family and Sue was able to open up a restaurant and catering business that featured Cajun and New Orleans cooking. The restaurant was located near a federal office building, served breakfast and lunch during the week and seafood dinners on Fridays. This was before Paul Prudhomme's fame and the "Cajun craze," and she credited the restaurant's popularity to Mobile's proximity to New Orleans (some 140 miles) and the use of fresh Gulf Coast seafood.

Sue moved back to California, to Sacramento this time and with children, when her husband left the air force and became a U.S. marshal. She missed home and flew back to visit New Orleans several times a year. She also missed running her own restaurant, but instead of opening another one she wrote, printed, and sold thousands of copies of an eighty-page cookbook, *Louisiana Sue's Cajun Cookin Made Easy*. The book reaches out to a broader public in various ways; it contains not only recipes but also a "Cajun crossword," a glossary of potentially unfamiliar Louisiana terms, and an eight-page allegory of Sue's life story, illustrated with line drawings of herself, husband, and children as a family of crawfish. The recipes themselves are sprinkled with asides to the neophyte, such as advice for thickening without flour in gravy and gumbo (using potatoes) for those who cannot eat flour or who have trouble making a roux.[19]

After Sue published her cookbook she made several appearances on regional television and radio outlets to promote it and to talk about Louisiana cuisine. She would bring along recordings of Cajun music, zydeco, and New Orleans rhythm and blues to use as background music for these appearances. It was on such a speaking engagement that the idea of herself producing a festival of food and music first occurred to her. Her travels took her to the Sacramento River outside the small town of Isleton, California, where "all that was missing was the Spanish moss" to remind her of Louisiana. Isleton also staged (and still stages) an annual Crawfish Festival where the focus was on food.

Sue was working at the Isleton festival in 1986 or 1987 as a coordinator when she first met Creole musician Mark St. Mary, who was playing there. St. Mary, a Chenier-influenced piano accordionist who lived in the Sacramento area, in turn became her entrée into the network of Creole musicians in northern California, putting her in touch with Al Rapone (Queen Ida's brother) and Danny Poullard. Not only Mark but the extended St. Mary family was instrumental in introducing Sue to the Creole community in northern California and to the local zydeco scene: Mark's brother Kirby "Lucky" St. Mary and uncle Arsene St. Mary played in his band, and his uncle Charlie St. Mary played rubboard with Danny Poullard. Through this family Sue was also able to meet Houston and Lena Pitre, who along with their daughter Olivia Guillory organized the zydeco dances at St. Mark's Church in Richmond. Sue volunteered to help at some of the St. Mark's dances, mopping floors and whatever else needed to be done.

By 1989 or 1990 Sue had the public exposure from her cookbook and the community connections she needed to produce the first festival of her own at Travis Air Force Base in Fairfield. St. Mary, Poullard, and Rapone supplied the music for the weekend while Houston Pitre and others helped with the food.

> When we started at Travis, I said I need to find Louisiana people. I want 'em cookin'. I wanted the *real* Cajun and Creole influence, and the Cajuns are hard to find, because they don't group up out here. Like the Creoles stayed focused, they stayed within themselves, and there are whole pockets of Creole people, you know, and their families no matter what part of California you go into. It's not just like one isolated person. Like they know each other in Stockton, they're in Fresno. If you meet a Cajun, he doesn't know where the other Cajuns are. But the Creoles know where everybody is, so that was my link into the families and through that my first Travis festival. I started looking around for a dance instructor, couldn't find anybody.

To teach dance lessons, she eventually found Irene Tenney, a Berkeley resident from Argentina who was booking some dances in the area for bands traveling from Louisiana.

Around the same period as her first festival, Sue had some significant upheavals in her personal life, including a divorce and the deaths of both her parents. She had not danced in fifteen years, but she started driving to the Bay Area twice a week just to dance. She also helped Tenney with some of her events and started producing more of her own.

In 1992, the same year that Freida Fusilier gave her first public musical and storytelling performances at the Sacramento Jazz Jubilee and California State Fair, Sue and her partner Russell Ardoin founded a membership organization called the West Coast Cajun and Zydeco Music and Dance Association (WCCZMDA). As stated on a 1994 membership application form, "the purpose of this organization is to define and recognize the accomplishments and efforts of musicians, dancers, producers and supporters of Cajun, Creole and zydeco music and dance on the West Coast." Derivative objectives included "to pass a good time as often as we can"; "document the origins of Cajun and Creole music on the West Coast"; "helping the bands by getting their music to record companies, radio stations, and other venues"; "encouraging dance instructors to get us more dancers"; "coordinate an awards dance to honor the pioneers, past and present, for their efforts"; and "setting up a scholarship fund to help young musicians to learn and continue the tradition of Cajun and zydeco music." For a nominal fee, members received a T-shirt with the WCCZMDA logo and discounts at events produced by Louisiana Sue and others.

While there was clearly some enlightened self-interest at work in the founding of WCCZMDA in terms of building an audience for Cajun music and zydeco in northern California (with visions of creating a circuit up and down the coastal states of California, Oregon, and Washington for bands touring from Louisiana), the association did also achieve many of its stated objectives in its first few years. Sue drafted Freida Fusilier early on to write a history of Cajun music and zydeco on the West Coast. Jolene Adams, a recent graduate of the University of California, Berkeley from Houma, Louisiana, quickly joined the project as second author. Together, the two Cajun women embarked on a community oral history research project, interviewing twenty-four people about how Cajun music and zydeco came to California and flourished, including several Creole community members. An attempt was made through telephone interviews to include the perspective of the large population of Creoles in the Los Angeles area (southern California).

Fusilier and Adams self-published the results of their work in the form of a spiral-bound, forty-eight-page booklet titled *Hé, Là-Bas! A History of Louisiana Cajun and Zydeco Music in California* (Fusilier and Adams 1994). The history booklet was not an end in itself; rather it was intended as an adjunct document to the ceremonial recognition of the older musicians while they were still alive to receive it. The WCCZMDA held its first annual Awards Dance in November 1993, at which Louisiana Sue and Russell Ardoin presided. In the twelve months after the first WCCZMDA awards dance, the *Hé, Là-Bas!* booklet was published, and Adams, a linguistics major in college, returned to Louisiana to work for CODOFIL, and later for the Acadian Memorial in St. Martinville. The WCCZMDA awards dance continued for another three or four years, playing a temporary but important role in bringing together Louisiana French immigrants and those who had just come to the dance as a leisure activity, and doing so in a way that educated the leisure enthusiasts about the contribution of the immigrants to the cultural expressions they were enjoying.

By 1994 Louisiana Sue's business as an "event specialist," as she described herself on her business card, was in full swing. She self-produced festivals three months in a row, April (Fifth Annual Napa Cajun Gumbo Ya Ya), May (Cajun Crawfish Festival, in Vallejo), and June (Tardi Mardi Gras and Crawfish Fest, in Roseville), and presented stages at other festivals and fairs, including the Sacramento Jazz Jubilee in May with the Zydeco Flames, a Bay Area band. At the Napa festival of that year she debuted her Cajun Back Porch theme stage, hosted by "Miss Freida Fusilier" and featuring "jam sessions," "cultural presentations and authentic Cajun folklore." At this same festival the following year were added two more stages with their own billings, Planet Zydeco (with some futuristic stage props) and a Mardi Gras Cafe with blues and Dixieland music (suggesting a New Orleans theme).[20]

Her strategy for marketing and audience development for the music was straightforward: "they'll come for the food and stay for the music. But we've gotta

Dancers at Napa Festival, 1996. Photo by the author.

feed them first. . . . There are more eaters than dancers." She would hire a dance instructor to give lessons on waltz, two-step, and line dancing at her events to maximize the chances that the "eaters" (newcomers to Louisiana French culture) would become "dancers" and therefore buy bands' recordings (to practice their dance steps at home) and attend another dance or festival in the near future.

Sue produced more events in the 1990s than can be enumerated here. Other outdoor ventures included a Dance Ranch series at a rural location outside of Vacaville that was cancelled after two weekends of low attendance, and a Cajun Harvest festival. The Cajun Back Porch stage set made the rounds of county fairs. After some financial setbacks at her own festivals due to bad weather, she moved to minimize such risk by producing more indoor events: an eight-hour Mini-Fest on a Sunday afternoon in Suisun, a Bayou Room music and dance venue on weekends at an inn in Vacaville, and costume dance parties for Halloween and Mardi Gras.

When I interviewed her in 1997, Sue had recently begun booking Cajun and zydeco bands at the Orleans Casino in Las Vegas, a run that began with the casino's

Louisiana Sue at West Coast Cajun and Zydeco Music and Dance Association Mardi Gras dance, Suisun, California, circa 1997. Photo by the author.

grand opening in 1996 and lasted into early 1998. The bands that played there, who were booked for a week at a time, came from northern California (Crawdaddy, Tom Rigney, Zydeco Flames, Gator Beat, Al Rapone), southern California (Lisa Haley, Kent Menard), and also bands from Louisiana who were less established at that time (Tony Delafose, Lil' Brian and the Zydeco Travelers, Thomas Fields, Chubby Carrier). She explained her role in this enterprise as a response both to financial opportunity and to cultural pride.

> I could sit back, now that I have this account, which is a major account, and say, OK, I'm gonna hire the commercial side of this, have no problems, I don't even have to physically be there. I can send the contracts out, collect my commission, and live happily ever after. That's the money side of that. But there's a certain pride that says, well yeah, I could do that, but, what if I worked a little bit hard[er] and I paid my own ticket, and I flew back to Vegas whenever one of those dance bands needed me, and we still had French-speaking, downhome, grassroots music in Vegas, right up there with the big showtime ones. That's making less commission, spending more time, why am I doing that? I've asked myself that. And it comes from a certain pride. And I've seen it in Freida [Fusilier], I've seen it in Kent [Menard], I've seen it in Richie [Domingue]. We just get that way. And when it's done right, we don't boast, we

don't do anything, we just smile.... The crossover bands have better marketing skills, better management qualities, and better professionalism than I can want to ask for. That's why I ask myself, then why am I doing this? If I can get paid same money—same money—with less grief and headache, and it goes down deep into your soul and it's pride. So I don't want to change your music but I want you up there, I want you to have a CD cover, I want you marketed.

Sue's approach to helping bands to succeed in the casino environment was to coach them on dress, presentation, and audience interaction.

What I've tried to do is find a way to make what we have, the grassroots music, commercial without commercializing it. That is the fine line I walk. [So the band learns] steps and presentation. I said, I'm not going to change one note of the music. I might change your clothes, and how you stand when you do 'em, but I'm not going to change the music. Let's just put it on the plate prettier. Because all of the American bands that have marketed themselves better and have presented our music on that pretty plate have gotten somewhere. And that's the only thing they do differently. So hey, let's not fight that. Let's just put the parsley on the plate. Let's not set up in a dance formation. Let's have five people up front, or four if you've only got five people in your band. The only person in the back is the drummer, but give him a mic and let him talk, and let him sing backup vocals. The one-mic, I'm-gonna-sing, you're-gonna-dance, they're-gonna-play—don't work.

These adjustments in presentation of the music may have been eased by hiring musicians individually and putting together a band expressly for this initial run. First, Sue was able to get Cajun accordionist and singer Kent (also known as Kenny) Menard, who lived in southern California and was available for work but did not have his own band. He brought a guitarist he knew, and they hired a bassist and drummer who had never played Cajun music or zydeco before. Menard and Russell Ardoin rehearsed the band for a week to learn the music, at the same time they were working out details of clothing and dance steps. By the night of the casino's grand opening, they were ready.

This was a multimillion-dollar casino, they were opening, they had a big fireworks display that night on December eighteenth. [Where] we were, the stage is right off the front door. These big doors have brass alligators on them. And these big huge glass doors open up, and off to the side right there is the lounge with no walls. I mean, when they say "the lounge," they mean the lounge area. Because you're playing out to the entire casino. And I said, when those doors open they're just gonna run right past us to see this big, absolutely gorgeous hotel. And I had thought about it and I had packed beads and all kind of throws that I had had. Mardi Gras throws, in these suitcases. And when I got there, the marketing man says, well we have beads. We have beads all over the place, we're giving them away! Ooh, I said, get me some and I'll throw 'em. Because I figured, well this will be good, it's called the Orleans. So he brings me one bag of beads, which has got maybe, you know, six or ten dozen in it or whatever. And I looked at him and I said, this is it? And he said, well I can't find them. I said fine, and they were just opening. I had like ten or fifteen gross of beads in my car, and I sent for them. I said, get me my beads! We're gonna throw beads! So the fireworks went off at seven o'clock and when the last bu-bu-bu-booms went off, the doors popped open because seven o'clock is when their license was in effect. The doors fly open and fifteen thousand people start rushing in! And I went to the side of the stage and started throwing beads, and it looked like a herd of cattle turned to face me. The look on my face must have been unbelievable! I had never seen anything like that. And everybody put their arms up—that made the front page of the newspaper in Vegas. But they stopped dead in their tracks and started yelling for beads and dancing with us. And it was phenomenal, it was something I will never forget.

After Ramon and Ardoin's bands had been playing at the Orleans for three months (when our interview took place), certain patterns of audience interaction had developed. They found that their audience consisted not only of casino and hotel guests, but also people who lived and worked in Las Vegas, especially entertainment and construction workers. Some of these local patrons were also transplanted Cajuns and Creoles who would come to dance, especially on Friday nights.

By the time Sue's run in Las Vegas was over, the field research for this book had mostly been completed. Her relationship with Russell Ardoin ended, and she was focusing more on a business partnership with Dana DeSimone (see ch. 7) around the regular Friday night zydeco dances in Alameda. Thus, although her pace of activity has slowed as she has taken on other kinds of work, she has continued to present Louisiana French music to the public.

Ralph "Bobby" Gradney[21]

Bobby Gradney ("My real name is Ralph Gradney, but a lot of people know me by Bobby") is best known among northern California dancers as a food vendor at dance events and as former proprietor of Bobby's Back Door BBQ, a restaurant and dance venue in Richmond that flourished in the late 1990s. I interviewed him in the year 2000 when the restaurant was still open for business and hosting dances on Thursday nights.

Gradney was born in 1942 in east Texas, "in a little town they call Raywood between Beaumont and Houston, down Highway 90." When I asked him if both his parents were Cajun, he responded this way:

> My mother was French and Irish, my grandfather was French, his daddy came from France. And I also got Choctaw Indian in me. My mother's daddy, they were from Louisiana, they moved to Texas early—1918, 1920, I don't remember. And loaded on the train. And my grandfather came, it took him a week with a wagon and an old sow [laughs]. And they say as soon as he got out in Texas that old sow had pigs the same night. You know, one of those old, true stories. Took him a week from Lake Charles to Raywood, Texas with a team of horses and a wagon.

Bobby's mother (née DeVille) was perhaps seventeen when she took the train to Texas with her family where her father rejoined them. Shortly thereafter, she married Bobby's father, Rayfiel Gradney.

Like his mother, Bobby's father was a Louisiana native who relocated to Texas. "He was French. French and Indian. My grandfather, his dad was [one of] three brothers moved from France together in the eighteen hundreds. But my grandfather was born in 1869. And he was telling me the story—he couldn't talk English too well, he speaks French—that he heard about those Jesse James guys, he used to talk about all of that, Jesse James, but he didn't know who they were, you know? He lived to be ninety-nine years old." Bobby never learned any family stories about why his ancestors came over from France.

In the farming community where he grew up, the Gradney family was not the only one to have relocated from Louisiana. He was the tenth of eleven children, six brothers and five sisters, most of whom attended the small schoolhouse nearby.

> You see, my mother tell me, it's several families moved from Louisiana to Texas. The Fontenots, the Griffins, the Gradneys, which was me, and Trahan. Several Frenchmen coonass moved to Texas and they had their own church, and they formed their own school. They paid the teacher, they called it a little red-top school. Everybody went to school there. There was a community, and everybody was related to the same people, you know, it was all relations, and it all just built up from there. Some of my older brothers and sisters went to that little school. I went to another school, it was a high school. They had a regular school when I came through. I finished school in '61.

Bobby first met Danny Poullard, who was a few years older and living in nearby Beaumont, when Danny came to Bobby's school to play sports.

Bobby's father died at the age of forty-two, after which his mother raised the family on her own. There was a lot of work to do on the forty-seven-acre family farm.

> We had our own cattle and hogs, chickens, everything. We raised cotton, corn, hay. We had horses. We couldn't afford a tractor, we had horses and mules to work the farm with. I thought it was hard work at the time, but it was beautiful. I look back now, I wish I could do it again. I remember a Seven-Up truck passing down there, I'm picking cotton in the field, I'd say I hope you don't get in a wreck, but just drop me a bottle of soda out here! You know, just a hot soda, I'd really... but we couldn't afford it, we didn't have any money. Now I can drink all the soda I want and I got sugar diabetes. [laughs] But it was a good life.

He also helped his mother in the kitchen. "I learned to cook beans and mustard greens, everything. I like to eat, so I learned how to cook early. She taught me a lot, yeah. I learned how to make sausages from her, boudin, cheese, all that. I added my own seasoning, but the basics was from her. Gumbo, boudin, you name it. Stews, jambalaya." However, the most popular dishes in his restaurant—barbecue pork and beef—he did not learn from his mother, although they did smoke meats on the farm.

> My mom didn't know anything about barbecue. Tell you the truth, we didn't even barbecue. We always had fifteen, twenty head of cattle though. All we had was bean and rice, bean and rice, or roast. I didn't know what filet mignon was until I came to California. Everything was bean and rice. Cut up those steaks, you know? I remember canning meat, in jars. She told me how to process the sausage and they'd have some grease hogs, so many hogs for grease, pull out the grease, the lard, so many for meat. And different types of hogs. They way they'd do the sausage, they put some grease there and put the sausage on and smoke 'em. I remember the bacon. They'd put away and salt it down, salt pork for the beans and stuff, in the wintertime. Washing it out and smoking it. Sometimes we'd smoke, leave it hanging in the smokehouse, we might smoke it for a week or so. Slow smoke everything. But it's funny. Now my sausage, the sausage I make now myself, I could smoke in five hours, a beautiful smoke, golden brown. We didn't have refrigeration in those days, you see?

Bobby's mother spoke French with her children at home when they were young. "When we was going to school, my mother, we would speak French at home. But we'd go to school and we'd talk French among our people, you know, and big kids would make fun of us that didn't speak French, so we got embarrassed. So my mother started speaking in English. So, the little bit I know, it's a bad deal now, but at the time we was embarrassed [laughs] to speak French.... But I know better now though, you know. I would know more. I know all those bad words, yeah [laughs]." According to Bobby, there was no discipline from the teachers at his Texas school against children who spoke French during the school day. It was peer pressure that motivated them to speak English almost to the exclusion of French.

He remembers hearing Cajun music and zydeco when he was young, both live and on the radio. He feels that he did not really learn to dance until much later, as an adult in California.

> We had some guys called the Broussards used to play the accordions. It was just accordion they had, they had the little house dance in the yard. They had one or two musicians. My dad used to play the violin, but I don't remember. He wasn't a musician, just mess around with it at home. We had a radio station out of Port Arthur, Texas, every Saturday for one hour. And I used to listen to that and dance at home by myself, you know. Dance with a chair, anything. They had a lot of Cajuns in Port Arthur, Texas, you know. That's about an hour from where I grew up at. Around the Gulf, around Beaumont. And we looked forward to listening to that on Saturdays during the day on radio. And then I learned more about the dance zydeco out here, in California. But my mother knew about it. Her favorite song was "Jolie Blonde." One of the best one that plays it now that I like, I don't like the rest of his music, but I like his "Jolie Blonde"—Buckwheat. You know that movie, *Big Easy*? At the end when they got married that song, "Jolie Blonde," that's Buckwheat's song. Beautiful song.

In addition to Louisiana French music, he enjoyed listening to rock and roll, artists like Little Richard and Chuck Berry. A few years later, he came to admire the music of James Brown.

For fun, Bobby and his brothers participated in rodeo, both bareback and bull riding. They also had a reputation for rowdy behavior, which eventually led to Bobby's decision to move to California after high school. "The sheriff of Liberty County asked [my brothers], he said 'I'm not runnin' you boys out of town, but could you at least change counties?' [laughs] So, that drove us to San Francisco." Bobby had just finished high school and gotten married when he found himself practically alone on the family farm. By then his mother and brothers had all moved to San Francisco, and he and his wife followed them a few months later.

I just moved out here just to start living, a new life, and the first job that I had was at this restaurant, Scotty's Drive-In in San Francisco at Divisadero and Golden Gate. This guy that my older brother went to school with in Texas, they weren't related, but he knew him, so he wanted me to go to work for him. Ninety dollars a week, that was some big bucks for me! And he had his daughter train me about two hours one night, next night he turned me loose by myself. I was scared, but I did it. Cook, and everything by myself. Sold beer. I was scared but I mastered it. I was bad, I mastered the hell out of it. He was proud of me. I made him some money, too. Had a lot of fun. We had a charcoal grill, and I'd have me a few beers and I'd take the spatula, made six or eight hamburgers and I'd take the meat and the spatula like this [mimics holding spatula with right hand in an upward motion], hit my arm like that [stops upward motion by clapping down on his right arm with his left hand], and all of 'em would flip over and the flame would come over, and they'd be choo! choo! He thought that was a big deal. Like the Japanese, Chinese do it, that was my own little show.

Bobby then worked in Burbank (southern California) as a mechanic for a year, after which he came back when he had an opportunity to buy the drive-in restaurant where he had worked before. After not quite a year he tired of the restaurant business and moved on to a job driving trucks in Richmond.

After working in Richmond a short time, he moved there and settled in the East Bay. He spent the bulk of his working career with a petroleum tank firm, unloading liquid products from ships and barges onto tank trucks and tank cars at Richmond's seaport facility. He retired from the firm as a foreman some twenty years later after developing a case of vertigo that prevented him from working any longer.

During the years that he worked in the Richmond petroleum industry, Bobby also made sausages in his garage and sold them to people he knew. Although one of his brothers had been to occasional dances where John Semien had played, no one in his family became very active in Bay Area's Louisiana French dance scene until Bobby's divorce. After that, he started going to church dances and "loved it." Although St. Mark's parish was close to where he lived in Richmond, he specifically mentioned All Hallows parish in San Francisco as one where many dances were held. Once in this social network he met Louisiana Sue, who learned of his cooking talents.

Thus it was that after he retired, Gradney started a catering business called Bobby's Cajun Kitchen. "I used to work with Louisiana Sue. She did some festivals, I did some catering there with that, yeah. I did Santa Rosa Fairgrounds three years in a row, fourteen days at a time. Boy, that was kind of tough. I did some on my own, I did gumbo for five hundred people at [Great] American Music Hall one time for Chris [Strachwitz]. I did several things for him. He buys sausage from me and might have his own little gig at his shop there."

In 1996 Bobby expanded his operations with the help of his oldest daughter by opening a restaurant in the back of bar named the Alvarado Gardens in Richmond, leasing the space from the bar owner. The bar stretches lengthwise from front to back. From the front door facing out onto San Pablo Avenue (a major commercial thoroughfare), one would walk in and first pass the bar with stools on the left, restrooms on the right; then a linoleum dance floor area with bandstand on the right; then tables where restaurant patrons ate and dancers sat when not dancing; and finally a back hallway with a window on the right where one could place a food order and peer into the restaurant kitchen where the food was prepared. At the end of the back hallway is a door leading out to a small parking lot. The layout of the place gave him the idea for what to name his restaurant. His explanation surprised me:

> Bobby: Bobby's Back Door and Cajun Barbecue. The reason why, a lot of people say, I just picked that name out of the sky. I called it that to direct people to the back where the parking is. I said Bobby's Back Door, so I figure they'll come to the back door and see the parking and find a place, you know? That was my intention.
> Author: So it didn't have anything to do with the song?
> Bobby: No, huh uh. What song? No.
> Author: D. L. Menard has a song called "The Back Door."
> Bobby: No, no, it doesn't have anything to do . . . I was just trying to show directions to the people to come to the back door to find a place. Yeah, that was the reason.

So the reference to Cajun musician D. L. Menard's 1960s regional hit song, "The Back Door" (*La porte d'en arrière*) was an unintentional but appropriate inside reference for a venue that featured live music and dancing to Louisiana French dance music once or twice a week for the five years or so that it was open. Bobby's new wife Lisa added decorations on the walls: fish nets, photos that they took themselves of the shrimp fleets of New Iberia, Louisiana, and of sugar cane fields, Mardi Gras masks, and photos of musicians.

The success of Bobby's Back Door Barbecue exemplified Louisiana Sue's saying, "they'll come for the food, they'll stay for the music." The restaurant was open every day and did a brisk lunch business, whereas Louisiana French dance music was only heard once or at most twice a week (with live blues sometimes on other nights). Because there was no wall or door between the bar and the music and the bar owner did not want his regular patrons to have to pay a cover charge, Bobby

"Famous People & Bands That Eat at Bobby's" sign, 1995 Napa Festival. Photo by the author.

could not collect a cover charge to pay the band and keep any profit. Instead, he offered bands a modest fixed amount and had them pass the hat during band breaks to supplement their income for the evening. Thus neither Bobby nor the bar owner derived any income directly from the music. From a business perspective, the music was ancillary to the food.

Bobby's barbecue regularly received high marks from reviewers. All of the lessons he learned from his mother in cooking and meat preservation served him well in his second career. With this knowledge he also brings very specific opinions and ideas about what he wants:

> Five years ago, I didn't know the first thing to put in barbecue sauce. A lot of people say this is all right, but I had a cousin in Texas, he died with his recipe. If I had his recipe, I'd throw mine away. That was some good stuff. He'd throw the meat away and just eat the bread and sauce. [laughs] Oh, it was good, yeah. But he wouldn't tell anybody. Mine's not bad. See, a lot of people use this molasses. Have you noticed most a lot of your barbecue has a glaze on it where you put the sauce? I don't have

that. I don't use molasses. There's no glaze on it. That's sweet, I don't like that sweet taste. I go away, it might be a week or so before I eat [my own sauce], it might be a little piece of biscuit and sauce. I say hey, this is some pretty good stuff. You know, to myself. Just check it out, see if it's still hangin'.

He also preferred to have an outdoor barbecue pit for the flavor it gave, but city regulations required him to move it inside.

The moving of the barbecue pit was just one of many factors that caused Bobby dissatisfaction in his situation at the Alvarado Gardens. The kitchen was too small for the restaurant to be able to offer as full a variety of dishes as he would have liked; for example, seafood dishes were a rarity. Then there was the fact, already mentioned, that he could not work out an agreement with the bar owner to ask a cover charge for live music. Bobby did eventually close his restaurant at the Alvarado Gardens bar and open another one, Bobby's Cajun BBQ, a no-frills storefront elsewhere in Richmond. The new location offers the same range of food as his previous operation but without the capacity for live music or dancing.

Richard Domingue[22]

Musician and songwriter Richard Domingue (1947–2005) was born in a small country hospital in Rayne, Louisiana. Richard's Cajun father met his Irish American mother in Oregon circa 1945 and brought her back to Louisiana, where they started a family of four boys and one girl. Richard spent most of his childhood in Louisiana. His father tried to escape poverty by working in the steel mills in Pittsburgh, where the family moved in 1948 for three or four years, but his father got fired, "probably because he didn't get along and probably a little bit was cultural." So they returned to Louisiana for good after that, living mostly around Lafayette. Richard's mother took ill when he was nine years old and died when he was fourteen. He was the oldest and took over raising his younger siblings while his father worked. He was driving by the time he was fourteen; "We had a little French woman I'd go pick up at noon from school, and she'd cook and I'd take her back at night." His father, who had a college education, found financial success working in the oil industry.

French was spoken on his father's side of the family up to but not including Richard's generation. "Probably if my mother had been Cajun, we would have been speaking French in the house. But there was a huge kind of a inferiority complex that the Cajuns had about the French, because the French is not a written language. So it's really, totally slang, and it's totally different depending on what little town you're in and what little family.... Dad told me he couldn't understand some of the French even in Breaux Bridge."

Once back in Louisiana, the family would go to nearby Duson almost every weekend to visit his paternal grandparents. Richard's grandfather Lucas Domingue was an important early musical influence.

> He was hard core, real hard core Cajun. He didn't speak English that well. I think he only went to the sixth grade. My grandfather was a Cajun musician most of his life. And they did a mix of Cajun music and Dixieland. And he was interested in all of the instruments, not just the Cajun music. It was cool because he had a country store in a little town called Duson, which is between Rayne and Lafayette. It's like a one-stoplight town, but they had the main store. He had all of the old oil dust on the floor, that kind of kept the dust down in the stores. It gave it a particular smell. But as you walked in the store, the store was rectangular, up on the left hand side in the back, in the corner, maybe fifteen feet by fifteen feet he had a canned-goods setup. Canned goods went up to the ceiling and behind that he had his music. So he had a piano back there and he used to make guitars. He hand-made guitars out of two-by-fours of plywood and he retuned 'em. He was kind of an inventor. He tuned 'em the same way that I think tenor guitars are tuned, like straight fifths or some damn thing. And then he had a triple-neck guitar that he had developed out of two-by-fours, and one was like a mandolin, and one was a bass, and a regular guitar in the center. They had little pickups on 'em. So he was heavily involved in the whole music scene. I mean it was just a part of his life. Same way with a lot of Cajuns. It's kind of what they did when they weren't working. By that time he wasn't playing that much. He was just kind of fussing around. He played professionally when he was younger, I think, in his twenties and thirties, but then they got into the store and got busy and stuff. But he always, always, always was messing with music, so I basically got a lot of my inspiration from him.

At his grandfather's suggestion, Richard took some piano lessons starting at age six, and his siblings took piano instruction as well. Richard did not get personally involved with Cajun music until much later.

> My dad didn't like Cajun music at all. So I was raised around Ray Charles. That's all he listened to was Ray Charles, and then he'd take us to the James Brown concert. But of course Cajun music is always there. It was always on the radio. It was on the TV shows Saturday morning, KLFY, they'd broadcast a live show. And of course

at that time it was also segregated, so you weren't getting any of your black artists, either, but they were extremely popular among the Cajuns, always had been. It was just a real complex, very interesting musical scene, because you had everything, not just Cajun. You got funk, you got blues, you got ballads, you got all your swamp pop guys. So all that stuff was on the radio and Louisiana basically had its own top 40. There were songs you would hear on the radio that we thought they were national hits. But they were regional songs. So the music was just very fertile, sort of contained in this bubble. It's like a swamp bubble that goes from New Orleans over to Houston. That whole area, if you drive through there when you hit Houston you'll run into this humidity bubble. [laughs] Seems like nothing ever gets out of there! It's a funny spot, man.

He does not remember exactly how he learned to dance, only that he was young when he learned. "I was raised dancing to Clifton Chenier and the Meters. So those guys used to come through Lafayette all the time. And I used to drive by Clifton's house every day, going to school." Buckwheat Zydeco played at his high school prom. He remembers that black bands would play for white dances, but not the other way around.

Richard graduated from high school in 1965, and life in the segregated South—at a time when the civil rights movement was in full swing—made him restless. His unease led him first to the West Coast and then to the other side of the country for college at Harvard.

When I was seventeen I didn't want to be in the South anymore, after my mother's death I was pretty upset about the whole thing. And at that time, I was getting hip to the racism and the edge and the anger. And civil rights was just brewing and my dad wasn't a racist type guy. So it was like a war zone. When I'd walk to school, you just didn't walk in certain neighborhoods. And they weren't just black, you had your working-class white neighborhoods that were just as violent. It hadn't been desegregated yet, so I was raised in the segregated South. But you know how your instincts are, when you experience that level of suffering that everybody has—on both sides, you know, I mean it's no fun being a slaveowner with a whip, that doesn't feel good. And it doesn't feel good being whipped. So on both sides you could start to experience the amount of suffering that was involved, and the difficulty and working with that is pretty amazing. So I think it got a little too much and when I was seventeen I left and I told my dad I was going to hitchhike out. And he gave me a 1950 Chevrolet. So I drove that out to Oregon where my mother's folks were and I worked out there for six weeks. And I ran into an uncle there and I didn't know what I was going to do. And he said well why don't you go to the East Coast and go to some Ivy League school? And I said [hesitating] OK.

Richard does not know how he got accepted, except that Harvard was making an attempt to diversify its student body at the time. Once he arrived there, he did not like it. The cultural adjustment was not easy. He found it a "soulless place," suited either for high-level intellectuals or future power brokers. "Your roots-type people, we rolled through there, I think, got what we wanted, and left and never looked back."

Richard remembers getting "seriously depressed" while he was at college, and considered enlisting in the military to go fight in Viet Nam. Instead, a friend convinced him to go study abroad in France, where after a year he had learned to speak French.

> So I studied French in France and learned French there. Man, I was so happy, I came back [to Louisiana] and I started talking French and they wouldn't talk to me. And it really pissed me off to no end, I couldn't believe it. I mean these guys first of all wouldn't teach us French, and then when we actually go out of the way to learn French.... But it wasn't their fault. They were just sort of humiliated because I had learned high French or something, Parisian French. And then it wasn't a big step to learn Cajun. It's not as big a jump as most people think. There's probably three or four hundred words that are key.

After his time in France, Richard finished his bachelor's degree in philosophy and returned to Louisiana. There, he learned to speak Cajun French with persistence and the help of the Rev. Msgr. Jules Daigle's Cajun dictionary.[23]

Once back in Lafayette, a long-haired Richard managed to avoid the draft and do some antiwar protest work, through which he met a black trumpeter named Wallace Hammond. This musical connection led to work playing guitar with local blues and funk bands. A couple of years later he became seriously ill, lost weight, and had a "general spiritual crisis." When he had recovered enough he packed up and drove to California, ending up at a Zen center that Jakusho Kwong Roshi was establishing at that time.

The onetime philosophy major would find a home at the Sonoma Mountain Zen Center from approximately 1975 to 1982. There he meditated in the mornings and evenings, worked during the day as a carpenter, and continued to play music.

> Because of politics, I was interested in community life. And I had been involved in political communities that had sort of disintegrated. And of course, being Cajun,

there's always that sort of community orientation, you know? So I went up there and just got interested in the whole community life and the meditation practice, and had started to deal with some of the internal issues that had come up all along: my mother's death, the crisis of going through an East Coast university and it didn't make any sense. You weren't going to be a doctor, lawyer, Indian chief, so here you were out on the streets again just like you were before. So there was no way to put all those pieces together, plus all the emotional stuff with the racism and general kid stuff. So I ended up staying there for about six or seven years. Playing some music still, always was playing some guitar. I started to become a carpenter when I got out here. My grandfather's people had been carpenters. So that's when the whole thing started to make sense in terms of what I was going to do with who I was. Because I was a manual laborer–type guy, was not an intellectual-type guy. And I was a musician.... So then things started making more sense. [laughs] I said OK, now I can make a living being a carpenter and I can play a little music on the weekend. This is a good thing! Just doing construction and playing music on the weekends, just like a regular coonass! Just like they always do, just like grandpa done, all the people before.

Shortly after moving out of the Zen center, Richard met his wife Carolyn. She had a daughter from a previous marriage; they then had two children of their own. As a musician he played blues, R&B, and "other roots music" for a long time before coming around to Cajun music. He was aware of Queen Ida but did not participate in the network of Louisiana French immigrants. Eventually, though, the "Cajun craze" caught up to him, such as Rockin' Sidney Simien's pop hit, "Don't Mess With My Toot Toot."

I don't remember how it happened, but eventually people were asking me to play Cajun music, or zydeco music. They knew I was from south Louisiana. And the music was starting to become popular, sort of coming up, and I didn't realize that there were that many people here that were into it. So the music, I think, through "Toot Toot" and some of those other songs had started to gain a certain level of national prominence. Besides your local powerhouse scene here. But I was always on the fringes of it, I don't know why. At one point, about seven or eight years ago [prior to 2000], I said, well, OK, let's just go for it. And I had my own band, I'd been running my own bands for ten or fifteen years. So I knew how to keep a band together and book jobs and pay people and write songs and all of that stuff. So it was just a question of shifting over, and learning the songs in the tradition like you do with anything, and studying with the people that know the stuff. I went back to Louisiana and took accordion lessons from a guy named René Stutes in Duson, that was a friend of my grandmother's. So I went and taped him, and he was a beautiful cat, man. Real simple, old style, not anything complex like what Danny [Poullard] does. Danny is extremely talented. I mean, he's on another level.

Richard was therefore mostly self-taught on accordion, working from his tapes of René Stutes and an instruction tape on Cajun accordion that France's Gérard Dôle put out on Folkways Records.[24]

With accordion in hand, in the early 1990s he began incorporating Cajun and zydeco numbers into the repertoire of his band Gator Beat. The band had been together since the mid-1980s and already had a following in Napa and Sonoma counties, where they played most of their engagements. An important part of the band's profile even through its progression of musical styles was an emphasis on original songwriting.

> My whole goal is to be a little bit like Boozoo or Professor Longhair, where you have a body of maybe twenty-five or thirty songs that are just your own songs and maybe some of them are unique and maybe others aren't that great, or real generic. I don't have a big attitude about it, but I felt like I always wanted to have a sound. And this is the way the band sounds, and nobody else sounds that way and if you want that sound you gotta go see that band. And you'll probably get some kind of regional popularity and you'll develop a decent following if you follow that kind of creative push.

In 1996, Louisiana Sue had the assignment to book zydeco bands for the Sacramento Jazz Jubilee. After a booking fell through with another local musician, Sue turned to Gator Beat. "She knew I was from Louisiana, and I'm sure she knew I wasn't that good. Which I wasn't at that time, in terms of the music, you know. But I could always sing even if I couldn't necessarily play the accordion that well. So I always had French." Sue asked Gator Beat for a Mardi Gras CD specifically to sell at the Sacramento festival, and they recorded *Mardi Gras Fever*, their first album with three songs (out of ten) composed by Richard. They were well received at the festival, as evidenced by follow-up invitations to play at other traditional jazz festivals and by Louisiana Sue to play at the Orleans Casino in Las Vegas. The next year they produced a second CD, *See Ya Later, Alligator*, that featured nine songs Richard wrote. In 1998 they traveled to Louisiana to play at the Breaux Bridge Crawfish Festival.

For all his interest in the French language and his fond memories of his grandfather's store and of Cajun community life, Richard did not feel the need to restrict himself to anyone's notion of a traditional musical style. While part of the band's repertoire fell within the conventional framework of waltzes and two-steps, other songs featured beats and hooks inspired by New Orleans street music or R&B. A saxophonist was a regular member of his band, and he used a pennywhistle on one or two numbers. Some songs alternated back and forth between French and English, a technique also employed by Queen Ida. Appropriately enough for a band based in northern California wine country, one of the band's most popular original songs is "Zydeco Wine." All of these moves appeared to be part of a concerted effort to reach out to audiences who have not come to dance necessarily or even to hear Louisiana French music, whether it be at a traditional jazz festival or a casual gig where music is not the main focus. "I got involved in telling people stories about the music and sort of educating and entertaining people about the music and the culture, and it really took off." The traditional jazz festival circuit became a strong source of income that allowed the band to produce their recordings. In addition to playing on stage, festivals hired them to play a street dance outside the festival, open to the public in an attempt to reel in a younger crowd to the festival itself (or after the festival is over).

Gator Beat also played occasionally for dances in the Bay Area at some of the venues where the Cajun and zydeco dance regulars go, but such gigs were the exception for them. Unlike most of the northern California Cajun or zydeco bands, they emphasized original songwriting and a show package over playing predictable sets of standards from the Louisiana French dance hall repertoire that California dancers tend to prefer. In this respect the band in the area most akin to Gator Beat is Tom Rigney and Flambeau, a lineup headed by a former fiddler for Queen Ida that paradoxically has been quite popular with the dance hall regulars at Ashkenaz and elsewhere. "We didn't [initially] go down into that Cajun/zydeco scene because I knew that the music that we were creating wasn't their traditional copy bands. But now, because people do have ears and people do have a sense of what's original, we're at a point now where it's carrying us instead of me having to carry it. People come out, we have lots of work. We've developed a certain amount of popularity and a certain amount of originality, so that's great. I managed to accomplish what I wanted to do."

Development of the Northern California Scene, 1985–2005

Prior to the "craze," live Cajun or Creole music could be heard in the Bay Area mostly at the church dances that took place about twice a month, with occasional dances at Ashkenaz in Berkeley starting in 1976 and dates at other clubs. The musicians available to play were also few in number: John Semien was active until around 1980, and Danny Poullard remembered only two other accordionists who would occasionally play at house parties when he first arrived circa 1961. Clifton Chenier started visiting occasionally in the mid-1960s. When she was just starting to play in public in the mid-1970s, Queen Ida and her brother Al Rapone would play for dances with some frequency, but when her career took off she was on tour most of the time. That left the Louisiana Playboys, with Danny Poullard, to play the bulk of the dances. This was the Cajun-zydeco scene that the first folk dancers found when they happened upon Cajun dancing in the early 1980s (see ch. 7). There were also a few folk musicians in the 1960s and 1970s who were learning some Cajun songs and incorporating them into their recordings and coffeehouse performances (see ch. 6). The mid-1980s saw the beginning of significant growth of the scene by all measures: venues, events, dancers, and bands. The Cajun craze itself provided a baseline of economic demand for the music among the general public. Another factor was the increasing amount of attention Danny Poullard was giving to teaching others how to play the music, which increased the number of musicians to supply live music.

With increased popular interest in Louisiana French culture in the 1980s came increased business opportunities. Event promoter Leonard Iniguez started holding dances regularly at DeMarco's 23 Club in Brisbane, a country music bar just south of San Francisco where Betty LeBlanc would later have her events. The 23 Club had a reputation as a honky-tonk where several country music stars had played over the years, which made it especially suitable in some people's minds as a place for Louisiana French music to be heard. Musician Billy Wilson occasionally hosted a masquerade party, which he dubbed the Grand Alligator Ball, at the Jack London Club in Oakland until the facility was condemned in 1993, at which point he helped inaugurate the Friday night zydeco dances at the Alameda Eagles' Hall. Suzy Thompson recalls the Alligator Ball phenomenon:

> There were these irregular *happenings*, that's the only way I can describe them, in Oakland at this *really* funky place called the Jack London club which I think must have been a whorehouse about a hundred years ago. And downstairs there was a bar, and upstairs all these little rooms, you know, and then in the back, the guy who owned it lived there, and you'd go outside and down some steps and there's another area and down some other steps and there's another building that looked like it was gonna fall down.... And Bill Wilson and some other people would put on these events there, and they were called Gator Balls, where they'd decorate the whole inside, and then they'd have about five different bands playing different kinds of music. And we played there some. I think that a certain number of people got turned on to the Cajun music from coming to those, too, because that cast its net pretty wide. It was a truly amazing experience. The first time we went to one, Corinna was

a baby and we actually went out, you know, we had a babysitter and got dressed up. We opened the door and walked in and my first thought was that when *I* was little and my parents would get dressed up to go out, this was the place I imagined that they were going to. There was confetti and decorations and the band playing, and people drinking, and people all dressed up, and Mal Sharp was going around with a microphone interviewing people, and it just was like this incredible party! I never saw anything like it before.[25]

Business was good but in general still not easy; the longevity of Ashkenaz and Eagles' Hall as places to dance stands in contrast to the dozens of shorter and longer runs of dances at other venues over the years. Because of all the media coverage of the Cajun craze, proprietors of venues for live music in the Bay Area were open to booking Cajun and zydeco bands, but they would often be disappointed with the financial results. Not only did dancers require more space for dancing than many clubs provide, but as a group they exhibited unusual characteristics, as Billy Wilson describes in this 1995 analysis:

> The people who habituate this kind of music are the kind of people who don't drink, they don't want to spend a lot of money going to a show, because they want to go three, four, five, six times a week. A big-time band could come into town and charge twenty-five bucks to get in, because they're only going to be around once a year, and the people will come and do that. This is a different type of scene. You've got a scene where, um, the dancers are hooked on it. They no longer can stay home and watch TV, that's just not possible, you know? If it's out there to be had, they'll be out there having it. What they need is a lot of real estate on that floor. They need that area of real estate to be free of cigarette smoke, and they need a good band that's gonna play hot tunes for a whole night, and a place to park their car. So, obviously, any bars and clubs are basically out. This is another thing that neither the bands nor the clubs have learned yet. The clubs are well aware of the myth that zydeco is hot. So I can call any club in town and book a gig, unless it's one of the gigs that we've already burned down. [laughs] Because, "Oh, oh, yeah, that stuff's supposed to be hot, I've been reading about it in these articles that people are writing." And so they'll book it. Then the dancers come, and they don't buy anything. They'll pay, they'll pay their money to get in, they'll pay a decent price to get in. You can charge more than the two or three dollars that some places want to charge.[26]

With so many exacting requirements, it is no wonder that so many clubs and restaurants booked Louisiana French music two or three times and then gave up. The cover charge could not be too high or people would not attend, but it had to be high enough to make up for the lack of food and beverage receipts—which, at Ashkenaz for example, would be miniscule at Cajun dances compared to other nights that featured reggae or West African music.[27]

Cigarette smoke and alcohol are parts of the experience of dancing in Louisiana (as they were at the church dances in California) that outsiders as a group preferred to filter out. The state of California has since banned smoking in all public indoor spaces, so the presence of smoke is no longer a factor that differentiates one venue from another. Explanations for the collectively abstemious nature of the dancers fall into the category of speculation. I would hazard to guess that the influence of alcohol gets in the way of a particular kind of dance experience that outsiders find enjoyable about Cajun and zydeco dancing that is qualitatively different from Cajun and Creole experiences. I believe this singular focus on the physical activity of dancing to the exclusion of other aspects is what Dana DeSimone encapsulates when he says, "I used to be this dance snob, thinking, 'Aw, I only gotta dance.'" The impulse to rush the dance floor on the band's first song at the church dances is another indicator of this focus.

One sign that the Cajun craze has perhaps passed its peak in northern California is the fewer number of festivals with Louisiana themes compared to the 1990s, when such events were Louisiana Sue's primary business. During the height of the craze, weekend-long outdoor events such as Franklin Zawacki's Bay Area Cajun and zydeco festivals (circa 1988–94), brought several bands from Louisiana and generated a certain level of contagious excitement about the music among outsiders who may have been hearing it for the first time. The festivals that have survived into the new millennium, such as the Ardenwood Festival, have adopted the more economically sustainable approach of bringing one or two groups from the Gulf Coast and filling in the rest of the schedule with local bands. Another event that does this is the Isleton Crawdad Festival, where Louisiana Sue first made a connection with the local Creole community (and which credits significant technical assistance in its early years from organizers of the Breaux Bridge Crawfish Festival in Louisiana).[28]

The story of how Freida was hired to perform by the Sacramento Jazz Jubilee, and of her ambivalence about it, represents a nexus of various types of controversy that have recurred in the Northern California Cajun and zydeco scene over the two decades since it has grown beyond the immigrant community. What she called "the bastardization of my culture" refers to the willingness of the event producer to hire a performer to fill a slot labeled "zydeco" with little regard for musical quality or fit to the category (she plays Cajun music, not zydeco) and the willingness of the public to consume and accept the entertainment as labeled. She

Sign outside Hot & Spicy Restaurant, Old Sacramento, 1998. Photo by the author.

sees the same sort of misrepresentation and misperception in the presentation of Cajun food to an uncritical California public, which is why she had initially resisted going to see Beausoleil—she had thought they were going to be an American band playing a rough approximation of Cajun music until she heard the name "Doucet." Louisiana Sue talks of having to walk a "fine line" between staying close to the culture that she knew and presenting something that the general public would accept, and this was a line that both Sue and Freida found themselves walking. The Hot and Spicy restaurant where Freida played regularly for some time was located in the touristic heritage district of Old Sacramento, a special district of the city built to suggest the Old West and geared to shoppers and tourists, where the Sacramento Jazz Jubilee usually stages some of its events. The restaurant advertised its cuisine to passersby as "The Cajun Taste of Old New Orleans!"—a staple misrepresentation conflating Cajun culture with New Orleans that was also present at the Orleans Casino.[29]

An interesting contrast to the Hot and Spicy's promotion of hyper-self-conscious consumption of Cajun commodities is Bobby Gradney's naming of his restaurant, Bobby's Back Door BBQ, whose inside reference to Cajun culture was so unself-conscious he wasn't even aware he was making it. Many who enjoyed music in his restaurant appreciated it for its unpretentiousness, and indeed a lack of pretension or self-consciousness is often welcomed as a sign of authenticity, recalling Rousseau's "wound of reflection." The topic of self-consciousness arises often when the Cajun craze is discussed, as generally is true in situations where authenticity is at issue and the preservation of heritage is under discussion.[30]

Concerning the rise of cultural tourism in southwestern Louisiana in the 1980s, Barry Ancelet wrote:

> There are inherent problems, such as self-consciousness and misinformation. On a recent fishing trip with a friend, I found myself sitting in a Cajun brand boat, using Cajun-brand crickets and grabbing a Cajun-brand beer from a Cajun-brand ice chest filled with Cajun-brand ice.... Cajun musician Marc Savoy was asked recently if he regretted that the Cajuns had been discovered. He answered, "What's worse is that the Cajuns have discovered themselves." On the other hand, it is unreasonable to expect the Cajuns to remain lost somewhere in the nineteenth century. If we are going to open ourselves to the outside, we should at least try to do it well and in our own terms.[31]

Here again Louisiana Sue's "fine line" appears, as well as "a certain pride" she took in doing things her way. Another angle on these same issues (again from Marc Savoy) is an outcry against "born-again Cajuns" who were born into the culture but attempted to disown it until it became fashionable:

> The problem however, is that because of this break in the continuity of all cultural aspects, the vision, attitude and understanding of these nouveau Cajuns have changed and are totally different than of those who never abandoned it in the first place. The imagery I use is the one of grandpa's old buggy that has been under the barn for 100 years and has been preserved by the traditional grandson's attitude of stewardship. The tourist came over for a look at the old buggy that the steward lovingly shows off in its original condition, but they can't quite connect with its original state or comprehend how it functioned or what its meaning is. The "born-again" knows what to do to make it noticeable. He paints it a flashy red color, puts rubber tires in place of the iron wheels, covers up the cracked, worn, leather seats with nauga-hide, and voila—instant success by distortion of the real thing. I have always noticed that the people who grew up immersed in their culture and have always continued to embrace it in good times as well as bad are the ones less likely to impose any changes. They are satisfied with it as it is and love it for that reason.[32]

Clearly, the path to representing Cajun and Creole cultures to the outside world is strewn with pitfalls for insider and outsider alike. Judging from their comments above, Freida, Sue, and Richard all were aware of the potential problems and decided (with some musical trepidation on the part of Freida and Richard) that they would make the effort to improve upon the misrepresentations they saw all around them.

Returning to the topic of social capital and the observation from the beginning of this chapter, that Cajuns in California have or had no social network of their own: Freida Fusilier had been pursuing her interests in travel and other cultures for years when a viewing of the film *Belizaire the Cajun*, followed by seeing Beausoleil perform live near her home in Sacramento, reminded her of the interest she had taken in her own culture when she was younger. Her Cajun network consisted mostly of friends and family back in Louisiana until she needed to find someone to teach her how to play the accordion her brother had built for her, when she contacted Chris Strachwitz's record store in order get in touch with Danny Poullard. Louisiana Sue was working on her own in Sacramento, promoting her cookbook and her knowledge of Louisiana cuisine, when she discovered the Isleton Crawdad Festival and through it met Mark St. Mary, her initial personal contact with the local Creole community. From that first contact she was able to strengthen relationships by volunteering at church dances and to leverage the social capital then available to her to produce her own festival at Travis Air Force Base. After that first experiment, a divorce propelled her to start attending dances regularly in the Bay Area and to involve herself further in event production. Divorce likewise was a catalyst for Bobby Gradney, who had known of the church dances going on nearby but had never felt sufficiently motivated to attend prior to his change in marital status. A second life change, a health problem that required him to retire from the oil industry, created the time for him to pursue his interests in food, while the dance scene provided him the business opportunities. Like Bobby, Richard Domingue knew of "your local powerhouse scene here. But I was always on the fringes of it, I don't know why." For him, the wake-up call was when people started asking why his band was not playing Louisiana hits like Rockin' Sidney Simien's "Toot Toot." As with Freida, the long arm of popular culture pulled him back to reflect on his ethnic group of origin. None of these four individuals was connected to a parallel social network of Cajuns who had resettled in California, which supports the idea that there was no such network. In contrast to the Creoles, Cajuns appear to have arrived in a trickle instead of in waves, in numbers perhaps insufficient to achieve a critical mass necessary to form a regional web of friends, relatives, and acquaintances. Until they succeeded in making connections and establishing trust, they would be able neither to draw on nor to contribute to the store of social capital that did exist in northern California. Freida and Louisiana Sue were initially so far removed from the existing dance scene that they had to go through quasi-public intermediaries (Down Home Music Store, Isleton Crawdad Festival) to get to it. Bobby and Richard were familiar enough with the dance scene that they knew how to access it, but chose not to do so until external circumstances (life changes, demand for new music driven by currents in popular culture) pushed them toward it.

Among sociologists who study leisure, it is well known that milestones in the life course are a major determining factor in people's choice of activities. Freida's brother in Louisiana took up accordion-building after his divorce. For Bobby and Louisiana Sue, the dance scene represents more than a leisure pursuit—it has also been part of their livelihood—yet each talked about attending dances after their divorces for the sheer enjoyment of dancing. The act of dancing is, after all, "a darn stress relief," as Betty LeBlanc says. The dance scene provides the opportunity for human physical contact and for social ties that may be perceived as a comforting community. For those so inclined, it also serves as a field for meeting other single and divorced individuals eligible for new relationships. The courtship element is a motivator for many dancers who enter the scene, the majority of whom are over forty years of age.[33]

The diversity of musicians and dancers who have come into the scene since the mid-1980s far outstrips the term "revivalist" that I applied to the musicians profiled in chapter 6 and the dancers in chapter 7. By no means have most of the outsiders since then had a previous interest in "folk music" or "folk dancing." They come from another kind of partner dancing such as salsa or West Coast swing, or some other kind of dancing (one woman interviewed had tap dancing lessons as a child, for example), or from no dance background at all. I would apply a more general term like "leisure enthusiast" to the dancers who have come to the scene more recently, some of whom seem attracted to the dances on their own terms rather than what they signify for some mildly exotic culture in another part of the country. In other words and as I have written elsewhere, it's not always about touristic fantasies: "We could be virtually there or actually here."[34]

On the other hand, I would hesitate to apply the label *leisure* to what the musicians do, since many of them have spent far too much time learning and applying their craft for it to be called a hobby even if most of them do not make a living at it. They too come from a variety of musical backgrounds and deserve a chapter in their own right. Multi-instrumentalist Billy Wilson was born in Fresno and raised in Bakersfield, where he developed interests in rock, country music, and bluegrass. In addition to working on his accordion playing with Danny Poullard, he studied steel guitar with onetime Bob Wills sideman Vance Terry and played bass in Bay Area blues bands. When it came time for him to form his band Motordude Zydeco, he drew on his contacts from all of these genres. Other country musicians who have come through the scene include Sam Siggins, former drummer and bassist with the California Cajun Orchestra, and the late Ed Luckenbach, also a student of Poullard's. Another student at Danny's garage conservatory was accordionist Maureen Karpan, who had taken classical piano lessons and played in her school band growing up in Minnesota, then took an interest in Cajun music after living in New Orleans for a summer. She formed a whole band, Frog Legs, from musicians that she had met in Poullard's garage (including Luckenbach on guitar and

Billy Wilson playing steel guitar at DeMarco's 23 Club, Brisbane, California. Photo by the author.

Marty Jara on fiddle), and went on to play with other groups including the Creole Belles, Delilah Lewis's band. Drummer David Hymowitz played in the California Cajun Orchestra after it recorded its second album and with a host of other bands over the years; after growing up drumming jazz, rock, and blues and playing with synthesizers, serious injury forced him to regroup. Friend Bobby Klein, a jazz and blues bassist who also danced and played zydeco himself, introduced David to the music as a way for him to meet people and get some exercise.[35]

While Poullard's influence on the scene was enormous, it was not universal. Musicians who came from other directions include two fiddlers who were alumni of Queen Ida's band and started their own groups: Annie Howard (Tee Fee) and Tom Rigney (Sundogs, Flambeau). One of the area's most popular zydeco bands, the Zydeco Flames, pulled their personnel mostly from the local blues scene, a continuation of the Oakland blues that Bob Geddins and Chris Strachwitz had recorded decades earlier. Piano accordionist Bruce Gordon started as a blues pianist who first heard Clifton Chenier's *Louisiana Blues and Zydeco* album while a jazz student at the Cornish Institute in Seattle. Sufficiently inspired by Chenier's example to brave the ridicule of his fellow jazz students, he obtained an accordion and started learning to play zydeco on it. When he moved to the Bay Area, he

Lloyd Meadows and Bruce Gordon performing at Slim's in San Francisco, circa 1989–90. Photo by Gary Canaparo.

played some blues (on the Hammond B3 organ for blues jams at Eli's Mile High Club in Oakland, for example) and continued to work on the accordion at home until he met Lloyd Meadows, a strong blues singer who had already been introduced to the rubboard and to singing zydeco by Billy Wilson. Gordon and Meadows formed their own piano accordion/rubboard duo that became the nucleus of the Zydeco Flames. Guitarist Frank Bohan joined them in 1990, after Gordon saw Frank play with his blues band, Freeway Frank and the Hot Wires, at a club in San Francisco and invited him to join them. Bassist Timm Walker was an acquaintance of Gordon's from the blues jams at Eli's, and drummer William Allums had played mostly gospel music before he joined the group.[36]

This quintet of highly competent musicians did not approach zydeco as a folk music; Frank Bohan's comments reveal a blues aesthetic that overlaps with a part of Louisiana French music different from that which appealed to the revivalist musicians profiled in chapter 6:

> But the thing that attracted me to zydeco was when I listened to Clifton Chenier, basically what he did with zydeco was a faster beat, it was little bit spicier, a little bit less folk and more urban. If you listen to the bands that Clifton played with, they were always blues bands, basically. They had Danny Caron, and that guy could rip

on guitar, so there was nothing timid or folky or plinky-plinky when it came time to play guitar. Now if you extend that out to listen to Buckwheat, listen to CJ, listen to Beau Jocque's band. That's my favorite zydeco band, Beau Jocque, bar none. What a loss to have him pass away. I tell you what, I was in Lloyd's car the other day and he played a Beau Jocque tune and I looked at him and I said, man these guys are the shit! These guys can rip! And I don't listen to zydeco music when I'm home, it's not what I listen to for enjoyment. I play it and I love playing it. But when I was in his car I was like, Yeah! My belt was going back and forth, I was . . . That's what I'm talking about, that's what I like about zydeco music and you don't hear that in a lot of styles of music, that ability to just shake, get in there and shake your guts up. And I like that part about any kind of music. If I feel my guts moving around or if I feel like crying or screaming or "Whoa!" or something like that, that's the kind of music I like. That's what I liked about zydeco. So yeah, that's the blues.[37]

The interaction among the Creole community, revivalist musicians, and dancers made for a tidy story in the previous chapters compared to the myriad paths to the scene glimpsed here. The processes for the creation of bridging social capital have diversified and, as they have done so, the average strength of social ties has probably weakened. Whether or not this is a bad thing is open to interpretation. One might surmise that weakened social ties forecast a disintegration of the scene. Social capital theorists, on the other hand, maintain that weak social ties are actually good for bridging social capital, because they allow the nimble realignment of alliances that can adjust for changing conditions. For example, one band of musicians breaks up and two new ones form, or a dance venue ceases operations and another is improvised within weeks. There seems to be a happy medium somewhere between an extreme of bonding social capital, where group membership is closed and hostile attitudes toward outsiders develop, and a watered-down bridging situation where ties are so weak and trust among actors so low that group action becomes impossible. So far the northern California dance scene has managed to find such a middle ground.[38]

As for the future of the scene, the only certainty, of course, is change. As trends like the folk song revival, international folk dancing, and the Cajun craze fade further into the historical distance, they will cease to be directly relevant—but bits and pieces of them will remain woven in the fabric of national and regional cultures, and history may repeat itself in the form of another revival once sufficient time has elapsed. Danny Poullard's passing left a huge hole that is still being mended. The region's current resident go-to musician, André Thierry, plays contemporary zydeco in contrast to Poullard's more conservative Cajun sound. Aspiring musicians seeking instruction now look primarily to summer camps to improve their

André Thierry performing at Ardenwood Festival, 2006. Photo by Sue Schleifer.

craft, and they commission workshops from touring musicians. Jam sessions still get organized, but no one has embraced the local master musician–teacher role like Danny did, and there is no guarantee that anyone will. Likewise there is no certainty that Arhoolie Records and Down Home Music will outlive Chris Strachwitz, although his Arhoolie Foundation may continue in some capacity. If the scene is to continue and thrive, it will likely be not through emulating past models but by, to borrow Charlie St. Mary's expression, "doing something we ain't never done before." If social ties are maintained, creative individuals will be able to inventory the resources available to them and use their social capital to improvise whatever new strategies are needed to sustain the scene.

Ending Reflections

This book has focused on the Cajun music and zydeco scene in northern California with a dual emphasis throughout: the scene as a unique and significant development within the history of Louisiana French music, and the scene as a microcosm for the reception of the music and dance in popular culture at national and even international levels. Unique and typical elements must be viewed together in order to understand the whole. A comparative study of dance scenes in other cities might have revealed further insights on the nature of a typical dance scene, but it was not feasible for me and it would not have afforded the depth of coverage I was able to devote to this single context. It is my hope that, to the extent I was able to document what has transpired in the northern California scene, future writers of cultural history will be able to draw on what I have found here and on the rich material in the individual profiles.

I see the unique value and interest of the northern California scene as twofold. One aspect is the significance of some of the individuals involved to the history of Louisiana French music as a whole—performers such as Queen Ida, Danny Poullard, and André Thierry as well as interpreter/curators such as Les Blank and Chris Strachwitz. The reader who has gotten this far will recognize that these individuals did not succeed on their own, that there have been many others named here who contributed directly or indirectly to the success of these individuals or who deserve some recognition in their own right, and there have been many more I was not able to mention.

The second aspect of the scene's uniqueness is its setting in northern California. I want to be careful here in deference to Creoles and others in southern California who carry on Louisiana French music there and whose activities I did not have the wherewithal to investigate myself. Some of what I want to say may apply to them as well, and it has to do with the notion, going back at least to the Gold Rush, that California is a place one goes to reinvent oneself. It is a place, perhaps, where Zygmunt Bauman's insight that most of us are now vagabonds goes without saying. Louisiana Sue gets at this quality in her comments: "Now, some people moved out here [to California] for that reason, because nobody knows who you are and your business. Where everybody knows [you], I didn't have a name, I was either Freddy or Irene's daughter, or somebody's niece, that's the essence of who you were. Out here, I became no one. But then you turn into yourself. It has its good points and its bad points, but I hated it." Paul Strogen experienced the same situation in a different way: "[C]oming from a small town, I didn't think much about community then. I was constantly surrounded by all these relatives and aunts and uncles. And you couldn't get away with anything. . . . So when I got out of there I just left it all behind." The several California natives profiled in this book felt no less free to relocate and reinvent themselves as little or as much as they saw fit. For the Louisiana French people who moved here, to continue with their culture of origin was a conscious choice not all of them made, which made it that much more significant to those who did choose to go on dancing and making music in this way. As unreligious as the music is, the spiritual side of self-reinvention often seen in California ("an imaginative frontier exceptional in the history of American religion," as one writer described it) has also had a role to play. Dancer Louie gets his massage therapist credentials from the National Holistic Institute. David Nadel grows up in a Jewish family in southern California, moves to the Bay Area, starts his own folk dance coffeehouse, calls it Ashkenaz, remodels it after an Eastern European synagogue, and runs it not as a Jewish community center but as a monument to world peace through music and dance of many cultures. Richard Domingue moves out from Louisiana and finds a home at Sonoma Mountain Zen Center, a residential community dedicated to Japanese Soto Zen practice led by a Chinese American teacher. He later joins the Pacific Zen Institute and sets their traditional chants to new music of his own composition. Emily Preston founds her own spiritual community in the 1880s in northern Sonoma County, which fades away after her death—and a group of hippie musicians and artisans with their own ideas about transcendence come to inhabit the Preston Ranch property several decades later.[39]

The northern California scene has also been susceptible to pop cultural influences from without—rhythm and blues star James Brown was as well known to Richard Domingue in Lafayette as he was to Dana DeSimone and Bobby Gradney in San Francisco—which makes it as much typical as it is unique. The casting of Cajun music as folk music during the 1950s and 1960s, the introduction of the zydeco music of Clifton Chenier and others through blues channels of distribution, and the multimedia octopus of the Cajun craze all gave ample opportunity for Bay Area residents, the rest of the country, and many in Europe who had never met a Louisiana French person to experience something of the culture and to want to learn more.

With pop cultural phenomena such as the Cajun craze, as with affinity groups generally, it is much easier to describe how, what, and when things happened than to explain why. Typically it is futile directly to ask outsiders why they are so engrossed in a culture that is not their own. When Laušević put this question to those whom she calls Balkanites (Americans fascinated with Balkan culture), "the reply I was first given was, almost without exception, a variation of 'I really don't know,' often pronounced slowly in a soft, almost whispering voice with the emphasis on *really*." Occasionally when I explained the nature of my research at the beginning of an interview, an interviewee would try to be helpful and offer their own explanation of the Cajun craze or of their own attraction to it, but I soon found that I learned more when I steered the interview away from theorizing and toward specifics about the context in which the interest arose and about other types of music and dance the person enjoyed. When some did reflect on why they were so drawn to Cajun or Creole music, the answer was usually a variation on "I don't know." Recalling her experience of hearing the Balfa Brothers in concert, Suzy Thompson said, "I just cried through their whole set. I was really just emotionally overwhelmed by their music, for some reason that I never will understand." Bruce Gordon heard a Clifton Chenier recording for the first time and "it was an instantaneous calling." When I asked Eric Thompson how he had been drawn into one of his other musical interests, he responded, "I heard it and I thought it was really cool," with a level stare and tone of voice to indicate his final answer on that line of inquiry. Ken Keppeler probably came closest to answering the question "why" at the end of chapter 6: "all the music expresses the same emotions and the same desires, and as musicians we are just looking for pathways for our own emotions and lives, to bring some joy to others and to give them glimpses of their own lives had they been raised in a different human culture." In their defense, I would say that asking these musicians and dancers why Cajun or zydeco is not unlike asking a songwriter to explain the meaning of her song or a writer the meaning of his novel. Small wonder, then, that the answers are not straightforward. Dana DeSimone said that dancing saved his life, Delilah Lewis suggested with some irony that the fiddle "ruined" her life, and I think they were both pointing to the same thing, Keppeler's "pathways for our own emotions and lives."[40]

Another route to understanding why affinity groups form are the ideas about modern pleasures and postmodernity discussed in chapters 1 and 2. Although at first I thought it lacked much explanatory value, Slobin's characterization of affinity groups—"charmed circles of like-minded music-makers drawn magnetically to a certain genre that creates strong expressive bonding"—distills in a phrase much of what I have been attempting to elucidate here. The disenchantment that follows from living in modern society leads some to seek re-enchantment through folklife, to cast new charms on themselves and those around them. The traditions that get used by affinity groups may be seen as the result of historical happenstance, the opportunities presented by available cultural materials, and the local network's topography of social capital. The aesthetic disposition of the individual for certain musical sounds also plays a role, and I have tried to foreground this aspect in the profiles. Returning to Marc Savoy's automotive analogy of grandpa's old buggy, although one's choice of buggy (Cajun, Balkan, Irish, etc.) may be somewhat an arbitrary matter of taste (and I'm sure many practitioners would object to that characterization), if the vehicle is getting you where you want to go ("strong expressive bonding"), you keep it and maintain it. Perhaps you make some modifications to increase the mileage, and your fellow buggy owners may not admire your choice of seat coverings, but it works and it's yours. I have tried to suggest here that the psychological satisfaction that folklife provides is at least of the same sort, if not always the same depth or intensity, for ethnic insiders and outsiders alike.[41]

The blurring of insiderness and outsiderness leads me to my final point, which has to do with the limited utility of categories—ethnic, musical, and otherwise. To learn the nuances of what the terms Cajun and Creole have meant over time and to various groups of people has been no small undertaking, and I am glad that I absorbed as much as I did for the additional appreciation it has given me (and, I hope, the reader) of Louisiana French culture and the extent to which it has often been misrepresented in popular media. I find all of this knowledge not so helpful in social situations, however, where it is much easier to spot a Louisiana French person by speech pattern than to predict by skin color or other cue if he is going to self-identify as Cajun or Creole or something else. In conversation I generally avoid the question altogether unless the subject comes up; as Ray Stevens said, "I won't name them because they can give their own description of theirs." Ray also said, "You're looking at a so-called Creole. In my opinion, there's no such thing as that." When I asked Bobby Gradney if both his parents were Cajun, he did not correct me but responded with a detailed answer in which he did not use the word "Cajun" once. Louisiana Sue, who has devoted much thought and effort to cultural representation, was careful to talk about the various parts of her background (Isleño, Cajun, German) without producing a single label for herself. The confusion around the terms "Cajun" and "Creole" discussed in chapter 2 reflects a complex social and historical situation, and the appropriate use of intellectual rigor is not to organize them and mount them for display but rather to understand them in their ecological context, use them when appropriate, and avoid making them a *raison d'être* for study.

For to make much over who or what is Cajun and who or what is Creole is to revert to an essentialist view of identity that reinscribes racism, among other things. I find that splitting hairs over whether a particular musical performance should be considered Cajun music or zydeco to be equally futile, and for the same reasons. Danny Poullard's career of playing Cajun music addresses this very point: if a Creole plays it, is it still Cajun music? His answer would be, you bet it is. There are also Cajuns who play zydeco (i.e., Creole music), of course. In a classroom I might lecture about stylistic differences between Cajun music and zydeco generally, but outside of the pedagogical context I am not sure that it is useful to make a great study of them.

Another, less racially charged example of the scholarly urge to categorize music illustrates the point. In jams at Danny's house, he often would end one tune and start another without verbal comment. Occasionally I would ask him right after he finished a number, "What do you call that one?" Sometimes the answer was a single title like "Step It Fast," other times he gave two or three alternate titles, and yet other times he could not give any. Anyone who has dipped into the research literature on tune families or tried to do their own research on tune variants is well acquainted with this phenomenon. The names, the categories are useful up to a point, then we must let them go lest they get in the way. The question is not whether you call it Cajun or zydeco, "Jolie Catin" or "Eunice Two-Step," Louisiana music or California music, but can you play it and can you dance to it? On such a practical basis can Louisiana French music serve as a bridging medium to sustain itself and the people who make it into the foreseeable future.

Notes

Chapter 1. Prelude: Down At The Twist And Shout

1. Carpenter 2003, p.c. Michael Doucet remembers that "the place, the club of people, the group of people were called Twist and Shout. And we used to play at a VFW, just like in Louisiana." The club would bring Beausoleil up to play for a dance, and Doucet recalls meeting Carpenter at one of these events before she received her major recording contract with Sony. Later, when she approached him to make the record, he agreed (Doucet 2004 interview).

2. Clifford 1992, 1997. For other examples of this type of ethnographic analysis of popular song, see Cheesman 1995, Martinez 1995, Busteed 1998.

3. Ancelet and Morgan 1984, 16; Brasseaux 1992. In this book the term *American* is used only for this Louisiana French meaning of it; if it appears in quotes, this is only as a reminder to the reader of this special meaning. Where the more usual sense of the term is needed, i.e., pertaining to the United States of America, "United States" or "U.S." will be used.

4. Parsons 1993.

5. Meintjes 1990 (on Paul Simon); Taylor 1997 (on other world music collaborations).

6. Doucet 2004 interview. According to him, the production and arrangement of the song were all due to Carpenter and John Jennings, her guitarist and production partner. He modestly claims his only contributions to the arrangement in the original recording were the opening fiddle solo passage and a suggestion for how to end the song. What he would not say, and yet what presumably was the case, was that he and Breaux and Ware were there in part to establish the Cajun two-step rhythmic foundation for the performance, and Carpenter's professional musicians were able to fall right in behind.

7. Seeger 1977; Small 1998; Doucet 2004 interview. "Musicking about music" is my own phrase inspired by the combination of Seeger's ruminations on speech about music and Christopher Small's coinage and explication of the verb form *musicking*.

8. Kelly and Godbey 1992, 14.

9. Csikszentmihalyi 1988, 34.

10. Csikszentmihalyi 1988, 34.

11. Leblanc 2000 interview.

12. Ancelet, *et al* 1991, 46–49.

13. Thompson and Thompson 1997 interview.

14. Doucet 2004 interview. The live recording from Carpenter's Super Bowl performance does not end this way. For more on creative use of the Cajun accordion's idiomatic possibilities, see DeWitt 2003.

15. Gupta and Ferguson 1997, 37; MacCannell 1999, 8.

Chapter 2. Identity Issues, Research Methods, and Ethnography

1. Hall 1989, 10.
2. Bendix 1997; Emoff 1998.
3. Bendix 1997, 17, 7, 159–87.
4. Kivy 1995, 1–12, 108.
5. Brasseaux 1991, 67; Hebert 1993; www.acadianmemorial.org 2006; Brasseaux 1987; Brasseaux 1992; Brasseaux 1989; Bernard 2003; Brasseaux 1988.
6. Dominguez 1986, 15, 150, 152.
7. Ancelet and Morgan 1984, 16.
8. Whatley and Jannise 1981, iii.
9. Olivier and Sandmel 1999, 15.
10. Spitzer 1986, 23; Brasseaux et al. 1994, 4–5; Rogers 1993, 4; Tregle 1992, 141; Dormon 1996, 169.
11. See Brasseaux 1991 for a detailed breakdown of where the Acadians dispersed in the decades following their 1755 expulsion. Only a fraction finally settled in Louisiana.
12. Dormon 1983, 63–71.
13. Dormon 1983, 70.
14. Bernard 2003, 18–19, describes the wartime atmosphere.
15. Dormon 1983, 35; Louisiana Writer's Project 1941; Means 2003.
16. Bendix 1997, 113–15.
17. Cantwell 1993, xv; Bendix 1997, 8.
18. Kirshenblatt-Gimblett 1998, 52; DeWitt 1999.
19. Savoy 1984. Prior to the recording era, there are earlier eyewitness accounts of music-making and even musical transcriptions of Creole folk songs, such as in Allen, Ware, and Garrison's 1867 volume, *Slave Songs of the United States*.
20. Lomax 1987; Lomax and Lomax 1941; Lomax 1942, Album V; Whitfield 1939; Bendix 1997, 146–49. See also on discography: Rounder 1842, 1843.
21. Ancelet 1989a, 19–20; personal communications with musicians; Spitzer 1986, 325; Tisserand 1998, 51–65.
22. Spitzer 1986, 320–21; Ancelet and Morgan 1984, 73. Swallow LP-8003-2; Rounder 6009; Arhoolie/Folklyric 7007.
23. Ancelet 1989a, 27–32; Ancelet 1989b, 4–5; Hall 1991, 35.
24. Stivale 2003; Frith 1996, 121–22.
25. Bauman 1996, 18, original emphasis.
26. Bauman 1996, 19; Hall 1989, 16.
27. Titon 1993, 222.
28. Sue Schleifer, former executive director of Ashkenaz, p.c.
29. Bauman 1996, 29.
30. Bernard 2003, 114.
31. Bernard 2003, 124; Ancelet 1992.
32. Kershaw 1991, 242; Bendix 1997, 89–94, 105–18, 142–45, 163–67; Bernard 2003; Schweid 1999.
33. Marcus and Fischer 1986; Clifford and Marcus 1986; Clifford 1988.
34. Burnim 1985.

35. Stivale 2003, 9–39.
36. Henry and Le Menestrel 2003, 2.
37. Le Menestrel 2003, 121–23.
38. Dundes 1980, 7–14 (folk groups); Slobin 1993, 36–60, 104–8 (affinity groups); Jordan-Smith and Horton 2001.
39. Fusilier and Adams 1994.
40. Burnim 1985, 445.
41. Kearney 1995; Clifford 1997.
42. Gupta and Ferguson 1997; Clifford 1997, 209.
43. Titon 1980.
44. Bourdieu 1986, 245. Bourdieu, in the context of his work on French society, when writing about cultural capital was usually referring to Culture with a capital C, associated with formal education and the higher social classes. Having acknowledged his original intent, I see no reason not to apply the term to the kind of enculturation that produces "distinctive value" but in a multicultural context where assumptions of upward social striving may not always apply. I would argue that while ethnic solidarity, pride, and appreciation of cultural differences by outsiders may not equate to wealth, power, and prestige in any straightforward way, they are still potentially of "value" and therefore qualify as capital. Crafts, Cavicchi, and Keil 1993; DeNora 2000, x, 46–74, 109–50.

Chapter 3. Music, Dance, and Social Capital

1. In the description of this house dance, the names of all parties have been changed except for the musicians and my companion (now my wife), Sue.
2. See Tisserand 1998, 23–38, for eyewitness accounts of Creole house dances in Louisiana; Guillory 1990, 165.
3. Putnam 2000, 19–21.
4. Putnam 2000, 93–94.
5. Putnam 2000, 22.
6. This basic model of social capital formation is proposed in Edwards, Foley, and Diani 2001, with the emphasis on trust added by another contributor to that same volume (Wood 2001, 261).
7. Bourdieu 1986, 250, emphasis added.
8. In addition to the musicians profiled in this book, there are several others who lived in California at least for a time, many of them in southern California: Ambrose Sam, Wilfred Latour, Joseph "'Tit Lou" Eaglin, Jo-El Sonnier, Mark St. Mary (Fusilier and Adams 1994).
9. Wilson 1995 interview.
10. Dart 1995, 14.
11. Edwards, Foley, and Diani 2001, 1–14, 266–79; Slobin 1993, 107. Unfortunately for the reader, the terms that Slobin coined for commerce and enthusiasm ("banding" and "bonding") do not map cleanly to Putnam's "bonding" and "bridging." Most of what Slobin discusses falls under Putnam's "bridging" rubric.
12. Putnam, et al. 2003, 9.
13. Kripal and Shuck 2005 (on the human potential movement).

Chapter 4. Wartime and Postwar Creole Migration to California

1. Bernard 2003, 3–22; Ancelet and Morgan 1984, 27; Ancelet 1989b, 5. Many thanks to Philip Flavin for confirming the meaning and use of the Japanese proverb.
2. Dormon 1983, 80–81.
3. Dormon 1983, 79–90.
4. Dormon 1983, 35–39; Bernard 1996, 39; Taylor 1997, 23–26; Emoff 1998; Stivale 2003.
5. Woods 1989, 5–11; Dormon 1996, 173–75.
6. All information in this profile, unless otherwise noted, is taken from Queen Ida's autobiographical cookbook, *Cookin' with Queen Ida* (Guillory 1990).
7. Fusilier and Adams 1994, 23.
8. Levine 1975.
9. GNP Crescendo GNPS-2101, GNPS-5-2131, GNPS-2147.
10. Fusilier and Adams 1994, 31.
11. Fusilier and Adams 1994, 24.
12. Gleason 1969, with thanks to Michael Tisserand for bringing my attention to this review (Tisserand 1998, 206).
13. La Louisianne LLC-509.
14. Tisserand 1998, 211.
15. Fusilier and Adams 1994, 24; Tisserand 1998, 205; *Bayou by the Bay* 1980.
16. Broussard 1994 interview with Gary Canaparo.
17. Canaparo interview, 2004.
18. Broussard 1994 interview with Gary Canaparo.
19. Broussard 1994 interview with Gary Canaparo. "Big Pete" is further mentioned and identified in chapter 5.
20. All information in this profile, unless otherwise noted, is taken from a taped interview the author did with Ray Stevens on August 29, 2000, at Emil Villa's restaurant in Oakland, California.
21. Daniels 1990, 162–75; *ibid.*, 172.
22. Broussard 1993, 206; McBroome 1993, 92.
23. Tisserand 1998, 205.
24. McBroome 1993, 92.
25. Broussard 1993, 138, 205.
26. Louder and LeBlanc 1979, 324; Broussard 1993, 136.
27. Daniels 1990, 163; Spitzer 1986, 124.
28. Broussard 1993, 205–45.
29. Daniels 1990, 169; Self 2003, 104.
30. Broussard 1993, 172–77; Guillory 1990, 163; Daniels 1990, 222–25; McBroome 1993, 145–47.
31. Dauphine 1993; Ida Guillory, in *Bayou by the Bay* 1980.
32. Tisserand 1998, 203; Fusilier and Adams 1994, 14, 24; Poullard 1985 interview; Tisserand 1998, 211.
33. Tisserand 1998, 194; Arhoolie CD 313.
34. Bernard 2003, 18.
35. Ancelet, et al 1991, xiii; Guillory 1990, 43; Olivier and Sandmel 1999, 15; Brasseaux 1996; Spitzer 1986, 113.

36. Tucker 1995; Laird 2005; Canaparo interview 2004.

37. Ancelet and Morgan 1984, 82, 101; Savoy 1984, 194; Guillory 1990, 168, 176.

Chapter 5. Further Creole Migration and Bridging to Other Social Networks

1. Broven 1983, 29–35, 279, 318–19; Daigle 1987, 118; Savoy 1984, 152, 194; Daigle 1987, 118; Nyhan et al. 1997, 114.

2. Savoy 1984, 234–49; Broven 1983, 239, 241–44; Ancelet and Morgan 1984, 85–86, 119–27; Ancelet 1989a, 37–41.

3. Ancelet and Morgan 1984, 128–39; Ancelet et al. 1991, 167–70; Savoy 1984, 1–3; www.lsue.edu/acadgate/music/savoy.htm, January 1, 2007.

4. Ancelet and Morgan 1984, 143.

5. Ancelet and Morgan 1984, 145; Ancelet and Morgan 1984, 140–49; Doucet 2004 interview; www.grammy.com, 2007.

6. Ancelet 1989a; Broven 1987; Bernard 1996.

7. Wald 2000, 20.

8. Broven 1983, 109–13; Olivier and Sandmel 1999, 50–59; Savoy 1984, 369–91; Tisserand 1998, 90–147. Whether or not there was a style of music that could be considered "zydeco" before Chenier came along is a matter of ongoing debate, but suffice it to say the way Chenier played the accordion had never been heard before.

9. DeWitt 2003, 309; Ancelet and Morgan 1984, 93–99, 140–49; Sexton 2001.

10. I am indebted to Will Spires for sharing with me an interview that he did with Danny in 1985 that contains the majority of the biographical information here, supplemented by personal conversations that I had with Danny, mostly 1995–98. Although he would gladly play accordion into someone's tape recorder any time, Danny was difficult to pin down for formal taped interviews.

11. Poullard 1985 interview; Ed Poullard 2006 interview; Fusilier and Adams 1994, 26.

12. Poullard 1985 interview; Poullard, p.c.

13. Poullard 1985 interview; Tisserand 1998, 203, 206.

14. Poullard 1985 interview; Tisserand 1998, 207.

15. Poullard 1985 interview; Fusilier and Adams 1994, 27.

16. Wood 2006, 280–83.

17. Poullard 1995 session tape.

18. Tisserand 1998, 108–15; Poullard 1985 interview; Spires 1997 interview; Ashkenaz archives.

19. Poullard 1985 interview; Ashkenaz archives.

20. Thompson and Thompson 1997 interview; Senauke, p.c.; Ashkenaz archives.

21. Poullard, p.c.; Ashkenaz archives; Arhoolie 5035.

22. Willging 1999; Louisiana Radio Records CD5958. I attended the Augusta Heritage Center's Cajun/Creole Week in 1998 as an accordion student (not in Poullard's class), and returned the following year as an audience member to observe Danny teaching the advanced accordion class.

23. All information in this profile, unless otherwise noted, is taken from a taped interview the author did with Betty LeBlanc on September 5, 2000, at her home in San Francisco, California.

24. All information in this profile, unless otherwise noted, is taken from a taped interview the author did with Olivia Guillory (then Olivia Thierry) on January 6, 1995, at her home in Richmond, California.

25. The recollections of Olivia's mother "Mama Lena Pitre" are featured in Michael Tisserand's *The Kingdom of Zydeco* in a composite oral history of Creole house dances in Louisiana (ch. 2) and scattered throughout wherever zydeco in California is mentioned (Tisserand 1998).

26. Fusilier and Adams 1994, 15.

27. All information in this profile, unless otherwise noted, is taken from a taped interview the author did with Andrew Carrière on September 11, 2000, at his home in Oakland, California.

28. Rounder 6009.

29. Fusilier and Adams 1994, 31–32.

30. Levine 1975, 28.

31. DeWitt 2003, 308.

32. Thompson and Thompson 1997 interview.

33. Spires 1997 interview.

34. Poullard 2000 interview.

35. Wilson 1995 interview.

36. Ancelet and Morgan 1984, 82, 101; Savoy 1984, 194, 326.

37. Canaparo 2004 interview.

38. Wald 2000; www.arhoolie.com/history/index.html, August 13, 2006.

39. Hildebrand and Moore 1998, 109.

40. Hildebrand and Moore 1998; Collins 1998, 229–30; www.arhoolie.com/history/index.html, August 13, 2006.

41. www.arhoolie.com/history/index.html, August 13, 2006; Wald 2000; Tisserand 1998, 17–20; Arhoolie 1001.

42. www.arhoolie.com/history/index.html, August 13, 2006.

43. Thompson 1997 interview; Arhoolie 1001–1004.

44. Arhoolie 1009; Arhoolie F5003; Benicewicz 1999, Part 2; Broven 1983, 23–24; Tisserand 1998, 108–16. Independent folklorist Archie Green has peppered his work with the term "vernacular" as a substitute for the word "folk" in contexts where there was a need for "bridging differences where folk and popular forms interact; association with the practices of vast numbers of people; neutrality regarding causes and revivals" (Green 2001, 214). A similarly expanded use of the word "vernacular" was developed earlier by Kouwenhoven, concentrating on engineering, architecture, and the visual arts, with speculations on the word's application to jazz music (1948).

45. www.arhoolie.com/history/index.html, August 6, 2006; Benicewicz 1999, Part 2.

46. Broven 1983, 245; www.arhoolie.com/catalog/cajun.html, August 19, 2006; www.arhoolie.org, August 20, 2006; www.nea.gov/honors/heritage/Heritage00/Strachwitz.html, August 20, 2006.

47. Tisserand 1998, 213; Strachwitz 1997, p.c.; Spires 1997 interview; www.arhoolie.com/history/index.html, August 6, 2006; Benicewicz 1999, Part 2; Arhoolie 5035; Arhoolie CD 474; DeSimone 1998 interview; Selvin 1995.

48. Hollenbach 1984.

49. Interview with Les Blank and Maureen Gosling, 1986.

50. www.lesblank.com, August 27, 2006; Csicsery 1998.

51. Wald 2000, 5.

52. www.nea.gov/honors/heritage/index.html, August 30, 2006; Bendix 1997, 155–58; Putnam 2000, 24–26 (on declensionist narratives).

53. Horton 1984, 276, 278.

54. Bendix 1997, 102.

Chapter 6. Folk Revival Connection: The Musicians

1. Laušević 2007, 205.
2. Folkways FP 251, 252, 253; Cantwell 1996, 189; Cantwell 1996, 189–90; Cantwell 1996, 191–92; Arhoolie C-212.
3. Cantwell 1996, 294–97. Recounts of Balfa at Newport: Ancelet 1989a, 37–41; Ancelet and Morgan 1984, 29–30, 121–25; Ancelet et al. 1991, 161; Broven 1983, 243–44; Cohen 1995, 44–45. Other references: Schwarz 1998 interview; Ancelet 1989a, 39; Ancelet 1989a, 40; Bernard 2003, 105–8; www.nojazzfest.com/totem.html, March 9, 1998.
4. Folkways F-31035; Swallow 6011; Folkways FA 2626; Swallow 6056; Folkways 8361, 8362; Savoy and Schwarz 1990.
5. Schwarz 1998 interview.
6. Frankenstein 1965; Olivier n.d., 23–24 (original emphasis).
7. Bendix 1997, 76–90, 194–207; Stekert 1993; Strachwitz 2000.
8. www.bayouseco.com/interview.html, January 27, 2007.
9. Ancelet 1992, 258. Development of cultural tourism from the 1980s onward is discussed in chapter 8. Thompson and Thompson 1997 interview.
10. All information in this profile, unless otherwise noted, is taken from a taped interview the author did with Will Spires on August 26, 1997 at his home in Cotati, California.
11. The Hackberry Ramblers made their only appearance at the Berkeley Folk Festival in 1965. Event listings in the San Francisco *Chronicle* indicate that they performed daily June 24–27, and that a Friday morning panel on "Folk Music of Southwest Louisiana" was on the program. Expert discussion panelists billed as part of the festival that year included Charles Seeger, Gene Bluestein, Bess Lomax Hawes, Chris Strachwitz, and Alan Dundes.
12. Folkways F-31035; Swallow LP 6011.
13. All information in this profile, unless otherwise noted, is taken from a taped interview the author did with Eric and Suzy Thompson on March 4, 1997, at their home in Berkeley, California.
14. Weill 1972, 5.
15. Weill 1972, 5. Thompson interview, 2006. julianwinston.com/music/me_and_my_old_banjo2.php, April 25, 2006.
16. Spires interview. Weill 1972, 5. Thompson 1997 and 2006 interviews.
17. Any Old Time String Band, Arhoolie LP 4009 (1978), rereleased on Arhoolie CD 433 together with the band's 1980 LP on Bay Records (Bay LP 217). The 1980 album was made after Suzy left the band and had three more Cajun selections on it with Genny Haley and Kate Brislin on vocals. *Eric Thompson's Bluegrass Guitar*, Kicking Mule KM 215 (1978), rereleased on CD as *Thompson's Real: Bluegrass Instrumentals with Guitar*, Herringbone Disc ET 101. This album has a corresponding tablature book with the guitar solos transcribed. The Backwoods Band, *Jes' Fine*, Rounder 0128. Both Suzy's and Eric's musical accomplishments range significantly beyond Cajun music. These accomplishments are worth mentioning here as an indicator of the depth of musical experience that they brought to their Cajun music projects, especially to the California Cajun Orchestra. Eric played lead guitar on *Beatle Country*, a 1966 album of bluegrass Beatles covers by the Charles River Valley Boys produced in Nashville (Elektra EKL-4006). In the 1970s he played Irish music on the tenor banjo and organized the Graineog Celidh Band with Irish musicians Joe Cooley and Kevin Keegan, who lived then in San Francisco. Suzy played and recorded with The Klezmorim, an influential Berkeley-based klezmer revival band in the seventies, appearing on their second album, *Streets of Gold*, Arhoolie LP 3011, rereleased as Arhoolie CD 309.

18. Flying Fish FF-275; Arhoolie 5029; Calendar archives, Ashkenaz Music and Dance Community Center, Berkeley, California.

19. Arhoolie CD 5041. Musician credits on the Cajun numbers included Danny Poullard, Kevin Wimmer, Charlie St. Mary, and Beth Weil (bass). Musician credits on the other tracks included Laurie Lewis, David Grisman, Will Scarlett, and George Winston.

20. The California Cajun Orchestra, *Not Lonesome Anymore*, Arhoolie CD 356 (1991). Produced by Jody Stecher, Suzy Thompson, Chris Strachwitz, and Michael Doucet. Personnel on this album were as listed above, including Wimmer on second fiddle.

21. Fusilier and Adams 1994. Thompson 2006 interview.

22. Arhoolie CD-436. On this album Sam Siggins has moved to bass, Terry O'Dwyer is on drums, and Andrew Carrière does not appear.

23. Thompson 2006 interview.

24. Bluegrass Intentions, *Old as Dirt*, Native and Fine 906-4. Suzy Thompson, *No Mockingbird*, Native and Fine 906-7 (2003). Suzy Thompson, *Stop and Listen*, Arhoolie CD 517 (2005).

25. All information in this profile, unless otherwise noted, is taken from a taped interview the author did with Delilah Lee Lewis on August 30, 2000, at her home in San Francisco.

26. Sheet music: "Creole Belles," song by J. Bodewalt Lampe, words by Geo. Steiner. Detroit: Whitney-Warner Publishing Company, 1900.

27. Lasar 1999; Olivier n.d.

28. Olivier n.d.; DeWitt 2003b; Gleason 1965, 1969a; Doug Kershaw entry, allmusic.com, September 24, 2006.

29. www.gildedserpent.com/articles22/zaharrmemoirs1.htm, March 11, 2006; www.freightandsalvage.com/about, September 24, 2006.

30. Mike Seeger, liner notes to Folkways FA 2436, 10; Weill 1972.

31. Sefton n.d.

32. Bayou Seco 2006 interview; www.BayouSeco.com, September 25, 2006; Rooster 111.

33. Bayou Seco 2006 interview.

34. Bayou Seco 2006 interview.

35. Laušević 2007, 44–50.

Chapter 7. Folk Revival Connection: The Dancers

1. DeWitt 1999, 62, where I argue that dancers outside of the Creole community learning how to dance Cajun waltzes and two-steps helped to create a sense of place and a "new tradition" on the California dance floor. Oullette 1994, 7.

2. Goodale and Godbey 1988, 92–125; Cantwell 1996, 28; Laušević 2007, 75–89, 248–49; Kraus 1962, 2–6; Volk 1994; Cantwell 1996, 31.

3. Laušević 2007, 133–67.

4. Laušević 2007, 183–204.

5. www.westwind-folk.org/mission.html, January 18, 2007; Strogen 2000 interview; Ashkenaz archives; Geerdes 1997.

6. All information in this profile, unless otherwise noted, is taken from a taped interview the author did with Gary and Maryanne Canaparo on August 24, 2004, at their home in Sunol, California.

7. Canaparo 2006 interview.

8. All information in this profile, unless otherwise noted, is taken from a taped interview the author did with Paul Strogen on September 9, 2000, at Ashkenaz Music and Dance Community Center in Berkeley, California.

9. All information in this profile, unless otherwise noted, is taken from a taped interview the author did with Ron Rumney on September 12, 2000, at his home near Sonoma, California.

10. According to the Ashkenaz calendar archives, the Louisiana Playboys played five dates there (October 15, 1976; February 8, 1981; April 3, 1982; September 4, 1982; March 19, 1983).

11. Rumney 1999.

12. All information in this profile, unless otherwise noted, is taken from a taped interview the author did with Dana DeSimone on June 25, 1998, at Studio J in Berkeley, California.

13. I have reconstructed this chronology of changes in the Alameda dances with the help of handbills and dance calendars gathered during field research, as well as from personal recollections.

14. Guillory 1990, 201–2.

15. Ashkenaz archives.

16. Schmidt 1995 interview.

17. Elektra Nonesuch 9 61146-2, "Forty-One Days."

18. Plater et al. 1993, 36–39.

19. Laušević 2007, 46; Phillips 1997, Strogen 2000 interview.

Chapter 8. Later Gulf Coast Arrivals

1. Rosenberg 1993, 177–82.

2. Billeaudeau 1995, 66; Ramon 1997 interview.

3. In lieu of any discussion here, I point the reader to other sources concerning representations of Louisiana French culture in film (Allain 1989; Bernard 2003, 120–22, 132–33; Stivale 2003, 73–109) and print (Allain 1989, Gaudet 1989).

4. Bernard 2003, 114 (quoted in ch. 2), 122–23; Brasseaux 1989, 15; www.explore-br.com/mulates/home.htm and www.prejeans.com/html/history.html, March 21, 1998; Ancelet 1992, 259; Randol 1998, p.c.; Plater et al. 1993, 10; Gutierrez 1992, 14; Ancelet 1992, 258.

5. Bernard 2003, 96–97, 114; Ancelet 1989c, 111.

6. Smith 1989, 4–5.

7. Brasseaux 1988, 35–52; U.S. Congress 1977, 171–74, 220–31; Turnipseed 1998 interview.

8. www.nps.gov/can/, March 23, 1998; National Park Service n.d.; National Park Service 2000, 2001.

9. Smith 1989, 14; Bernard 2003, 119.

10. Guillory 1990, 199; Olivier and Sandmel 1999, 114; fil.net-connect.net/Home.html, March 12, 1998.

11. Sweeney 1991, ix; Spencer 1992, Broughton et al. 1994; Feld 1988; Meintjes 1990, 48; Taylor 1997, 28, 17. A new Grammy award category for Best Zydeco Or Cajun Music Album was announced in 2007, to be first awarded in 2008. www.grammy.com/PressReleases/397_412_TrusteeRelease.pdf, January 28, 2008.

12. Bernard 2003, 124.

13. All information in this profile, unless otherwise noted, is taken from a taped interview the author did with Freida Fusilier on March 23, 1997, at her home in Sacramento, California.

14. Rounder CD6060, "Nonc Willie."

15. The Loma Prieta earthquake occurred on October 17, 1989, at 5:04 PM local time. It was perhaps best known across the country for images of elevated highways and portions of the Bay Bridge that collapsed and for the interruption of Major League Baseball's World Series, which happened to be contested that year between the Bay Area's two teams, the San Francisco Giants and the Oakland A's.

16. Miller and Miller 1988.

17. All information in this profile, unless otherwise noted, is taken from a taped interview the author did with Susan Appe Ramon on March 22, 1997, at her home in Sacramento, California.

18. Throughout this book I have been using the term Creole as shorthand for black Creole or Creole of Color, two terms which themselves are sometimes used interchangeably and sometimes not. Sue's characterization of the Isleño ethnic group as "white Creole" reflects another dimension of this term, especially (although not exclusively) as it is used in New Orleans (Domínguez 1986).

19. Ramon 1986.

20. Festival flyers.

21. All information in this profile, unless otherwise noted, is taken from a taped interview the author did with Ralph "Bobby" Gradney on August 31, 2000, at Bobby's Back Door BBQ in Richmond, California.

22. All information in this profile, unless otherwise noted, is taken from a taped interview the author did with Richard Domingue on August 23, 2000, at his home in Sonoma, California.

23. Daigle 1984.

24. Folkways 8363, 8364.

25. Thompson 1997 interview, original emphasis.

26. Wilson 1995 interview.

27. Sue Schleifer, p.c. (regarding Ashkenaz).

28. www.crawdadfestival.org/c-history.html, February 2, 2007.

29. www.sacjazz.org/jubilee.html, February 3, 2007.

30. Bendix 1997, 8. Barbara Kirshenblatt-Gimblett, for example, traces a progression from self-evident to self-conscious Jewishness in the development of klezmer music (Kirshenblatt-Gimblett 1998).

31. Ancelet 1992, 264.

32. www.savoymusiccenter.com, February 3, 2007, "Ponderings Of A Reincarnated Neanderthal."

33. Kelly and Godbey 1992, 251–72; Betty LeBlanc 2000 interview, from longer quote that appears in chapter 1. For more on the courtship function of the dance scene, see the interview with Eric and Suzy Thompson in chapter 6.

34. DeWitt 1999, 78.

35. Wilson 1995 interview; Arhoolie CD 356; Karpan 2000 interview; Hymowitz 2000 interview.

36. Gordon 1995 interview; Bohan 2000 interview.

37. Bohan 2000 interview.

38. Putnam 2000, 22–24.

39. Davis 2006, 8; Domingue 2000 interview; www.pacificzen.org/pages/teachers.htm, February 19, 2007; Sefton, n.d.

40. Laušević 2007, 52; Thompson 1997 interview; Gordon 1995 interview.

41. Slobin 1993, 98.

Bibliography

Allain, Mathé. 1989. "They Don't Even Talk Like Us: Cajun Violence in Film and Fiction." *Journal of Popular Culture* 23, no. 1: 65–75.
Allen, William Francis, Charles Pickard Ware, and Lucy McKim Garrison. 1867. *Slave Songs of the United States*. New York: A. Simpson.
Ancelet, Barry Jean. 1989a. *Cajun Music: Its Origins and Development*. Lafayette: Center for Louisiana Studies, University of Southwestern Louisiana.
———. 1989b. *"Capitaine, voyage ton flag": The Traditional Cajun Country Mardi Gras*. Lafayette: Center for Louisiana Studies, University of Southwestern Louisiana.
———. 1989c. "The Cajun Who Went to Harvard: Identity in the Oral Tradition of South Louisiana." *Journal of Popular Culture* 23, no. 1: 101–5.
———. 1992. "Cultural Tourism in Cajun Country: Shotgun Wedding or Marriage Made in Heaven." *Southern Folklore* 49, no. 3: 256–66.
Ancelet, Barry Jean, Jay Edwards, and Glen Pitre. 1991. *Cajun Country*. Additional material by Carl Brasseaux, Fred B. Kniffen, Maida Bergeron, Janet Shoemaker, and Mathé Allain. Jackson: University Press of Mississippi.
Ancelet, Barry Jean, and Elemore Morgan Jr. 1984. *The Makers of Cajun Music (Musiciens cadiens et creoles)*. Austin: University of Texas Press.
Bauman, Zygmunt. 1996. "From Pilgrim to Tourist—Or a Short History of Identity." *Questions of Cultural Identity*. Ed. Stuart Hall and Paul du Gay. London: Sage Publications. 18–36.
Bendix, Regina. 1997. *In Search of Authenticity: The Formation of Folklore Studies*. Madison, WI: University of Wisconsin Press.
Benicewicz, Larry. 1999. "Chris Strachwitz and the Arhoolie Story, Part 1: The Early Years." www.bluesartstudio.com/NeueSeiten/pageA54.html, August 13, 2006.
———. "Chris Strachwitz and the Arhoolie Story, Part 2: In the Field." www.bluesartstudio.com/NeueSeiten/pageA58.html, August 13, 2006.
———. "Chris Strachwitz and the Arhoolie Story, Part 3: Branching Out." www.bluesartstudio.com/NeueSeiten/pageA63.html, August 13, 2006.
Bernard, Shane K. 1996. *Swamp Pop: Cajun and Creole Rhythm and Blues*. Jackson: University Press of Mississippi.
———. 2003. *The Cajuns: Americanization of a People*. Jackson: University Press of Mississippi.
Billeaudeau, Lisa. 1995. "Vous Allez Oust! Cajun Migration to California." M.A. thesis, California Institute of Integral Studies.
Bourdieu, Pierre. 1986. "The Forms of Capital." In *Handbook of Theory and Research for the Sociology of Education*. Ed. John G. Richardson. New York: Greenwood Press. 241–58.
Brasseaux, Carl, Keith P. Fontenot, and Claude F. Oubre. 1994. *Creoles of Color in the Bayou Country*. Foreword by Clifton Carmon. Jackson: University Press of Mississippi.
Brasseaux, Carl A. 1987. *The Founding of New Acadia: The Beginnings of Acadian Life in Louisiana, 1765–1803*. Baton Rouge: Louisiana State University Press.

———. 1988. In *Search of Evangeline: Birth and Evolution of the Evangeline Myth*. Thibodaux, LA: Blue Heron Press.

———. 1989. "Four Hundred Years of Acadian Life in North America." *Journal of Popular Culture* 23, no. 1: 3–22.

———. 1991. *"Scattered to the Wind": Dispersal and Wanderings of the Acadians, 1755–1809*. Lafayette: Center for Louisiana Studies, University of Southwestern Louisiana.

———. 1992. *Acadian to Cajun: Transformation of a People, 1803–1877*. Jackson: University Press of Mississippi.

———. 1996. "Creoles of Color in Louisiana's Bayou Country, 1766–1877." In *Creoles of Color of the Gulf South*. Ed. James H. Dormon. Knoxville: University of Tennessee Press. 67–86.

Broughton, Simon, Mark Ellingham, David Muddyman, and Richard Trillo, eds. 1994. *World Music: The Rough Guide*. London: Rough Guides.

Broussard, Albert S. 1993. *Black San Francisco: The Struggle for Racial Equality in the West, 1900–1954*. Lawrence: University Press of Kansas.

Broven, John. 1983. *South to Louisiana: The Music of the Cajun Bayous*. Gretna, LA: Pelican Publishing Co.

Burnim, Mellonee. 1985. "Culture Bearer and Tradition Bearer: An Ethnomusicologist's Research on Gospel Music." *Ethnomusicology* 29, no. 3: 432–47.

Busteed, Mervyn. 1998. "Songs in a strange land—ambiguities of identity amongst Irish migrants in mid-Victorian Manchester." *Political Geography* 17, no. 6: 627–65.

Cantwell, Robert. 1993. *Ethnomimesis: Folklife and the Representation of Culture*. Chapel Hill: University of North Carolina Press.

———. 1996. *When We Were Good: The Folk Revival*. Cambridge, MA: Harvard University Press.

Carpenter, Mary Chapin. 1990. "Down At The Twist And Shout." *Shooting Straight in the Dark*. CBS 46077 (sound recording).

Cheesman, Tom. 1995. "Intersubcultural Dialogue on Husband-Killing: 'Elise,' A Popular Ballad in Nineteenth-Century Germany." In *Ballads and Boundaries: Narrative Singing in an Intercultural Context*. Ed. James Porter. Los Angeles: UCLA Department of Ethnomusicology and Systematic Musicology. 87–100.

Clifford, James. 1988. *The Predicament of Culture: Twentieth Century Ethnography, Literature, and Art*. Cambridge, MA: Harvard University Press.

———. 1992. "Traveling Cultures." In *Cultural Studies*. Ed. Lawrence Grossberg, Cary Nelson, and Paula Treichler. New York: Routledge. 96–116.

———. 1997. *Routes: Travel and Translation in the Late Twentieth Century*. Cambridge, MA: Harvard University Press.

Clifford, James, and George E. Marcus, eds. 1986. *Writing Culture: The Poetics and Politics of Ethnography*. Berkeley: University of California Press.

Cohen, Ronald D. 1995. *"Wasn't That a Time!" Firsthand Accounts of the Folk Music Revival*. Metuchen, NJ: Scarecrow Press.

Collins, Willie R. 1998. "California Rhythm and Blues Recordings, 1942–1972: A Diversity of Styles." *California Soul: Music of African Americans in the West*. Ed. Jacqueline Cogdell DjeDje and Eddie S. Meadows. Berkeley: University of California Press. 213–43.

Crafts, Susan, Daniel Cavicchi, and Charles Keil, eds. 1993. *My Music*. Middletown, CT: Wesleyan University Press.

Csicsery, George Paul. "The First Family: Les and Harrod Blank." *Express: The East Bay's Free Weekly*. 24 April 1998: 7–8.

Csikszentmihalyi, Mihaly, and Isabela Selega Csikszentmihalyi, eds. 1988. *Optimal Experience: Psychological Studies of Flow in Consciousness*. Cambridge, UK: Cambridge University Press.
Daigle, Pierre Varmon. 1987. *Tears, Love, and Laughter: The Story of the Cajuns and Their Music*. 4th ed. Ville Platte, LA: Swallow Publications.
Daigle, Rev. Msgr. Jules O. 1984. *A Dictionary of the Cajun Language*. Ville Platte, LA: Swallow Publications.
Daniels, Douglas Henry. 1990. *Pioneer Urbanites: A Social and Cultural History of Black San Francisco*. Berkeley: University of California Press.
Dart, Mary McNab. 1995. *Contra Dance Choreography: A Reflection of Social Change*. New York: Garland Publications.
Dauphine, James G. 1993. *A Question of Inheritance: Religion, Education, and Louisiana's Cultural Boundary, 1880–1940*. Lafayette: Center for Louisiana Studies, University of Southwestern Louisiana.
Davis, Erik. 2006. *The Visionary State: A Journey Through California's Spiritual Landscape*. Photographs by Michael Rauner. San Francisco: Chronicle Books.
DeNora, Tia. 2000. *Music in Everyday Life*. Cambridge, UK: Cambridge University Press.
DeWitt, Mark F. 1998. "The Cajun and Zydeco Music and Dance Scene in Northern California: Ethnicity, Authenticity, and Leisure." Ph.D. dissertation, University of California, Berkeley.
———. 1999. "Heritage, Tradition and Travel: Louisiana French Culture Placed on a California Dance Floor." *world of music* 41, no. 3: 57–83.
———. 2003. "The Diatonic Button Accordion in Ethnic Context: Idiom and Style in Cajun Dance Music." *Popular Music and Society* 26, no. 3: 305–30.
———. 2003b. Review of *Luderin Darbone's Hackberry Ramblers. Early Recordings: 1935–1950*. Arhoolie CD 7050. *Yearbook for Traditional Music* 35: 220–21.
———. 2006. "Heritage, Tradition and Travel: Louisiana French Culture Placed on a California Dance Floor." In *Accordions, Fiddles, Two Step and Swing: A Cajun Music Reader*. Ed. Ryan A. Brasseaux and Kevin S. Fontenot. Lafayette: The Center for Louisiana Studies, University of Louisiana at Lafayette. 115–37.
Domínguez, Virginia. 1986. *White By Definition: Social Classification in Creole Louisiana*. New Brunswick, NJ: Rutgers University Press.
Dormon, James H. 1983. *The People Called Cajuns: Introduction to an Ethnohistory*. Lafayette: The Center for Louisiana Studies, University of Southwestern Louisiana.
———. 1996. "Ethnicity and Identity: Creoles of Color in Twentieth-Century South Louisiana." *Creoles of Color of the Gulf South*. Ed. James H. Dormon. Knoxville: University of Tennessee Press. 166–79.
Duke, Jerry C. [1988]. *Dances of the Cajuns (Louisiana and Texas)*. San Francisco: Duke.
Dundes, Alan. 1980. *Interpreting Folklore*. Bloomington: Indiana University Press.
Edwards, Bob, Michael W. Foley, and Mario Diani, eds. 2001. *Beyond Toqueville: Civil Society and Social Capital Debate in Comparative Perspective*. Hanover, NH: Tufts University/University Press of New England.
Emoff, Ron. 1998. "A Cajun Poetics of Loss and Longing." *Ethnomusicology* 42, no. 2: 283–301.
Feld, Steven. 1988. "Notes on 'World Beat.'" *Public Culture* 1, no. 1: 31–37.
François, Raymond E., collector, transcriber, and annotator. 1990. *Yé Yaille, Chère! Traditional Cajun Dance Music*. Lafayette, LA: Thunderstone Press.
Frankenstein, Alfred. 20 June 1965. "Recordings of Folk Artists." *San Francisco Chronicle*, sec. This World: 31–32.

Frith, Simon. 1996. "Music and Identity." In *Questions of Cultural Identity*. Ed. Stuart Hall and Paul du Gay. London: Sage Publications. 108–27.

Fusilier, Freida Marie, and Jolene M. Adams. 1994. *Hé, Là-Bas! A History of Louisiana Cajun and Zydeco Music in California*. Sacramento, CA.

Gaudet, Marcia. 1989. "The Image of the Cajun in Literature." *Journal of Popular Culture* 23, no. 1: 77–88.

Geerdes, Clay. 1 January 1997. "David Nadel [1946–1996]." *Anderson Valley Advertiser*, 1, 10.

Gleason, Ralph J. 25 June 1965. "On the Town: How It Is at The Folk Festival." *San Francisco Chronicle*.

———. 29 June 1965. "On the Town: Folk Cult's Bid to Deal With Reality." *San Francisco Chronicle*.

———. 20 October 1969. "Rhythm: A Festival That Poses Questions." *San Francisco Chronicle*. 34.

———. 27 October 1969. "On The Town: A Really Festive Music Festival." *San Francisco Chronicle*. 46.

Goodale, Thomas, and Geoffrey Godbey. 1988. *The Evolution of Leisure: Historical and Philosophical Perspectives*. State College, PA: Venture Publishing.

Green, Archie. 2001. *Torching the Fink Books and Other Essays on Vernacular Culture*. Foreword by Robert Cantwell. Chapel Hill: University of North Carolina Press.

Guillory, Ida, with Naomi Wise. 1990. *Cookin' with Queen Ida*. Rocklin, CA: Prima Publishing.

Gupta, Akhil, and James Ferguson. 1997. *Anthropological Locations: Boundaries and Grounds of a Field Science*. Berkeley: University of California Press.

Gutierrez, C. Paige. 1992. *Cajun Foodways*. Jackson: University Press of Mississippi.

Hall, Stuart. 1989. "Ethnicity: Identity and Difference." *Radical America* 23, no. 4: 9–20.

———. 1991. "The Local and the Global: Globalization and Ethnicity." In *Culture, Globalization, and the World-System: Contemporary Conditions for the Representation of Identity*. Ed. Anthony D. King. 19–39. Binghamton: Department of Art and Art History, State University of New York at Binghamton. 19–39.

Hebert, Timothy. 1993. *Acadian-Cajun Genealogy: Step by Step*. Lafayette: Center for Louisiana Studies, University of Southwestern Louisiana.

Henry, Jacques, and Sara Le Menestrel, eds. 2003. *Working in the Field: Accounts from French Louisiana*. Westport, CT: Praeger.

Henry, Jacques M., and Carl L. Bankston III. 2002. *Blue Collar Bayou: Louisiana Cajuns in the New Economy of Ethnicity*. Westport, CT: Praeger Publishers.

Hildebrand, Lee, and James C. Moore Sr. 1998. "Oakland Blues." *California Soul: Music of African Americans in the West*. Ed. Jacqueline Cogdell DjeDje and Eddie S. Meadows. Berkeley: University of California Press. 104–23.

Hollenbach, Margaret. 1984. "Herzog's Burden—Blank's Dreams." In Les Blank and James Bogan, *Burden of Dreams: Screenplay, Journals, Reviews, Photographs*. Berkeley: North Atlantic Books. 255–59.

Horton, Andrew. 1984. "A Well-Spent Life: Les Blank's Celebrations on Film." In Les Blank and James Bogan, *Burden of Dreams: Screenplay, Journals, Reviews, Photographs*. Berkeley: North Atlantic Books. 266–81.

Kearney, M. 1995. "The Local and the Global: The Anthropology of Globalization and Transnationalism." *Annual Review of Anthropology* 24: 547–65.

Kelly, John R., and Geoffrey Godbey. 1992. *The Sociology of Leisure*. State College, PA: Venture Publishing.

Kershaw, Andy. 1991. "North America—Introduction." *The Virgin Directory of World Music.* 1st Owl Book ed. Ed. Philip Sweeney. New York: Henry Holt. 241–43.

Kirshenblatt-Gimblett, Barbara. 1995. "Theorizing Heritage." *Ethnomusicology* 39, no. 3: 367–80.

———. 1998. "Sounds of Sensibility." *Judaism* 47, no. 1: 49–78.

Kivy, Peter. 1995. *Authenticities: Philosophical Reflections on Musical Performance.* Ithaca, NY: Cornell University Press.

Kouwenhoven, John A. 1948. *Made in America: The Arts in Modern American Civilization.* Newton Centre, MA: Charles T. Branford.

Kraus, Richard. 1962. *Folk Dancing: A Guide for Schools, Colleges, and Recreation Groups.* New York: Macmillan.

Kripal, Jeffrey J., and Glenn W. Shuck, eds. 2005. *On the Edge of the Future: Esalen and the Evolution of American Culture.* Bloomington: Indiana University Press.

Laird, Tracey E. W. 2005. *Louisiana Hayride: Radio and Roots Music Along the Red River.* New York: Oxford University Press.

Lasar, Matthew. 1999. *Pacifica Radio: The Rise of an Alternative Network.* Philadelphia: Temple University Press.

Laušević, Mirjana. 2007. *Balkan Fascination: Creating an Alternative Music Culture in America.* New York: Oxford University Press.

Le Menestrel, Sara. 1999. *La voie des Cadiens: Tourisme et identité en Louisiane.* Paris: Belin.

———. 2003. "Tourist and 'Cajun From France': The Shifting Identity of the Anthropologist." In *Working in the Field: Accounts from French Louisiana.* Ed. Jacques Henry and Sara Le Menestrel. Westport, CT: Praeger. 121–38.

Levine, Peter. 2 March 1975. "They Call It Zydeco." *San Francisco Examiner and Chronicle,* sec. California Living: 24–29.

Lomax, Alan. 1942. *Folk Music of the United States.* Washington: Library of Congress (sound recording).

Lomax, Alan J. 1987. "Introductory Liner Notes." On *Louisiana Cajun and Creole Music, 1934: The Lomax Recordings.* Produced by Barry Jean Ancelet and Michael Doucet. Ville Platte, LA: Swallow Records (sound recording).

Lomax, John, and Alan Lomax, collectors and compilers. 1941. *Our Singing Country: A Second Volume of American Ballads and Folk Songs.* Music ed. Ruth Crawford Seeger. New York: Macmillan.

Louder, Dean R., and Michael Leblanc. 1979. "The Cajuns of East Texas." *Cahiers De Géographie Du Québec* 23, no. 59: 317–29.

Louisiana Writer's Project. 1941. *Louisiana: A Guide to the State.* American Guide Series. Sponsored by The Louisiana Library Commission in Baton Rouge, Louisiana State University, Federal Works Agency, and Work Projects Administration. New York: Hastings House.

MacCannell, Dean. 1999. *The Tourist: A New Theory of the Leisure Class.* New foreword by Lucy Lippard. Berkeley: University of California Press.

Marcus, George E., and Michael M. J. Fischer. 1986. *Anthropology as Cultural Critique: An Experimental Moment in the Human Sciences.* Chicago: University of Chicago Press.

Martinez, Jesus. 1995. "Tigers in a Gold Cage: Binationalism and Politics in the Songs of Mexican Immigrants in Silicon Valley." In *Ballads and Boundaries: Narrative Singing in an Intercultural Context.* Ed. James Porter. Los Angeles: UCLA Department of Ethnomusicology and Systematic Musicology. 325–38.

McBroome, Delores Nason. 1993. *Parallel Communities: African Americans in California's East Bay, 1850–1963*. New York: Garland.
Means, Nathaniel. 2003. "Forging Identity: African American, Cajun, and Anglo American Folkways in WPA Guides to the Deep South." *Louisiana History* 44, no. 2: 211–23.
Meintjes, Louise. 1990. "Paul Simon's *Graceland*, South Africa, and the Mediation of Musical Meaning." *Ethnomusicology* 34, no. 1: 37–73.
Miller, Larry, and Mike Miller. 1988. *You Can Play Cajun Accordion: Designed for Beginners*. Revised ed. Iota, LA: Pointe Au Loup Publishing.
National Park Service. 2000. *Cane River Creole National Historical Park: Draft General Management Plan/Environmental Impact Statement*. U.S. Government Printing Office.
———. 2001. *Cane River Creole National Historical Park: Final General Management Plan/Environmental Impact Statement*. U.S. Government Printing Office.
Niles, John D. 1995. "The Role of the Strong Tradition-Bearer in the Making of an Oral Culture." In *Ballads and Boundaries: Narrative Singing in an Intercultural Context*. Ed. James Porter. Los Angeles: UCLA Department of Ethnomusicology and Systematic Musicology. 231–40.
Nyhan, Pat, Brian Rollins, and David Babb. 1997. *Let the Good Times Roll! A Guide to Cajun and Zydeco Music*. Portland, ME: Upbeat Books.
Olivier, Barry. n.d. "Folk Music at Berkeley 1956 to 1970." Evanston, IL: Berkeley Folk Festival Archive, McCormick Library of Special Collections, Northwestern University Library.
Olivier, Rick, and Ben Sandmel, photographer/author. 1999. *Zydeco!* Jackson: University Press of Mississippi.
Oullette, Dan. 1994. "Ragin' Cajun." *The Monthly* (Emeryville, CA) 25 (3): 5–9.
Parsons, Clark. 1993. Interview with Mary Chapin Carpenter. *Nashville Scene*.
Phillips, Jim. 1997. "Notes from the Prez . . ." Emeryville, CA: *California Friends of Louisiana French Music Newsletter* 2, no. 4: 2–3.
Plater, Ormonde, Rand Speyrer, and Cynthia Speyrer. 1993. *Cajun Dancing*. Gretna, LA: Pelican Publishing.
Putnam, Robert D. 2000. *Bowling Alone: The Collapse and Revival of American Community*. New York: Simon and Schuster.
Putnam, Robert D., and Lewis M. Feldstein. 2003. *Better Together: Restoring the American Community*. New York: Simon and Schuster.
Ramon, Susan Appe. 1986. *Louisiana Sue's Cajun Cookin Made Easy: Cajun and Creole Dishes Anyone Can Fix With Little Fuss; Fantastic Foods and Folklore From the Kitchens of New Orleans*. [Sacramento, CA.]
Rogers, Kim Lacy. 1993. *Righteous Lives: Narratives of the New Orleans Civil Rights Movement*. New York: New York University Press.
Rosenberg, Neil V., ed. 1993. *Transforming Tradition: Folk Music Revivals Examined*. Publications of the American Folklore Society. Urbana, IL: University of Illinois Press.
Rumney, Ron. 1999. "President's Message." Emeryville, CA: *California Friends of Louisiana French Music Newsletter* 4, no. 3: 1–2.
Savoy, Ann, compiler and ed. 1984. *Cajun Music: A Reflection of a People*. 3rd ed. Eunice, LA: Bluebird Press.
Schweid, Richard. 1999. *Hot Peppers: The Story of Cajuns and Capsicum*. Rev. ed. Chapel Hill: University of North Carolina Press.
Seeger, Charles. 1977. "Toward a Unitary Field Theory for Musicology." *Studies in Musicology, 1935–1975*. Berkeley: University of California Press. 102–38.

Sefton, W. M., ed. and compiler. n.d. *Recollections of Nineteenth- and Twentieth-century Communal Life at Preston Ranch.* Unpublished manuscript.
Selvin, Joel. 1 October 1995. "A 35-Year Spin: Arhoolie Records celebrates anniversary with concerts from blues to Tex-Mex." *San Francisco Chronicle.*
Sexton, Rocky. 2001. "The Cajun-French Music Association: Negotiating and Transmitting Tradition." *The 46th Annual Meeting of the Society for Ethnomusicology.*
Slobin, Mark. 1993. *Subcultural Sounds: Micromusics of the West.* Hanover, NH: Wesleyan University Press.
Small, Christopher. 1998. *Musicking: The Meanings of Performing and Listening.* Hanover, NH: Wesley University Press/University Press of New England.
Smith, Valene L., ed. 1989. *Hosts and Guests: The Anthropology of Tourism.* 2nd ed. Philadelphia: University of Pennsylvania Press.
Spencer, Peter. 1992. *World Beat: A Listener's Guide to Contemporary World Music on CD.* Chicago: A Cappella Books.
Spitzer, Nicholas R. 1986. "Zydeco and Mardi Gras: Creole Identity and Performance Genres in Rural French Louisiana." Dissertation, University of Texas at Austin.
———. 1996. "Mardi Gras in L'Anse de 'Prien Noir: A Creole Community Performance in Rural French Louisiana." In *Creoles of Color of the Gulf South.* Ed. James H. Dormon. Knoxville: University of Tennessee Press. 87–125.
Stekert, Ellen J. 1993. "Cents and Nonsense in the Urban Folksong Movement: 1930–66." In *Transforming Tradition: Folk Music Revivals Examined.* Ed. Neil V. Rosenberg. Urbana: University of Illinois Press. 84–106.
Stivale, Charles J. 2003. *Disenchanting Les Bons Temps: Identity and Authenticity in Cajun Music and Dance.* Durham, NC: Duke University Press.
Strachwitz, Chris. 2000. Foreword to *40th Anniversary Collection, 1960–2000: The Journey of Chris Strachwitz.* El Cerrito, CA: Arhoolie Records CD491 (sound recording).
Sweeney, Philip. 1991. *The Virgin Directory of World Music.* 1st Owl Book ed. New York: Henry Holt.
Taylor, Timothy D. 1997. *Global Pop: World Music, World Markets.* New York: Routledge.
Tisserand, Michael. 1998. *The Kingdom of Zydeco.* 1st ed. New York: Arcade.
Titon, Jeff Todd. 1980. "The Life Story." *Journal of American Folklore* 93, no. 369: 276–92.
———. 1993. "Reconstructing the Blues: Reflections on the 1960s Blues Revival." In *Transforming Tradition: Folk Music Revivals Examined.* Ed. Neil V. Rosenberg Urbana: University of Illinois Press. 220–40.
Tregle, Joseph G. Jr. 1992. "Creoles and Americans." In *Creole New Orleans: Race and Americanization.* Ed. Arnold R. Hirsch and Joseph Logsdon. Baton Rouge: Louisiana State University Press. 131–85.
Tucker, Stephen R. 1995. "'Louisiana Saturday Night': A History of Louisiana Country Music." Dissertation, Tulane University.
United States Congress. 1977. Hearing Before the Subcommittee on Parks and Recreation of the Committee on Interior and Insular Affairs, United States Senate, Ninety-Fourth Congress, Second Session, on S. 3546: A Bill to Authorize the Establishment of the Jean Lafitte National Park in the State of Louisiana, and for Other Purposes. Washington: U.S. Government Printing Office.
Volk, Terese M. 1994. "Folk Musics and Increasing Diversity in American Music Education: 1900–1916." *Journal of Research in Music Education* 42, no. 4: 285–305.

Wald, Elijah. 2000. Program notes to *40th Anniversary Collection, 1960–2000: The Journey of Chris Strachwitz*. El Cerrito, CA: Arhoolie Records CD491 (sound recording).

Weill, Rita. 1972. Liner notes to *Berkeley Farms: Oldtime and Country Style Music of Berkeley*. New York: Folkways FA 2436 (sound recording).

Whatley, Randall P., and Harry Jannise. 1981. *Conversational Cajun French 1*. 1st Pelican ed. Gretna, LA: Pelican Publishing.

Whitfield, Irène Thérèse. 1939. *Louisiana French Folk Songs*. Baton Rouge: Louisiana State University Press.

Willging, Dan. 1999. "Digging at the Roots of Creole Music: D'Jalma Garnier of Filé." *Dirty Linen* 80.

Wood, Richard L. 2001. "Political Culture Reconsidered: Insights on Social Capital from an Ethnography of Faith-Based Community Organizing." In *Beyond Toqueville: Civil Society and Social Capital Debate in Comparative Perspective*. Ed. Bob Edwards, Michael W. Foley, and Mario Diani. Hanover, NH: Tufts University/University Press of New England. 254–65.

Wood, Roger. 2006. *Texas Zydeco*. Photography by James Fraher. Austin: University of Texas Press.

Woods, Frances. 1989. *Value Retention Among Young Creoles: Attitudes and Commitment of Contemporary Youth*. Lewiston, NY: Edwin Mellen Press.

Discography

A-2-Fay 001. Motordude Zydeco, *Motordude Zydeco*. Oakland, CA: A-2-Fay Records, 1993.
A-2-Fay 002. Zydeco Slim, *Zydeco Slim featuring R.C. Carrier*. Oakland, CA: A-2-Fay Records, 1995.
A-2-Fay 003. Motordude Zydeco, *Big Oakland*. Oakland, CA: A-2-Fay Records, 1995.
Arhoolie 1001. Mance Lipscomb, *Mance Lipscomb: Texas Sharecropper and Songster*. Chris Strachwitz, producer. El Cerrito, CA: Arhoolie Records, 1960.
Arhoolie 1002. Big Joe Williams, *Tough Times*. Chris Strachwitz, producer. El Cerrito, CA: Arhoolie Records, 1960.
Arhoolie 1003. B. K. Turner, *The Black Ace: B. K. Turner and His Steel Guitar*. Chris Strachwitz, producer. El Cerrito, CA: Arhoolie Records, 1960.
Arhoolie 1004. Melvin Jackson, *Lil Son Jackson*. Chris Strachwitz, producer. El Cerrito, CA: Arhoolie Records, 1960.
Arhoolie 1009. *Zydeco*. Chris Strachwitz, editor and annotator. El Cerrito, CA: Arhoolie Records, 1967.
Arhoolie 3011. The Klezmorim, *Streets of Gold*. El Cerrito, CA: Arhoolie Records, 1978.
Arhoolie 5029. Savoy-Doucet Cajun Band, *Les Harias: Home Music*. Arhoolie Records, 1983.
Arhoolie 5035. Michael Doucet, Danny Poullard, and Alan Senauke, *Cajun Jam Session*. El Cerrito, CA: Arhoolie Records, 1989.
Arhoolie C-212. *Folksongs of the Louisiana Acadians, Volumes 1 and 2*. Harry Oster, collector. El Cerrito, CA: Arhoolie Records, 1984.
Arhoolie CD 313. Clifton Chenier, *Live at St. Mark's*. Chris Strachwitz, producer. El Cerrito, CA: Arhoolie Records, 1989.
Arhoolie CD 331. *J'ai été au bal: I Went to the Dance, Volume 1*. Chris Strachwitz and Maureen Gosling, eds. El Cerrito, CA: Arhoolie Records, 1990.
Arhoolie CD 332. *J'ai été au bal: I Went to the Dance, Volume 2*. Chris Strachwitz and Maureen Gosling, eds. El Cerrito, CA: Arhoolie Records, 1990.
Arhoolie CD 356. California Cajun Orchestra, *Not Lonesome Anymore*. Jody Stecher with Suzy Thompson and Bob Shumaker, producers. El Cerrito, CA: Arhoolie Records, 1991.
Arhoolie CD 418. Savoy-Doucet Cajun Band, *Live! At the Dance*. Chris Strachwitz, producer. El Cerrito, CA: Arhoolie Records, 1994.
Arhoolie CD 433. Any Old Time String Band, *I Bid You Goodnight*. Chris Strachwitz, producer. El Cerrito, CA: Arhoolie Records, 1996.
Arhoolie CD 436. California Cajun Orchestra, *Nonc Adam Two-Step*. El Cerrito, CA: Arhoolie Records, 1995.
Arhoolie CD 474. Clifton Chenier, *The Best of Clifton Chenier: The King of Zydeco and Louisiana Blues*. Chris Strachwitz, producer. El Cerrito, CA: Arhoolie Records, 2003.
Arhoolie CD 525. The Creole Belles (with Andrew Carrière), *Cajun and Creole Traditional Music*. El Cerrito, CA: Arhoolie Records, 2008.

Arhoolie CD 5041. Eric and Suzy Thompson, *Adam and Eve Had the Blues*. John Lumsdaine with Eric and Suzy Thompson, producers. El Cerrito, CA: Arhoolie Records, 1989.

Arhoolie F5003. Hackberry Ramblers, *Luderin Darbone's Hackberry Ramblers: Louisiana Cajun Music*. El Cerrito, CA: Arhoolie Records, 1963.

Arhoolie/Folklyric CD 7007. *The Roots of Zydeco-Amédé Ardoin, "I'm Never Comin' Back."* Chris Strachwitz, producer. El Cerrito, CA: Arhoolie Records, 1995.

Carryon 6010. Gerard Landry and Friends, *One Day on the Porch*. New Orleans: Carryon Productions, 2006.

Elektra EKL-4006. Charles River Valley Boys, *Beatle Country*. Nashville, TN: Elektra Records, 1966.

Elektra Nonesuch 9 61146-2. Boozoo Chavis, *Boozoo Chavis*. Terry Adams, producer. New York: Elektra Entertainment, 1991.

Flying Fish FF-275. Blue Flame String Band, *Blue Flame String Band*. Chicago: Flying Fish Records, 1982.

Folkways 8361. Dewey Balfa and Tracy Schwarz, instructors, *Traditional Cajun Fiddle: Instruction*. Folkways Records, 1976.

Folkways 8362. Dewey Balfa, *Cajun Fiddle, Old and New*. Tracy Schwarz, recorder and annotator. Folkways Records, 1977.

Folkways 8363. Gérard Dôle, *Traditional Cajun Accordion*. Folkways Records, 1977.

Folkways 8364. Gérard Dôle, *Cajun Accordion, Old and New, Vol. 2: Instruction*. Folkways Records, 1979.

Folkways F-31035. New Lost City Ramblers, *Remembrance Of Things To Come*. New York: Folkways Records, 1966.

Folkways FA 2436. *Berkeley Farms: Oldtime and country style music of Berkeley*. Mike Seeger, producer. New York: Folkways Records, 1972.

Folkways FA 2626. Quatre Vieux Garçons, *Quatre Vieux Garçons*. Folkways Records, 1984.

Folkways FP 251, 252, 253. *Anthology of American Folk Music*. Harry Smith, ed. New York: Folkways Records, 1952.

Gator Beat GTBTA2-CD. Gator Beat, *Mardi Gras Fever!* Sonoma, CA: 1996.

Gator Beat GTBTA3-CD. Gator Beat, *See Ya Later Alligator*. Sonoma, CA: 1997.

Globe GLO-027. Various artists, *West Coast Mardi Gras Party*. Mill Valley, CA: Globe Records, 2001.

GNP5-2197. Queen Ida Guillory, *Cookin' with Queen Ida and Her Zydeco Band*. Los Angeles: GNP-Crescendo Records, 1989.

GNP5-2203. Myrick Freeze Guillory, *Nouveau Zydeco*. Los Angeles: GNP-Crescendo Records, 1991.

GNPS-2101. Queen Ida Guillory, *Queen Ida Plays Zydeco*. Los Angeles: GNP-Crescendo Records, 1976.

GNPS-2112. Queen Ida and the Bon Temps Band, *Queen Ida and the Bon Temps Band: Zydeco a la Mode*. Los Angeles: GNP-Crescendo Records, 1977.

GNPS-2147. Queen Ida and the Bon Temps Zydeco Band, *Queen Ida and the Bon Temps Zydeco Band: On Tour*. Los Angeles: GNP-Crescendo Records, 1982.

GNPS-2172. Queen Ida and Her Zydeco Band, *Queen Ida and Her Zydeco Band: On a Saturday Night*. Los Angeles: GNP-Crescendo Records, 1984.

GNPS 2181. Queen Ida and Her Zydeco Band, *Queen Ida and Her Zydeco Band: Caught in the Act!* Los Angeles: GNP Crescendo Records, 1985.

GNPS-5-2131. Queen Ida and the Bon Temps Zydeco Band, *Queen Ida and the Bon Temps Zydeco Band: In New Orleans*. Los Angeles: GNP-Crescendo Records, 1980.
GNPS5-2158. Queen Ida and Her Zydeco Band, *Queen Ida and Her Zydeco Band: In San Francisco*. Los Angeles: GNP-Crescendo Records, 1983.
Herringbone Disc ET 101. Eric Thompson, *Thompson's Real: Bluegrass Instrumentals with Guitar*. Berkeley: Herringbone Disc, 2000.
La Louisianne AT7071. Andre Thierry and Zydeco Magic, *A Whole Lotta Something*. La Louisianne Records, 2004.
La Louisianne LLC-509. John Semien and His Opelousas Playboys, *John Semien and His Opelousas Playboys*. Lafayette: La Louisianne Records, n.d.
La Louisianne LLCD-1007. Aldus Roger, *Aldus Roger: A Cajun Legend*. Lafayette: La Louisianne Records, 1993.
Miss Freida and the Cajun Fusiliers. *I've Got a Sou in My Shoe*. Sacramento, CA: 1998.
Miss Freida and the Cajun Fusiliers. *Old Songs and New Stories*. Sacramento, CA: 2000.
Native and Fine 906-4. Bluegrass Intentions, *Old As Dirt*. Albany, CA: Native and Fine Records.
Native and Fine 906-7. Suzy Thompson, *No Mockingbird*. Albany, CA: Native and Fine Records, 2003.
Rooster 111. The Delta Sisters, *Music From The Old-Timey Hotel*. Rooster Records, 1981.
Rounder 0128. The Backwoods Band, *Jes' Fine*. Cambridge, MA: Rounder Records, 1979.
Rounder 6009. *Zodico: Louisiana Créole Music*. Nicholas R. Spitzer, recorder, producer, photographer. Somerville, MA: Rounder Records, 1979.
Rounder CD 1842-1843. *Louisiana Cajun and Creole Music, 1934: The Lomax Recordings*. Barry Jean Ancelet and Michael Doucet, producers. Cambridge, MA: Rounder Records.
Rounder CD-6060. Bruce Daigrepont, *Petit Cadeau*. Cambridge, MA: Rounder Records, 1994.
Swallow 6011. Balfa Brothers, *The Balfa Brothers Play Traditional Cajun Music, Vols. I and II*. Floyd Soileau, producer. Ville Platte, LA: Swallow Records, 1990.
Swallow 6056. Dewey Balfa, fiddle, *Souvenirs*. Louisiana: Swallow Records, 1985.
Swallow LP-8003-2. *Louisiana Cajun and Creole Music, 1934: The Lomax Recordings*. Barry Jean Ancelet and Michael Doucet, producers. Ville Platte, LA: Swallow Records, 1987.
Warner Bros. 9 25447-2. Paul Simon, *Graceland*. Warner Bros. Records, 1986.
Zydeco Flames-VS01. Zydeco Flames, *Hot Offerings*. Berkeley: 1993.
Zydeco Flames-VS02. Zydeco Flames, *Burnin' Up The Tracks*. San Anselmo, CA: 1995.
Zydeco Flames-VS03. Zydeco Flames, *The Heat is On*. San Anselmo, CA: 1996.
Zydeco Flames-VS04. Zydeco Flames, *Zydeco Flames Live: Smokin' at the Plant*. Berkeley: 1998.
Zydeco Flames-VS05. Zydeco Flames, *Bank the Fire*. San Anselmo, CA: 2003.

Filmography

Always For Pleasure. Filmed, edited, produced, and directed by Les Blank. El Cerrito, CA: Flower Films and Video, 1978.
Bayou by the Bay. Produced and directed by Hal Rowland and Glenn Switkes. Berkeley: School of Journalism, U.C. Berkeley, 1980.
Belizaire the Cajun. Directed by Glen Pitre. 1986.
The Big Easy. Directed by Jim McBride. 1987.
The Blues Accordin' to Lightnin' Hopkins. By Les Blank. El Cerrito, CA: Flower Films and Video, 1969.
Chulas Fronteras. By Les Blank. With Maureen Gosling. El Cerrito, CA: Flower Films and Video, 1976.
Del Mero Corazon. By Les Blank. El Cerrito, CA: Flower Films and Video, 1979.
Dry Wood. By Les Blank. With Maureen Gosling. El Cerrito, CA: Flower Films and Video, 1973.
Garlic is as Good as Ten Mothers. By Les Blank. With Maureen Gosling. El Cerrito, CA: Flower Films and Video, 1980.
God Respects Us When We Work, But He Loves Us When We Dance. By Les Blank. El Cerrito, CA: Flower Films and Video, 1968.
Hot Pepper. By Les Blank. With Maureen Gosling. El Cerrito, CA: Flower Films and Video, 1973.
How to Play the Cajun Accordion: With Marc Savoy and Tracy Schwarz. Produced by Ed McKeon. Eunice, LA: Bluebird Films, 1990.
Interview with Les Blank and Maureen Gosling. Interview by Kevin Bender. Berkeley: University of California, Berkeley, Office of Educational Television and Radio, 1986.
It's Got To Be Rough and Sweet: Arhoolie Records 25th Anniversary Party. Produced by Chris Strachwitz. El Cerrito, CA: Arhoolie Video 402v, 1985.
J'ai Été Au Bal (I Went to the Dance). By Les Blank, Chris Strachwitz, and Maureen Gosling. El Cerrito, CA: Brazos Films/Arhoolie Productions, 1989.
Marc and Ann. Produced and directed by Les Blank. El Cerrito, CA: Flower Films and Video, 1990.
Spend It All. By Les Blank. With Skip Gerson. El Cerrito, CA: Flower Films and Video, 1971.
Yum! Yum! Yum! Produced and directed by Les Blank and Maureen Gosling. El Cerrito, CA: Flower Films and Video, 1991.

Interviews

Bayou Seco (Jeanie McLerie and Ken Keppeler). Interview by Mark DeWitt, 2006. Email.
Bohan, Frank. Interview by Mark DeWitt, 8 September 2000, San Anselmo, CA. Audio recording.
Broussard, George. Interview by Gary Canaparo, 1994, Sunol, CA. Audio recording.
Canaparo, Gary and Maryanne. Interview by Mark DeWitt, 24 August 2004, Sunol, CA. Audio recording.
Canaparo, Gary and Maryanne. Interview by Mark DeWitt, May 2006. Email.
Carpenter, Mary Chapin. Interview by Mark DeWitt, 2003. Email.
Carrière, Andrew. Interview by Mark DeWitt, 11 September 2000, Oakland, CA. Audio recording.
DeSimone, Dana. Interview by Mark DeWitt, 25 June 1998, Berkeley, CA. Audio recording.
Domingue, Richard. Interview by Mark DeWitt, 23 August 2000, Sonoma, CA. Audio recording.
Doucet, Michael. Telephone interview by Mark DeWitt, 12 June 2004, Oakland, CA–Connecticut. Audio recording.
Fusilier, Freida. Interview by Mark DeWitt, 23 March 1997, Sacramento, CA. Audio recording.
Gordon, Bruce. Interview by Mark DeWitt, 10 October 1995, Berkeley, CA. Audio recording.
Gradney, Ralph Bobby. Interview by Mark DeWitt, 31 August 2000, Richmond, CA. Audio recording.
Guillory, Olivia. Interview by Mark DeWitt, 9 January 1995, Richmond, CA. Audio recording.
Hymowitz, David. Interview by Mark DeWitt, 12 September 2000, Albany, CA. Audio recording.
Karpan, Maureen. Interview by Mark DeWitt, 25 August 2000, Berkeley, CA. Audio recording.
Leblanc, Betty. Interview by Mark DeWitt, 5 September 2000, San Francisco, CA. Audio recording.
Lewis, Delilah Lee. Interview by Mark F. DeWitt, 30 August 2000, San Francisco, CA. Audio recording.
Poullard, Danny. Interview by Will Spires, 10 March 1985, San Francisco, CA. Audio recording.
Poullard, Danny. Interview by Mark DeWitt, 8 September 2000, Fairfield, CA. Audio recording.
Ramon, Susan Appe. Interview by Mark DeWitt, 22 March 1997, Sacramento, CA. Audio recording.
Rumney, Ron. Interview by Mark DeWitt, 12 September 2000, Sonoma, CA. Audio recording.
Schmidt, Linda. Interview by Mark DeWitt, 9 February 1995, Berkeley, CA. Audio recording.
Schwarz, Tracy. Interview by Mark DeWitt, 13 January 1998, Berkeley, CA. Audio recording.
Spires, Will. Interview by Mark DeWitt, 26 August 1997, Cotati, CA. Audio recording.
Stevens, Ray. Interview by Mark DeWitt, 29 August 2000, Oakland, CA. Audio recording.
Strogen, Paul. Interview by Mark DeWitt, 9 September 2000, Berkeley, CA. Audio recording.
Thompson, Eric and Suzy. Interview by Mark DeWitt, 4 March 1997, Berkeley, CA. Audio recording.
Thompson, Eric and Suzy. Interview by Mark DeWitt and Sue Schleifer, 27 April 2006, Oakland, CA. Audio recording.
Wilson, Bill. Interview by Mark DeWitt, 6 January 1995, Oakland, CA. Audio recording.
Wimmer, Kevin. Interview by Mark DeWitt, 21 September 1997, Lafayette, LA. Interview notes.

Index

Page numbers in *italics* refer to illustrations.

Abshire, Nathan, 25, 76–77, 83, 104, 112, 149
accordion. *See* instruments
Adam, Jolene (née Adams), vii, 34, 214
aesthetics, viii, 113–14, 120–21, 129–30, 150, 177, 193–94, 240–41, 245–46
affinity group, 34, 197, 244–45
Alameda, Calif., 64, 135, 187–88, 196, 218
American (term for outsiders to ethnic group), 5, 14, 33, 249n3
Ancelet, Barry Jean, 123, 199, 235–36
Anthology of American Folk Music, 118, 157
Ardoin, Amédé, 24–25, 61, 63, 76
Ardoin, Black (Lawrence), 170
Ardoin, Bois Sec (Alphonse), 25, 61, 76, 88, 98–99, 104, 110, 112, *122*, 126, 131, 142, *147*, 151, 158, 198
Ardoin, Chris, 170
Ardoin, Morris, 147
Ardoin, Paul "Chipso," 185
Ardoin, Russell, 198, 208, 213–14, 217–18
Arhoolie Records. *See* Strachwitz, Chris
Ashkenaz Music and Dance Community Center, viii, 3–4, 34, 47, 60, 84–86, 98, *99*, 107, 117, 135–36, 138, *158*, 163, 172, 176–77, 179, 183–84, 187, 192, 196, 231, 233–34, 244
authenticity, 5, 18–19, 30–31, 51, 98, 109–10, 113–14, 120–21, 214, 235

Balfa, Christine, 153, 158
Balfa, Dewey, 28, 76–78, 84–85, 114, 119–20, *122*, 125–26, 129, 133–36, 143, 149, 153, 184
Balfa, Rodney, 77, 84, 125, 134, 158
Balfa Brothers, 25, 76–77, 111–12, 119–20, 124–25, 127, 131, 133–34, 153, 158, 245. *See also* Bolfa, Will

Ban, Agi, 139, 193
bands: Bayou Seco, 159; Poullard, Poullard, and Garnier, 88
  in California: Any Old Time String Band, 134–35, 255n17; Aux Cajunals, 139, 154; Bayou Croakers, 156; Bayou Pon Pon, 151, 156, 192–93; Blue Flame String Band, 85, 135; Blues de Bayou, 128; Cajun Coyotes, 151; California Cajun Orchestra, 60, 85–86, 91, 97–98, *135*, 136, *139*, 153, 188, 192–93, 238–39; Creole Belles, 98, 151, 239; Frog Legs, 102, 238; Gator Beat, 175, 198, 216, 230–31; Louisiana Playboys, 59–60, 71, 73–74, 81, 83–86, 91, 100, *106*, 111, 127, 143, 164–67, *170*, 176–77, 184, 190, 192, 232, 257ch7n10; Motordude Zydeco, 187–88, 193, 238; Opelousas Playboys, 54–55, 57–60, 71, 81, 100, 154–55; Sauce Piquante, 102; Tee Fee, 3, 7, 239; Zydeco Flames, 188, 214, 216, 239–41, *240*; ZZ and the Bad Boys, 150, 193
  in Louisiana: Beausoleil, 4–9, 19, 41, 78, 85, 123, 149, 205–6, 235, 237, 249n1, 249n6; Filé, 88; Hackberry Ramblers, 25, 109, 120, *122*, 124, 154–55, 255n11; Lawtell Playboys, 96
Basile, La., *13*, 25, 57, *58*, 59, 61, 80, 93
Bauman, Zygmunt, 27, 29, 243
Beau Jocque, 61, 65, 91, 93–94, 186, 241
Bendix, Regina, 18–19, 23–24
Berkeley, Calif., 3–4, *15*, 16, 34, 40, 66, 83–86, 98, 102, 109–12, 124, 127–28, 131, 133–35, 138, 140, 153–57, 163–64, 171, 187–88, 213, 255n17; dance style associated with, 161, 177. *See also* University of California, Berkeley

INDEX

Berkeley Folk Festival. *See* festivals
Bernard, Shane, 29–30, 51, 199, 201
Blank, Les, 45, 83–84, 107, 111–16, 153; *The Blues According to Lightnin' Hopkins*, 111–12; *Dry Wood*, 112; *Garlic Is As Good As Ten Mothers*, 84, 113–16; *Hot Pepper*, 79, 112; *J'ai Éte Au Bal*, 85, 110, 112, 137; *Marc and Ann*, 112; *Spend It All*, 111–12, 114; *Yum! Yum! Yum!*, 112
blues: associated with zydeco, 33, 46, 55, 111, 214, 223; and dance, 192; as emotion, *8*; Oakland, 107–8; revival, 16, 45, 85, 109, 113, 117, 119, 121, 128, 134–37, 142, 197, 238–41. *See also* zydeco
Bluestein, Gene, 143, 151, 255n11
Bluestein, Jemmy and Evo, 143, 150–51
Bohan, Frank, 240–41
Bolfa, Will, 77, 125, 158
Bourdieu, Pierre, 38, 45, 251n44
Breaux Bridge, La., *13*, 89, 149, 199, 201, 226, 230, 234
Brisbane, Calif. *See* DeMarco's 23 Club
Broussard, George, 54, 57, 59–62, *61*, 71, 73–74, 85, 100, 104, *105*, 137, 164–67
Brown, James, 182, 221, 226, 244
Buckwheat Zydeco, 93, 201, 221, 227, 241

Cajun: coonass, 199, 219, 229; craze, 29–30, 117, 196, 198–203, 232–38; definition of, 5, 20; desire to become, 26, 32, 114–16, 159–60, 180; ethnic history, 19, 21–22, 49–51, 79, 250n11; migration, 197, 205, 219, 221–22, 227–29; rehabilitated image of, 4–16, 49–51, 107, 118–19; stereotypes of, 23, 30–31, 51, 114, 199; as umbrella term, 4
Cajun culture: foodways, 4, *7*, 8–9, 110, 112, 199, 210–15, 220, 222–25; religion, 22. *See also* Cajun music; dance; French language; Mardi Gras
Cajun French Music Association (CFMA), 79, 120, 137
Cajun music: blues influences, 76, 78, *127*, 149, 202; instrumentation, 25; languages sung, 25. *See also* Louisiana French music
California Friends of Louisiana French Music (CFLFM), 47, 99, 170, 177, 181

Canaparo, Gary, 55, 58, *61*, 73, 82, 84, 90, *105*, *106*, 163–68, *166*, *170*, 190, *191*, 193–95, 240
Canaparo, Maryanne, 163–70
Cantwell, Robert, 23–24, 118, 162
Carpenter, Mary Chapin, 3–12, 14, 26, 28, 34, 78, 249n1, 249n6, 249n14
Carrier, R. C., 95
Carrière, Andrew, 60, 96–99, 103, 132, 137–38
Carrière, Bébé (Joseph), 25, 61, 96–98, 110, 147, *148*, 151
Carrière, Calvin, 58, 96
Carrière, Dolon (Éraste), 25, 96, 99, 110, 147
Castillo, Diana, 185, 187, 194
Catholic church: as Creole social nexus in California, 70–71; as location for dances, 45, 47, 52, 60–61, 63, 71, 93–94, 104, 111, *170*, 173–74, 177–79, *191*, 195–96, 234
Catholic parishes, northern California: All Hallows, 57, 71, 81, *90*, 136, 167, 173, 196, 222; St. Benedict's, *105*; St. Francis of Assisi, 71, 136, 167, *170*, 173, 177, 196; St. Mark's, 71, 93–94, 104, 136, 167, 173, 190, *191*, 196, 212; St. Michael's, 91
Chavis, Boozoo, 61, 79, 91, *122*, 169, 177, 186, 193–94, 230
Chenier, Clifton, 28, 54, 58, 60–61, 65, 71, 78–79, 89–90, 93–95, 100, 104, 108–13, *122*, 154, 164, 167, 184, 192, 202–3, 211–12, 227, 232, 239–40, 244–45, 253n8
Chez Panisse, 60, 84, 115, 127
CODOFIL, 50, 199, 214
country music: American, 6–9, 53, 66, 73, 78, 85, 117, 121, 136, 141, 190, 232, 238; Cajun, 25, 78. *See also* Nashville, Tenn.
Creole: definition of, 5, 20, 51, 63, 72–73, 258n18; ethnic history, 21–23, 49–51; image as "black Cajun," 57; migration, 29, 47, 57, 59, 67–72, 75, 80–81, 90, 93, 97, 182–83, 197; phenotype, 62–63, 68, 80, 246; white, 20, 258n18
Creole culture: customs, 42–43, 52–53, 63, 91–93, 167–68, 173–74, 254n23;

folktales, 51; religion, 22. *See also* Creole music; French language; Mardi Gras
Creole music: history, 24–25, 61–63, 76, 88, 96; style, 25, 58–59, 61. *See also* Louisiana French music; zydeco
Crowley, La., *13*, 25, 96, 143–44, 146
cultural capital, 38–39, 45, 47, 251n44

dance: codification of style, 165–66; contests, 91, 174; etiquette, 173–74, 179; family traditions, 166–67; learning, insider, 52, 89–90, 93, 204, 210, 221, 227; learning, outsider, *8*, 28, 104–7, 146, 167, 173, 176–78, 184–87, 193–94, 256n1; teaching, 65–66, 95, 184, 187–90, 194–95, 213; zydeco style, 65–66. *See also* Catholic church; folk dancing; house parties
Delafose, John, 93–95, 167, 177, 185–86
DeMarco's 23 Club, 73, 91, *92*, 187, 232, *239*
DeSimone, Dana, 181–90, 194–96, 218, 234, 245
Domingue, Richard, 216, 225–31, 236–37, 244
Doucet, David, 145, 157
Doucet, Michael, 4, 6–7, 9, 12, 14, 77–79, 85, 110–11, 117, *122*, 123, 147, 149, 157, 205–6, 249n1, 249n6
"Down At The Twist and Shout," 3–17, 19, 78; complete lyrics for, 7–8
Down Home Music Store, 111, 207, 237, 242
Duke, Jerry, 184, 187

Eagles' Hall (Alameda), 107, 188, 196, 218, 232–33
East Palo Alto, Calif., 71, 136, 167, *170*, 173, 177, 179
ethnicity. *See* Cajun; Creole; identity; Isleño
ethnography, 4–6, 14, 16, 36–39, 118, 163, 249n2; songwriting as, 3–16, 249n2
Eunice, La., *13*, 25, 77, 80, 82, 123, 126, 134–35, 137, 143–46, 157–58, 186, 200–1

Felton, Junior, 60, 84–85, *105*, 164–65
festival, 46, 50–51, 84–85, 96, 111, 115, 117, 130, 140, 142, 179, 187, *191*, 196, 198, 200, *209*, 210, 213–16, *216,* 231, 234; of American Fiddle Tunes, 88, 151–52; Ardenwood, 169–70, 234, *242*; Augusta Heritage Center, 88, 95–96, 102, 120, 253n22; Bay Area Blues, 55; Berkeley Farmers' Market, 98; Berkeley Folk, vii, 57, 120–21, 124, 154–55, 255n11; Breaux Bridge Crawfish, 230, 234; *Festival International de Louisiane*, 201; *Festivals Acadiens*, 77, 91, 119, 137, 174; Isleton Crawdad, 212, 234, 237; Lark in the Morning, 129, 151, 157; National Folk, 77–78; New Orleans Jazz & Heritage, 46, 119, 211; Newport Folk, 76–77, 119; Plaisance Zydeco, 65, 186; Sacramento Jazz Jubilee, 207–8, 214, 230, 234–35; San Diego, 125, 133–34; San Francisco Ethnic Dance, 184; Smithsonian Festival of American Folklife, 122; Stern Grove, 74; Sweet's Mill, 129, 143, 156–57
film: *Belizaire the Cajun*, 205, 237; *The Big Easy*, 198, 221; *Louisiana Story*, 157. *See also* Blank, Les
folk dancing: Balkan, 162–63, 172, 174, 178, 183–84, 190, 192, 196–97, 244; clogging, 118, 183–84, 186; contra, 11–12, 46, 178; Greek, 163, 171–72, 176, 178, 180, 183–84, 192; international, 117, 161–63, 172, 176, 178, 190, 192, 194, 197; Israeli, 178, 192; Mandala club, 163, 172–73, 176, 184, 190; polka, 171, 180; square dancing, 11, 84–85, 118, 136, 162, 171, 178, 182, 192; Turkish, 171–72. *See also* Ashkenaz Music and Dance Community Center
folk music: bluegrass, 85, 117, 120–21, 130–31, 134–36, 238, 255n17; Irish, 126, 131, 255n17; old-time, 85, 117, 124, 126, 129, 131–32, 134–35, 138–39, 156, 159
folk revivalists: politics of representation, 159–60; recordings by, 119–20, 134–35, 155–56; summer music camps, 132–33, 140, 143, 151–52, 156

Fontenot, Canray, 25, 76, 78, 80, 88, 98, 104, 110, 112, *122*, 126, 134, 142, *147*, 149, 151, 158
Fontenot, Freeman, 25, 61, 80
François, Raymond, 149, 158
Frank, Keith, 65, 91, 93, 170, 186
Freight and Salvage Coffeehouse, 85, 128, 134, 155
French language: as ethnic marker, 5, 17, 20, 22, 45, 57, 69, 72–73; as first language, 22, 37, 51–52, 62, 80, 88–89, 93, 203, 220–21; local dialects, 50, 199, 225–26, 228; preservation efforts, 12, 50–51, 78; public policy against, 22–23, 49, 52, 72, 203; as second language, 77, 96, 157, 182–83, 204–5, 228; spoken in public, 50, 204–5, 208; use in military, 49–50, 80; use in song, 6, 9, 12, 24–25, 33–34, 58, 61, 74, 76, 78, 88, 99, 109, 119, 159, 183, 208–9, 216, 230–31. *See also* radio
Frugé, Wade, 110, 126, 129, 134, 145, 149
Fulson, Lowell, 79, 108
Fusilier, Freida, vii, 34, 56, 197–98, 203–9, *209*, 213–14, 216, 234–38

Garnier, D'Jalma, 88
Geddins, Bob, 107–8, 110, 239
Gleason, Ralph, 57, 155
Gobart, Ullus, 73, 81, *84*, *90*, 91, 100, 105, 167, 177, 179
Gordon, Bruce, 239–40, *240*, 245
Graceland (Paul Simon album), 6, 201–2
Gradney, Ralph ("Bobby"), 169, 218–25, 235, 237–38, 246
Grammy Awards, 4, 6, 56, 78–79, 202, 257ch8n11
Guillory, Ben, 57, 60, 81–82, *82*, 84–85, 91, 100, 127, 164–65
Guillory, Ida (née Lewis). *See* Queen Ida
Guillory, Myrick "Freeze," 56, 177
Guillory, Olivia, 92–96, 188–89, 212
Guillory, Ray, 54, 190

Hall, Stuart, 18–19, 26–27
heritage, 18, 24, 74, 88, 113, 122, 165, 235; parks, 200, 202
hippie, 11–12, 111, 133, 153, 168, 181, 244
Hopkins, Lightnin', 108–9, 111, 113
house parties, 35, 40–48, 52–54, 56, 60, 63–65, 90–91, 93–94, 96, 146, 167–69, 174, 210–11, 251n2
Hymowitz, David, 239

identity: and civil rights movement, 50–51, 79, 153, 197, 227; constructivist view, 27–31; essentialist view, 17–27, 100, 246; ethnicity, 5, 19–23, 27, 32, 44–46, 50–51, 79, 100–1, 112, 119, 199, 200, 202, 251n44; gender, 53–55, 73–74, 114, 145, 204–6; insider/outsider, 5–14, 17, 20, 26–38, 46, 77, 107, 117, 121, 173, 179, 193, 201–2, 234, 236, 238, 241, 243–46, 251n44; Jewish, 20–21, 63, 146, 153, 244, 258n30; Louisiana French, as pan-ethnic category, 5, 25, 100–1; the Other, 27–28, 32–33, 202; researcher, 31–36. *See also* American; Cajun; Creole; Native American
instruments: accordion, 8, 12, 14, 25, 34–35, 41–42, 50–51, 53–60, *55*, *58*, 73–74, 76–83, 85–88, 94, 96–102, 104, 120, 130, 143, 145, 155, 164–65, 183, 190, 206–8, 229–31, 237–40, *240*, 249n14, 253n8, 253n22; fiddle, *3*, 7–8, 57, 59–60, 77–78, 88, 93, 96, 117, 119–20, *122*, 124–31, 133–52, *148*, 156–59; rub board, 42, 137, *166*, 185, *240*; steel guitar, 25, 140, 238, *239*; triangle, 97–98, 119
Isleño, 200, 209, 246, 258n18

jam sessions, vii, 35–36, 40–42, 81–83, *84*, 86–87, 93–94, 102, 117, 127–28, 146, 154, 167, 201, 214, 240, 242, 246–47
Jara, Marty, 102, 239

Karpan, Maureen, 102, 151, 238–39
Keppeler, Ken, 121, 128, 147, 157–60, *159*, 245
Kershaw, Doug, 57, 131, 155
Kilpatrick, Blair, vii, 102
Kirshenblatt-Gimblett, Barbara, 24, 258n30

Lafayette, La., 3, 7, 8–9, 13, 76–77, 88–89, 91–92, 137, 157, 186, 199–201, 225–28
Lake Charles, La., 13, 41, 51–52, 57, 64–65, 97, 109, 168, 182–83, 185, 219
Landry, Gerard, 86, 192–93
Laušević, Mirjana, 117, 159, 162, 196, 244
Lawtell, La., 13, 25, 41, 56, 59, 96–97, 147
Leblanc, Betty, 10, 88–92, 105, 232
leisure, 5, 9–10, 43, 50, 162, 197, 214, 237–38
Lejeune, Iry, 25, 50, 76, 98
Leopold, Frannie, 128, 134, 157
Lewis, Al. *See* Rapone, Al
Lewis, Delilah Lee, 98–99, 123, *128*, 129, 140–54, *144*, *147*, *148*, 193, 239, 245
Lewis, Elvina (née Broussard), 51, 53, 59
Lomax, Alan, 24–25, 154
Los Angeles, Calif., 30, 47, 54, 56, 67–68, *68*, 71, 80, 108, 111, 121, 124, 163, 214
Louisiana French music: debates over style, 100–1, 253n8; harmony, 12–13, 42; history, 24–26, 75–79, 108–11, 118–23, 127, 137–38; improvisation, 87, 165–67, 193–94; instrumentation, 8; interaction, 87; languages sung, 12; learning, insider, 54, 56, 78, 81–83, 97–98, 104, 149, 192–93, 207, 229–30; learning, outsider, 34–35, 102, 119, 123–34, 141–43, 147–53, 157, 192–93, 238–40; melody, 35, 83, 87, 127–28, 138, 142, 151, 246–47; non-dance contexts, 85; popularity, 43, 45–46; rhythm, 9, 42, *190*; style, 25, 60–62; teaching, viii, 81, 86–88, 102–3, 120, 128, 142, 147, 149, 152, 253n22; yelled interjections, 9, 137. *See also* Cajun music; Creole music; dance; folk revivalists; instruments; jam sessions; zydeco
Louisiana Sue, vii, 188, 197–98, 208–18, *216*, 222, 230, 234–38, 243, 246
Luckenbach, Ed, 102, 238

Mamou, La., 13, 25, 76, 118, 123, 142, 186, 201
maps: Central Northern California, 15; Southern Louisiana, 13
Mardi Gras, 26, 50, 54, 112, 157, 184, 186, 214–16, *215*, *216*, 223, 230

McBride, Cheryl, 185
McGee, Dennis, 19, 24–25, 78–79, 120, 125–30, *127*, *128*, 133–34, *144*, 144–46, 148–49, 151, 153, 158
McLerie, Jeanie, 128, 134, 142, 147, 157, *158*
Meadows, Lloyd, *240*, 240–41
Menard, D. L., *122*, 134, 137, 223
Menard, Kent ("Kenny"), 188, 216–17
military: impact on ethnic identity, 49–50, 63–64, 126, 228; impact on migration and employment, 29, 63–64, 75, 80, 90, 171
Mulate's, 149, 179, 199
music. *See* Louisiana French music

Nadel, David, 138, 161, 163, 172, 183, 187, 192–93, 244
Nashville, Tenn., 6, 78, 255n17
National Endowment for the Arts (NEA), 28, 56, 78, 113, 122, 127, 135
Native American, 5, 52, 66, 72, 80
New Lost City Ramblers, 45, 119–20, 123–25, 130–33, 154–55
New Orleans, La.: association with Cajun culture, 3, 6–9, 12; and Creole identity, 20–21, 73, 258n18; dancing in, 185, 194, 201, 238; as destination to perform or record, 24, 56, 90, 157, 199; as film subject, 107, 112; history, 200, 209; jazz, 107–8, 214; Mardi Gras, 184; marketing images of, 215–18, *235*; rhythm and blues, 192, 212, 231. *See also* festival; tourism

Oakland, Calif., *15*, 62, 64, *68*, 68–71, 79, *105*, 107–8, 115, 130–31, 140, 142–43, 148, 163–64, 232, 240
Olivier, Barry, 120–21, 124, 154–55

Palo Alto, Calif., *15*, 81, 130. *See also* East Palo Alto, Calif.
Pitre, Davis (David Pitre/Petri, "Big Pete"), 61, 93–94, 104, *105*, *106*, 190, *191*
Pitre, Houston, 93–94, 104, 212–13
Pitre, Lena, 68, 93–94, 104, 212, 254n25
postcolonialism, 4–5, 32

Poullard, Danny, viii, 35–36, 59–60, 71, 80–88, *82*, *84*, *90*, 95, 97–105, 111, 122, 127–28, 133–39, *135*, *139*, 142–43, 145, 147–48, 151–53, 164–65, 167–68, 173, 175–77, 184, 192–93, 207, 212–13, 220, 230–32, 237–39, 241–43, 246, 253n10, 253n22
Poullard, Dorence ("Dorsina"), 80, 138
Poullard, Edward, 82–83, 88, 137, 145, 147, 152
Poullard, John, 80, 82, 101–2, 127, 138
Poullard, Ruby, 81
Preston Ranch, 131–33, 156–57, 244
Prudhomme, Paul, 112, 199, 212
Putnam, Robert, 43–44, 251n11

Queen Ida, 33, 43, 46, 51–56, *55*, 59–60, 69–75, 79, 85, 112, 117, 137, 161, 164, 167, 183–84, 190, *191*, 192–93, 201, 229, 231–32

race: and American attitudes, 126, 153–54, 173–74, 176, 195–96; and Cajun attitudes, 126, 153; and Creole attitudes, 73, 165, 168; discrimination in California, 64, 70; discrimination in Louisiana, 64, 69–70, 73; and musical style, 100–1, 246–47
radio, 3, *7*, 52–53, 73, 98, 107, 111, 131, 137–38, 163, 171, 184, 201, 203, 212–13, 221, 226–27; French programming, 12, 50, 80; KPFA (Berkeley), 83, 85, 111, 142, 154; KVMR (Nevada City), 208; *Prairie Home Companion* show, 135; *Rendezvous des Cajuns* show, 137, 201
Ramon, Susan (née Appe). *See* Louisiana Sue
Randol's, 179, 199
Rapone, Al, 51, 53–56, 59, 74, *135*, 212–13, 216, 232
Read, Cheese, 110, 134, 149
revivalism: defined, 28. *See also* folk dancing; folk revivalists; heritage
Richard's Club, 146, 186, 195–96
Richmond, Calif., *15*, 42, 64, *68*, 68–69, 71, 93, 104, 136, 167, 173, *191*, 212, 222–25

Rigney, Tom, 175, 216, 231, 239
Rinzler, Ralph, 76, 119
Robertson, Robbie, 166, 185
Robertson, Shirley (née St. Julien), 185–6
Rockin' Dopsie, 89, 201–2
Roger, Aldus, 76, 83, 101–2, 104, 108, 138, 145, 204
Rothfield, John, 98, 132, 207
Rumney, Ron, 173–74, 176–81, 194–96

Sacramento, Calif., *15*, 205, 207–9, 212–14, 230, *235*, 237
San Francisco, Calif., *15*, 43, 52–55, 57, 60, 67–71, *68*, 74, 81, *90*, 91, 97, 111, 127, 134, 136, 151, 162–63, 167, 171–73, 176, 178, 181–84, 187, 221–22, *240*
San Leandro, Calif., *15*, 64, 70
Savoy, Ann (née Allen), 28, 76–77, 110, 112, 134–35, 146–47, 153, 157
Savoy, Marc, 28, 77, 83, 85, 110–12, 120, *122*, 126, 134–35, 143, 146, 153, 157, 231, 236, 245
Savoy, Wilson, 110
Savoy Music Center, 135, 142, 145–46, 150, 201
Schmidt, Linda, 7, 192–93
Schwarz, Tracy, 28, 119–20, 125, 129, *144*
Seeger, Charles, 6, 154, 249n7, 255n11
Seeger, Mike, 119, 125, 133, 153, 155–56
Seeger, Pete, 121, 130, 154
Semien, Joe, 56–57, 98
Semien, John, 43, 53–60, *58*, 64, 71, 73, 81–82, 90, 97–100, *106*, 137, 164–65, 190, *191*, 222, 231
Semien, Louis, *84*, 168, 190, *191*
Senauke, Alan, 85, 111, 135, 139
shuffle (dance rhythm and step), 105, 149, 161
Siggins, Sam, 103, 136–37, *139*, 170, 238, 256n22
Simon, Paul. *See Graceland*
Slim's Y-Ki-Ki, 146, 195
Slobin, Mark, 47, 245, 251n11
Small, Christopher, 6, 249n7
Smith, Mayne, 139–41, 154, 156
social capital: bonding, 44–45, 48, 241, 245, 251n11; bridging, 44–48, 84, 107, 241, 247, 251n11; civil society, 46–47;

defined, 43; *machers* vs. *schmoozers*, 43–44; reciprocity, 43, 103; social networks, 29, 37, 39, 41, 43–49, 53, 60, 70, 72, 80–81, 95, 103, 123, 153, 160–61, 195, 197–98, 212, 222, 229, 236–37, 245; trust, 43–45, 48, 237, 241, 251n6; using, 45–48, 103, 212, 236–37, 242. *See also* cultural capital

songs: "Bernadette," 147, 151–52; "Blue Runner," 148; "Don't Mess With My Toot Toot," 229, 237; "Diggy Liggy Lo," 131, 155; "Eunice Two-Step," 42, *58*, 247; "Fifi Poncho," *58*, 192; "J'ai Passé Devant Ta Porte," 42, 97; "Jolie Blonde," *8*, *9*, *58*, 75–77, 221; "Lafayette Two-Step," *58*, 83; "Madame Faielle," 148; "Parlez Nous à Boire," 119, 124, 133, 155

Spires, Will, 81, 101–2, 123–30, *128*, 134, 142–44, *144*, 148, 153, 155–56, 190

Spitzer, Nicholas R., 25, 69, 73

St. Martinville, La., *13*, 19, 186, 200, 209–10, 214

St. Mary, Charlie, *82*, *84*, *90*, 91, 103, 105, 136–37, *139*, 164–68, *166*, 193, 212, 242

St. Mary, Junior, 167, 185

St. Mary, Lucky, 185, 192, 212

St. Mary, Mark, 55, 86, 190, *191*, 212–13, 237

Stevens, Ray, 62–67, 70, 72, 246

Strachwitz, Chris, 28, 45, 71, 79, 83, 85, 107–14, 116, 118, 121, 123, 131, 137, 153–54, 164, 223, 237, 242, 255n11. *See also* Down Home Music Store

Strogen, Paul, 171–76, 179, 195–96, 243

swamp pop, 51

Tabak, Steve, vii, 102

Taylor, Timothy, 51, 202

television, 30, 83, 98, 155, 204, 208, 212; KLFY (Lafayette, La.), 76, 226

Tenney, Irene, 187, 213

Texas, 41, 43, 49, 67, 69, 107–9, 111, 113, 194, 219, 222; Beaumont, *13*, 52, 80, 82, 127, 220; Houston, 75–76, 96, 108–9, 227; Port Arthur, *13*, 80, 221; Raywood, 219–21

Thierry, André, 42, 94–96, 186, 241–43, *242*

Thierry, Chasya, 94, 96

Thierry, Jason, 95

Thompson, Eric, 11–12, 85, 101, 103, 109, 123–25, 128, 130–31, 134–40, *139*, 153–57, 245, 255n17

Thompson, Suzy (née Rothfield), 11–12, 85, 98, 101, 103, 123, 128, 131–40, *139*, 142, 153–54, 156–57, 207, 232–33, 245, 255n17

Titon, Jeff Todd, 28, 37

tourism: boom in Louisiana, 28, 30–31, 123, 145, 197–201; in California, 235; cultural impacts of, 29–31, 179–80, 195–96, 199–201, 236; dancer-tourists, 48, 119, 179–80, 195–96, 201; environmental, 199; historical, 19, 200; indirect ("virtual"), 5, 14, 195–96, 198, 214–18, 223, 235, 238; international, 145; and modernity, 14; as pilgrimage, 9, 196; role in Cajun craze, 4–5, 9, 16, 45–46, 198, 202. *See also* heritage

Twist and Shout (music club), 4, *7*, 11, 249n1

"Twist and Shout" (song). *See* "Down At The Twist and Shout"

two-step (dance rhythm and step), 3, 4, 6, *7*, 9, 14, 105, 161, 173, 189–90, *190*, 194, 215, 249n6, 256n1

University of California, Berkeley, vii, 34–35, 107–8, 125, 130–31, 154, 163, 171, 214

University of California, Los Angeles, 110, 163

University of Louisiana at Lafayette (University of Southwestern Louisiana), 204

waltz, *8*, *9*, 11, 14, 58, 90, 104–5, 127, 161, 171, 173–74, 177, 194, 215, 230, 256n1

West Coast Cajun and Zydeco Music and Dance Association (WCCZMDA), 34–35, 213–14, *216*

Wilson, Billy (Bill), 46, 86, 94, 103–4, 136, *139*, 151, 188, 192–93, 232–33, 238, *239*, 240

Wimmer, Kevin, 103, 136–37, 153

world music, 30–31, 51, 122, 163, 192, 201–2

Young, Allie, 77, 125, 134

Zawacki, Franklin, 174, 234
zydeco: blues influences, 53, 61, 78–79, 109, 166, 227–29, 239–41; blues musicians playing, 60, 165; history, 20, 26, 42–43, 78–79, 108, 203–4, 253n8; at jazz festivals, 230–31; in Las Vegas, 215–18; meaning, 10, 190, 193–94; style, 60–62, 65–66, 74, 93, 95, 175, 177, 185–87, 189–90, 240–41, 246. *See also* Creole music; dance; Louisiana French music

www.ingramcontent.com/pod-product-compliance
Lightning Source LLC
Chambersburg PA
CBHW030337240426
43661CB00052B/1662